Screen Culture

New Directions in Media History

Richard Butsch, *Screen Culture: A Global History*
John Nerone, *The Media and Public Life: A History*

Screen Culture

A Global History

Richard Butsch

polity

First published in 2019 by Polity Press

Polity Press
65 Bridge Street
Cambridge CB2 1UR, UK

Polity Press
101 Station Landing
Suite 300
Medford, MA 02155, USA

ISBN-13: 978-0-7456-5324-2 (hardback)
ISBN-13: 978-0-7456-5325-9 (paperback)

A catalogue record for this book is available from the British Library.

Library of Congress Cataloging-in-Publication Data

Names: Butsch, Richard, 1943- author.
Title: Screen culture : a global history / Richard Butsch.
Description: Cambridge, UK ; Medford, MA : Polity, 2019. | Series: New directions in media history | Includes bibliographical references and index.
Identifiers: LCCN 2018035712 (print) | LCCN 2018049986 (ebook) | ISBN 9781509535866 (Epub) | ISBN 9780745653242 | ISBN 9780745653242 (hardback) | ISBN 9780745653259 (paperback)
Subjects: LCSH: Mass media–History–20th century. | Mass media–History–21st century.
Classification: LCC P90 (ebook) | LCC P90 .B89 2019 (print) | DDC 302.23009/04–dc23
LC record available at https://lccn.loc.gov/2018035712

Typeset in 10.5 on 12 pt Sabon
by Toppan Best-set Premedia Limited
Printed and bound in Great Britain by CPI Group (UK) Ltd, Croydon

For further information on Polity, visit our website:
politybooks.com

*In memory of my sisters, Ruth and Peggy,
and in appreciation of Ava and Noah as living inspirations.*

Contents

Acknowledgments   viii

Abbreviations   ix

Introduction: A Screen Culture History   1

1   American Cinema to World War I   21

2   Global Cinema, 1900–1920   38

3   The Hollywood Studio Era, 1910s–1940s   65

4   Global Hollywood, 1920s–1950s   83

5   Western Television in the Broadcast Era, 1945–1990   116

6   Post-Colonial Television, 1960s–1990s   145

7   Digital Media in the New Millennium   172

8   Using Digital Media   190

9   Globalized Media in the New Millennium   205

Notes   226

Index   298

Acknowledgments

In researching and writing this book I have striven to see the forest, but also to see the trees well enough to see how they make a forest. To do this, I have had to rely on sources produced by thousands of scholars, many not directly cited, from whom I have accumulated knowledge and insights over decades that allowed me to see the trees and the forest. I wish to thank those scholars.

I also wish to thank a few by name whose work and reflections have helped me through this project and to whom I am grateful: Richard Abel, Katherine Fuller, Sonia Livingstone, Richard Maltby, Virginia Nightingale, Janet Staiger, Silvio Waisbord, and anonymous reviewers for Polity Press. Further, I could not have done the research for this book without the help of Rose Hilgar, who tracked down and obtained for me, often beyond the call of duty, innumerable books and articles, primary and secondary sources through inter-library loans. Finally, as always, I thank Ava Baron, whose unstinting support and insightful guidance from beginning to end enabled me to find my way through the forest to a book manuscript.

Abbreviations

NYT   *New York Times*
MPW   *Moving Picture World*
HJFRT   *Historical Journal of Film, Radio and Television*
Annals   *Annals of the Academy of Political and Social Science*
ILWCH   *International Labor and Working Class History*

Introduction: A Screen Culture History

When the leading American broadcast television network of the time, NBC, introduced color television in the 1950s they promoted it as 'living color.' The great divide between print and screen is this 'living' quality of moving images. Moving images long pre-dated film. There were a variety of mechanical devices that did this. But these never went beyond the novelty phase, mostly occasional toys for a very few, very rich. On the other hand, in the early twentieth century, film quickly became a mass medium and moved beyond novelty to narrative story-telling. Over the century, television and recently the internet and smartphones were added. Now screen media, as they are collectively called, are as pervasive a part of our lives as breathing and present stories as ubiquitous and enveloping as reality. Now internet and smartphones are 'living' in a second sense too, not only moving or active, but also interactive. As pervasive as they have become, screens could not but have an influence on culture. This book explores the history of that culture.

Media are purveyors of culture, distributing images and ideas to millions of individuals, providing a common experience across numerous and dispersed groups. Even while people differ in their interpretations of the same video representations, they begin at the same starting point, a 'preferred' reading. Such widely disseminated representations provide a glue for modern societies.

Over a long history, critics have assumed powerful effects of screens upon their viewers, shaping their ideas and behavior. But research over the past four decades has made it clear that we cannot presume

that media messages are consumed whole and uncritically by audiences. Yet, neither can we assume that mass-consumed texts (their visual, oral, and symbolic content), when pervasive and persistent, have no impact at all. So the book includes examination of screen industries and screen texts. At the same time, screens and screen messages are of no consequence unless people integrate them into their lives. Thus we must examine meaning-taking and meaning-making by audiences and other actors situated in everyday life, where cultures are made, expressed, and experienced.

This book provides a global history. It examines screen media and their audiences in multiple nations across five continents in order to reveal how screen culture developed under diverse circumstances, and how it flows across nations. Underlying the idea of globalization is the assumption that everything is connected, that people, actions, events, conditions in one part of the world are connected to those in other parts of the world. Screen media very clearly have been global since the early days of moving pictures. To better understand the growth and pervasiveness of screen media we need to understand their global reach. The global is a larger version of more local processes of cultural intrusion and resistance, such as a small town's resistance to big city ideas expressed in a movie. Thus the cultural geography of place, local, national, and global, which weaves through the history in multiple and varying ways.

What is Screen Culture?

The term 'screen' includes screens for film, television, video games, computers, and smartphones, what Graeme Turner and Jinna Tay describe as first, second, and third waves of screen technology.[1] Screens are about images more than language, a modern form of visual culture. Excluded by the term are media that rely primarily on senses other than the visual, in particular the sound media of audio recording, radio, and voice telephone. Also excluded are live performances that are not mediated by a screen. Second, screen implies *moving* images, or what often is termed 'video,' excluding or at least limiting photos and other static visual arts. Third, I have excluded screens used almost entirely for text as did early PCs, email and the internet – the internet term 'web-page' is a remnant of that era. The internet entered screen culture when it evolved beyond email and text to predominantly video websites. Mobile phones entered screen culture when smartphones added video and internet capabilities. While earlier mobile phones had screens, these were for display of text, like early PCs. Smartphones advanced the convergence of film, television, computers, and phones and made video content mobile.

'Screen culture' as a term, first appeared in trade and academic books during the mid 1980s, and had a boost in the mid 1990s, according to a Google Books Ngram search. The term has been used loosely and imprecisely to describe something arising from screen media, most often the video images on film or tv. Popular press writers use the term as if screen images shape culture, rather than culture serving as a context for screen use. I will look less at the screen and more at its context, the shared ideas and practices of people in front of the screen, and what explains those. I will examine the interaction between the organizations and people who have produced the consumer technology – e.g. the movie theater, the tv set, the smartphone – and the images on the one hand, and those who are using the technology and viewing the images, on the other. This interaction is more abstracted and impersonal, but nevertheless real and consequential.

Consequently, I will use a literal interpretation of the term. Screen *culture* is the shared ideas expressed by producer and audience practices using these media and texts. What makes it culture, above all, is that it is the *lived* culture that arises when people interact with and through screen media. As everyday life fills with screen activity – averaging nine hours per day for American adults in 2017 – screen becomes an increasingly important aspect of the broader culture, infiltrating and influencing all other elements.[2]

Screens: Image and Language

Through the twentieth century, media have become predominantly images rather than worded representations. Advances in print technologies and changes in advertising strategy substantially turned newspapers and magazines to visual imagery; television supplanted radio; and most recently, imagery has challenged text on computer and smartphone screens.

The value of word versus image was controversial long before the twentieth century. W. J. T. Mitchell stated that the history of Western discourse on images is "about the *fear* [sic] of images ... the political psychology of icons, the study of iconophobia, iconophilia, and the struggle between iconoclasm and idolatry." Leading English literati as well as religious moralists opposed 'spectacles' as inferior to textual representation. Shakespeare's contemporary Robert Greene was known for his spectacles popular with audiences, such as a whale's mouth from which the character of Jonah arrived on stage. But the famous actor Richard Tarelton was admired for his quick wit in response to

picture is worth a thousand words

shouts from the audience. Ben Jonson and John Locke too favored word over image.[3] Also in the seventeenth century, Protestant Non-Conformists objected to the visual performance on stage as deceptive lies, although they considered the written text of plays to be morally acceptable. One of the first acts of the Commonwealth government in 1642 banned theatrical performances, even as it allowed printing and reading playscripts.[4] In the nineteenth century, Charles Lamb and Romantics such as Samuel Coleridge continued the tradition of pre-ferring playscript over stage performance. When modern mass media arrived in twentieth-century America, reactions to radio were uniformly positive, while film and television were often treated with moral and aesthetic hostility. Reviving this criticism recently, media theorist Neil Postman regretted that America had changed from a print culture to a screen culture.[5]

At the same time, reactions varied with types of visual culture. Visual art has held a preserved space where a select canon of images has been granted special status.[6] Stage has been divided between 'legiti-mate' drama that relies primarily on the word, and comedy and musical theater that has relied more on spectacle. The long form of feature film, requiring a more complex story and characters, was considered superior to short-form television programming – television was described as a vast wasteland in the same era that auteur theory was recasting film as an art form. Nevertheless, it is the screen that has appealed to the masses, has colonized our everyday environment, and has become increasingly integral to our everyday culture. This should not be entirely surprising since the visual is nonlinear, amorphous, and contextual – much like everyday lived culture – while text is more linear and formalized. Images are more holistic, while words are more precise. Visual representation is more akin to the subtlety of everyday practice of culture, which depends on implicit visual cues far more than on explicit oral or written instruction.

Culture

All this brings us to the term 'culture,' famously described by Raymond Williams as "one of the two or three most complicated words in the English language … mainly because it has now come to be used for important concepts in several distinct intellectual disciplines," includ-ing anthropology, sociology, history, cultural and media studies. It is important to understand culture because it is the fabric of everyday life upon which societies are built and histories unfold. That is to say, culture, as it is experienced and expressed in everyday life, is most influential. So-called high culture, art, and literature, intellectual culture, or any sort of culture is important only so far as it is incorporated into everyday interactions. To understand the significance of screen culture, we must concentrate on lived culture or culture as practice, where ideas are expressed, shared, and activated.[7]

Put simply, culture is shared ideas; and objects and actions symbolize these ideas.[8] Functionally, shared ideas, a shared understanding of the meaning of things, enable a group of people to coordinate their actions with each other. Culture exists only through interactions among people. Interactions both depend upon and express the shared ideas. In interacting, people interpret the meaning of others' actions and in turn convey meaning in their own actions. Through this dance of meaning, people confirm their shared ideas. Thus, cultures are not fixed and finished things, but fluid and continually negotiated.

Nor is culture singular. Any group interacting with each other on a regular basis develops a culture among themselves. Couples, families, circles of friends, and other associates typically develop unspoken assumptions about what is appropriate appearance and behavior, how each is to be treated, who is a leader and who followers. In small groups, members regularly re-negotiate such assumptions, through arguments, resistance, and feelings talk. So too, nations of millions are bound together by a common culture, mediated by large organizations, communication systems, and goods distributed and consumed nationally, all of which circulate and confirm shared meanings. Millions internationally may share aspects of a common culture across national boundaries through the flow of communication and goods that represent cultural values norms and beliefs.[9] Between these micro and macro extremes are numerous other cultures, in layers, levels, and interstices, such as cultures of class, gender, ethnicity, religion, etc.[10]

The plurality of cultures is especially pertinent to the discussion of global-local distinctions. The term global culture is an imagined singular culture that homogenizes and threatens to dissolve the distinctiveness of other cultures. At the same time this dichotomy presumes that local cultures are numerous, particularly focusing on geographic cultures. The term 'local,' however, is used vaguely, creating confusion about which local cultures are meant – national, ethnic, neighborhood or family.

None of these cultures is total in the sense that all the members of a group live solely within one culture. We each and all participate in a variety of cultures each day as we move from group to group and situation to situation. Multiple cultures are woven together by individuals participating in diverse cultures. Even in isolated groups such as hunter-gatherer bands, peasant villages, or nomadic herdsmen, anthropologists often find distinct subcultures for men and women. In cosmopolitan cultures of urban areas people encounter many cultures in a typical day. As anthropologist Lila Abu-Lughod observes: "because [television's] cultural texts are produced elsewhere and inserted into local households, communities, nations – confirms for us the need to rethink the notion of culture in the singular."[11]

Lastly, culture is not an individual creation, but is the product of collective, coordinated action of many people enacting and enforcing the same expectations, values, and beliefs. Those collective, coordinated actions constitute social structure. Therefore we cannot examine and explain culture without also discussing social structure, in this case the economic, political, and global structures that shape the production and reception of screen media and their images.[12]

Context: Place and Situation

Culture happens when people gather in places and engage in situations where they interact, create, and express that culture. While the two terms, place and situation, are close relatives, it is useful to distinguish them. A geographer's term, place is a space populated with things – interiors with walls, floors, and furnishings; streetscapes of buildings, pavement, signs, a forest or farm – that identify it as a *particular place*. A place becomes the setting for a situation when peopled with actors, their dress, props, and statuses, who build a shared understanding of it in order to align their interactions with each other. Place is grounded in *location*; situation in *interaction*. The meanings of places and situations and the things within them are fabricated by the actors in the process of interacting.[13]

The complex of meanings thus constructed is culture. The meanings are not created sui generis, but are based on the culture(s) people bring with them to this place/situation and use – as raw material we might say – to guide their interpretation of it and of the actions of others, and to choose their own purposes and actions in constructing a culture for that situation and those participants. Where and when a place is influences which people and what cultures arrive there. The more cosmopolitan the place the more diverse – and the more work is involved in aligning actions and constructing a shared definition of the situation.

Places are fixed to a particular location. Situations are portable to the degree to which a particular place is inessential to the interaction. Cultures are even more portable, since people carry cultures into a situation. The physicality of place gives culture fixity. Without some fixity, culture would be useless, since its purpose is to give us some predictability in our daily life and interactions, a frame within which actors can assess how to act. At the same time culture needs to be fluid to fit the situation and interactions. Being mindful of place as well as situation, we are then sensitized to the dual nature of culture as both fixed and fluid.

Places are more durable, residues of past actions; situations more ephemeral, people in the midst of acting. Actors enter places and create situations. Situations arise as actors engage and evaporate when they depart. In one place, many situations may occur. In a plaza, several may emerge simultaneously. In a school building, days are full of some situations, nights with others. Places are the artefactual fabric of culture at large, its distinctive character that enables us to identify what and where it is. If we are familiar with the culture, the artifacts tell us what they are for, what we are expected to do with them. Situations are the momentary processes of culture writ small in our everyday lives.

Two important contrasts of places keep appearing throughout this history, that between urban and rural, and between Western and post-colonial societies. Both also involve contrasts between industrial and agricultural economies, as well as contrasting representations as modern or traditional cultures. At the same time, these contrasted places are linked to each other by capitalism and imperialism.[14]

Cities tend to be centers of greater specialization, while rural country dwellers, notably small farmers, of necessity tend to depend upon doing most things themselves. Cities have long been characterized as places of hurry, anonymity, and loneliness, while small town and rural setting have been depicted as stagnant and claustrophobic, due to little privacy and peer pressure to conform, although having more sense of community.[15] Cities initially arose as government centers, but have grown into markets that stimulated consumption. During the last two centuries, much, mostly Western-inspired discourse has characterized Western societies as being similar to cities in such respects, and colonial peoples similarly to rural communities.

Characterizations that contrast modern and traditional values, and link them to differences between city and country, recur across many societies and are central to modernization and national-building efforts of post-colonial nations. As will be seen, screen media often have been recruited to serve these efforts. Tradition and modernity have been ideal types used to capture dimensions along which societies vary. Tradition was often conceived as an idealized community contrasted to the alienation and anonymity created by urbanization and industrialization. Of course, while tendencies may differ between cultures, differences are not dichotomous, and individuals within a culture may exhibit a broad range on the same dimensions, sometimes such that variation within a culture may rival variation between cultures.[16]

Places and Screens

Screens are things; they occupy and are contextualized by places in which they sit, such as a tv in a home or a waiting room. We talk about screens in terms of place, such as going to a movie, going on the internet. Where we watch is therefore important: at home, on a bus, in this or that country or continent. Mobile screens such as smartphones can be carried from place to place, as the bus moves.

What we witness on the screen is itself a place, metaphorically, fictively, realistically. Screens are like windows in a place that enable us to see into another place. Immersive media places, like movie theaters, help us imaginatively to leave the viewing place and be transported into the place in the screen. Watching in the home, on the other hand, we are immersed in domestic life. Interactive screens conjoin the two places. With the internet and smartphones, we can pass through those windows and engage in real time with people and events in that other place, while continuing to be and act in the first place. The relation between these spaces can create a variety of problematic social and cultural situations as well as opportunities. Thus, the complaint since television began, "Stop watching that screen and look at me ..." Numerous cartoons since the 1950s have caricatured this situation.[17] Decades ago, phones made a limited, aural tear in the space, but the smartphone screen has greatly increased availability of distracting attractions and bi-spatial interactions.

Screen presence and use changes the definition of the situation. Conversation arises in a waiting room, but is stultified by a television turned on. At the same time, social interaction may incorporate and shape their meaning. Turning off the tv can 'put it in its place' and restore conversation. All this will be discussed in Chapter 8.

As an example of a place, a situation and a medium, take an empty storefront in 1908 New York City on a local neighborhood shopping street where one might encounter neighbors and friends. For a nickel one can enter. The interior is filled with about a hundred motley chairs. It is dark, a moving light image of people doing something is projected on a sheet or improvised screen. It flickers. The people are dressed casually and come and go. They chat and eat, talk at the images on the screen. This is a place and a socially defined situation. The people share a definition of it as a nickelodeon and act accordingly. The situation includes props such as the informal decoration and furnishings, projector and screen, darkness. The entry price communicates its casual nature. The images tell them it is light entertainment, a novelty, not serious work.

Compare this to a large, lavish theater downtown where the people on the street are more likely strangers and more formally dressed, whether for work or a night out. The entry fee in 1920 is a dollar, a sufficient expense to mark this as a special event. The lobby is luxuriously decorated with marble, mirrors and chandeliers. The auditorium is filled with chairs upholstered in velvet and bolted to the floor in rows. It is dark and a projector lights up a screen. All this communicates very different expectations of behavior.

Compare this again to a television in a home in the 1950s, a domestic situation with yet other props, cues and behavior, or to people almost anywhere today using mobile media, such as a smartphone. Each of these examples involves a medium in a situation, and people attending to that medium or sometimes ignoring it. The situation defines the medium and what to do with it; at the same time the medium redefines the situation. To understand media and their audiences, their cultures, we need to understand the processes through which the media and their contexts are socially constructed by place and in situation.

Life with and without Screen Media

To understand the development and turns of screen cultures over time, we must begin with an historical baseline of life before the arrival of screen media. Today, for surprisingly many in the world, daily life is filled with screen media, their sights and sounds. They are ubiquitous and have become the *context* of our lives. Just a century ago, however, the only screen media were silent films, available only in a movie theater and leaving 'life' outside. Screen media history involves three dimensions of change in everyday life, changes in people's use of time, changes in what may be called leisure skills, and changes in isolation from the larger world. Time spent using media meant less time used elsewise. Such displacement also meant collective loss of skills in activities no longer passed down to younger generations. Third, media brought the outside world into even remote communities, where traditionally information had been passed on largely by word of mouth. These changes in everyday life were part and parcel of larger historical changes, from domestic production and a culture of subsistence to industrial production and a culture of consumption.

The changes occurred unevenly depending upon people's different social and geographical locations, as capitalist industrialization spread across the global landscape over the past three centuries.

From Domestic to Industrial Production

Concomitant with the spread of screen media in capitalist economies, subsistence production by families for their household use was steadily displaced by industrial mass production to sell to consumers, turning useful things into commodities for sale, and replacing utility with profit as the purpose and drive. The specific directions of development depended upon timing and circumstances particular to each society. Scholars have debated the differences in capitalist development in early modern Europe, colonial and post-colonial societies, and post-Soviet Eastern Europe.[18] But once under way, the structure of industrial capitalism pushed toward some common changes. Industrial capitalism separated production from consumption, work for pay from leisure to consume. Before industrial capitalist mass production became dominant, most families produced most of their own sustenance and pleasures.

In the nineteenth-century US, many people built their own homes, made their own clothes and processed their own food. As there was little separation between work and home or between personal relations and market relations, there was also little separation of work and leisure. Capitalist production grew piecemeal by colonizing ever more aspects of life and replacing 'home-made' with factory-made goods produced and sold for a profit. The process pushed and pulled people from subsistence living to working for a wage and buying what they needed.[19]

The process transformed cultural production as well. In the past, people made toys, music and entertainment for their own enjoyment As recently as the early twentieth century, in isolated valleys of the Appalachian mountains of the eastern US, there was a rich folk music culture in which most of the population were musically skilled in singing and playing instruments as part of everyday activity, and many made their own instruments. It was such music cultures that American record companies mined to create the commercial forms of country music and 'race' music.[20]

As with national markets, globalization proceeded, industry by industry; for example, from textiles to oil in the nineteenth century, autos to television in the twentieth. The unique economic properties of cultural products like movies sometimes aided their export.[21] In much of the world the transition from pre-capitalist villages to industrial production has often been rapid, compared to that in the West.

In some cases, screen media seemed to arrive all at once. But that growth logic can be retarded or diverted by other forces, most notably by the state. In particular, post-colonial governments often developed and operated screen media as an alternative to capitalist development. This will be discussed in Chapters 2, 4, 6, and 9.

Cultures of Consumption

To continue expansion, industrial capitalism needed to commodify new areas of life and stimulate consumer demand. This meant promoting a culture of consumption for homes, families and individuals. In tandem with the commodification of production, Western cultures began to shift their emphasis from a parsimonious work ethic to increasing approval of consumption as a way of life. Consumption in this sense however did not mean literally to consume or to use; it referred to a narrower, market sense of purchase.

Western European and US businesses began in earnest to promote consumption and reshape upper-middle and upper-class culture in the mid to late nineteenth century, when they turned shopping and purchasing into pleasurable leisure. Pioneering retail entrepreneurs created feminine urban shopping districts in New York, London and Paris, including department stores, theaters and other amusements, and supplanted the previously masculine markets near docks and factories. This signaled a new culture of everyday experience for urban middle- and upper-class women centered on spectacle, sensation and indulgence.[22] From this it grew into mail-order businesses that reached even small villages and farmhouses with enticing catalogs of images of things to buy, from shovels to ladies' wear. By the end of the nineteenth century, commodification and consumption were well established in Western cultures.[23]

Screen media arrived in the US just when this culture of consumption was broadening. Motion pictures were not only consumption in themselves, but also ideally suited to display and promote consumption. Early movie theaters greatly increased the market for purchasing entertainment, making it available at low cost and at convenient locations, so that vast sections of the working class, who previously could not regularly afford commercial entertainment, could now do so. In addition, 'moving pictures' could depict people engaging in the pleasures of consumption, to a greater degree than static department store displays and print advertising. By the 1920s films had changed to longer feature-length and had shifted from working-class to upper-class characters and settings. This allowed displays of lavish lifestyles based on consumption. Producers began contracting with manufacturers to prominently feature their products within the sets of the film. At the same time, movie 'palaces' combined both witnessing the spectacle of consumption in the movies and temporarily enjoying an hour or two in luxurious surroundings, a sort of fantasy consumption.[24] Consumption was intensifying.

Intensification is indicated by increased time spent to acquire and use commodities. How people use their time reflects cultural priorities and values. American time-use research has revealed that screen media strikingly increased the amount of time spent consuming commercial entertainment, due mostly to its wide availability and affordability.[25] Through the twentieth century, screen media accounted for a steadily increasing portion of the waking day in the US, even for working-class people. Movie-going consumed an hour or two per week until the 1950s, when television multiplied that to four hours a day. Recently, smartphones with internet connection have made screen media use almost a continuous activity. That meant other activities, such as socializing, community activities, recreation and sleep increasingly had to compete for time and attention. In general, leisure became less participative and less communal; social interaction became less face-to-face and more mediated. What does this reveal or reflect about cultural changes? At minimum, time use patterns reveal that Americans have chosen consumption of screen media over non-commercial social interactions or solitude.

Globalization contributed another element to consumption. It gave rise to intersticial higher classes or class fractions situated between their native culture and a hegemonic or global culture arriving with global commerce, as will be discussed. For these groups, culture was becoming less insular and more cosmopolitan, and presumed familiarity with multiple cultures. As sociologist Zigmunt Bauman writes, "The sign of belonging to a cultural elite today is maximum tolerance and minimal choosiness. The principal of cultural elitism is omnivorousness – feeling at home in every cultural milieu, without considering any *as* a home, let alone the only home."[26] Globalized media enabled and enhanced such cosmopolitan consumption.

At the same time, the values of a culture of consumption were not universally accepted. As was noted, the pleasures of consumption at first were directed toward upper-middle and upper-class women, and were criticized for distracting these women from their domestic responsibilities. But those same classes more vociferously condemned expenditures for pleasures by working classes that they feared encouraged rebelliousness.

British sociologist Stanley Cohen identified recurring patterns of reaction to incipient social and cultural changes of all sorts, which he labeled 'moral panics.'[27] Such reactions accompanied the spread of each new visual medium. Regardless of the era, continent or culture, these triggered public debates and moralistic outcries, especially by higher-status groups, against their popularity among women, children, lower classes and castes, subordinated races and tribes and other lower-status groups. In the earliest phase, optimists focused on utopian possibilities of the new technology. But shortly, others expressed alarm, predicted and publicized bad consequences, stirred a moral panic and called for some civic regulation. However, panics faded away as people became accustomed to the medium. This is not to say that there was no basis for either optimism or pessimism, but both tended to be overstated.[28]

Media panics are seldom about large structural changes, since these are not immediately evident in people's everyday lives. Structural issues more often are addressed in political debates concerning the society and the state. But reactions by a broad swathe of people tend to be about things they can see – or think they see – affecting their own family or community. Even when calling for a national solution, these are local issues. Both euphoria and hysteria are invariably in relation to visible impacts on people's everyday lives and immediate circumstances, while long-term and broader social economic and political effects tend to be less noticed and reacted to.

In some cases reactions have been framed as nationalist causes. American film companies stirred fears that French films in the 1900s and 1910s were endangering the nation (Chapter 2). Post-colonial variants focused on cultural imperialism weakening native cultures and nation-building agendas (Chapters 4 and 6). Again, the fears were often a response to the real popularity of screen media among lower-status populations.

Nationalism, Colonialism, and Global Media

Globalization is place and situation writ large. So far, we have focused on screen media at the ground level of everyday life. The issues discussed above, as already noted, applied as well to the development and reception of screen media across the globe, but under differing circumstances and in different eras. Larger structural forces, such as capitalism, imperialism and nationalism, have driven media developments, economic and cultural hegemony, and reactions to them at the national and international level.

Global media distribution grew upon a broader global trade system with deep historical roots. To understand this context, we need to briefly review the linked histories of the formation of nation states, nationalism, colonial empires, and post-colonial nations. Media have played a part in these as a means of persuasion or, seen from another perspective, as fostering a national culture. These developments were uneven, in some places advancing a century or more ahead of others. But the general pattern still applies.

Global media hegemony began with the dominance of Western European companies and countries exporting films to their colonies and to the US before World War I. The war disrupted their dominance, allowing US companies, then settling in Hollywood, to consolidate control of the American domestic market. After the war, Hollywood quickly extended its reach to European markets and much of the rest of the world, a hegemony which was compounded by export of American television programming after World War II. Only recently has this hegemony begun to be challenged, as several nations vie for regional dominance and even begin incursions into Europe and the US.

Post-colonial media institutionalization arose in the context of this history. Film, radio and television were perceived by many governments as powerful tools for reshaping culture, forging national identity, fostering nationalist allegiance, and binding the nation to the state. For these purposes, governments controlled and often owned and operated such media within their territories. However, as Western imperialism receded and transnational corporations ascended, global media arose less as instruments of nationalism than of trade. This includes trade in media content as commodities in themselves, and media as advertising platforms for all commodities and for a culture of consumption. Most recently, multiple centers of media production, export and exchange have arisen, contesting Western hegemony and establishing regional dominance. The book will follow this history as it has moved from film to television to digital screen media (see Chapters 2, 4, 6, 9).

Globalization has always been about trade. When traders came with military escorts it became conquest. Global trade is as ancient as civilizations.[29] Ancient empires, such as Persia or Rome, grew by absorbing adjoining territories, transferring goods from periphery to center and then re-distributing them. As modern European nation-states emerged, they were able to acquire and hold colonial empires of non-contiguous territories, often separated by oceans, at far greater distances from the homeland than the adjacent territories of ancient empires. By the sixteenth century a handful of Western European nations had created modern colonial empires and organized the world into parallel, hierarchical systems of trade between European ruling nations and their respective colonies. By 1900, few peoples and little territory lay outside this system.[30]

Colonial rule required occupiers on the ground. Posted throughout the colonial world they constituted an early global bourgeoisie. They and their governments did much to sustain their home cultures in foreign places – exclusive enclaves, children sent home for their education and enculturation, and rulers imposing their home culture and language on colonial government. Appended to this colonial class were the native populations who served and conducted trade with colonials, their governments and businesses. Such in-between population necessarily were familiar with both the colonial's culture and language as well as their own native culture and language. This in-betweenness produced some blended cultures among this class, as well as tension and conflict.

By the mid twentieth century, colonial systems were being challenged by powerful independence movements and by the rise of multi-national corporations.[31] After World War II, Western powers began to re-order the world system with international pacts such as the Bretton Woods monetary agreements, and organizations such as the World Bank. Unlike the competing imperial networks before, this new system allegedly gathered all nations into one open-market trade system, but one of dramatic economic imbalance, with the US at the top, the former European imperial states as its allies, and the rest of the globe gradually slipping from their control. In the same era, the largest corporations in the most multi-national industries, such as oil,[32] changed from multi-nationals that were based in one nation while doing business in many, to become transnational companies without financial interests and allegiance tied to any one nation. The transition to transnational corporations, including media corporations, has been a victory of private over public, since public was by definition circumscribed by national boundaries, while private companies were free to range across the globe wherever they could find profit. At the same time, this did not leave nations powerless. Certainly, strong central governments of large, rich nations have continued to wield great power militarily, politically and economically.

European Nationalism

Coinciding with their formation out of feudal landholdings and fealty relationships, early modern European states engaged in processes to forge unified nations at home.[33] Max Weber recognized that states cannot effectively operate using force alone when he defined the state as an institution with a monopoly of *legitimate* power within a territory. Territorial control by the nation-state demanded discourses to justify its authority. Nation-building is not a once-and-done effort, but requires an apparatus of on-going legitimation to counter disintegrating forces. The creation of a nation required the creation of a unified culture through new narratives, new traditions, new histories and new myths. As one Italian unification leader phrased it, "We've made Italy; now we must make Italians." Modern European states constructed imagined nationalities coterminous with their territorial boundaries to replace feudalistic pyramids of social relations as the glue of society.[34] This entailed defining all subjects as one people and securing their allegiance to the national state.

Defining 'who we are' was buttressed with the creation of traditions ('what we share') and history ('what we did together'). This was accomplished through laws and schools, public celebrations for citizen participation, public monuments as ever present reminders, and through the preservation of 'heritage,' the physical detritus of the past, including buildings, battlefields, and artifacts in museums, given special new meaning.[35]

Strategic use of media propagated these ideas to the masses. Before the twentieth century the medium was print. But its capacity to reach the masses was fore shorn by illiteracy and language differences. The twentieth century visual and aural media promised to overcome some of these limitations. European nations quickly adopted these new media as valuable tools of nationalism. They introduced state policies to tailor film, radio, and television to these purposes through subsidies for domestic producers and trade barriers against imports, and the establishment of broadcasting as a government controlled public service.[36]

Post-Colonial National Unity

Among its many injuries, colonialism created problems of identity for colonial peoples. European rulers created artificial boundaries for their colonies, disregarding traditional tribal territories.[37] The consequences of this persisted after independence. Substantial ethnic minority populations within nations and tribal allegiances across boundaries made constructing a unified national culture more difficult.

In such circumstances, independence movements had to choose between fighting one or two wars: a war of independence against the colonial ruler to establish an independent nation within existing colonial boundaries, and another to redraw boundaries with multiple adjacent nations to create an entirely new map based upon tribal unification. The latter has almost always been sacrificed to the former, due to a necessity to become functionally a nation, in order to negotiate with their colonial ruler and to deal with a world divided into nations.

The principal experience upon which national identity could be built was to define the nation, its population and culture, as opposite to their colonial rulers, different but not inferior. Such a strategy was inherently reactive, in contrast to pro-active and aggressive early modern European nationalism. At the same time, these new nations continued to be economically linked to Western technologies and markets.

These contradictory pulls toward and away from the West contributed to an "inherent contradictoriness in nationalist thinking" for both independence movements and post-colonial governments. Thus, post-colonial historian Partha Chatterjee argues that nationalism developed in these nations, even before independence, through a bifurcation of the 'material,' that is, the economic, the state, science, and technology; and the 'spiritual,' the national culture constructed from tradition, religion, and so on. Control of the former was relinquished to colonial rulers. The latter was insulated from colonial control. Yet over generations of colonialism, Western ideas nevertheless had changed the 'spiritual,' as well – to such a degree that even ancient classics were neglected. Western concepts of nation, individualism, and scientific rationality had become, in historian Dipesh Chakrabarty's words, "both indispensable and inadequate".[38] Western ideas had to be identified, but could not simply be excised or the whole cloth would be damaged. They had to be de-constructed, their universality disclosed as provincialism, making room for non-Western ideas, while not discarding the West entirely.

In an effort to address these contradictions, post-war programs of nationalism constructed new histories of the nation and its peoples, and folklore revivals enshrined fragments of people's cultures while discarding other aspects seen as impediments to modernization. At the same time, nationalist movements adopted Western technology and modernist values (sometimes capitalist, other times socialist), justifying this as necessary to the strength of the nation and a patriotic duty of every citizen.[39] While modernization took priority in earlier post-colonial development, by the late twentieth century, populist ideological programs took precedent, in some cases resulting in a wholesale discard of all things Western, rather than the complexity and subtlety proposed by post-colonial studies and other de-Westernization intellectuals.[40]

Given its perceived importance for nationalist agendas, governments often subsidized the costs of media infrastructure and production of content, in contrast to the American commercial model. Nevertheless recently, just as some nations have heightened their anti-Western stance on culture, they have opted to retreat from government-supported media and shift to a neo-liberal for-profit model, as discussed in Chapter 6.[41]

From White Man's Burden to Modernization Theories

Western colonialism had defined colonial peoples, cultures and socie-ties as backward and colonization as improvement and uplift, that Europeans were the drivers of history and their subjects were the objects of history. As Edward Said explained, Western discourses orientalized the East in order to occidentalize the West and hid the complexity of the relationship.[42]

Western post-war modernization theory and policies continued these social Darwinian presumptions. Arising with de-colonization and post-colonial nation-building, and in the midst of the cold war, it was an instrument with two edges, continuing to define these new nations as culturally backward peoples, while promising economic progress for them at the same time. After World War II, development planning was promoted by American and Soviet technocrats alike, and conflated Western with 'modern' science and technology. Post-colonial societies were conceived as earlier universal stages of economic and political development, with the expectation that technological industrialization was the way forward, whether as capitalist or socialist states.[43]

Consequently, governments launched massive efforts to persuade native populations to shed their traditional culture and adopt modern values, motives and goals. Modern values privileged quantifiable mate-rial gains over traditional satisfactions, social relations and spiritual beliefs. While Western development plans promoted progress through individualism and achievement motivation, post-colonial nation-building emphasized individual sacrifice for the good of the nation.[44] As anthro-pologist William Mazzarella succinctly phrased it:

> ... postcolonial elites within those new nations tended to legitimate their own custodianship of the development ideal – the urgent *need* for development – on the grounds that the vast majority of their less privileged compatriots had so far failed to manifest the [necessary] forms of modern consciousness that had purportedly been achieved in the developed West.[45]

One notable example of modernization theory was psychologist David McClelland's claim that the lack of achievement motivation – in effect, aspiration for upward social and economic mobility – kept poorer nations poor. Judging other cultures using the values of

Western capitalist societies, he concluded that these cultures were preventing Western modernization. As late as 1997, another influential theorist, Alex Inkeles, still denied the ethnocentricity of these theories.[46]

Recently, cosmopolitanism, a cultural outgrowth of globalization, has become another challenge to nationalism. It echoes the suggestions of modernization theory that nations need to shed their traditional cultures and open up to Western ideas. It advocates cultural relativism in which peoples of differing identities and cultures live and let live in the same geographic, social, and political spaces. However, given the continuing wealth and power differential between the West and most post-colonial nations, operationally cosmopolitanism buttresses Westernization more than Western acceptance of post-colonial cultures. It does this in part by turning social relations into market relations and conceiving people as consumers in global markets.[47]

Organization of the Book

This book entails a double structure, one of time, another of space. It is a history of the arrival, rise to dominance and transformation of the principal screen media, from film to television to digital screens. Second, it is a history of spatial differences in media development across nations and the global ebb and flow of media hegemony, and of cultural differences in audiences' use of media and interpretations of their texts. Comparisons across time and space reveal some surprising similarities as well as differences. At the same time, the book will trace two linked developments: on the one hand, the rise and fall of American cultural hegemony; on the other, the consistency among nations of audiences constructing their own cultures out of materials of screen entertainments and, beyond the West, engaged in this process with an ambivalence toward the West and its modernism. Given the uniqueness of historical moments, chapters vary in the attention to production and the texts it produces on the one hand, and audiences and the cultures they produce on the other, depending on which forces are more pertinent to the times and places and the issues discussed. The book examines both the global and the local, that is, at ground level how audiences and others create screen culture through their everyday social interactions in using screen media or reacting to it, and at the national and international levels how screen industries, from the beginning, pursued international markets and established cultural hegemony, and how governments promoted and reacted to those markets and that hegemony.

To make all this manageable, as well as to create a continuing thread through the chapters, I have focused on a few notable national examples to encompass a global history. The primary criteria for these selections are cultural power and market size or population. Population is concentrated in a few nations that constitute half the world's population, which therefore have a great global impact. China has 1.4 billion people; India has 1.25 billion; the EU member nation population is 500 million; the US is 300 million; Brazil 200 million; Nigeria 175 million.[48] This list includes the nations that historically have exercised international cultural power through media, and nations that seem poised to exercise a comparable power as well. Consequently, woven through the chapters are the histories of media developments in the US, Europe, China, India, Brazil, and West Africa, and their relationships to each other.

Film was the first screen medium. Cinema overturned the pre-screen world of live entertainment. Film shared the media spotlight of this era with the aural medium of radio. But it stood above all as *the* popular visual medium. The story of film in the first half of the century is also primarily about Western cultural hegemony. This history is explained in Chapters 1 through 4. By the mid 1950s the second screen medium, television, was established. Television became the quintessential mass medium, with nightly audiences far larger than film. Hollywood became the supplier of much prime-time programming, so television and film had a close but complicated relationship in shaping screen text. Again, the story begins with the US and Europe and moves outward, as post-colonial governments subsidized development in their own nations. Chapters 5 and 6 tell this story.

Toward the end of the century, a complex of new communication devices and infrastructure overturned the film and television worlds. Digitization tied all screen media together, so that the same texts and images were available on multiple platforms and users could shift from one to the other seamlessly. This media interconnectedness also merged industries from film and television to computers and telephone, and provided the groundwork for huge multi-media, global corporations to form. At the same time, these new media were mobile and interactive, and peoples of many nations, previously on the margins of screen media, were now active participants. Chapters 7 through 9 tell these stories.

1

American Cinema to World War I

Moving pictures projected on a screen appeared first as a novelty in the mid 1890s US. It was one among a variety of entertainments in vaudeville halls, amusement parks, circuses and other traveling shows. Within a decade, thousands of new venues showed films exclusively, cropping up in vacant storefronts with rudimentary furnishings and equipment. They became known as nickelodeons for their cheap admission. For the first time, a commercial entertainment was becoming available almost every day, often morning to night, in almost every town, large or small, and affordable to almost every American. Such availability of commercial entertainment was new for the vast majority of people.[1] Watching entertainment was supplanting participation in it, and purchased entertainment was replacing home-made.

Movies increasingly gained a permanent place in the built environment and the culture. Within another decade, these makeshift places were being supplanted by theaters with raked floors and fixed seats, either converted from former drama or variety houses or newly purpose-built for movies. The films themselves increased in length from a few minutes to an hour or more, telling more complicated tales. They became a new form of fiction, alongside print, before radio and less expensive than stage. Millions took advantage of the new availability and the new fiction to become movie-goers.

Such widespread availability and popularity could not but influence culture. A culture specific to movies and movie-going, a screen culture would emerge from this new experience, as would broader cultural changes, propelled by great structural changes in the whole society. This new screen culture did not go unnoticed, especially when numerous poor and untutored were flocking to the movies. Early on, journalists, reformers, government officials and elites of all sorts began to ask whether movies were changing people, culture and society for better or worse.

With a century of hindsight, we address what screen culture arose around movies and movie-going at the time, and what influence that did have on the broader culture. We will lay the groundwork for understanding screen culture by examining its development in the US, by far the largest film market at the time. Screen culture is not simply film texts and their manufacture, but a living culture that people made and expressed *collectively*, as audiences and more. This was especially true in this era when audiences were most active and much discussed in public discourse. Therefore, audiences and the circumstances of their audiencing will be the primary focus here. We will begin with local culture and conditions before film, then with the arrival of film and its incorporation into that context by its audiences and by the communities beyond the theater.

Historical Context

Sociologists Robert and Helen Merrill Lynd, in their classic Middletown studies, provide before and after snapshots of a small midwestern industrial city around 1900 and again in 1923, with which we can measure changes before and after the arrival of movies.[2] The population of 20,000 in 1900 was overwhelmingly white and native born. The first automobile arrived in 1900 at a time when most townsfolk walked to work and for relaxation on a Sunday afternoon; only a few well-off families used a horse-drawn carriage. Traveling players (minstrels, stock companies, circuses) occasionally arrived for a one-night stand in towns like this and nearly the whole town would attend. The Lynds commented, "To be sure, the spectacle-watching habit was strong upon Middletown in the nineties. Whenever they had a chance people turned out to a 'show,' but chances were relatively few" – fewer than 125 performances for the entire year. In small towns like Middletown across America, such shows were staged at the main street opera house, typically a second-floor room with a flat floor to facilitate multipurpose use that hosted meetings of local groups, local dances and traveling players.

In the absence of commercial entertainment, pianos and print served middle-class families for diversion in the home. Girls were expected to play the piano to entertain their family and their guests at home; and it was a common practice for one of the family to read to everyone during the evenings. Working-class men and women had less leisure time and the Lynds noted little more than to say they read, but less.[3]

By the early 1920s Middletown had two passenger cars for every three families, and motoring beyond the town center became a new form of leisure which was especially popular among teens. Movies had made entertainment a permanent fixture and a regular part of the week instead of a special event. The town had grown to a population of 38,000. The Lynds reported for 1923:

> ... nine motion picture theaters operate from 1 to 11pm seven days a week summer and winter; four give three different programs a week, the other five having two a week; thus twenty-two different programs with a total of over 300 performances [per week] ... About two and three-fourths times the city's entire population attended the nine motion picture theaters during July 1923, the 'valley' month, and four and one-half times in the 'peak' month of December.

Movies made commercial entertainment an everyday presence even in this small midwest industrial town. Children attended more than other family members and often without their parents. The Lynds claimed that the automobile and the movies had a "decentralizing tendency" on the family, allowing children and teens to enjoy recreation without their parents. By the mid 1920s, automobiles, movies and radio were thought by local businessmen to reduce community participation, as people did things more often as individuals, families, or small groups.[4] Film histories have documented similar stories in other regions. The trade magazine *Moving Picture World* heralded fancy new movie theater buildings even in small cities.[5]

At the same time, the change depended upon place. Half the US population still lived outside even small towns of 2,500, and rural life in 1920 remained much as it was in 1900. Movie houses in nearby towns and cities were not readily accessible. Many rural families were still on the margins of a money economy and consumer culture, still producing much of their own food, shelter and clothing. Even those who were not poor bought few things compared to urban dwellers. For purchases, they often relied on credit from local merchants until harvest, when they were paid for their crops. While for the urban family the nickelodeon was a short walk from home, for rural families any commercial entertainment required traveling miles by horse on dirt roads that were seasonally impassable. Even mail was infrequent then. During winters, many endured long periods of isolation. For them, movies were less familiar and important than radio a decade later, which brought timely weather information and regular entertainment into their homes. Rural families most often continued to amuse themselves, using inherited skills and resources to tell stories and make music and toys. Only as paved roads, electrification and radio brought the world into rural homes and lives, did the gap between rural and urban life begin to lessen.[6]

At the other extreme, even before 1900, big cities with sufficient populations to supply a steady stream of customers had well-established, permanent, purpose-built venues for entertainments of varied prices and tastes, in a variety of neighborhoods and even languages. By comparison, in small cities, populations were too few and cultural modernization too muted to sustain anything but intermittent visits by itinerant players. At the turn of the century, much was made of the differences between big cities and small cities and towns in rural settings far from metropolitan centers. A wide range of writers from novelists to journalists to sociologists around the turn of the century took note of the psychological impact of cities' density, constant stimulation and anonymity, and a whole genre of writing dwelt on the suffocating society of small towns and the lonely and dangerous anonymity in big cities.[7]

Some recent scholarship focusing on big cities explains the rise of cinema as an aspect of a singular larger cultural phenomenon, urban modernism or modernity. According to such theses, urbanization and industrialization created "constant sensory change, nervous stimulation, feverish stress, speed," psychological states that produced alienation and reshaped the culture. But the term elides examination of social and economic structures such as capitalism and class differences or specific cultural changes underlying the label.[8] Around the turn of the twentieth century, compelling historical forces were bringing deep and broad structural changes to the US: industrial capitalism, urbanization and immigration. At the end of the nineteenth century, American industrial capitalism was becoming concentrated in the hands of huge corporations that matured and solidified in this era, establishing a new structural foundation to the society that would displace and gradually marginalize the agricultural, localized world that preceded it. Urbanization was increasing with it. In 1900 a quarter (26%) of the population lived in cities of 25,000 or more; in 1920 that had risen to more than a third (36%). Historian Olivier Zunz put it in his study of Detroit at the turn of the century:

> Central to the formation of modern North American society has been the growth of a vast urban industrial complex, extending from the Eastern Seaboard to the Great Lakes region, which began in the 1870s and reached maturity in the 1920s ... A modern urban world, with

new dimensions ... Simultaneously, large business corporations accomplished an organizational revolution in mass production and distribution
techniques.[9]

This "industrial complex" required labor that was supplied by an
equally vast wave of immigration. During 1900–1920, half of all
foreign born in the US resided in the northeast and an additional
30–40 percent in the midwest where Zunz's complex arose. By contrast,
the stagnant agricultural economies of the South and West attracted
relatively few foreign born.[10]

Fear of this massive population of immigrants, so visibly congregated in dense neighborhoods of large cities, was substantial, ranging
from conservatives to progressives. They and their neighborhoods
became targets of moral panics and policing, racial theorizing and
eugenic policies, the temperance movement, and other regimes of
control.[11] A racial eugenics movement applied the new tool of IQ
testing to racial distinctions and advocated compulsory sterilization
and restrictive immigration laws. At the same time, progressives exhibited ambivalences between sympathy on the one hand, and abhorrence
of their tastes and values, on the other.[12]

It was amid these deep historic changes and moral panics about
them that moving pictures arrived. Inevitably that first screen culture
would be influenced by these contexts, much as they would be in
other nations and times.

Early Moving Picture Exhibition

Moving pictures were first introduced as part of established entertainments, and in the context of their managerial and audience practices.
While timing and details vary, film exhibition in North America and
Western Europe, as well as in colonial capitals and ports around the
world, originated at nearly the same time in the mid 1890s and followed similar paths of development – a prime example of a globalized
market.[13]

From the mid 1890s to the early 1900s what attracted audiences
was their fascination with the novelty of a moving image. Films of
this period recorded mundane everyday events, documentaries of
notable events, demonstrations of new inventions and curiosities, film
tricks, and simple comic scenes. Films were short, often as little as
five minutes, and audiences would watch several at a sitting.

Such novelties had long been a part of stage entertainment. In early
nineteenth-century US drama theaters, the typical bill included brief

performances before, between and after the featured play, in part to keep audiences focused on the stage and out of trouble. Variety entertainments such as minstrelsy, vaudeville and burlesque evolved from this. When film arrived on these stages it was simply another act in a variety bill. Operators touring outside big cities exhibited the new phenomenon just about anywhere that they could obtain darkness and admission charges – in meeting halls or tents, at circuses and country fairs.

Film pioneers began exhibitions in 1896 in order to demonstrate their fascinating new moving-picture projectors. Early equipment manufacturers – Thomas Edison in the US, and George Melies, Louis Lumière, Leon Gaumont, and Charles Pathé in France – began making films in part to sell their equipment.

Anyone who had the modest initial capital to buy film-making equipment – roughly $100 in the mid 1890s, equivalent to $2500 in 2015 – could begin making films. Since films of this time were mostly of actual events, they required little specialization and little costs to film: no script, no sets or costumes, no writers, directors or actors, and no editing. To make a film, a single person could set up a camera at a parade, sport event, or even on a town street and start the film rolling. Slightly more complicated 'trick' films required a performer or two, a few staging tricks and editing skills to create illusions such as people disappearing or floating through the air. Production was in the artisan tradition that pre-dated industrial mass production; the artisan engaged the entire production process from conception to finished product. Early pioneers had to invent the first film-making techniques. In some cases, the film-maker was also the exhibitor, traveling from place to place with his camera, projector and collection of films.

By the turn of the century, the novelty of a moving picture was wearing off.[14] In cities, big-time vaudeville houses began to drop them from their bill. If film was to survive commercially, it needed a new form of appeal. To sustain people's interests, exhibitors and producers turned to fictional narrative. Filming single-scene comic sketches typical of variety acts made the shift to narrative easier. At first, any local actors or amateurs and minimal scenery and props would suffice. But the demand for stories soon led to more narratives, taken from dramatic plays and print fiction, and to longer, more expensive films.[15] Producers increased production of story films, and developed montage strategies to help audiences follow the story, inserting title and dialog boards in silent films to explain the action and announce scene shifts. By 1908, 96 percent of total American production was narrative comedy and drama.

Paralleling the development of narrative film, several factors coalesced to support exhibition spaces dedicated exclusively to moving pictures: Sufficient production and a system of rental exchanges or wholesalers could supply enough new films for continuous showings and frequent program changes. With this supply source, a small entrepreneur could rent a vacant storefront on a busy street and install a projector, a screen and a couple of hundred chairs, all available at relatively modest costs. A nickel admission was modest as well, about a quarter of a laborer's hourly wage and thus affordable even to the working class.

Nickelodeons spread so rapidly and created such demand that they fueled further development of narrative films. Narrative films were better suited to rationalizing production and deliver on the regular schedule needed by nickelodeons, since they could be manufactured on schedule. Such mass production required increased speed and efficiency. But at first, American film producers could not keep up with the growth of nickelodeons. A shortage in 1906 enabled European film companies, who were pioneering longer narrative films, to expand their US market. In 1907 two thirds of films released in the US were European, with the French company Pathé alone accounting for a third of the entire market. They briefly established hegemony in the American film industry and across the world, making film into a global industry, as described in Chapter 2.

Urban Nickelodeons and Neighborhood Audiences

For many, the nickelodeon's sheltered space in crowded urban neighborhoods had its own attractions, aside from the moving pictures. A Progressive reformer noted in 1909 that "Certain houses have become genuine social centers where neighborhood groups may be found any evening of the week [and] where the regulars stroll up and down the aisles and visit friends." Such stories reporting the animated behavior, talkativeness and sociability of audiences in working-class nickelodeons, were frequent in the popular and trade presses. American social historians have documented many examples of working-class audiences adapting nickelodeons to their own needs and purposes, including community meetings as well as sociability.[16]

However, such sociality in theaters pre-dated nickelodeons. Before film, it was common at cheap theater entertainments, particularly at drama, variety and puppet shows that working classes could afford. Audiences often included women and children, as well as men. Immigrants from a wide range of cultures, including East European Jews, Poles, Italians, and Chinese, reportedly were lively and vocal in their favored haunts. Drama critic and writer John Corbin, slumming at a cheap theater in New York's Little Italy in the 1900s described their habits, "They would speak to you on the slightest pretext, or none, and would relate all that was happening on stage." Sicilian men were avid and vocal attendees at puppet theaters that performed Renaissance Italian epic poems about crusades and other battles, one episode each night running for months. Arts critic Carl Van Vechten described Yiddish theater audiences too as busily talking, eating and drinking. A cartoon of the time contrasted the 'uncouth' behavior of Lower East Side, Yiddish-speaking Jews in disarray at a theater to respectable uptown audiences sitting quietly. Chinese audiences in San Francisco were described in similar ways in books published in the late nineteenth century. At the venerable Bowery Theater in 1911, then called the Thalia, playwright and critic Channing Pollock reported the same sociability. Before they became nickelodeons, urban buildings were used as meeting halls for working-class inhabitants. The informality and familiarity of the storefront and its furnishing contributed to an at-homeness for audiences. Moveable chairs were familiar from saloons and one's own kitchen. Minimal and inexpensive decoration, lax management policies and few employees to police behavior, as well as cheap admission, further cued attendees that sociability fitted the situation.[17]

Sociologist and urban designers have long observed the importance of public spaces in the cityscape where people could congregate for sociability.[18] Sociability is an asset of the community as a whole, which increases trust among residents, likelihood of public discussion of community issues and collective action to resolve those, as well as overall desirability as a place to live.[19] European plazas, arising as destinations in organically developed cities, served such functions. But most American cities in the nineteenth century adopted a grid street system whose straightaway avenues favored un-hindered movement and transportation over congregation and sociability. They lacked plazas, small parks and playgrounds. In tight-packed 'tenement districts' even street space itself was at a premium. By the end of the century, the Progressive playgrounds movement argued that immigrant children especially lacked public spaces in their neighborhood to make them into 'good citizens.' The reformers planned to supervise the children's play and shape them into the white upper-middle-class American ideal.[20]

In large American cities, space was scarce. Men had their saloons; nickelodeons offered space for women and children as well. Nickelodeons had several attractive features over playgrounds, parks, settlement houses and other public spaces offered by upper-middle-class

WASP reformers: first, they were more numerous and convenient; second, they were indoors sheltered from cold and rain; third, they were not supervised by well-meaning reformers trying to Americanize these immigrants; fourth, adults could converse among themselves while supervising the children; and fifth, they could enjoy the movies.

Socializing in urban nickelodeons, as various ethnic groups did, was a practical adaptation of a new public space to the needs of residents. In neighborhood theaters, one was more likely to know others in the audience. Such neighborhoods tended to be more homogeneous and self-contained, due to the fact that immigrants who did not speak English found it easier to live, shop and even work within their own native-language communities. Consequently, they more likely knew their neighbors, not by virtue of longevity – there was significant turnover, people leaving to seek work elsewhere – but by virtue of a native-language social network. One might be inclined to talk to a stranger in this circumstance, as they may have the neighborhood, acquaintances and home country in common. Thus, in Corbin's experience, "they would speak to you on the slightest pretext."[21]

Spellbound in Darkness

If nickelodeons were an opportunity for sociability, then what did moving pictures mean to their audiences? We need to distinguish impact on cultural practices from readings of movie text. As a place, nickelodeons constituted a substantial expansion of the availability of entertainment from an occasional event to a part of daily life, the female equivalent to the homosocial saloon. Early cinema audiences defined that in itself as positive enough that they would pay for it from meager incomes. As cultural texts, moving pictures constituted the first great leap into the virtual reality of moving images, beginning a century of screen that substantially increased mediated visual experience. They made the unfamiliar familiar. They enabled audiences to visualize places and witness events that previously they could only read about. The film brought a wider view of the world within their financial, geographical and social reach.

What then was the cultural impact of film texts? As a general rule, we may expect that the more activity reported among audiences, the less they are attending to and absorbed in the text, and thus are likely to be less influenced by it. In the nickelodeon era, working-class patrons frequently went for the 'place' more than the 'play.'[22] On the other hand, the middle and higher classes did not need movie theaters for sociability; for that they could afford other spaces, such as clubs and their more spacious homes. Yet the films themselves still held an attraction which, combined with middle-class norms of propriety, made these audiences less sociable and more attentive to the films. For them, the 'spell-binding'[23] effect may have been more noticeable, especially as narrative films grew to feature length that required sustained attention. Class difference in attention-span is not at issue here, especially as immigrants from rural cultures were accustomed to extended story-telling during long winter nights.[24] Thus audience differences in sociability versus attention to the film would seem to derive from social contexts, not from audience attention span. Nevertheless, a darkened room invited movie-goers' immersion in an alternative reality and heightened the experience of 'being there.' It could stimulate imagination, hope, ambition, discontent or resistance, depending on audience members' inclination or social location.

Darkened theaters originated before moving pictures, at electrically lit drama theaters that the upper and upper-middle classes frequented, enabling the introduction of dramatic realism and the 'fourth wall' separating audiences from actors. This experience was heightened in movies by the fact that actors were mere light images, not living persons with whom audiences could interact. Moreover, it created a disjuncture between inside and outside the cinema that segregated the screen culture experience from everyday reality. For movies, the fourth wall was not the proscenium, but the doors to the theater.

Grander, purpose-built theaters also promoted a subdued audience more absorbed in the film. By the 1910s, American movie theater managers sought a 'better class' clientele and employed larger staffs to police and prevent any disturbance. Higher admission also announced this as a formal event calling for appropriate behavior. Even lower-income clientele would have considered it a special occasion, not to be spoiled by the noise and spontaneity of sociability. These several developments helped to shift movie-going expectations away from sociability to silence in the theater.

Public Reactions

With the appearance of low-priced, store-front theaters on neighborhood shopping streets in large cities in the 1900s, movies quickly gained a reputation as the 'working man's amusement.' Most of urban American stage entertainment was already class-segmented into separate markets, such as melodrama versus legitimate theater and small time versus refined vaudeville. Specifically, nickelodeons became identified with immigrant working classes in urban tenement districts of the largest cities, notably New York, Philadelphia and Chicago, principal destinations for immigrants and where early film production first flourished – and incidentally where opinion-makers and print media were concentrated. Muckraking journalist and future publisher of the *Chicago Tribune* and the *New York Daily News*, Joseph Medill Patterson characterized the new phenomenon in the *Saturday Evening Post* in 1907, "The nickelodeon is tapping an entirely new stratum of people, is developing into theatergoers a section of population that formerly knew and cared little about the drama ... foreigners attend in larger proportions than the English speakers."[25]

Outside large cities, film audiences typically included the whole community, a mix of classes within a single exhibition space, just as stage audiences had been in the nineteenth century.[26] But in the largest cities, a lower-class image stuck to nickelodeons and was persuasive to many contemporaries, be they reformers or film investors and producers. Consequently, there were significant calls for and efforts to 'improve' nickelodeons, their films, and their reputations, by attracting respectable middle-class audiences.

Such reactions were not new. Nineteenth-century commercial entertainments, from drama to vaudeville, and print from illustrated news to the yellow press, aroused hopes and fears when they first became popular. Parents, religious leaders, cultural authorities and others feared these as challenges to their influence and authority and to accepted values and beliefs about reality, life, morality, justice, and equality, shaking the foundations of social norms and social order. Moreover, such fears typically involved higher classes, who had the power to impose their own social norms upon lower classes.[27]

Reactions to the popularity of movies at the turn of the twentieth century in the US occurred in the context of broader elite concerns about growing urbanization, immigration, and commercialization causing 'hyper-stimulation' among the 'anonymous masses,' as described above. Adding to this around 1900, rapid diffusion of new consumer technologies, such as electricity, automobiles, and telephone, was changing the daily lives of the affluent. Movies epitomized the consumer culture and, even more concerning to elites left and right, they were affordable to working classes and their children.

Movies arrived amid a major shift in moral panics, from concerns about women to concerns about children. Through much of the nineteenth century, upper and upper-middle-class women symbolized the respectability of their families, husbands, and fathers. Numerous books depicted city streets as dangerous places; etiquette manuals advised women what to avoid and how to behave to shield themselves in public. However, around the turn of the century, concern shifted to children, particularly working-class children, and their parenting. This shift also was spurred by concerns that immigrant children would be future citizens and voters, and therefore it was important to 'Americanize' them into the values of the upper-middle class.[28]

The working-class response to these concerns, by and large, was to choose entertainment over uplift. Marketing won over reform, continuing the general failure of Progressive reform attempts to regulate, plan, and control the leisure of the working class; the fun offered by commercial entertainment was more attractive. This further cemented the image of movie-going as a habit of the working classes and immigrants.[29]

The association with the working class made nickelodeons and moving pictures disreputable in the eyes of the middle and upper classes. In the US, concerns first arose about *where* movies were viewed. Reformers focused on the potential for immorality in darkened nickelodeons, especially by men preying upon teenage girls. Quite soon concern about place was supplanted by concerns about immoral ideas in films 'implanted' in the minds of 'youths,' i.e. teens, leading to crime and ruinous sex. Elites critical of cinema typically imagined the audiences as crowds of uneducated, impressionable working-class and immigrant adults as well as children, all susceptible to ideas suggested by movies, and contrasted them to the respectable and higher-class, 'well-behaved' good citizens of strong character who could resist such suggestions. These concerns gave rise to regimes of control, such as licensing and censorship.[30]

Pursuing the Middle Classes

In1908, *Moving Picture World* (*MPW*), editorialized that, "... manufacturers must watch carefully the quality of their pictures or the better class of patrons will turn against the motion picture and the profits seriously reduced." Decision-makers in the film industry, including producers, distributors, exhibitors, and trade journalists, were aware that the 'respectable' public perceived nickelodeons as working-class establishments and considered them disreputable. Industry leaders also believed that the upper middle class was a more profitable clientele. Therefore they pursued a marketing strategy to seek the respectability and profits of the middle class. This strategy had recurred from drama theater to minstrelsy to vaudeville since the 1840s. The movie industry repeated this strategy not only for profits, but also to avoid government regulation and censorship.[31]

Marketing to higher-income classes was linked to the development of purpose-built movie theaters. It also added to the trend to feature-length films that met aesthetic and moral standards of respectability.[32] By 1910, *MPW* claimed that a transformation had begun. In 1911, an article noted that, "Not since the moving picture became the photoplay has there been released in a similar space of time more truly notable pictures than those in the past six months." A *MPW* editorial asserted: "It is the unanimous experience [of exhibitors across the nation] that the picture is ascending higher and higher in public favor and the better class of people are being attracted to it, and that there is a growing distaste for that which is not elevating and refining." *MPW* also claimed that better movies enabled theaters to charge higher prices. In 1912 a columnist claimed that movies were thriving in scores of theaters that showed pictures exclusively, charging 15 to 25 cents. Consequently, the first 'movie palaces' were sited in middle-class neighborhoods near commuter lines. Exhibitors redefined their audiences as patrons and themselves as good members of the neighborhood community.[33]

The success in seeking respectability and the middle class had significant consequences. The toll on stage entertainment was striking, contributing to the decline of most live stage entertainment that might have competed with the movie industry for audiences and dollars. The impact was greatest on companies touring outside the major cities. American theater impresario Robert Grau claimed that "conditions in the one-night stands are simply unbelievable; cities of 50,000 are without a single legit place of amusement, the regular theaters all being used for moving pictures or what is called 'pop' vaudeville." *Billboard* estimated that, in 1910, there were approximately 1,500 theaters of the one- or two-night stop for road shows; by 1925, only about 600 remained. Between 1909 and 1915, the number of touring companies plummeted from about 300 to 100 per year and never recovered. By 1913 movies also were affecting big city theaters. Three of the biggest investors in stage entertainment, the Shubert Brothers, Klaw and Erlanger, and F. F. Proctor announced shifts to the movie business.[34] All this represented the loss of jobs for thousands of performers, stage hands, and ancillary workers.

Film Text and Culture

Film introduced a new scale of audiences, measured in millions, instead of thousands. Given the sheer numbers of people and their frequent attendance, it would seem that the collective representations and narratives of early films was likely to influence culture. Such influence would be greater if the same theme recurred across many films, repeating the same representations again and again. Repetition makes an idea seem pervasive and persistent, suggesting that everyone thinks it, so it must be true. Film scholars have focused primarily on the influence of single films, actors or directors upon film texts. But in order for film to have a broader impact, pervasive themes must be shared by numerous films over extended periods of time.[35]

Some film historians have placed American films within the context of American cultural history and argued for it as an expression *of* that culture, as well as an influence *upon* that culture.[36] In the Hollywood studio era, studio moguls cautiously avoided taking any lead in cultural change and preferred to follow the mainstream culture. The nickelodeon era, however, may have allowed more flexibility and openness in shaping film text. This was the era of director and director-unit production, before the specialization and assembly line production of the Hollywood studio system. The director had full authority in making decisions and played a significant part in the actual work, from script-writing to camera work to editing. Films were cheap to make, under $1,000, so bad decisions were less costly, allowing directors greater leeway as they invented this new medium and conceived ways to tell stories on film. Because production was less centralized, this enabled them also to make films suited to their audience constituency, which often was working class rather than mainstream middle class.[37]

Representing Class and Gender

One factor influencing film texts during this era was the particular social lens through which directors told the stories. Many of them were familiar with working-class experience. Often they were mechanics accustomed to working with their hands. Several, such as D. W. Griffith, could not only draw upon this experience for stories, but also had a personal interest in doing so. For this and other reasons, films of the nickelodeon era more often told their stories from the view-point of working-class or less powerful people, rather than from that of people in positions of authority or affluence.

Many films of this era featured a working-class protagonist, set in working-class workplaces or neighborhoods, who challenged authority, according to historian Steven Ross, who examined some 600 movies made between 1905 and 1917. Comedies frequently chose as the butt of humor upwardly striving, middle-class husbands and their wives, and pompous bosses, owners, and authority figures, while working-class characters were often the irreverent pranksters bursting their balloon and getting away with it. The working class was portrayed as unburdened by the stuffiness of their 'betters' and as escaping their authority. Moreover, comedy was the most popular genre at nickelodeons, so these subversive texts had large audiences.[38]

Second in popularity was melodrama, including all its permutations, such as the evil landlord, the chase films, westerns, and a variety of serials. These films frequently depicted the gross inequity between extravagant, often immoral, rich villains and honest, hard-working poor. In addition, these melodramas depicted the working-class "as middle-class people without money ... idealized versions of how the middle class ought to behave ... clean, respectable, hard-working, virtuous, kind, and supportive of family."[39] In other words, working-class people were imagined as sharing the same values as the middle class, making them seem less threatening and more appealing to middle-class audiences. As we will see in later chapters, such positive depictions of the working class in comedy and melodrama would not last in film or television. Gender and class were interwoven in movie serials. In the 1910s, American producers introduced serials as a new form of melodrama targeting young women workers, as well as some for an even younger market of pre-adolescents.[40] These serials presented stories of adventure and featured heroines rather than male heroes. Serial films were about twenty minutes long and typically adapted from popular serialized stories in magazines and dime novels. Sometimes, film and novel were promoted, published and screened simultaneously.

The episodes in magazines and films appeared weekly or monthly and were first produced in the waning years of nickelodeons before Hollywood took hold of the industry. In 1914 a reformer noted that, while New York City girls from affluent families were filling the seats for stage matinees, young working-class women were 'crazed' about the movies and particularly these serials. The 'matinee idol,' the lead in romance plays, was the object of affection of more affluent play-going girls. However, working-class girls were reading dime novels and watching movie serials starring adventurous working heroines – whose romance was secondary to her overcoming dangers and striving for success. Serial titles themselves advertised the excitement: *Hazards of Helen, Perils of Pauline, Adventures of Kathryn*, all releases in 1914. Young women were portrayed as civil-war spies, detectives, telegraph operators, and railroad workers. They endured and overcame chases, fires, and villains. The actress who played Helen was known for her risky stunts, such as running atop a fast-moving train.[41] The appeal to working-class girls would seem to be not only the adventure, but the underlying independence of the characters, since their own autonomy was circumscribed by low wages and persisting patriarchal traditions.[42] At the same time, the heroines often ended up married, a realistic outcome for the era.

In New York City, these serials were part of a distinct working-class 'ladyhood' constructed by young working-class women. The young women in the audiences were striking for better wages and work conditions, wore cheap high heels that middle-class women shunned, and forged their own style culture from commodities within their income reach. Dime novels and movie serials complemented this assertive femininity. It also was a collective culture. As with any serial form, fans would end up consuming episodes out of order, which likely heightened the importance of the participative experience. They talked among themselves about the stories and shared their fashion sense with their workmates. They also used the nickelodeon as a place to meet and talk with young men as well as friends. The heroine characters contradicted the middle-class notion of femininity as passive, probably both reflecting and contributing to cultural changes in gender and affirming working-class women's own definition of femininity.[43]

Screen Culture and Culture

When movie exhibition was a business of small-scale independent nickelodeon operators, requiring little capital to enter the business, audiences had more say in their use of the spaces. When film was easily and cheaply made, and distributed by the foot, the film was not paramount and audiences' need for sociability defined the situation. Moreover, its definition as a working-class space also succeeded in demanding film topics suitable to this circumstance. The screen culture was of the audiences' making more than of business manufacture. From nickelodeon to nickelodeon, the experiences and subcultures were as similar or different as the cultures of the various neighborhoods or towns. Yet in places as different as ethnic urban neighborhoods and small towns in rural countryside, they shared common needs for diversion and sociability, and similar audience spontaneity and volubility established the place as their own. Likewise, during hours when they predominated, women and girls bent the definition to suit their particular needs, and films depicting heroines followed suit.

As the business began to develop and institutionalize, the voices of audiences were less strong, and the industry more. The move from nickelodeon to theater and from short one-reelers to feature films, the moral panic and the re-branding, together transformed screen culture from a creation *by* working-class audiences into one fashioned *for* the

American upper-middle class. The principal places and their representations, and their enforcement of certain values and norms changed from ones welcoming working-class people to ones disciplining them. The principal films paralleled this, changing from frequent positive representations of working-class characters to themes preferable to upper-middle class clientele. Theaters and films serving working-class clientele – still a large source of income and profits for the industry – continued, but were limited, compared to the nickelodeon era.

Ironically, this marginalization of working-class movie-goers' influence occurred in the same decades in which these workers were forming stronger unions and gaining higher wages, shorter hours and better working conditions. But it also was a time of growth of the upper-middle, white-collar class of professionals and managers and the size and power of the corporations that employed them. Also, it was a time of an emerging culture of consumption built on and by these corporations to draw the population increasingly into purchasing rather than making their lives.

2

Global Cinema, 1900–1920

Film exhibition began as a global phenomenon, arriving almost simultaneously in the mid 1890s in many large cities around the world, not only New York, London, and Paris, but also cities such as Shanghai, Cairo, Bombay, and Buenos Aires as well. Traveling showmen presented their own collections of films as part of vaudeville and other stage entertainments. Outside major cities, showmen presented films in tents and open-air arenas at fairs and other temporary sites. Shortly, in the largest cities, permanent, film-only theaters began to proliferate.

Decades of Hollywood dominance give the appearance that film history was always one of American cultural hegemony. But the pre-Hollywood, pre-World War I history is marked by European film dominance in the US and around the world. Early film screen projection as a technology and an entertainment was an innovation of Europeans as much as, or more than, Americans. A conjunction of circumstances led to European film companies capturing much of the American exhibition market in this era. Moreover, their position in colonial empires enabled them to gain control of nascent markets across the rest of the world. Only in the 1910s did American film companies recapture their domestic market, and begin to dominate markets in Europe as well as around the world.[1]

The development of film exhibition in the US varied. While equivalent exhibition spaces may have arisen in many countries, their numbers and duration seem to have differed from one place to another. It would be inappropriate to call this the nickelodeon era in all nations. Certainly, in the US nickelodeons were a widespread phenomenon and their rapid spread widely commented upon. Britain experienced some of this, but to a lesser degree and for a briefer time. France even less so, and Italy less again. India, on the other hand, had cheap venues early on, mostly temporary tent affairs, not unlike the traveling showman at fairs in rural areas of Western nations. China indicates yet another story, in which cheap movie venues in the 1910s and 1920s remained part of amusement houses limited to the largest cities.

Information on audiences, what they did in these spaces, and how they responded to the films in this era, is often fragmented. The relatively robust body of research in the US is an accident of history. Progressive reformers were struck by nickelodeon's popularity among urban working classes, and documented numbers, locations, and conditions of these venues and recorded observations of the audiences. Their concerns stirred broader discussion in newspaper and magazine articles. That trove of first-hand testimony was used in the 1930s by a couple of film historians, Benjamin Hampton and Lewis Jacob, who wrote the first histories. Then it lay dormant until it was revived in the 1970s by a new generation of working-class historians. As a result, we are fortunate to have a fairly good base of research on early film audiences in the US.[2] By comparison, Italian film exhibition and audiences appear to have involved a substantially smaller portion of the population. Moreover, there seems to have been less public discussion about the impact of film and film-going, and thus less visible and more scattered first-hand documentation.[3]

To understand cross-nation variations we must examine some of the economic, political, and cultural contexts of these countries, including general economic development, globalization and market hegemony, urbanization and industrialization, the income of lower classes and affordability of cinema to them, war and other instability, colonial policies and conditions, government stability, and social, cultural, and moral movements affecting film and exhibition spaces. We will examine such contexts to understand audience responses and film's cultural implications, and to compare that to globalization discussed in later chapters.

Early European Film Culture

The development of national film industries depended not only upon technological and commercial innovation and infrastructure, but also upon the economic demand for film and film-going that the nation's population could generate – that is, how many people who liked and could afford to go, and how often. The technology of cinema offered the potential for a low-cost commercial entertainment, but would require a large population who could purchase such entertainment on a regular basis and could find a cinema within convenient distance. If industrial prosperity was shared by the masses, it could create sufficient demand for affordable commercial entertainment, and cinema in particular. For example, European visitors to the US in the mid nineteenth century were struck by the fact that American manual workers attended commercial entertainments while those of their home nations, with lower wages, could not.[4] In general, film exhibition thrived in cities, where sufficient numbers were near enough to a cinema to make attendance convenient and regular. Therefore we begin by looking at the degree of widespread prosperity in urban industrial nations.

Among Western nations, the US, Britain, and Germany increased their shares of world industrial production exponentially in the nineteenth century. Industry in France grew some, while growth in Italy, Eastern Europe, Russia, and Japan was relatively stagnant.[5] At the turn of the twentieth century, when cinema was new, Britain was among the greatest industrial powers, rivaled only by the US and Germany, and was particularly strong in shipping and export. It also ruled the world's largest colonial empire, encompassing about a fifth of the world population. Britain colonized or controlled almost all of eastern Africa from Egypt to South Africa, much of south Asia from the Near East to India to Canton (now Quangzhou), Shanghai, and Hong Kong. Canada, Australia, and New Zealand, with British and Irish majority populations, also were part of the empire, although with a greater degree of self-governance. This vast empire supplied great wealth to fuel industrialization, which had had a substantial head start over the US and Germany. Unification of Germany came only in the late nineteenth century and only belatedly did it build a world empire, mostly in Africa; on the other hand, the US had sufficient market size within its borders that made export less necessary for corporate profits in the late nineteenth century.

Working-class wages in Britain rose in the last two decades of the nineteenth century, leveling off around 1900. About the same time, a nascent welfare state began to undergird a working-class standard of living.[6] This enabled the British working class to spend modestly on commercial entertainment. Paralleling its earlier and greater industrialization, Britain was more densely populated and urbanized than France and Italy. These factors favored a growth in demand for urban commercial entertainments such as pubs, music hall, and especially movie theaters, given their substantially cheaper admission price.[7]

In the early twentieth century, France was much more an agricultural society than Britain. Historian Eugen Weber stated that in the 1860s, "… nowhere in England could one find anything approaching the distance that separated the [urban industrial] departments of Nord and Seine-Inferieure, say, from [rural] Lozere and Landes." Even in the 1890s, there was still comment on the striking gulf between rural and urban France. Lack of secondary transportation and long-standing social, political and cultural differences had slowed the spread of modernization to rural areas. Moreover, the course of industrialization diverged from Britain. Large-scale industrialization was slow to develop in France; instead it had a relatively smaller industrial and proportionally more artisanal working class. High quality production on a small scale was favored culturally over mass-produced quantities. At the same time, the Third Republic considerably expanded public education, health care, and social welfare from 1890 to 1910, boosting the industrial working-class standard of living.[8]

With this support, a proportionally smaller urban working class of skilled artisans had a standard of living that was sufficient to sustain a market in Paris for neighborhood café concerts, the French equivalent of Britain's music halls, and later, a market for the nascent film industry. Some of the Parisian working class was even beginning to participate in the consumerism of large department stores. But little of this extended to smaller cities and towns. Even while the bourgeoisie outside Paris had their local opera and theater, others mostly were left to their own folk entertainments. A guide to such towns in 1901 noted that "… diversions are rare." Instead, the Third Republic fostered a cultural class divide, with the haute bourgeoisie supporting a high culture, and other classes, with the arrival of local cinema theaters, transitioning to a nationwide, mass-produced popular culture.[9]

In both France and Italy, dominant contemporary discourses depicted the rural peasantry as backward and retarding modernization. But in Italy, rural poverty was more severe; many landless agricultural workers, even in the north, had a status not unlike peasants. Even less industrialization, with a quite small industrial workforce, meant that there was not the robust urban working class that marked the early years of film in the US and Britain. Also, the nation was relatively newborn, as political unification of the peninsula was completed only in 1870. Italy remained culturally diverse even after unification. Even in Piedmonte, the heart of the unification movement, people continued to speak Piedmotese. On the other hand, many elites believed that film could help instill a sense of national identity and modernize the culture, so that there was political and financial support for film production. Consequently, despite being more rural and less industrialized than Britain or even France, Italy became an early center of feature-film production, if not consumption.[10]

So the key factor differentiating the spread of film exhibition in these countries was the size and income of the working class.[11] Britain had a proportionally larger, urban working class who could afford cinema, while fewer working-class people in France and Italy could attend. An analysis of a cross national survey of industrial manual-worker families' expenditures in 1889–1890, just a few years before the arrival of film projection, supports this conclusion. Economic historian Gerben Bakker concluded from this survey that US workers' incomes were roughly 30 percent higher than those in Britain and Britain's 30 percent higher than those in France. These suggest that higher incomes in the US indicate a large population who could afford amusements. But this is complicated by the fact that, at the same time, expenditures on recreation and amusement in the British and French samples was proportionally more than three times higher than in the US (3.5–4.0% v 1.1%).[12] This suggests that a larger portion of the population on lower incomes in Britain and France had opted to purchase amusements by foregoing other expenditures. This reduced, but did not erase, the cross-national differences in film-going markets. Thus, US and, to a lesser extent, British film manufacturers were less dependent on exporting their films to make a profit, while France and Italy were more dependent on export. This necessity probably partly accounts for early French international film hegemony.

This connection between film industry development and the working class was due to the fact that film exhibition's greatest advantage was its cheap admission price. It was affordable for a much larger sector of the working class than previous commercial entertainments.[13] This does not mean that it appealed more to the working class than to other classes, as implied by the common labeling of it as a 'working man's amusement,' nor that working-class people were necessarily the largest portion of the audience. But it does suggest that cinema exhibition was more successful in places of greater industrialization and urbanization, more in the US and Britain than in France and Italy, and more in the West than elsewhere. Place, then, was an impor-tant determinant of availability as well as affordability of the new screen medium of film. In addition, a whole range of cultural capital and cultural constructions would distinguish what films were distrib-uted, how and where, to what audiences, and how audiences behaved in and made use of those venues and reacted to the films, to which we will turn below. But first, we will address the issue of relative dominance of various national film industries.

From French to Hollywood Hegemony

For at least the first two decades of the twentieth century, the US was the largest market for moving picture exhibition, so large that Ameri-can companies found it difficult in the 1900s to supply the rapidly

growing market, as discussed in Chapter 1. Consequently, much of
the film exhibited in the US was imported. Indicating the potential
profitability of such a large market, Charles Pathé, founder of the
French film company, described its size, "… their huge interior market,
which, concerning box office revenue, represents forty to fifty times
the French one, thus three quarters of the world market."[14]

One may have expected that British film companies would have
been in the forefront of export to such a large and lucrative market.
Still a dominant world power and industrial economy, and their shared
language and relatively greater cultural compatibility should have given
Britain a distinct advantage in the US market. In addition, Britain had
the world's largest empire and shipping business and thus was well
positioned to support export businesses that could have been directed
toward the US. Demonstrating such export potential, American films
companies initially chose British agents for distribution in Europe
and across the rest of the world. Finally, Britain had an early start in
film, due to a group of pioneering British men in the 1890s who built
their own equipment, made their own movies and exhibited them.[15]

But earlier concentration of the French industry gave it an advantage in export, and a smaller, less developed, home market gave it
strong incentive to export. From 1895 to 1903, continental European,
mostly French, companies' share of the US market grew to about 50
percent, and remained high until the 1910s. One commentator claimed
that, by 1907, 80 percent of film footage shown in the US was foreign.
The French film company, Pathé Frères supplied more films to the US
than any other company, including any domestic US company. By
1906, Pathé was the largest French film producer, and was becoming
vertically integrated, including a large chain of theaters. Its domestic
dominance provided a base to become a powerful exporter, from
which it gained 60 percent of its revenues by 1907. At its peak, Pathé
accounted for between 50 and 70 percent of the world film market.
Pathé's biggest market by far was the US, where it sent three fourths
of its film prints, and supplied a third of all films shown in the US.
Its size enabled it to produce in quantity to fill the demand of rapidly
growing American nickelodeons. Pathé claimed to release six new
films per week in 1906, and seven in 1907, a rate of production
American companies could not match. Eastman Kodak, which manufactured approximately 90 percent of all film negative footage world-
wide at the time, claimed that Pathé accounted for two thirds of all
footage of positive film stock sold in the US. Moreover, much of the
trade at that time considered Pathé films to be superior both in filming
quality and entertainment value, and were in such demand that major
American companies duplicated Pathé films without permission and
sold the duplicates widely.[16]

Italy's film export to the US was second only to France's.[17] Its film production grew rapidly from 1908 to the beginning of World War I by gaining financial backing from aristocrats and venture capitalists. However, Italian companies were not as large, centralized and consolidated as in France. Italian film production was divided among centers in Turin, Milan, Rome, and Naples, reflecting regional differences and dialects. Infrastructure for domestic distribution and exhibition too were lacking. Nevertheless, Italian film companies benefited from a rich subject matter for films familiar across Europe and the Americas. About 1909 they began to produce films based on literary adaptations and historical epics glorifying ancient Rome and the Risorgimento. The films emphasized set design and historical verisimilitude. Moreover, given the limited domestic market, export was important to profitability from these feature-length films. Between 1907 and 1914 Italian films were successful in Britain and the US. Italian émigré communities in Britain were avid patrons of later Italian epics, such as *Quo Vadis*. Such epics established Italian film companies as significant suppliers to the US in the early 1910s. But Italian companies never gained the dominance and world-wide market of Pathé.[18]

Transition to Hollywood Hegemony

In 1907 American companies began to challenge Pathé's dominance. As one part of this campaign, they, the movie-censorship movement and the press began to frame French films in terms of morality and national interests, painting Pathé with the stereotype of the French as risqué and immoral, and thus a danger to children and young women, who were believed at the time to be the most devoted and vulnerable movie-goers. This occurred amid a general cultural unease about changes, such as massive industrialization, urban growth, and a huge wave of immigration mentioned in the Introduction.

By 1910, European film-makers' share of the US market declined to about 20 percent, and by 1915, to less than five percent. Due to the war, European producers were strained to find the venture-capital necessary to cover the increased costs of feature films. Moreover, hostilities between European nations shrank the broader European market that existed before the war. By the end of the war, many European film companies were financially weak, and some were bankrupt. French film production reverted to a 'cottage industry,' conceived and promoted as artisanal instead of mass production.[19]

Between 1913 and 1918 some American producers, most notably Jesse Lasky's Famous Players studio (the future Paramount Pictures), shifted to feature films of three or more reels, cast well-known actors and advertised widely, sharply increasing film costs that put further pressure on declining European companies. The emerging Hollywood studios also benefited from three substantial advantages over other companies: through exclusive contracts they bound to them the most successful creative talent (actors, directors, etc.); they established favorable relationships with American financiers for reliable financing; and an entire infrastructure of ancillary services and organizations nearby provided easy access to necessary and specialized skills and services. Meanwhile, European creative talents were defecting to Hollywood for greater opportunities. Even before the war, American companies had begun to establish their own presence in Europe, with their own in-house, overseas distribution branches instead of using British agents. By 1919, objecting to American block-booking practices and startled by Famous Players establishing a British branch to produce films, British exhibitors petitioned their government to stem the 'American invasion.' Yet, by the early 1920s European distribution was increasingly controlled by American companies. Despite substantial government protections, not one European company capable of rivalling the Americans emerged in the remainder of the twentieth century.[20]

Summing up the change, in 1924 *The New York Times* stated: "A few years ago there was a flurry, almost a panic, among American photoplay producers because of a threatened invasion of the home market by European producers … The invasion turned out to be only a foray: American audiences decisively showed their preference for photoplays 'made in America.' More than this, foreign audiences – in Europe, South America, Africa, and Asia – are reported as showing the same preferences."[21]

American companies were able to tip the balance in their favor because of the size of their domestic market. Smaller populations and lower incomes in home markets for European film producers made it difficult to be financially profitable. The difference was particularly great for film. First, it is the home market in which a company's films are most culturally compatible. This became more important with the shift to feature films in the 1910s, as extended narratives are more culture-specific. Second, a larger home market spreads production costs over more ticket sales. The greatest cost of production, called 'sunk costs,' was in making the master copy of the film.[22] Duplicating this for distribution costs much less, making the cost of a movie 'sold' to twenty million viewers only slightly greater than to two million viewers. As production costs rose with the trend to feature films, US companies increasingly had a financial edge, even over leading European companies like Pathé. The escalation of costs also hastened the demise of weaker American companies and increased concentration and integration in the American industry. The surviving larger, stronger American companies were able to invest even more in production, marketing, and distribution, making their films more attractive than those of their foreign competitors.

The problem of sunk costs was even greater for film companies serving smaller language communities. With a population of five million at the turn of the century, Sweden exemplified this situation. Industrialization began rapidly in the 1890s, along with an advanced technological infrastructure, including the first fully electrified city in Europe. Sweden repeated the same pattern in exhibition development as larger nations, traveling exhibitors first, followed briefly by storefront nickelodeons and then permanent cinemas beginning about 1907. But as film-making became more expensive, Sweden did not have the population to generate sufficient domestic demand; nor was there a substantial Swedish-speaking diaspora market for export. Consequently, Swedish productions never accounted for more than 17 percent of feature films shown even in Sweden. American films became dominant there in 1916 and from 1918 to the 1950s never dipped below 50 percent of all films there.[23]

Hollywood's 'invasion' of Europe began to raise specters of cultural hegemony and its alleged threat to home values and heritage. There were two inversely related responses to film in these times and in various European nations: reactions by mass audiences in theaters, and moral panics by elites and authorities about those audiences and the feared effects of the films on them. This brings us to the subject of audiences and the screen cultures they made.

Places and Situations of Movie-Going

Whether in the US and Europe or the east and south, it is notable that the diffusion of urban exhibition followed some similar patterns, from sites of variety entertainments, to a range of movie-only or movie-featured venues.[24] The first film exhibitions were traveling shows, offering the technological novelty of moving pictures, often as a part of other amusements, such as variety shows in urban areas or at fairs and circuses in rural areas, or at any available location where a showman might set up his projector and screen for his collection of films.

The similarities in early exhibition arose mainly from the entertainment environment that pre-dated the arrival of film in many nations. Well-established, modestly priced variety entertainments had their own dedicated venues in cities of many nations: variety and vaudeville in the US, music hall in Britain, café-concerts in France, and café-chantants in Italy. In Shanghai, tea houses, and amusement halls served a similar purpose.[25]

These entertainment venues succeeded as part of an economic transition to industrialization in which markets were displacing subsistence production and consumption; and a cultural transition from values of the Protestant ethic emphasizing work and production, to values emphasizing pleasure and discretionary consumption.[26] Especially in urban settings, wage workers labored year-round with no 'fallow season' to develop self-entertainment skills, while commercial entertainments were increasingly available at low prices. These conditions provided the foundation for a mass base of consumers that suited the growth of film. At the same time, pursuit of more profitable customers with more disposable income, who did not wish to rub shoulders with the *hoi polloi*, led to market segmentation of film exhibition along class lines. In Britain and France, as in the US, exhibitors announced their preferred clientèles through the symbolism of the theaters in which the films were shown. Buildings, their location, decoration, and management policies signified the situation as intended for persons and behaviors of a certain class and cultural capital.

General descriptions of early British movie exhibition could be mistaken for descriptions of the situation in the US at the time.[27] There were three principal types of urban venues: music halls, storefronts and other easily acquired urban spaces, and, in small cities and towns, any available public hall that a showman could rent for a night or two. In Birmingham permanent cinemas were replacing traveling exhibitors by 1908. Numbers of licensed exhibitors grew rapidly to 64 in 1915. The general pattern was of a large number of small, inexpensive cinemas on the shopping street in working-class neighborhoods and a few large-capacity cinemas downtown, representing a wide range of investment from 400 to 10,000 pounds. Most were locally financed, but nine were lavish downtown theaters owned by national chains. Attendance was based on price and convenience more than on a particular film.[28]

Audiences were class segmented in theaters by neighborhood location. A contemporary report expressed class snobbery about a children's matinée in one middle-class neighborhood cinema: "They are not gutter urchins, but clean and neatly dressed youngsters from good middle-class homes." Others described children at a working-class cinema, noisy in and outside, who "relieved themselves where they sat."[29]

At the same time, there seems to have been some small but distinctive differences from the US: store-front nickelodeons did not become as numerous nor as predominant in Britain, and film exhibition in music halls was more common and persisted longer. This may have been due to music hall being more widespread and more identified with the working-class than vaudeville was in the US. In 1908, at the peak of the US nickelodeon craze, music halls were the overwhelmingly predominant commercial sites for film exhibition in London.[30] On the other hand, there were some nickelodeon-type venues. A London journalist observed in 1909 widespread happenstance conversions of commercial spaces, similar to the US, in which, "nearly every small hall which was formerly carrying on a precarious existence with dancing classes, lectures, and meetings, has been seized upon by the enterprising living-picture *syndicates*, repainted, relit, and newly furnished to blossom out as cinemas, picture palaces, 'picture dromes,' and 'electric palaces.'" Birmingham too had a landscape of small neighborhood 'picture palaces' that sound like smartened-up nickelodeons, not unlike the trend in the US to 'improving' nickelodeons around the same time.[31]

A more rapid spread of upscale purpose-built theaters for film in Britain pre-empted further spread of nickelodeons. As the business quickly proved to be both lucrative and permanent, numbers of purpose-built cinemas soon proliferated; so too did investment in 'classier' decoration and furnishings. The shift to purpose-built cinema theaters seems to have occurred earlier than in the US. In 1908, Provincial Cinematograph Theaters was formed to open fifteen plush theaters in cities outside London, with restaurants, cloakrooms, and lounges for reading to attract an affluent audience. By 1911 two thirds of commercial venues were purpose-built cinemas.[32] It seems that nickelodeons were not as numerous in Britain because they were more quickly superseded by purpose-built theaters than they were in the US.

More clearly, British film exhibition consolidated earlier than in the US, with the development of financial "syndicates." Due to the cinema-building boom of 1909 to 1914, roughly half of all cinemas were in the hands of large, incorporated businesses with greater financing. The growth of incorporated ownership was aided by the 1909 Cinematographic Act, which required stricter building codes and more retrofitting too costly to small investors; fire licensing in 1910 that favored theaters with raked floors added to this trend.[33]

In sum, it appears that British syndicates arose earlier and could raise the capital more easily and quickly, and thus could finance construction of more purpose-built cinemas sooner. By contrast, in the US, film companies did not have direct backing of banks at the time, as did British exhibitors and French and Italian film manufacturers.[34] So in Britain, the place and circumstances in which people viewed movies changed earlier, which would mean that audience practices and screen culture would too, a matter to which we will return.

By 1889, Parisian manual workers could afford a range of commercial entertainments. For a franc or so, the price of a drink at a café concert, people could see some of the best singers, comics, and other variety entertainers. These cafés were plentiful in the 1890s and ranged from simple neighborhood homosocial spaces with skilled manual workers and lower-middle-class shopkeepers as their steady customers, to a few larger, fancier ones on the boulevards frequented by prosperous bourgeoisie. At the neighborhood cafés men kept their hats on, smoked cigars and were raucous, singing along and throwing cherry stones at poor performers. Some claimed that prostitutes frequented these places as well. Family friendly cinema would soon rival these male haunts.[35]

As in other Western nations, moving picture exhibition began in Paris in the 1890s at café concerts, boulevard variety theaters (admission a half franc), and street fairs. By 1905, movie-only venues showing fictional narrative films were supplanting the variety format. By 1910 café concerts were disappearing, allegedly due to competition from automobile recreation, boulevard theaters – and movies. Boulevard theaters themselves were soon closing and converting to movie theaters that were available in a range of plushness. Industrial factory workers were less identified with the artisans' neighborhood café and turned instead to film as their entertainment. By 1914 film was the most popular and profitable commercial entertainment in the center of Paris, including at the internationally famous Folies-Bergère.[36]

The French film-making business consolidated even sooner and more thoroughly than did that of the British. Beginning in 1906, Pathé established an extensive exhibition chain, with cinemas in Paris and regional capitals such as Lyons, Marseilles, Bordeaux, and Toulouse. Other entrepreneurs followed Pathé's lead and upgraded exhibition by converting existing spaces in shopping and entertainment districts into cinemas. Advertising for these theaters aimed at a 'respectable' cross-class, family market. A second wave of building in Paris began in 1911, more than doubling the number of cinemas in two years, including several cinema palaces. The more numerous and earlier appearance of purpose-built cinemas, their centralized planning, financing, and ownership, combined with seeking a middle-class clientele, appears to have skipped the hyper-competitive era of nickelodeons that occurred in the US.[37]

The development from temporary and multi-use sites to purpose-built movie theaters and class-distinct urban theaters constituted not only relocation of places of movie-going, but also redefinition of the situation of movie-going. The cultural implications of different places of exhibition depended upon, on the one hand, the definition of the situation implied by the building and its management, and on the other, the interpretation audiences gave to that situation. The meanings of both place and situation are revealed in actual audience practices, a subject to which we now turn.

European Audiences

In London, a decade before World War I, while cinemas still were referred to as 'poor man's theaters,' moving pictures were gaining popularity among the middle class as well. Exhibitors and audiences alike labeled particular cinemas as either for 'the better classes' or the working class.[38] Such class segregation is significant, since class-homogeneous audiences are more likely to respond in class terms to both the venue and the film texts. The working class used movie houses as alternative public venues, at least in the very short term, just as they had done in music halls and pubs, and as had occurred in the US. Such events, however, should not be considered a characteristic of theaters themselves, but rather of certain neighborhoods that were defined and defended as homogeneous working-class, ethnic bastions, such as London's East End, New York City's Lower East Side, and other working-class quarters around the world. Theaters were simply part of a larger stake in class-conscious definitions of 'us versus them.'[39] At the same time, attention to this large body of research on working-class communities and audiences should not lead us to forget that such homogeneity applies equally to other class neighborhoods as well, such as enclaves of the very rich, or middle-class suburbs, or even various bourgeois or upper-middle class subcultures in artist/hip or academic neighborhoods.[40]

Much as in the US, British working-class families and adolescents attended cinemas, even if it meant less to spend on necessities. However, working-class patrons went less for a particular film than for the experience of movies in general and time in the cinema to socialize or escape a cramped apartment and crowded streets. Mothers peeled potatoes while watching; children translated inter-titles for their parents. The cheapness, handy locality, and continuous showing meant that they could attend any time and just as they were, well matched to their overburdened lives and limited resources.[41]

Movie-going was popular among British working-class children and adolescents as well. They were boisterous and littered the floors with peanut shells. One exhibitor reported a local tradition of children throwing orange peel at the piano player. In showings of *Perils of Pauline*, they reacted vocally to the scenes on screen. Women found serials appealing. All this much the same as what was reported in the US about the same time.[42]

One consequence of the quicker consolidation of exhibition in Britain and France may have been a briefer phase of the 'alternate public sphere,' when working-class and immigrant audiences commandeered the space for their own socializing and entertainment, as in the American nickelodeon.[43] As we will see in the chapters on the Hollywood era, British adult audiences in the 1920s and 1930s had quieted significantly, and settled into watching the movie; more so in posh downtown theaters than in neighborhood houses or small town theaters.

The 1910s in Paris was a time of a building boom for boulevard cinemas, including many in working-class industrial neighborhoods like Montmartre. Cinema attendance grew manyfold during World War I, with women and working classes constituting a large part of the audience. Working classes tended to prefer their neighborhood cinemas to theaters in the bourgeois city center. Their cinemas were places of social congregation and active participation contiguous with the neighborhood. By the 1920s they were using their cinemas as their own public sphere. Given their dependence on working-class patrons, especially during the war and post-war recovery, exhibitors in these neighborhoods cooperated in allowing their cinemas to be used for a wide range of community events, including meetings and preparations for actions of political parties, unions, and consumer organizations, fundraising for various social causes such as war veterans and widows, and those displaced by the war, for bomb shelters during the war, even for neighborhood beauty contests with local contestants and local audiences voting. For example, Dufayel department store sales-girls used a cinema near the store as their strike headquarters. Such vibrant and vital community use, combined with the localness of the clientele, suggest that movie-going itself must have been a communal event, with familiar faces and shared circumstances.[44]

Unlike these working-class neighborhood cinemas, large cinemas in Paris' central entertainment district were frequented by the bourgeoisie and rarely hosted such community events. Also, in stark contrast to the reality of activist women in working-class cinemas, bourgeois cinephiles and other elites stereotyped working-class women movie-goers in the mid 1910s as gullible followers of adventure serials and their stars, and dreamers hoping to become actresses themselves.[45]

Outside Paris, screen culture was under-developed. There was still a gulf between provincial rural life and life in Paris. Some regions were untouched by industrialization to the degree that the people made no distinction between capitalists and workers, seeing city merchants and artisans alike as the same bourgeois, city-dweller class, with servants drawn from the peasant countryside. Given the limited transport, traveling entertainment was difficult in rural areas, and given the poverty in these regions, there was little market for cinema. It was at most an occasional treat, not entirely absent in provincial cities, but insufficient for a distinct culture to grow, except for those few vicariously attached to the screen culture of Paris via magazines.[46]

Elite Reactions

Film cultures include multiple discourses in a discursive field, in which various interpretations contest meanings of film, exhibition sites, and movie-going. These include discourses of industry decision-makers in production and exhibition and the trade press, discourses among audiences in theaters and beyond, and discourses among broader publics, expressing hopes and fears about film and its audiences.

Across Western cultures, elite public reactions to the popularity of movie-going were directed at lower classes and framed as matters of national character.[47] At first criticism focused on the place of exhibition, citing lack of ventilation, dangers of fire, and darkness that abetted indecent behavior. As film became story-telling, concerns shifted to its message. Drawing on theories of crowd psychology, some claimed it affected people with susceptible minds and weak character, allegedly the lower classes, women and children. Just as French films had been attacked by American film companies as a threat to the nation, now American film imports were accused of threatening the national character and culture of European nations. A common thread in these criticisms was elite concerns about maintaining control of the masses.

Concerns in Britain about the dangers of cinema reflected the structural and cultural circumstances of the era. The Victorian and Edwardian eras were rife with middle- and upper-class discourses about the industrial working class. Before film, a moral crusade arose concerning working-class music hall, in much the same way as in the US about stage entertainments. But while in the US, moral entrepreneurs seemed to fear above all the massive wave of immigration of eastern and southern Europeans into the US at the turn of the century, in Britain in the Edwardian era they worried most about an assertive working class. Thus, a stuffy middle class in the late nineteenth century feared the decline in acceptance of their "class, religious, and moral norms."[48]

In the 1910s, middle-class crusaders targeted the working class and particularly youths, considering their different values and norms a direct threat to their own moral hegemony. Before 1906, there was little complaint about morally objectionable films in religious weeklies that later participated in the crusade. Between 1906 and 1914, crusaders were objecting to the immorality of film content. In 1912, the industry responded by creating its own British Board of Film Censors to pre-empt outside censorship. Turning attention to the cinema house, during the first three years of the war 1914–1917, the weeklies attacked what they believed to be sexual indecency among audiences. They feared that the war was loosening sexual mores among soldiers and working girls. In response to these concerns, the film industry Cinematograph Trade Council requested that the National Council of Public Morals investigate whether cinema was corrupting youth. While acknowledging that films produced a "generally unwholesome influence on the young," the report disclaimed that darkness in theaters led to indecent behavior or that films about crime led young boys to imitate them. The Council recommended a film coding system to identify good and bad films. By 1917, however, public support for the crusade began to fade and London film censorship boards rejected demands for censorship as being out of step with the changing norms of the times.[49]

Discussions in France during this period similarly depicted working-class audiences as undesirable crowds vulnerable to suggestion. More an institutional response than public outcry, the large Catholic publisher La Bonne Press, founded in 1883 to counter secular policies of the Third Republic, chose in 1905 to counter the bad influences of movies by producing their own films to be shown in Catholic schools. Rather than condemning film wholesale, instead they distinguished morally good films from bad, supporting the good while censoring the bad. Long-standing consequences of this approach were production codes that labeled films as suitable for children or not.[50]

In France there also was a substantial movement to distinguish between good and bad films on aesthetic grounds, between art and mass culture. An aesthetic reaction to low-brow cinema and its audiences that blended nationalism and class-snobbery began to emerge before World War I and became institutionalized after the war with industry and government cooperation. An early cinephile movement sacralized their version of French film and feared its artistic potential was endangered by mainstream film culture. As in Britain and other nations, cultural and political elites saw twin dangers of film: on the one hand an invasion in the form of American films and film stars was deemed aesthetically inferior; and on the other, working-class taste was influenced by this, so degrading national culture. Cinephiles attacked the sector of French film industry that pandered to this class with *cine romans* (film novels) and serials that "intoxicated" their audiences with "mediocre emotions." Some cinephiles in the early 1920s hoped "to restore the prestige of French cinema" by educating working-class movie goers "... about beautiful films, explaining to the crowds cinema's artistic possibilities."[51]

In Italy too, cinema had become associated with the masses in the trade press. A 1908 newspaper in Turin, the industrial center of Italy, criticized these early theaters in much the same terms as critics of urban working-class nickelodeons in the US, describing them as, "lightless and airless premises, backshops, basements, trying to get some profit by paying lower rents." This referred to cinema-chantants, similar to the small-time vaudeville-nickelodeon hybrids that appeared for a brief time in the US. A moral reform movement reacted to these combination stage and film shows, claiming that they were a degraded and immoral version of the higher-priced café-chantants. Cinema trade magazines also opposed them, claiming that they were bad publicity for the film business, much as the trade press in the US had claimed about cheap vaudeville-movie combination houses. But less like the US and more like Britain, there was a difference in circumstances: "theater chains were already numerous," which indicated an early industry consolidation with a monetary interest in respectability.[52]

This grew into broader anti-cinema campaigns. Films themselves were attacked as immoral, sensationalist, and a public danger. Citing broad educational and cultural concerns, defenders of theater and high culture argued that film images were supplanting the written word. One even predicted that movies "will replace written stories, until we have to abolish the alphabet completely, as a useless curiosity." At the same time, the Catholic Church hoped to use film to promote its own religious and moral values. Following the lead of the French Catholic publisher, Italian dioceses began about 1908 to encourage production of religious films to show in schools and other educational settings.[53]

This pattern was repeated in smaller European nations as well. In Sweden, even before feature films appeared, concern about film content arose when children began to flock to Sunday matinees, where they could see films with violent content. In the largest cities, censorship was introduced. In Hungary, conservatives reacted against film as Western modernism. They gained political influence after World War I, and in 1928 a government decree prohibited licenses for cinemas in towns of 1,000 or fewer people to protect naive and culturally 'immature' folk and preserve 'authentic' national culture in rural areas from intrusion by mass culture.[54]

In the US, moral panics about early film focused on the dangers of dark theaters and immoral films on children and subordinate classes and races. European nations added panics about the invasion of American films and culture. Next we discuss colonial settings, where colonial administrations were focused on the dangers of commercial films generally upon the obedience and malleability of natives, and typically couched this in terms of racial hierarchy.

Colonial Contexts

In these early years, film markets beyond North America and Europe were not more than ten percent of world film sales. Even as late as 1931, Europe and North America accounted for nearly 80 percent of all movie theaters world-wide for roughly 20 percent of the world population.[55] But while non-Western markets were not significant financially for European and American companies, film and who controlled it would become significant not only economically, but also culturally and politically for other nations and regions.

Moving-picture exhibition first arrived in the 1890s in major port cities around the world. Shortly after the Lumière brothers debuted their projector in Paris, they sent film, projectors, and operators across the globe. By 1906, Pathé had offices not only in most European capitals but also in Moscow, Odessa, Calcutta, Singapore and Shanghai, and in South America and Africa. Film exhibition in these entrepots recapitulated the changes in the West from novelty to narrative films and from traveling exhibitors in variety halls to purpose-built movie palaces, and repeated the time-worn marketing strategy to make entertainment respectable in order to draw a more profitable middle-class audience with more disposable income.[56]

Since film technology was first developed in North American and European nations, it is not surprising that commercial exploitation also began at the same time on both continents. But, given that this was the height of the European colonial era in Africa and Asia and US influence in South America, film also arrived at the same time elsewhere around the world through entrepot cities.[57] European entrepreneurs initially came to entertain the communities of Western colonials. As mentioned in the Introduction, colonials posted throughout the colonial world did much to sustain their home cultures in foreign places. Early film exhibitors served this purpose, often excluding natives, except for high-level officials. Nevertheless, film drew the attention of curious natives in these cities who constituted a secondary market for traveling exhibitors and native entrepreneurs.

Film arrived along with other artifacts of Western culture and society, such as automobiles, architecture, dress, books, even in some cases law and government. These port cities were the contact points between colonizing nations with their cultures of modernity and the indigenous populations and cultures. Everywhere, film was seen as the essence of modernity, posing promise and threat.

Across Asia, Africa, and South America, cinema was almost exclusively an urban and largely middle and upper-class phenomenon, a small portion of the population. For them, movie-going was an extension of European-American screen culture, looking at the world through European or American eyes, rather than a national cinema culture. Indigenous films and industries were stymied by limited markets and the dominance of European and American imports. For example, before World War I, Pathé already had become the dominant film supplier to Latin America where imported films filled the metropolitan cinemas with narrative fiction films. Native film-makers succeeded only in niche markets by appealing to nationalist pride with documentaries of the natural wonders and the aristocracies of their country. After the war, they could not compete with the resources of American companies to produce higher-cost feature films and the shift to sound.[58]

For the most part, cinema remained a small presence in these societies at least until the 1920s, even in major urban areas and for decades elsewhere. For the vast majority of the native population cinema remained inaccessible, affordable only on rare occasion, and then more a novelty than a familiar experience, in some cases until independence and state-funded television. In parts of Africa it was as late as the 1940s; some villages in Cuba's Oriente Province reputedly not until the 1960s. Rural poverty and undeveloped infrastructure, products of colonialism, stood in the way. Consequently, we will postpone to later chapters discussion related to colonial propaganda film and native film culture.

We will now concentrate on two cultures and continue their thread in succeeding chapters: China and India, the two most populous societies and recently two of the new centers of film and television production. China and India in 1900 both had very large populations, the vast majority poor peasants engaged in subsistence farming. Industry was under-developed and overshadowed by colonial trade. India was a classic case of imperial colonial rule. China ostensibly had an independent government, but Western powers controlled the major port cities, while the central Chinese government had a weak hold on the rest of the country. There was also stark contrast in political stability and order. In the first half of the twentieth century, China witnessed the end of emperors and establishment of a republic, then two decades of civil war and Japanese invasion sweeping over much of the country. India under British rule experienced no revolution, civil war or invasion on the scale that occurred in China, until the Partition. Film arrived and arose within these economic and political circumstances. While the two nations faced similar economic challenges, differences in film entertainment development was due at least in part to the differences in political turmoil. Bollywood and exhibition beyond the major cities began fairly early on, while film production was slow to grow in China and its markets restricted to a few major cities, mostly coastal ports.

China, from Emperor to Republic

The deep historical and cultural context preceding the arrival of film in China includes two centuries-long conditions. One was its population density and the limited arable land to feed it. China had to feed about a quarter of the world's human population on less than a tenth of the world's arable land. Consequently, nine tenths of crops were for human consumption and only four percent for feeding animals. This resulted in a shortage of draft animals that could have relieved rural human labor. The heavy dependence on human labor dictated small-scale agricultural production. The consequence was a land of closely spaced peasant villages, whole villages living off land the size of a single American Midwest family farm. Second, China has a two-thousand-year history of centralized government and a common Confucian culture. An equivalent in the West would have been as if the Roman Empire had continued to rule the European continent and the Mediterranean, even while the power of that central government may have ebbed and flowed. While China had a population of diverse peoples, the power of the central government and the continuity of unification and national identity were notably greater than the Indian subcontinent. China had a rural culture, with landlords and peasants alike rooted on the land near their ancestral homes. Cities were primarily governmental administrative centers that represented external political and legal power disliked by locals. Rural life was valued as the true China and cities as appendages to that.[59]

However, from the mid nineteenth century changes in coastal cities began to upset the traditional relation of urban to rural. In major port cities, European imperial powers and the US carved out 'spheres of influence' that led to lopsided treaties and trade agreements and ceded increasingly greater rights to these powers. Western intrusions brought commercialization and some industrialization to these areas, making them places of opportunity that attracted immigrants from the countryside. At the same time, Western commerce and technology arrived packaged with Western ideas that clashed with traditional values, and stimulated movements promoting as well as opposing Western modernization.[60]

Commercialization even affected theater and the arts. Literati and artists traditionally had served as government officials, the mandarin class, and had painted and wrote as forms of self-cultivation. In the late nineteenth century young artists and writers began to move to foreign concessions and make a living by selling their works. In another form of commercialization, in Shanghai, traditional opera began to emphasize spectacle and sensation in order to attract larger audiences and sell more tickets.[61]

The attraction of peasants to the city was due to their relative chances of survival. Even lowly workers in these port cities had better incomes than village peasants. At the same time, the ancient fear and disdain for cities created mixed feelings on the part of transplanted villagers, so that they retained many aspects of their village life and culture. As historian Hanchao Lu put it:

> if we step away from the fashionable boulevards and look into the back alleys where the majority of the people of Shanghai lived, we witness another image – a less publicized but more realistic picture, and one that may be regarded as *not* modern. Calling it an urban village with a small-town type of life would be more appropriate ... not unlike what one might see when viewing a rural village.[62]

In these cities, cheek by jowl with the West, a hybrid 'yangjingbang' culture arose among the middle-class Chinese. It was among these that an interest in film arose as part of this culture. This new amusement gained acceptance initially by framing it as a new 'electric' form of traditional 'shadow-play' puppet shows, whose traditional style was incorporated into some early Chinese film productions.[63]

Film exhibitions in China first took place in variety entertainment venues of Shanghai teahouses and amusement halls. Halls sometimes contained multiple smaller venues in one building where, for about five cents gold, one could visit a cinema or two, plus stage dramas presented in different dialects for provincial migrants who understood only their native dialect. The rooms were unheated and furnished with benches and small tables, with tea and other refreshments and hot towels served during the performance. Similar to the West, these locations were considered by traditional Chinese to be a bit risqué, although some women did attend. Peking police regulations required women to be seated separately, unless escorted in stalls. The audiences consuming the new mass culture were predominantly 'emerging white-collar class' and 'middle-brow,' neither poor nor powerful, although there were tea-houses and seating suited to varying pockets.[64]

Histories give little mention of nickelodeon-type venues that might have catered to a manual labor population, unlike that in the US, Europe, and the Indian four-anna movie venues described below. The first movie house in Shanghai, Hongkew Theatre, built in 1908 by a Spanish showman, Antonio Ramos, was a sheet-iron structure with 250 seats, but its origins and location suggest something more than a nickelodeon. Other early movie theaters were also built and operated by Westerners. Ramos became an agent for Famous Players-Lasky, and built a chain of theaters.[65]

It appears that cinema did not develop in China as an urban, working-class amusement, as it had in the US and Britain, in part because there was little industry to produce a proletariat. As a result, it seems to have arisen as a different sort of film culture, aligned with the peculiar situation of the entrepot middle class, not foreign nor Chinese, but something in between. Chinese films in the 1920s would become a mélange of Chinese and Western bits. Chinese literati criticized its low-brow pop culture and attempted to create a cinephile community, although less successfully as in France due to weak government support.[66]

However, even as an urban Chinese bourgeoisie exposed to Western ideas and films was growing, the native population in these port cities was a tiny portion of the nation's population. In 1910, the urban population, interior as well as port cities, was probably well under ten percent of the whole population; even as late as 1953 it was still only 13 percent. Moreover, rural peasant poverty remained, so that the vast majority of peasants across the nation most likely could not afford film exhibition.[67]

Neither did peasants have access to cinema. The US Department of Commerce reported in 1927 on the film industry in China and American film business there, and repeatedly emphasized the limited distribution of films. There were very few theaters, confined to port cities, and a very small amount of film exported to China in 1913, only 190,000 feet. At a generous estimate of 50 feet per minute, that is only about 70 hours of new film, including multiple copies, to be distributed across the whole country for the entire year.

The report listed several obstacles to expansion. Rural poverty severely limited market demand for commercial entertainment. Political instability made it 'hazardous' to invest in extended distribution and exhibition efforts there. The lack of rail and paved roads required "six months for film to go the distance of 1,600 miles," for the round trip from Shanghai to Chungking (now Chongqing) in Western China, and ten days by boat up the Yangtze River to Hangkow (now Wuhan). There was no electricity for lighting the projector or charging batteries in most places. Lastly, Chinese peasants were not familiar with stage performances; the only entertainment familiar to villagers was amateur street performances of folk song and dance dramas amid crowds on special occasions.[68]

The lack of theaters makes it highly unlikely that exhibition and viewing could have been any more than a rarity in most places, even most inland cities, given not only the obstacles but also the sheer size of the population compared to the small numbers of copies of films there. This meant that early film clientele would have to be foreigners or Chinese elites and literate middle class with more than average income, a very small base for anything but a tiny and exclusive film subculture.

India under the Raj

By the turn of the century, the Raj, including what is now Pakistan, India, Bangladesh, and Burma, was ruled by the British government.[69] Large-scale agriculture was secondary to a peasant-village economy of subsistence agriculture and handicraft; large-scale industry was even more limited. In 1901, 90 percent of workers were agricultural; less than one percent were modern industrial. Moreover, industry was integrated tightly into and dependent upon the British empire's military needs and commercial network. From 1858 to 1930 the British Raj built an integrated rail system blanketing the subcontinent, the fourth largest network in the world, but based on a priority of military over commercial. Railroads were well-developed for moving products to ports as well as for military transport, but may not have been effective as an integrated national transportation system.[70]

The sub-continental population at the turn of the century was over 250 million (six times that of the UK), most of whom were peasants living under feudal conditions. A small educated English-speaking class, about one hundred thousand natives, were educated to serve in the government bureaucracy. Thus there was a double inequality, between British colonials and native Indians, and between higher class and caste, educated, English-speaking Indians, and the mass of illiterate poor. At the same time, the culturally heterogeneous subcontinent was divided by further inequalities rooted in religions, languages, and regions. Finally, women were severely restricted by laws and traditions. These multiple dimensions of inequality would shape Indian film content, exhibition spaces, audience reception, and elite reactions.[71]

As in other entrepot cities, film arrived in Bombay (now Mumbai) in 1896, exhibited as a novelty at the elite English Watson's Hotel, which excluded all Indians, and at the posh Novelty Theater, which excluded Indian lower castes and classes. Film spread to other cities, but by 1901, the novelty of film wore off among privileged Indians and attendance was declining. In 1902, J. F. Madan, a Calcutta importer and entrepreneur, began movie exhibitions in tents to attract a new audience, the urban masses displaced from their traditional villages and unable to afford other entertainments. Tent cinema soon expanded to villages beyond Calcutta, creating a new four-anna admission class of movie-goers. Four annas would have been one and a half percent of gross monthly wages for carpenters and four percent for laborers.[72]

The potential market for exhibition in these humble settings may have been rather large. Tent exhibition was adaptable to travel through towns and villages to reach the vast rural population. Also, the scale of wages suggests that movie-going would have been occasionally affordable for manual workers' families. Government statistics indicate that in 1900, skilled carpenters earned about 16 rupees (256 annas) per month and agricultural laborers about six rupees. However, income and affordability for film varied substantially, since there were notable differentials in the prosperity of different rural regions depending upon climate, crops, and transport to export markets. In poorer areas, lean times meant famine, losing land, and selling children into bondage. Entertainment would seem out of the question for these people.[73]

By 1910, longer feature films of European classics attracted Indian audiences, even though Western film style was contrary to that of traditional Indian theater, which was built around rituals and music with religious and magical significance. Indian film production did succeed by offering films based on such traditions. The first Indian-made feature films depicted familiar and popular Sankrit legends from the *Mahabharata* and *Ramayana*, presented with moral messages appealing to Hindi audiences. Within a decade, such 'mythological films' became the dominant Indian film genre, accounting for 70 percent of all Indian productions in 1923. Some early Indian films were similarly based on other ethnic and religious traditions, such as tales from Persian-Arabic traditions, and historical films set in the Mughal and Sultanate eras of Muslim rule.[74] These various links to subcontinent history and culture led to culturally distinct film styles that later evolved into what is now identified as Bollywood masala.

South Indian exhibitors believed that mythological films enhanced the respectability of movie-going, due to their religious basis. They reported that such films drew Indian women and family audiences, whose very presence constituted respectability. A government official stated that "Hindu women have a natural reluctance to go to any public affair, to attend any show in a public place ... [at film theaters] there are about a dozen sitting in a roped off section or behind a purdah." But women composed a substantial portion of the audiences for mythologicals. In addition, women brought their families, multiplying admissions further. According to one report, these films attracted audiences that were "60 per cent poorer classes and wage earners, 25 per cent ladies, and 15 per cent literate Indians."[75] The presence of women and their families leavened the audiences.

Early films, theaters, and audiences in India were segregated along multiple lines of respectability: Western films for Europeans in theaters excluding Indians and for the English-speaking two percent of Indians at posh theaters; and Hindi mythological for the masses at lower-class venues that were "dank and seedy [with] hard, creaky, wooden seats" and the stench of a toilet in the lobby. Even into the 1920s exhibitors catering to English-speaking Indians objected to screening Hindi mythological films on the ground that they attracted lower-caste and class Indians who were "dirty and stinking" and that this would require thorough cleaning of the theater before the 'better class' would return. We will discuss this continuing class divide further in Chapter 4.[76] The 1928 Indian Cinematograph Committee, appointed by the colonial government and composed of British and Westernized Indian elites, also noted audiences chewing betel leaves and seated on the ground in 'corrugated tin sheds.' Through its lens of disdain for the masses, the Westernized Indian elite saw movie theaters as spaces of cultural difference.

In 1918, censorship began to excise sensitive political issues, including criticism of British rule. American films had risen from four per cent of film imports into India in 1913 to 95 percent by 1919. By 1927, 85 percent of films shown in India were imports. The British worried that American films might undermine the idea of white superiority. Ironically those who preferred American films tended to be English-speaking Indians who already identified with the West. The 1928 Committee, based on testimony from many Westernized Indians, reported concern that unsophisticated lower-class Indians would be vulnerable to American sexual and criminal mores in the films. To address this, censors imposed Victorian prudery, disallowing kissing, restricting where a cinema could be located, and imposing a heavy tax on ticket sales. At the same time, Westernized Indian elites were concerned about what they considered inferior Indian-made films, the themes of which were mostly Indian mythology and history. Among the Westernized middle class these films were considered negative cultural capital and to be avoided. All this was made embarassing by their own children, college students of the 1920s who enjoyed 'slumming' in theatre galleries, where they intermingled and adopted the rowdy behavior of non-Westernized Indians.[77]

Another film genre that concerned native elites was American adventure serials, which became popular in south India. Edison's *What Ever Happened to Mary* arrived in 1912, followed by Pathé's *Perils of Pauline* (1914) and *Exploits of Elaine* (1914–15) starring Pearl White, who established a new kind of action role for women. By the late 1910s Universal supplied the majority of adventure serials including *Broken Coin* (1915), *The Lure of the Circus* (1918), and *Elmo, the Mighty* (1919) starring Elmo Lincoln. White and Lincoln became the best-known movie stars in south India. A survey of Madras newspapers found that at least one and often more serials were showing throughout this period.[78]

Exhibitors claimed that serials appealed especially to the 'two-anna' crowd of the illiterate and young, since serials included many action sequences that required fewer inter-titles. One Madras exhibitor, future film director A. Narayanan, was more specific, stating that serial audiences were "70 per cent [illiterate] wage earners, 20 per cent middle-class and semi-literate and 10 per cent rich and literate." Throughout the 1920s, the British-owned *Madras Mail* severely criticized these serials as attracting lower-class patrons and displacing quality drama films. Using the language of crowd psychology, it described these audiences as addicted: "Once having acquired a taste for the serial, the masses find that they cannot shake it off." The newspaper contrasted these to drama films derived from literature:

> I hope that patrons of all classes will give the short dramas at the Elphinstone and Wellington good support. I would like to see the patrons of the dearer seats turn up in great force, for these films are, such as they are, more likely to please them than the masses who throng the cheaper seats. The short drama appeals more to one's sense of beauty and dramatic effect than the serial and the masses are, at present, mainly interested in the fighting and thrilling stunts, which the serial contains.[79]

While the lower classes differed in religion, language, and region, and antagonisms among themselves, elites saw them as one uniform mass, whether in Bombay, Calcutta, or Madras.

British colonial officials' fears about the bad influence of some films often combined with beliefs that films could be used for propagandistic purposes. Officials in England and India hoped to use film to maintain order and sustain the loyalty of Indian subjects. Early British-made documentary films about India presented imperial achievements, official visits, aristocrats' hunting expeditions, and military parades as spectacular displays intended to legitimate imperial rule. On the other hand, Indian-made mythological films suited the goal of nationalists to assert the superiority of Indian culture.[80]

In this early era of film, elite reaction, west, east, and south was to fear the effects of movies and movie-going on the lower orders, whether working classes in Europe, or low-income natives in European colonies and dependencies. Once Hollywood attained success exporting its films world-wide, elites in these societies responded with alarm to the popularity of this foreign culture among the same lower orders. Government responses thus linked the two issues of disturbance to stratification hierarchies and cultural invasion. This made problematic the desire for modern technology and industrial development on the one hand and upholding traditional culture and values on the others. These strains would continue as major issues for post-colonial nations after independence, as we will see in ensuing chapters.

3

The Hollywood Studio Era, 1910s–1940s

In 1926, William Seabury, General Counsel to the Motion Picture Board of Trade and the National Association of the Motion Picture Industry, quoted Thomas Edison saying, "whoever controls the motion picture industry controls the most powerful medium of influence over the people."[1] In this era film was *the* screen medium in America, a highly organized, vertically integrated oligopoly, with annual ticket sales in the billions. The basic characteristics of the industry, including its relocation in Hollywood, began to emerge by the mid 1910s. The mature economic and cultural formation, the Hollywood studio system, would remain dominant and essentially unchanged for three decades, until the US government dismantled the vertical integration and television arrived after World War II.[2]

A handful of Hollywood studios had centralized control of film production, distribution and exhibition. They shaped what films were made, how much each was promoted and distributed, and in what circumstances each was viewed. They even colonized other entertainments, such as the Broadway theater and recorded music industries, to feed its maul. Most important, the concentration of Hollywood decision-making and routinization of production resulted in a uniformity in style of Hollywood films from the 1920s to the 1960s. Noting this, French auteur François Truffaut said, "We love the American cinema because the films all resemble each other."[3] Such consistency and repetition did much to naturalize underlying viewpoints, values and beliefs encoded in these films, making them a greater influence on American screen culture and on American culture generally than they otherwise may have been.

At the same time, Hollywood succeeded in containing the controversy and criticism that had constituted a national discourse before this consolidation. Movie-going became a normal part of American everyday life. Audiences were uncontroversial and only sporadically surfaced in public discourse. This was demonstrated by the mild reception to the thirteen-volume Payne Fund Studies published in 1933, probably still the largest single research effort to document the effects of film on child audiences.[4] Consequently, there is less readily visible historical documentation of audiences in these years, since it is mostly buried in memoirs and business papers rather than reported in daily newspapers.

Place and situation played their part in creating an industry screen culture. Its location and concentration in L. A. – paralleling concentration of other industries, such as auto in Detroit, steel in Pittsburgh, clothes and publishing in New York – contributed to a distinctive culture among the Hollywood community whose influence would become nationwide through its films. Places of exhibition were controlled to a significant degree by Hollywood, from the architecture to films exhibited, as well as prices, policies, and management of audiences within those theaters. Once established, it became good business for Hollywood to make uncontroversial films featuring studio-manufactured movie stars that were stereotypes of mainstream American values and beliefs and that avoided questions about power and inequality in America and other sensitive issues.

What was Hollywood?

Hollywood in its heyday was: a geographic, cultural, and mythical place; a vertically integrated oligopoly of film production; an efficient production system based on a detailed division of labor and decision-making centralized at the top; a distinct 'classical' film style; films that predominantly reinforced the status quo, and were consistently non-controversial – except for highly profitable sex and violence; and an audience experience delivered and shaped by the spectator position framed in the films and by the theater environment in which the films were viewed. These features were not planned and introduced systematically, but arose from an accretion of incremental decisions that addressed immediate pressures and problems of the business. Taken together however, they produced a monolithic film culture that at its peak, presented a fairly consistent message to four billion American viewers each year, making it a powerful force in shaping culture.

We will review several factors composing the Hollywood studio system, including its location, industry concentration and integration, the production process, marketing and distribution. It was the product of these, the films that led to the *nom de plume*, the classical Hollywood cinema, consistent in style and general content through these decades.

Making Hollywood

Film-making in the US at first was concentrated in the largest cities at the time, New York, Philadelphia, and Chicago. Los Angeles was a smaller city, ranked seventeenth in population in the US, smaller than Buffalo, Milwaukee, Cincinnati, and Newark NJ in 1910. The move to Hollywood was not to serve a Western market. It had begun just as feature film and outdoor action series were gaining popularity, and in the midst of the industrial struggle between manufacturers licensed by the Motion Picture Patent Company (MPPC) and the Independents opposed to it.

As discussed in Chapter 1, the rapid growth of nickelodeons in the 1900s had required a huge expansion in film production, pressing existing companies to build studios and increase output, and attracting new entrepreneurs into film-making. One way which companies accomplished this was to multiply their film units. Previously, each manufacturer relied mostly upon a single director who led a team of personnel that ground out new films day after day. To increase production, companies established multiple units of this sort, the director-unit system of production, beginning in 1908, often with each unit specializing in a particular genre. For example, in 1911 independent Biograph had units led by D. W. Griffith, Frank Powell, and Mack Sennett.[5]

The established genre of short comedies was quite popular among nickelodeon audiences. But manufacturers needed something to supplement this without incurring great expense building new studios. Outdoor filming fitted this need. However, the centers of film production around New York and Chicago had limited days of sunshine and clement weather for filming. In winter when natural light diminished in the northern cities, companies sent director units to the southwest to continue filming. In 1911, *Moving Picture World* cited the advantages of southern California over other locations: good weather, a variety of exteriors, a good labor supply compared to other west locations, a growing number of other film firms located there along with the development of specialized services for film-making, and good train services to other parts of the nation. By 1915 Los Angeles was the principal American film production center, and by 1922 it accounted for 84 percent of all US film, making Hollywood synonymous with film.[6]

Among the first new products was the western film. By 1911, six film manufacturers had year-round units stationed in southern California, all specializing in westerns. Essanay alone had made fifty-two one-reel stories during the 1909/10 season. Cowboy films were well-suited to taking advantage of the outdoor landscapes in the Los Angeles basin. Westerns also were relatively inexpensive and quick to produce: outdoor filming required no scenery, and traveling troupes could hire local entertainers and cowboys at modest wages. Westerns also constituted a uniquely American genre to compete against European film imports for the American market.[7]

The western derived from and built upon dime novels and Wild West traveling shows already familiar to audiences. This, combined with the spectacle of western vistas and sensationalist stories, helped to make the genre very popular. Westerns developed as character studies focusing on an individual cowboy and his exploits in film after film, and with the leading actors promoted as stars. At first, these westerns featured sensational figures such as the outlaw James gang that had captured the imagination of the American public, renegades who "fought the system" as heroes, which no doubt added to their appeal to working-class audiences.[8]

More generally, Los Angeles geography was projected through Hollywood's films and publicity of the time. The landscape appeared – and continues to appear – in many films, not only westerns, but even in films fictionally located in places with entirely different landscape. The purported lavish and leisure lives of Hollywood personae became a part of the myth of Los Angeles easy living. This mythical construction was captured in a quote, "Here all life is better than anywhere else in the universe," a paradise in the desert. In this mythical construction, L. A. was reduced to Hollywood, and Hollywood culture became L. A.'s.[9]

From the era of the MPPC to that of the Hollywood studios, there was a turnover of the dominant companies. Its formation in 1909 led many excluded companies (the 'Independents') to join together in 1910 to form a competing distribution company, Motion Picture Distribution and Sales. These two factions formed a duopoly that dominated distribution, but also were engage in legal battles about licenses for motion picture patents. However, this was short lived. Longer narrative feature films of four or more reels became the norm by the mid 1910s, bringing a change in distribution from film exchanges renting short films priced by the *foot* to producers doing their own distribution and renting by the *film*. This induced a market turnover, where the two alliances began to dissolve, and the number of production companies specializing in feature films rose, while those who continued to concentrate on the older, short films for nickelodeons, declined.[10]

This enticed exhibitors and distributors, who had the money, to merge with film manufacturers, who had the future, to begin forming the vertically integrated studio system. Several Independents, including some studios in Southern California that had succeeded with cowboy films, merged in 1912 and formed the Universal Film Manufacturing Company to produce feature films. Famous Players-Lasky absorbed a film distribution company, Paramount, and eventually acquired control of three hundred first-run movie palaces in many large cities across the nation. Warner Brothers, Fox, and MGM each began with nickelodeons and film exchanges and in the 1910s and early 1920s acquired production companies. Through the 1920s, consolidation continued, so that by the early 1930s, five vertically integrated companies with production studios in and around Hollywood, constituted a powerful oligopoly that controlled the American industry from production to exhibition.[11]

Longer feature films required greater investment. Without ready access to capital, the film companies could not produce a steady stream of new films, nor expand their real estate empire of movie theaters. Film companies began to forge ties with major banking firms: Paramount with Kuhn Loeb; Fox with Prudential Insurance and other New York investors; MGM-Loews backed by DuPont; Warner Brothers by Goldman Sachs; RKO with Merrill Lynch. By the early 1930s almost all of the founders of the major studios no longer controlled their studios, often supplanted by financiers.[12]

During the 1930s and 1940s, the peak decades for movie-going in the US, the five controlled the "vast majority of first-run movie theaters in the 92 largest cities" with populations over 100,000. This ended in the late 1940s and early 1950s when the federal government forced divestment of their theater chains. Yet their power within the industry still continued.[13]

Industry concentration developed along with the industrialization of production. Just as other corporate industries at the time transformed work, Hollywood transformed film production from an artisanal process in 1910 into a detailed division of labor by 1920, concentrating major decision-making in the hands of higher-level executives and routinizing other decisions through formulaic application of rules and procedures. The demand for a steady flow of feature films to America's thousands of theaters provided substantial incentives for studios to increase speed and efficiency and lower the cost of production. Production could not be reduced entirely to an assembly line process, since each film is a unique product. But much of the work could be standardized, even in writing where the development of genre formulae could reduce the necessity of invention and creativity and replace it with the tried and true.

The major studios' 'central producer system' moved most decision-making from the director of a unit to specialized departments, with the producer coordinating all the work from planning and budgeting to production and post-production. The director was freed of much preparatory and other work, but stripped of much decision-making, was no longer in charge of his own team of workers, and instead concentrated on supervising the performance before the camera. For each film, the producer selected a team of contract employees (writer, director, cameraman, cast) from their respective departments to work with the director. Scripts were broken down into a pre-planned order of shooting of scenes, determining for each the set to be built, the wardrobe, minor casting, an estimated time and cost to shoot. Experts in specialist departments would design and construct sets and prepare wardrobe and makeup, before the scheduled date of shooting. Film processing, editing, and other post-production was also specialized. While all this varied from company to company, the general trend was to shift control from a director and his team to a producer and toward specialists with equipment and materials that could quickly design and produce what was needed with little supervision. In this way the skill gained from one film could be used to improve the quality and efficiency of the next.[14]

This all contributed inevitably to standardization of style and centralization of decision-making. Studio executives and their bankers decided what movies to make. Message was constrained by a desire to avoid controversial topics and remain safely in the mainstream, in the hope of assuaging moral entrepreneurs and politicians. At the same time, they allowed some leeway for sex and violence to boost ticket sales.

Making the Classic Hollywood Film

The oligopoly and organization of production led to a recognizable common film style.[15] Style refers to the techniques of narrative form and filming that are used to tell the story. Content or message refers not only to the story and characters, but how characters, their actions, events, and things express particular values, norms, and beliefs. Style or form and content are not separable, but rather integral to each other in complex and subtle ways. For example, narrative form tells a story from a particular point of view, which inevitably is freighted with value judgments. It also requires closure, and choosing a particular closure involves taking a normative position on the events, characters, and their actions.[16]

The classical style arose along with long feature films, the consolidation of the major studios, and the rationalization of production in the 1910s and 1920s. An overarching formula for Hollywood films became so established that it pre-determined how any story would be transformed into film. Visual, aural, and linguistic information conveyed through the camera and editing helped the viewer to follow the story. Narrowing the logic of the film and delimiting interpretation, characters were presented with a few consistent traits that also cued the story direction. Use of conventional and widely known stereotypes – and the culture embedded in them – aided this purpose, e.g. in the form of the familiar personae of stars and character actors typecast in these films.[17] The goal was more effective story-telling, enabling audiences to follow the story more easily, but it also made it easier to voluntarily suspend disbelief and thus skepticism or criticism. The darkened theater and its policing by ushers further reduced distracting sights and sounds and focused individuals on the film story and its characters.[18]

I am not suggesting that audiences, as a result, became involuntarily 'spellbound.' The studio created ripe conditions, but audience absorption is still volitional. After all, it was a common audience purpose to relax and just enjoy the movie. Moreover, people can choose to interpret or read films differently. Openness of a text to variant readings is of course a relative matter. The classical style necessarily had a degree of openness to reach broad and diverse audiences. Unfortunately, the concept of variant readings has been used to refer to *individual* interpretations of media messages. However, readings are socially and culturally important only when they are widely shared, *collective* interpretations. Moreover, cultural impact is significant only when a similar interpretive viewpoint is applied by many people to many movies, not only to a single movie. In other words, effective resistant readings need to be pervasive and persistent, just as with preferred reading representations.[19]

The classical style is based on individual character motives as the predictable driving forces in the story. But motives and their goals must have specific substance. As Bordwell et al. explain, most goal-oriented Hollywood protagonists are "a reflection of the ideology of American individualism and enterprise." In particular, American westerns presented a heroic, independent 'rugged individualist,' such as the Lone Ranger, or John Wayne and Clint Eastwood characters.[20] Individualism was at the heart of the most common goal of characters that appeared across genres, that of heterosexual romance, which approves individual choice of a mate rather than family match-making. Its appeal transcended many differences among Americans, providing a common, uncontroversial identification with the characters. Individualism is also part of the larger positioning in American films of the viewer as an American. Such films were considered a tool for Americanization of immigrants, or to promote American views abroad, representing the ideal American through simple and concrete stories.[21]

Yet another way in which film text projects a point of view is through the subject position implicit in the film. A story is always told from a point of view; classical film-making techniques do this literally by selecting the position of and the focus of the camera, and by editing and sequencing those frames. Film differs from live performance in this aspect. With live entertainment, audience members can choose what to look at and when – this or that actor, a stray cat strolling across the stage. With film, the camera and editing chooses what audiences can look at. Yet it does not draw attention to itself, but rather presents, "a solid fictional world which has simply been filmed for our benefit."[22]

Feminist film studies demonstrated how subject position may be an ideological tool, framing a male point of view through the filming and editing of the classical Hollywood film. But one may well find subject positions similarly representing the viewpoints of other dominant parties. What makes a subject position a matter of discursive power is control not only of what audiences see, but more broadly, *how* they see it, what valuations are made and what conclusions drawn. The story, the scripted words, the scene, the editing, as well as the camera, define the characters as well as a subject position through which to view the characters, a dual creation. As with other techniques, pointing the camera and editing film must have a substantive purpose, which links it to content. That is, the viewer is presented with a particular definition of a character from a particular subject position. For example, the western genre famously was created from the point of view of the white cowboy, and rarely from that of the native-American Indian, presenting a dilemma for native American audiences, to accept the white view and negate their own experience. Similar circumstances arise for African-American audiences watching a film with a white perspective, or gay viewers watching a heterosexual romance, and so on. It is not that subject position cannot be subverted, but that it is a presumption of the film that must be overcome.[23]

Finally, we must reiterate that film characterization and spectator subject positions are notable, not because they are found in one or another movie, but because they are typical of Hollywood films in general and align with other discourses and other institutional settings, e.g. concerning race and gender, education and the psychology of intelligence and persuasion, business and economic growth, that promoted similar points of view in this era. The same beliefs and values repeated across many films seen by many people over decades, helped to naturalize those values and beliefs and reaffirm them in the broader culture. Uniformity of film content arose from converging forces: the centralization of power within major Hollywood studios, the insularity of the Hollywood community, and the external political pressures upon Hollywood from other powerful organizations, such as Congressional committees, religious organizations, and reform groups.[24]

Marketing the Film

A film economist for the industry in 1931 stated, "… the real boss of studio picture production is the sales department … so many westerns, so many rough-stuff melos, so many comedies." Decisions about what movies to make were shaped more by box office receipts than aesthetics or morality. Some genres targeted audiences of particular regions, gender, or class. An assumption in the industry during the 1920s and 1930s was that film profits depended on appealing to women, who it was believed were the most avid movie-goers. Consequently, a large portion of films in the 1920s were melodramas and romances – often written by women or adapted from popular fiction by women. Product placement in films and the plush decoration of movie palaces targeted women.

The big studios' priorities for other demographics are indicated in their sequencing release of films. The studios distributed their films through a process known as zone-run-clearance by which movies featuring the big stars were released sequentially from first- to fifth-run theaters, from metropolitan downtown theaters to neighborhood and small-town ones. Distribution divisions defined their task as delivering the right movies to the right theaters at the right time. The major studios also used their power to exclude independent films from exhibition, reducing audience access to movies that may have offered an alternative voice in the 'marketplace of ideas.'

Not all movies were first-run fare. To ensure these movies paid for themselves, studios used their power to enforce block booking in which exhibitors could not choose specific movies to lease. As a consequence, independent exhibitors in small towns invariably at the end of these runs, persistently complained that their customers were not served well by Hollywood, and regularly sought less sophisticated, less racy, less modern films. These small-time theater owners and their local constituency tended to ally themselves with conservative crusades for censoring and monitoring Hollywood.[25]

Movie-star publicity was an important channel of marketing for major studios. American movie companies began creating 'movie stars' around the same time that film production was first being rationalized. The star enabled producers to differentiate their product, so that their film was not just another film by an impersonal studio, but a Mary Pickford film, for example. It also encouraged moviegoers' brand loyalty, to go to *any* Mary Pickford film. Publicity also generated more avid movie-going by fostering an apparent intimacy and para-social relationship with the star. This was premised again on the industry view that frequent moviegoers were primarily women and girls.

Stars were created by turning actors into celebrities. This was often instigated and sustained by the movie companies, conducted through the trade press, fan magazines and newspapers. The publicity projected an appealing off-screen persona that mirrored the typecast characters played by the actor in film after film. More broadly, the star system was an important apparatus in the production of screen culture. Stars were embodiments of archetypes that distilled norms, values, and beliefs of mainstream culture, e.g. about masculinity or patriotism. They also promoted consumerism: Publicity about the 'private' lives of stars accented the pleasures of consumption.

The problem for the movie industry was to control the discourse. If the press reported star behavior inconsistent with the persona the whole edifice risked collapse. The consolidation of the industry enabled major studios to wield power over stars, restricting even off-screen behavior, and over the press to prevent bad publicity. The movie press, dependent on industry sources, became accomplices in the process.[26]

Hollywood studios tried to avoid controversy and appease critics, even while testing boundaries of decency with violent and sexually suggestive scenes. From the nickelodeon days the movie business had been criticized by a wide range of moral entrepreneurs. Underlying their concerns typically was the crowd psychology assumption that lower-status groups (lower classes, 'inferior' races and immigrants, women and children) were vulnerable to the 'dangerous' influences of the movies. Invariably these concerns led to calls for film censorship of one sort or another. In the 1920s, a few highly publicized Hollywood scandals and risqué films led to a renewal of censorship initiatives. The big Hollywood studios moved to pre-empt this with the Motion Picture Production Code.[27]

The Production Code was complemented by another studio strategy to appear respectable and responsible, matinees. The most persistent criticism of film focused on children. Most critics and reformers were opposed not to movies per se but to the wrong movies with the wrong message for children. Matinees specifically for children separated children from inappropriate adult fare. Saturday matinees were at first instituted by local reform groups in the 1910s. While programs often did not appeal to adolescents, it did seem to work for younger children. Film serials delighted children during Saturday matinee programs at neighborhood theaters. The Hays Office launched its own national program in 1922, under the auspices of a board of national civic and religious organizations. The Office had compiled a year's inventory of mostly old films sometimes re-edited for children and provided them as a package to theater managers. The strategy preempted free exhibitions by churches, schools, and civic organizations, returning child audiences and their pocket change to the industry revenue stream.[28]

In 1929 Disney Studio adopted the matinee and billed it as a club for children, meeting each Saturday at a local theater. Disney built these clubs around their Mickey Mouse character with a club creed, club yell, club song, and a program of a Mickey Mouse cartoon, a feature film, and often contests and a stage show with local children performing. Loew's and Warner Brothers theater circuits soon introduced their own children's clubs. Hollywood studios gained local support by including promotion of local businesses. They posed as good corporate citizens helping to enculture the next generation of young citizens, while also promoting the consumption of goods of their own and others for a profit.[29]

'The Product': A Normative Message

Unlike the nickelodeon era in the US when many independent exhibitors attempted to attract a large, mostly urban, working-class clientele with films that might appeal to their point of view, the consolidation of the Hollywood studio system by the 1920s, meant that a small film community determined what millions of people would see. As we have seen, they controlled not only production, but distribution and exhibition as well, guaranteeing the major studios' films the largest audiences and independent films only limited engagements in small theaters. Even in neighborhood theaters the studios standardized management policies, homogenizing the movie-going experience.[30] Thus, rather than representing the diverse views and experiences of American people, Hollywood films collectively promoted consistent, persistent images and censored other views. Hollywood's goal of avoiding controversy translated into films that mostly reproduced and reinforced mainstream American values and beliefs. This also meant producing generally favorable representations of those who held these mainstream values.

This is not to say that Hollywood films were entirely homogeneous. Each film treated its story in its own way. The uniformity in message was not in the specific story told, but in elements, such as character types and the valuations given them, stereotypes and tropes familiar to American audiences and already naturalized from mainstream culture, that were incorporated in movie after movie. What made Hollywood's product important was its power to reinforce these already naturalized elements of the culture, if for no other reason than these familiar elements made films easier for audiences to understand. If an aspect of a scene contradicts audience expectations, then that aspect distracts attention from the progress of the narrative. Avoiding such problems leads to reinforcing the status quo, for example, of men over women, white over black, 'mental' over manual workers.[31]

There were films that diverged from the norm. Second-tier studios who were frozen out of first and second-run theaters controlled by the Big Five, specialized in genres for smaller niche markets at independent theaters. Republic Films revived serials in the 1930s for juveniles.[32] Major studio script-writers and directors pushed against commerce for their artistic freedom, their complaints frequent enough to become a cliché. But their successes in this conflict were despite, rather than because of, the industry structure, and typically reached only smaller audiences for modest box office returns.

Hollywood film became a significant voice in American culture and opinion. At its peak in the 1940s the industry sold about four billion tickets a year to a population of about 140 million, or nearly 30 tickets a year for every man, woman and child, far more than any other cultural form of the time, except radio. Thus Hollywood was a cultural presence in American lives. Its films mostly presented an image of America as mainstream and affluent upper-middle class. Other values or groups were mostly absent, relegated to roles supporting the mainstream viewpoint. Hollywood films commonly divided the world into good (white, capitalism, upper-middle-class men, and cowboys) and bad (minorities, socialism, working class, rebellious women, Indians). In such a world, violence was integral to the struggle between good and evil, used by both sides, and thus integral to the narrative. The overall effect was to value one group and way of life and to de-value all others, much as many of the major figures in the industry had erased their own immigrant backgrounds and changed their names in order to assimilate to the mainstream culture.[33]

A case in point is the representation of class in films of this era. As discussed in Chapter 1, in the nickelodeon era, when the industry was newborn and serving a large working-class clientele, films more frequently presented stories sympathetic to or from the point of view of working-class audiences. Even as films began to shift to feature length, there were still significant working-class messages in films.[34]

However, as increasingly grand theaters began to displace the store-front nickelodeon, and exhibitors increasingly sought a higher-class clientele, more 'sophisticated' feature films changed the message. By the 1920s the films and the movie palaces both projected ideas that wealth is good and fell silent about the inequities and exclusions of race, gender, and class. Historian Lary May observed, "In the teens and twenties producers dignified the moral revolution within the standards of the Anglo-Saxon middle class," stating that "more than 60 percent of the characters had roots in small towns and rural areas as well as the milieu of the older professions and small propertied middle class," rather than the industrial working class.[35]

In the 1930s, even while the Depression pushed conservative studio executives to produce films sympathetic to the plight of the common man, the films offered only individualistic solutions: to bear up and be good, not engage in collective actions such as strikes, protests, and political campaigns. The term itself, the common man, blurred class lines. Characters may have been 'plain folks' and 'men of the street,' but often not working class. Frank Capra wanted his movies to combat individual despair, not class exploitation. *One More Spring* (1935) featured an unemployed musician, an antique dealer, a chorus girl, and a banker. Other Capra's heroes included a journalist and a small-town banker who loaned money to small businessmen. The heroes tended more to be business people in small towns rather than blue-collar workers in factories and construction. Small business conservatism ran through these stories. A protagonist in *You can't take it with you* (1938) says, "I don't owe the government a cent." John Ford's oeuvre often featured family farmers and a nostalgia for a Jeffersonian rural life of individualism overcoming strife, in which spiritual satisfaction rather than victory over oppression is the goal. These films focused on personal relationships more than class relations between owners or bosses and workers. Even the sympathetic films avoided or opposed collective actions, and their heroes were elevated for their individualist principles, not for their part in social change. Workers often were depicted as basically good people misguided by agitators.[36]

Moreover, films addressing class issues of the Depression were 'poor performers' at the profitable first-run palaces that established a film's reputation and longer-run success.[37] Audiences at these theaters tended to be more affluent and thus less likely to identify with working-class problems. But more important, many in the audience at movie palaces were having a special night out and thus less likely to want to think about problems, more inclined to a screwball comedy than *Grapes of Wrath*.

Movie Palaces and Neighborhood Houses

By the 1920s, going to the movies had settled in as a widespread social and cultural practice. It served singles and young couples for cheap entertainment or date nights, parents for a night out without the kids and, on Saturdays, day-care for a dime to give parents a reprieve from parenting. The movie theater was a place where Hollywood and audiences' cultures met. The industry spoke in this era through the Hollywood-controlled theater and its management as well as through the films. Audiences, to varying degrees, paid attention to the film and abided by the house policies for audience behavior.

During the mid to late 1910s, some prosperous exhibitors converted closed vaudeville and drama theaters and constructed purpose-built movie theaters, advertising them as 'palaces' offering not just respectability, but luxury for higher ticket prices. By the 1920s, the metropolitan picture palace was well established. As Hollywood studios consolidated, these movie palaces were the first to show the most sought-after pictures featuring big-name stars. Theater chains, like Paramount, who were buying and building such theaters, aggressively advertised the movie palace experience. In the press, they completely overshadowed the thousands of unremarkable, smaller, and humbler theaters in metropolitan areas and in the many small cities and towns of the nation's hinterlands. In most cities they were concentrated in the downtown, although in larger cities, such as New York and Chicago, with more than one heavily trafficked shopping district, some movie palaces were also built on main streets of middle-class neighborhoods.[38]

For most people, going to these theaters with higher admission prices was a special, formal night out, for which they dressed up, arrived on time and behaved themselves. From what little documentation describes about movie palace audiences, they were relatively sedate and well behaved. They appear to have required only light managing, as the building itself seems to have conveyed an ambience that cued 'proper' behavior. A *New Yorker* cartoon captured this, with a child asking the parent in the lobby, "Does God live here?" Audiences were likely more inclined to arrive on time and to watch quietly and intently, more voyeuristic than participative. There were also plentiful ushers, from street to seat, to offer help, provide direction and occasionally enforce rules. The surroundings were not what most people were accustomed to – which was the point of their lavish interiors – so people were unlikely to behave as they might in a neighborhood house.[39]

But movie palaces, while receiving most publicity and representing a large share of box office receipts, accounted for a lesser share of attendance and represented only a small portion of all movie houses. In the US in the 1920s there were about a thousand picture palaces with seating capacity over 1,500 in fan-shaped auditoriums and elaborate décor, which accounted for eight percent of all US movie theaters. Another estimate put their numbers at five percent of all movie houses.[40]

Smaller, less lavish theaters were more typical in outlying and less prosperous neighborhoods of big cities and in smaller cities and towns. The hierarchical distribution system did not deliver movies to later-run theaters in urban neighborhoods and smaller cities and towns sometimes for weeks. But they had other advantages: Their modest architecture ($45,000 in 1929 for an 800 seat theatre, $1.2 million for the new 3,200 seat Paramount downtown), low prices (10–15 cents), plus the local independent owner, often a fellow townsperson, contributed to a more neighborly, relaxed atmosphere. Consequently theaters in working-class neighborhoods were well attended in the 1920s by a clientele that could less afford and was disinclined to attend the downtown theaters.[41]

Compatible with the informality was a common practice of arriving at the movie house not at the scheduled start of the show, but rather on the schedule of the household from which parents had to extract themselves, then staying for the next showing to see the first part of the show, and leaving when they reached the point in the film at which they first arrived, saying "This is where we came in." Such practice of beginning anywhere in the film and seeing the end before the beginning, combined with a regular coming and going during the screening, of course disrupted classical Hollywood narratives as well as audience absorption. This was routine for parents whose busy schedules did not afford them the opportunity to arrive on time. It also applied to children who walked to neighborhood theaters on their own and were unlikely to plan by the clock – unless it was the regular Saturday children's matinee. It applied less to dating teens and twenties but, even among them, a Saturday night date was the primary event; the movies were a good enough, yet inexpensive, choice for working-class dating. *Going* to the movies was the cultural practice; often the movie was secondary in these theaters. The characterization of movie audiences as 'spell-bound in darkness' simply did not describe American audiences in many circumstances.[42]

Small-town populations were less able to support specialized theaters, either in terms of types of entertainment or in terms of clientele. Consequently, even well into the movie-going era, theaters in smaller towns were likely to welcome any type of entertainment that might fill seats. These theaters were often locally owned and of little interest to the major chains. Instead of orienting their business to the national companies and attempting to emulate big city entertainment, they typically oriented their entertainment and policies to the local community that they served. For example, central and eastern Kentucky theater owners in the 1930s accommodated meetings and benefits of local groups, staged performances by local musicians, showed locally made newsreels, and chose movies from regional booking agents suited to the local taste, such as Will Rogers and western movies, and sometimes even scheduled tours by Hollywood western stars, such as Gene Autry.[43]

Entire towns and urban neighborhoods patronized the one theater – or in some cases two, segregated voluntarily or involuntarily on the basis of race or class. Either way, audiences tended to have a common identity as town folk or neighbors.[44] These local theaters had a screen culture somewhat reminiscent of nickelodeons, reflecting the local community rather than being imposed upon it from outside. Neighborhood audiences may have felt it was their theater. Consequently, these audiences sometimes required more active management. Ushers more vigorously enforced theater policies, especially with children and teens. Programs also included various participative activities to busy the audiences and keep them out of trouble.

One such activity in the 1920s was a community sing that seemed an equitable compromise between audience autonomy and theater management.[45] Community singing was not welcome in the posher movie palaces. But they were popular elsewhere: many people participated with enthusiasm, creating a feeling of togetherness. At the same time, management was orchestrating the activity, choosing the song, the organist setting the pace, drowning out conversation and other activities among audience members. Community sings, however, died with the introduction of film sound: Most musicians lost their jobs, including the organists who had led the singing.[46]

Film exhibition was transformed by two economic blows in the 1930s, the Depression and the arrival of sound. In the early 1930s attendance dropped. *Variety* suggested audiences were discontented, that "going to theater was no longer routine ... people go because there is something specific they want to see." *Motion Picture Herald* wrote that people threw things at the screen in protest. Movie palaces cut costs and prices to become more affordable, and neighborhood houses became rundown. Attendance began to improve by 1934 and rose thereafter until 1948.[47]

Audiences at 'lower order cinemas' had different film preferences than those at first-run palaces. The top stars were popular at first-run theaters as well as at lower rung cinemas, perhaps due to the publicity derived from successful openings. But tastes differed about many movies and stars. In big Eastern cities Chaplin and costume dramas, biopics and adaptations from stage did better; Will Rogers and Shirley Temple, westerns, and melodramas were not popular there. The reverse was true in small towns and other regions of the country. But other factors than the feature film affected attendance in lower-rung venues: weather, competing entertainments such as a circus, or other parts of the playbill such as a second feature, live entertainment, newsreel, short films, raffles, and give-aways. Letters to the *Motion Picture Herald* in the mid to late 1930s confirm these small-town preferences and effects on attendance.[48]

The coming of sound was a boon for the Hollywood-owned theater chains, giving them another advantage over smaller regional chains and independent theaters. The big studios obtained financing from Wall Street investors to install sound equipment in their theaters. But small owners and theaters were hard pressed to afford renovation for sound. Between 1928 before sound and 1935 after silent films disappeared, about a third of all theaters, overwhelmingly smaller ones, closed.[49]

Sound seems to have brought some change to patrons' behavior. Talking movies required audiences to listen, which in turn required a reduction in other sounds, such as live musical accompaniment and chattering audiences. With silent movies, audiences depended upon reading inter-titles to understand the action, and these were sometimes read to others by audience members. With sound, audiences had to hear the dialog that now included a good deal more detail. Sound furthered the 'spellbound in darkness' effect, adding another sense to be attended to, and discouraging social activity in favor of individual concentration on the film. While not universally silencing all audience members, to some degree it led to new norms of behavior, often enforced by audiences themselves.[50]

Despite the centralized power of the major Hollywood studios, their rationalized production and standardized film style, and their control of exhibition, American film culture remained diverse, ranging from downtown palace to neighborhood house, from big city to small town, and across regions; from one class to another, and from one race to another, as *de jure* and *de facto* segregation assured that black and white theater experiences were separate and distinct. As will be evident throughout this history, corporate forces of concentration repeatedly confronted forces of diversification, producing a veneer of national commonality over a plethora of local screen cultures. All groups were familiar with the names and stories from Hollywood and maybe accommodated those values, but each maintained their own preferences and shaped their own experience.

4

Global Hollywood, 1920s–1950s

In Europe by the end of World War I, narrative fiction films were well established as movie theater entertainment and audience habits too had settled in, along with a variety of regulations for censorship, theaters and their audiences. Cinema-going had become part of everyday life. However, European nations were confronted with the Hollywood juggernaut holding economic marketplace advantages on the one hand, and with European mass audiences often attending American films more than domestic films on the other hand. Political, economic, and cultural elites reacted strongly to this dilemma. European elites' fear of 'Americanization' became entwined with concerns about controlling their homeland working classes. As film scholars Richard Maltby and Ruth Vasey noted, the popularity of American films "... concentrated as it was, among women and the working class ... was, for bourgeois nationalism, a further threat ..."[1] This was paralleled by a similar fear about colonial native audiences' apparent attractions to American movies. Regardless of the degree to which mass audiences actually preferred American films, the fears built upon stereotypes of the masses and drove national and colonial film policies.

After World War II, the same dilemma confronted newly independent post-colonial governments trying to construct national identity and unity, and to extricate themselves from century-long cultural ties to their former colonial rulers. At the same time, American films and goods were arriving and gaining widespread popularity. In this circumstance, the masses' attraction to American culture both doubled and halved the difficulties. Consequently, screen cultures, films, and audiences were nodes of political discourse and hot debate, in contrast to the US, where movie-going had become uncontroversial.

To cover globe-girdling colonial populations, I will first discuss issues relatively common to most, and then provide a closer look at three nations, India, China, and Egypt, as prominent cases from distinct cultural regions. Other regions and nations, such as Nigeria and Brazil, became more prominent during the television era and will be discussed in Chapter 6.

American Film Hegemony

During World War I, European film companies' share of the American market was reduced to five percent, and American studios were becoming the dominant film suppliers to Europe and the rest of the world. By 1920 American film companies were gaining a third of their income from export. Will Hays, head of the Motion Picture Producers and Distributors of America (MPPDA) and spokesperson for the major studios, summed up Hollywood's plans for international distribution, "We are going to sell America to the world with American motion pictures."[2] By 1923 British films accounted for only ten percent of those shown in Britain, while in France, three fourths of films approved for screening were American films. The US Department of Commerce estimated that during 1925/6 American film exports totaled $8 million, while imports were $0.5 million. Of American exports, 40 percent went to Europe, with almost half of that to Britain, about a quarter to Latin America, 20 percent to the 'Far East,' and less than two percent to Africa.[3]

This world-wide expansion of Hollywood's market was part of an early stage of post-colonial globalization. Improved transport and communication widened and quickened international markets, as imperial government control of trade within separate colonial empires slackened. Western governments also aided development of multinational corporations to create and sustain markets. This included sponsorship of film industry exports.[4]

The size of the US domestic market gave Hollywood film companies several advantages in international film trade. First, once American companies controlled the US market after driving out European companies, they could amortize their production costs across a domestic market far larger than that of other nations. Having recouped expenses, they could then export films at lower prices, undercutting competitors such as French companies who depended more heavily on export income. Second, this large market enabled American studios to produce more expensive and appealing feature films than their foreign counterparts. This was recognized in a memo by an advisor to England's Gainsborough Films in which he stated that British film companies could not compete with Hollywood spectacles, musicals and drama due to the cost of their production, and that cheaper films, like westerns and crime stories, would appear ridiculous in a British setting. As a result, it was more profitable in Britain to distribute and exhibit American film than British films. Third, this large US market also attracted the best film stars, directors, and technical experts from European nations, such as Britain, France, and Germany, that made American films featuring these personnel more attractive when exported back to their home nations. Hollywood thus captured a cultural bonus that normally would go to domestic film companies. This talent drain simultaneously strengthened Hollywood while weakening its competitors. Lastly, the predominance of American films in European theaters, once established, made these films, and by extension American culture, familiar to European audiences, thus avoiding some of the 'cultural discount' that a foreign film usually suffered.[5] Thus, Hollywood benefited from a peculiar combination of cultural familiarity as well as exoticness.

European Responses

In the US before World War I, American film companies had led a campaign expressing alarm at the dominance of French films and their alleged immoral nature.[6] After World War I, European nations similarly objected to the dominance of Hollywood films in their countries and alleged that the films had ill effects on their people and their culture. There the reaction was more among elites and mobilized government efforts against a wide range of American influences. The responses involved specific economic policies as well as broader cultural defenses.

European governments constructed twin economic policies: to restrict exhibition of Hollywood films in their nation, and to subsidize an alternative supply of 'national cinema.' One proposal called for a pan-Europe response, a 'Europäische Monroe-Doktrin' proposed in 1924 by a German film magazine, *Lichtbildbühne*. The editorial began with the premise that:

> ... with the exception of the United States, no producing country in the world is in a position to get back its negative costs in its own country. Therein lies the weakness of each and every European film producing country against America – as long as they march separately.

It proposed reciprocal distribution agreements among European nations, an industry-specific precursor to the European Union. But the very nationalism that was the foundation of the reaction to the

American film invasion, at the same time undermined the cooperation proposed.[7]

The proposal was a grander version of a German government strategy in 1917 when it merged German studios into a subsidized film consortium, Ufa, to combat imports with top-quality historical dramas and Expressionist films produced with artisanal methods. For a time the strategy succeeded: German films accounted for 40 percent of all films shown in Germany. Italian film companies formed a similar private trust in 1919, which was absorbed in 1926 into one company, but had little success competing with foreign imports. As with Ufa, French companies and governments also pursued a strategy through the interwar period that emphasized the shift from industrial to artisanal film production and claimed the high ground of French art over American entertainment for marketing to Frenchmen. It too did not stem the tide of American films.[8]

In each case, the economic strategy was product differentiation – artisanal versus industrial film-making – to create a national cinema that would enhance the nation's artistic reputation in the industry. These reorganizations of the national industries, while economic in form, were in substance promoting political and cultural nationalism.

European governments, institutions, and elites defined the success of American films in their countries after World War I as a threat to their national cultures. As early as 1919, the British government complained publicly about the 'invasion' of American film and its method of block booking. In 1924 a British newspaper declared, "the British film industry is dying" due to the American invasion. French politicians and intellectuals characterized the American presence as a disease or a military conquest. A French writer in 1931 described film imports as "outposts of the American invasion installed at the gates of France, Italy, Germany, and all the nations of the Old World." Europeans feared that American films abetted a broader 'Americanization' of their culture, and especially influencing the allegedly more susceptible lower classes of their nations.[9]

The dominance of American culture in Europe by the early 1920s was relatively new. In the early nineteenth century Americans still read books and saw plays mostly written in Britain or Europe and European performers regularly toured the US. Later in that century, the most successful American performers began to tour Europe, but this represented only a small part of the art and entertainment consumed by Europeans, more a novelty than a treat. Only with the influx of numerous American films in the 1920s, did American entertainment become prevalent in the everyday lives of the Europeans.

A broad array of European elites and institutions responded by declaiming the intellectual, aesthetic, and moral superiority of their own culture, and linking these efforts to patriotism and citizenship. Going to a French-made movie, for example, was supposed to be not only enjoyable, but also culturally uplifting and a civic duty. Some warned about degrading national character and weakening national unity – at the same time dismissing the importance of class, ethnic, and regional inequalities.[10] The discourses presumed a hierarchy of tastes – inborn or bred – with the culture of the bourgeois elite defined as superior and synonymous with the nation, and the invading culture as well as domestic subcultures as inferior. The advisor to Gainsborough Pictures in 1930, mentioned above, claimed English cultural superiority to explain why English films could not compete with popular Americans crime movies, "We have no gang-warfare to speak of. We have no machine-gun battles in the street ... Lawlessness has no important status in England; we are too civilized."[11]

Consequently, the idea of a national cinema was advocated to represent the nation to its citizens. Governments subsidized filmmaking, censoring or even commissioning films to mold consistent, positive representations of the nation. The very idea of national cinemas of course presumed an antithesis, Hollywood, to which it was contrasted.[12]

A prime example of national cinema is a perennial genre, the English 'heritage' film. Films of classic novels and plays, for example, used historical dress, furnishings, houses, public buildings and scenic locations that were owned by the upper classes, canonizing upper-class culture as *the* English heritage. A national heritage movement began about the same time as commercial film exhibition: The National Trust for Places of Historic Interest and Natural Beauty was founded in 1895, and confined itself to the buildings and landscapes of the wealthy bourgeoisie of the seventeenth and eighteenth centuries. The films included other classes as accessories or background, as quaint and thoroughly English villagers, farmers or factory workers.[13]

In the 1930s, smaller British film companies tried a contrasting strategy to compete with American films. They appealed to class as much as nationalism with music and comedy films in the British music hall tradition and featuring music hall stars, most notably Gracie Fields. These films drew upon British working-class culture, in contrast to the heritage films, and were not intended for export. Both genres were successful – heritage among the middle class, comedies among the working class – and together the two celebrated and sentimentalized a common Britishness of their target audiences, transcending class in favor of national unity.[14]

European Movie-Goers

American film was more than an invasion. The films were appealing enough to be successful in many countries. *The New York Times* attributed the success to changes in audience preferences:

> A few years ago there was a flurry, almost a panic, among American photoplay producers because of a threatened invasion of the home market by European producers. Germany was the immediate cause of alarm. The invasion turned out to be only a foray: American audiences decisively showed their preference for photoplays "made in America." More than this, foreign audiences – in Europe, in South America, in Africa, in Asia – are reported as showing the same preference. Lloyd George is said to have made the statement that, "if the popularity of the American cinema continues, it will be a tremendous influence toward the Americanization of the world."[15]

Some say Hollywood benefited from the widespread international use of English. But in this era that would have made a difference only for a small public composed of a privileged and literate class who spoke English. Some scholars cite a 'universal' appeal that the classical Hollywood film seemed to have. As Richard Maltby and Ruth Vasay put it:

> Few French people wanted to be German, few Italians wanted to be British, but almost everybody wanted to be Gary Cooper or James Cagney, and Greta Garbo and Marlene Dietrich showed that you could, despite your nationality and even your accent. If Hollywood was a foreign country, it was also everybody's imaginative home ...[16]

Some research indicates that the popularity may have been due to economic hegemony, less the attraction to American movies than the lack of domestic films as an alternative – indeed, one could expect that people may be more inclined to domestic films expressing their own culture if there were sufficient supply.[17] If that was the case, then the fear of cultural hegemony was not well founded, but the fear nonetheless motivated cultural policies.

In addition, acceptance of American films was accompanied by other forms of social and cultural preparation. At least some Europeans were buying American consumer goods between the wars, including appliances and popular music. These multiple American products in their homes may have bred a familiarity that made understanding American movies easier.[18]

An underlying factor may have been the economic and social strain facing families in these years, from the toll of World War I to the inflation and aftermath in the 1920s, followed by the Depression and spread of fascism, and then World War II. American movies offered an escape from the stressful times; European movies by contrast tended to be more self-consciously cultural, educational or civic. Circumstances also favored movie-going generally, despite difficult times. Many workers had more time for movies. Workers had gained shorter working hours in the 1920s, eight-hour days, forty-eight hour weeks. Of course, unemployment followed during the Depression, giving too much spare time. Inflation in the 1920s put pressure on working-class families to have wives and daughters bring home wages. The strain on family budgets from both inflation and depression also made movie-going, among the very cheapest of entertainments, a practical choice. Daughters especially, with some independent income, also now had more opportunity for a treat like a movie.[19]

Class and Movie-Going

Hollywood invasion or not, the audiences' cinema experience was less about the pedigree of the film. It was other factors that differentiated the experience. These depended more on *where* family members went to see a movie.[20] As discussed in Chapter 3, location dictated ticket prices, how a theater was furnished and managed, what movies appeared there and whether as first or fourth run. Location also determined what class predominated in the audiences and how at home they felt. Ticket prices, furnishings, and the feature films chosen, each expressed what class was the preferred customer. Managerial practices stipulated the balance between service and supervision, depending upon the social class or age group expected. The selection of movies also indicated the anticipated class of clientele. In urban areas, audiences were segregated by neighborhood, and neighborhood determined the social class of the audience and their movie-going practices.

In working-class districts of Antwerp, Belgians went "almost in their pajamas" to their neighborhood houses, but for posher palaces in city center "you had to be dressed almost in a gala outfit" to enter. From the point of view of those who frequented the palaces, speaking about the smaller, plainer cinemas:

> We didn't go to the smaller cinemas. They were always packed and in our eyes a lesser kind of cinema. Because they would be belching, making noises, eating, and smoking, and that wasn't for us. That was

just too foul, it was the rabble having a party where one should just
go to see a film.[21]

For working-class audiences, movie-going was a matter of affordability, convenience, informality, and relaxation to escape the work
and worries of daily life. Most did not have the energy or inclination
for striving or cultural uplift, nor money for frequent 'nights on the
town.' For example, during World War I in neutral Netherlands,
movie attendance rose in part due to a lack of heat in homes from
a shortage of coal. Movie-going had gained popularity only recently
in the Netherlands, even though it had been popular in Belgium a
decade earlier. Teens were the majority of movie-goers during the
war, since they had replaced workers who had been conscripted into
the Army and had money to spend, even after contributing to the
family income. It is likely that teens were the rowdy men reported
at matinees who roared along with the MGM lion and sometimes
fought with each other.[22]

In Britain during the interwar years, movie-going was the most
popular entertainment. A post-war planning committee claimed that
more people attended the movies in a fortnight than all the spectators
for a whole season at Football League matches. Average weekly attendance was about 40–50 percent of the whole population through the
1930s and 1940s. Again, theaters favoring different film genres tended
to draw class-specific crowds. In the 1930s the working class of Bolton
in the Lancashire industrial region preferred comedies while higher-
class Brighton on the South coast tended to favor historical dramas.[23]

In France, the working class, even while rushing to see Hollywood
films in the late 1940s, grounded their interpretations of Hollywood
films in their own culture and experience. But again, working classes
attended their own theaters, which higher classes avoided, where they
could pay less, see their preferred genres and feel at home. Higher-
class locals scorned the aesthetics of the films and called the audience
at the working-class theaters 'riff-raff.'[24]

Children's matinees also tended to be class-segregated. In early
1930s Britain, newspapers reported that the relatively adult-free environment allowed children to make noise, run about, climb, crawl,
and throw things. As a solution to this, cinema chains introduced
clubs to control children, but at significantly higher admission prices
– six pence versus two. The higher-class Odeon circuit adopted the
Mickey Mouse Club for their theaters across Britain. Supervisors
planned events to hold attention and occupy kids, such as sing-alongs
and competitions for badges and prizes. But children's matinees were
not always well supervised and sometimes showed the same adult

films as the regular bill. Lower-price cinemas without club programs allegedly tolerated misbehavior. Newspapers even reported instances of precocious, business-like pre-adolescents running their own make-shift 'theaters' in basements and other places without licenses or adult supervision.[25] However, as often occurs, it is difficult to disentangle *bona fide* reports of bad audience behavior and their frequency from unsubstantiated rumors. What is clear from contemporary accounts is that middle-class children were not allowed to attend predominantly working-class cinemas.

Time and again, theater owners built and managers operated theaters to please a particular class of clientele – the theaters becoming an expression of that class's culture and taste. Similarly, the films offered drew different classes with differing tastes to different cinemas, thus self-segregating theaters by class. Many theaters, and more so, specific film genres, became identified with a particular race or age, but class is the most common distinction – even though writers seldom used the specific term.

Movies, Classes, and Moral Control

Whether or not working classes preferred American films, elites believed they did, and feared their cultural influence. Through the films, British film goers did become more familiar with American places and slang. A fan magazine stated proudly in 1921, "Already we know Texas as well as we know Barking Creek. We know what the Sante Fe railroad is, and how to eat grapefruit, and all about New York and 'Los' and the great northwest. We can say 'sure thing' as easily as we can say 'not 'arf.' We are partly American." Such effects confirmed elite fears that these films were a threat to their own culture, specifically a bad influence that interfered with elite efforts to 'uplift' lower classes.[26]

These fears often followed the pattern of moral panics and extended beyond objections to imported films to concerns about audience behavior itself, particularly among working classes. In the Netherlands, for example, a backlash against cinema began during World War I and continued after the war. Film profiteers were accused of promoting bad cinema lacking proper bourgeois values. Germans were blamed for imported sex films and for financing the 'palaces' where they were shown. Some moral entrepreneurs took it upon themselves to arouse public concern and mobilize action. European governments and film industries typically responded with investigations and expert opinions, usually leading to some sort of regulation.[27] Everywhere, reactions to the spread of film were based on a belief that films were powerful forces of suggestion. Even those who heavily criticized commercial films were eager to use film to shape the minds and behavior of lower classes and races, women, and children. These reactions presumed that audience behavior reflected individual deviance and social disintegration, and called for measures of social control.

The Catholic Church orchestrated the most widespread and well-organized responses to the popularity of movies. In France, Italy, Belgium, and the Netherlands there were notable Catholic pioneers, promoters, and enforcers of film morality ratings.[28] There were also systematic efforts to enlist film for 'positive' effect. In France, the Comité Catholique du Cinématographe was formed in 1927 to supply films suitable for Catholic audiences. As this was too expensive, instead they established a rating system that distinguished films based on their suitability for different audiences according to their education, Catholic religious training, and social status. These distinctions among audiences were based on nineteenth-century ideas about the strength of character of different groups, structured within a class hierarchy that allegedly enabled some, more than others, to resist the bad suggestions of inappropriate films.[29]

Similarly, the unspoken presumption in the earlier quote from the advisor to Gainsborough Films was that there were two British peoples, one that was 'civilized' and another that was attracted to American movies, and that American films interfered with efforts to 'civilize' the British working class. The advisor was not comparing American culture to British culture, but rather the mass culture of Hollywood consumed by the British masses to the taste and culture of the British upper and upper-middle classes. This was a common class discourse through the nineteenth and twentieth centuries in the US as well, but in Britain and Europe in the twentieth century it was also tied to concerns about Americanization. In other words, discourses against Americanization were closely tied to discourses about the waywardness of working classes and to regimes to control both. One cannot be understood entirely without the other.

The concern about working-class filmgoers was a chapter in a broad and enduring discursive field on class in Britain. There are numerous examples of British elites condemning the bad tastes and low morals of the working class and the need to educate and 'uplift' them. Typically, their stance was based on a belief that the working classes were vulnerable to corruption and this included susceptibility to film.

Iris Barry, British film critic and later film curator for the Museum of Modern Art in New York City, tried to reassure her readers that the fact that people liked Hollywood films did not mean Brits wanted to be like Americans.

It is true we are much more familiar with the American temperament and social habit because of the all-prevalent American films than we should be without it. But I am sure we do not love or respect the Americans more on that account. To know is not necessarily to admire.[30]

As has been the case repeatedly with popular culture, commercial discourse collided with elite discourses. Popular fan magazines, marketed to lower-middle and upper working-class women, presented a quite positive image of American culture and Hollywood, even excluding Hollywood scandals from their pages. Commercial discourses played to the market; elite discourses promoted their own cultural tastes and urged working-class people to reject their own culture.[31] Time and again such elite efforts to 'uplift' the working class have lost to commercial appeals to working-class tastes, in part, for that reason.

The problem with European elites' responses to American films was that they, wedded to their nationality and empires, attempted to resist Hollywood by forcing their choice of films on the working class, who preferred less stuffy Hollywood fare with "its freedom from academic constraint, its professionalism in the production of a vernacular culture." This same program of cultural uplift had failed in the US, when elites attempted to Americanize working-class immigrants. So what appeared on the surface to be contention between nations was underlain by class struggles over leisure and culture.[32]

In much of Western Europe cinema-going had become a year-round, weekly event for young and old, in small town and big city, among nearly all classes. Some films were 'must see' events by virtue of the fact that there was such wide-spread publicity and conversation about these films. It had gained an inevitability as an answer to the question, "what are you doing this weekend?" And most of those films were American films.

While there was much reaction by European elites, it is difficult to find evidence that American films undermined elite moral and aesthetic values. But there had long been an alternative, a folk culture of the people and *by* the people. Films, and American films in particular, served as a culture *for* the people, an industrial replacement for folk culture. For at least a substantial portion of European working-class audiences, Hollywood films were not only affordable and convenient, but also entertaining. In addition, the demographic patterns among audiences and their preferences in film and behaviors in movie theaters were similar to those in the US.

At the same time, however, it is not clear that European audiences took away the same ideas from these films as Americans may have, nor that the films 'implanted' ideas that displaced those of their native cultures. What is clear about film screen culture in Europe in this era is that its significance was less that it re-shaped local or national cultures, than that it was digested and absorbed into pre-existing local cultures differing by class, gender, and age, and that these subcultures, sometimes alternative or opposed to the nation's dominant culture, were seen by elites as becoming threats to their dominion. This contrasted to two centuries or so earlier when landed aristocrats, still secure in their power and station, participated freely in the popular culture of agricultural laborers or peasants.[33]

Colonial and Post-Colonial Markets: Africa, Asia, Latin America

By the early 1920s the Hollywood studio oligopoly had begun in earnest a program of global expansion, including Asia, Africa, and Latin America. The MPPDA was established in 1922 to expand sales abroad, as well as to coordinate industry public relations and lobby the US government at home. By the 1930s the major studios had extensive distribution networks on five continents. At the same time the largest market for US export remained Europe, far more than other continents. In the early 1930s, the US Department of Commerce estimated that there were 50,000 movie theaters in Europe and North America, 5,000 each in Latin America and Asia, and less than 1,000 in Africa. Africa, Asia, and Latin America accounted for roughly two thirds of world population at the time, but only 18 percent of theaters. Belgium, Austria, Sweden, and Czechoslovakia each had more theaters than all of Africa. Even the small population of Australia was a more important export market for British and American films than these continents.[34]

Reasonable transportation as well as concentrated populations with money to spend were essential to establish cinema as a medium for the masses. These were not the circumstances for most population in the pre-industrial agricultural societies of Asia, Africa, and Latin America. Most of the population was poor, particularly the rural population, and participated only marginally in a money economy, so that they could not readily constitute consumers and purchase tickets. Consequently, while elites were introduced to film in the 1890s in the principal entrepot cities throughout the world, it was not until the 1930s or 1940s, and in remote villages even later, before film became a part of the everyday lives of the mass of the population.

All of these factors were linked to the fundamental fact that these nations had long been subject to European powers, not only formally colonized peoples but also superficially independent nations, such as

China, most of Latin America, and parts of the Middle East. In both cases, economic and infrastructure development was shaped by the goal to extract raw materials and transport them from the hinterlands to port cities for shipping to the Western world. For example, railway construction in Turkey was financed privately by European companies in order to move goods to ports. Consequently, railroads were built without consideration of knitting the society together, and Turkey inherited this set of disconnected rails rather than a system to serve the new nation's needs. The benefits of colonial rail development have also been questioned about India, Central and West Africa, and Latin America. In Central Africa also, private companies built railways according to their commercial priorities.[35]

In addition to affecting these geographic and economic factors, colonialism was also heavily, even stridently cultural. Administrators posted throughout the colonial world constituted an early global bourgeoisie. As mentioned in the Introduction, far from home, they and their governments did much to sustain their home cultures in foreign places, in part to prevent them from 'going native.' They also imposed their home culture and language on the colony. Colonial governance was often conducted in the colonials' rather than the natives' language. In the interwar era, colonial governments also began to use the new media of radio and film to propagandize native populations. In myriad ways, natives were reminded every day that the ruler's culture was superior.

Again, as mentioned in Chapter 2, attached to the colonial class were native populations who served and conducted business with colonials, their governments and businesses. This in-between population, in order to fulfill their function, necessarily were familiar with both the colonials' culture and language as well as their own native culture and language. Between-ness blended the cultures, but at the same time, made them marginal to both, inducing a constant tension between the demands of the two cultures and peoples. Colonial officials expected their native servants and assistants to adopt their point of view, even when dealing with their own people, yet at the same time colonials treated them as an inferior race. Compounding this, fellow natives criticized their cooperation with and cooptation by colonials as a betrayal of their own origins. From this tension often arose resistance and independence movements. This resistance was sometimes evident in theaters.

Colonial Cinema, Urban Audiences: Africa

In most colonies and especially beyond the major cities, film did not arrive until the 1920s or later. It began as, and continued to be, commercial enterprises showing imported US and European feature-length films, albeit regulated by colonial governments. Even the largest colonial empire, the British, funded only documentary productions for propaganda and educational purposes, and that insufficient for a regular flow of new films for natives. The deficit was made up largely by Western commercial film industries.[36]

In the French Maghreb (Morocco, Algeria, and Tunisia), cinema theaters were predominantly located in cities where substantial French colonizer communities were located. Since indigenous film-making for the domestic market was practically non-existent before independence, the cinemas relied heavily on foreign imports from the US and Europe. In French West Africa (including the present sub-Saharan states of Senegal, Ivory Coast, Mali, and Niger) at the start of this era, there were cinemas only in a few major cities like Dakar, the colonial capital. These were commercial investments and catered to French colonials. Native Africans had not the income, leisure or free movement to enable access. Films were almost all from France and the US. After the 1920s, affluent urban native West Africans created their own alternative cinema experience by purchasing and showing films in their homes, cafés or other private venues. Still in the 1940s, cinemas remained limited to major cities. Similarly in British Southern Rhodesia (now Zimbabwe) films only reached the very few cinemas in the major cities, which charged high admissions, so that very few Africans could attend and most theaters prohibited Africans.[37] In South Africa, cinemas in urban neighborhoods were for whites only, although a few allowed blacks in the balcony.

Nevertheless, as more cinemas were built in the 1930s, urban native African audiences across central, west, and south Africa became avid movie-goers and adapted it to their local purposes. In French West Africa, city youths created distractions at the entrances to cinemas so others could sneak in and enjoy the fantasy, forge community, and confront the colonial state. In South Africa, by the 1930s a black section of Johannesburg had a range of cinemas from first-run in which higher classes attended and respectability reigned, to third-run where working-class audiences predominated. Cape Town's District Six was a working-class neighborhood of predominantly 'coloureds,' mixed with some Europeans and Africans before apartheid. It had a strong sense of community and a vibrant street culture, and movie-going was integral to this local culture. Cinema-going held a community standing not unlike the English pub. The local cinema owners let out their theaters for community events such as strike meetings and political protests, benefit performances for the unemployed and poor, as well as council meetings and even church ceremonies.

Concentrated in a few urban neighborhoods, these native movie-goers constituted an enthusiastic, local movie-going public. Nevertheless, as late as the mid 1940s, the percentage of the native populations attending movies every week was still quite small and was confined mostly to large cities and mining camps.[38]

Outside the major cities, itinerant shows entertained in mining towns. With a boom in Northern Rhodesian (now Zambia) copper mining in the 1930s, mine owners provided American westerns to large audiences, as many as a thousand migrant African miners, as an alternative to drinking and fighting when off work. Again here, commercial films were preferred by native Africans, even though heavily edited by colonial officials, missionaries, and mining companies. In South Africa in the 1930s an American missionary showed films, selected for their moral lessons, at mining compounds to black migrant workers. By the 1940s, a few cinemas were operating in black townships, and a government-funded mobile film unit toured rural black areas to show instructional films, e.g. advocating drinking tea instead of alcohol. This was curtailed in 1948 when *apartheid* was established, strictly censoring films and limiting film-going for native Africans.[39]

Native African audiences behaved in many ways similar to the nickelodeon audiences of the US. They used the cinema space to suit their own purposes and fitted to their own culture. For example, their reactions to films set in distant places, such as Europe or the American West, were vocal excitement and conversation, which was typical in their culture when encountering something novel. American cowboy movies appealed to young urban men because they especially admired the character of the heroes. Some even began to dress in the manner of these movie heroes. Mixed race, working-class audiences in Cape Town's District Six overwhelmingly chose American over British films, especially westerns, which had crowds "pushing and pushing to get in" and talking cowboy slang while waiting. Western themes even pervaded the New Year carnival. During showings, audiences were lively. People changed seats, sang along to music, and talked back to the screen, making "such a rumpus, man, people didn't restrain themselves." Auditoriums smelled of "orange peels, chips, and samosas."[40]

Where there was more than one cinema to choose from, urban movie-goers self-segregated into a class hierarchy of cinemas, based on price and strictness of enforcement of decorum. Skilled working-class families accepted some cinemas as respectable and safe enough for adolescent boys and girls to attend in mixed company. Food distinguished the rough from respectable: "you could take anything to the Star ... but not at the Avalon ... a more respectable kind of bioscope," said one informant.[41]

These examples from Africa, as well as others in India and China to be discussed below, illustrate some similarities and differences among colonial audiences. First, circumstances were similar: Cinema began and continued to be concentrated in major cities and remained a rarity in rural areas for decades. Second, as in the West, native audiences enjoyed movies, even documentaries, at first simply for the novelty, but soon for the stories they told. However, the stories they *took* from films were not necessarily the ones intended by the producers and exhibitors, but rather ones fitted to their own practical experiences and cultures. Mobile cinema crews exhibiting in rural areas were frustrated by the '*mis*-interpretations' of films by natives. Audiences focused on what was pertinent to them, such as a chicken walking through the midst of a scene, or reacting according to their culture, such as laughing at a cripple, rather than as the film-makers intended. Thus, where circumstances were similar for Westerners and native audiences, their reactions to western films coincided. Where circumstances or cultures differed, their reactions differed as well. Also, audience reactions differed as times changed. In Central Africa, native audiences were at first enthusiastic attendants at mobile cinema, then bored by seeing the same films again and again. Then as films became more transparently propagandistic, audiences resisted and protested the films' messages.[42]

What can be said is that, for the most part in the colonized world, cinema in this era remained an urban phenomena, and even there, for only a small portion of the population was it a part of everyday life as compared with the US and Europe at the time. Thus to the degree that there developed a screen culture in this era, it was a subculture among a select part of the native populations of these colonies. This is most evident when we compare that to the screen culture of the US and Europe, where cinema-going was a year-round, weekly event for young and old, in small towns and big city, among nearly all classes.

Colonial Propaganda Film

The fundamental purpose of colonialism and subaltern states was to extract wealth from colonies to enrich the ruling nation – a remnant of the mercantilism that pre-dated industrialization in Europe and the US. The sunset of European colonialism began during the interwar period, still shining brightly from its pre-war pride, but with colonial administrations adjusting to changing economics of colonialism and growing independence movements.

The prime question asked by colonial officials was: Did film fit their purpose? Colonialism necessarily meant a small occupying force subordinating a substantially larger native population. As a result, occupiers depended upon persuasion to gain cooperation and legitimize their power. Racialized discourses had long combined with impressive demonstrations of Western technologies and suppression of contradictory information to define the colonized as inferior and colonizers as superior. Film censorship and making films specifically for a native market were part of such efforts too.

European colonial policies presumed that film was a powerful shaper of minds, even overcoming individual will, and that colonial natives were especially susceptible. These were widespread beliefs among elites in Europe and the US at the time. Highly influential but unsubstantiated theories of crowd psychology claimed that women, children, lower social classes, and 'inferior' races were far more susceptible to suggestion that films could induce.[43]

Suppression of contradictory information took priority over the more expensive and difficult task of making original films specifically for native Africans. For this reason, colonial officials often censored films or scenes that they feared might "stir up the natives." In 1945, Belgium banned all Hollywood films in the Congo. In Southern Rhodesia the very small white population feared that films would stimulate violence by Africans. Through the 1920s there were increasing pressures to censor films seen by Africans. By the 1930s editing of commercial films for African audiences was so severe that it was sometimes difficult to understand the storyline.[44]

Film editing tended to conform to colonial propaganda about the superiority of Europeans over colonial peoples. For example, in Africa, English men and women seldom did manual labor, which was relegated to native Africans. Consistent with this, films edited for Africans seldom showed Englishmen at manual labor. In one instance, an African student studying in England wrote in the British Colonial Office newsletter about the contrast between depictions of Englishmen in films shown to blacks in Africa and the large English working class doing manual labor that she witnessed in England. She observed that others had the same experience in France and the US, contradicting what movies in Africa had led them to expect. Even when some documentary films showed English manual laborers, many native Africans refused to accept this as true, as it contradicted their own experience in the colonial setting, demonstrating the effectiveness of information suppression.[45]

In addition to censorship, colonial policies used film pro-actively to shape native African minds. British and French colonial offices established film units to research colonial native audience reactions and produce films specifically directed to them, and to establish traveling mobile cinema exhibition programs to reach this audience. When seen by native Africans, such Western films placed African audiences in the subject position of seeing their own culture and history through the 'colonizer's gaze.' The colonized were aware of such policies and often argued that colonizers used films to convince the natives of the superiority of their rulers and the benefits of colonization.[46]

The British colonial film program between the wars reported colonials observing and speculating about effects of films on black African audiences, about documentaries targeting Africans, and prospects of a successful mobile cinema program. According to testimony native Africans lacked sufficient intelligence, confused film enactments as the real thing, such as a close-up of a mosquito as being a giant mosquito; could not understand film techniques such as panning, flashbacks and jump-cuts; and could not place film events in their 'proper' context. Based on these assumptions, documentaries were made specifically for 'primitive' Africans. Similar observations and claims were made by French colonials and Belgian Congo authorities in the 1940s. Tales of ignorant African audiences persisted. These may have been apocryphal and unsubstantiated. Nevertheless, such tales circulated for decades as indicators of racial inferiority, justifying colonial rule.[47]

Whether apocryphal or true, such reports demonstrate the degree to which reaction to films depended upon the audience's definition of the situation. In the stories, the African audiences, unfamiliar with film, defined it, if only briefly, as a window through which they saw actual events as they occurred. British colonials defined it as a case of African inferiority, unable to recognize the representational nature of scenes on the film. In colonial India in the 1920s, Anglos and Westernized Indians described the Indian masses as unable to make sense of Western films, demonstrating their lack of intelligence. In the US, nineteenth-century stories had backwoods or immigrant 'green 'uns,' who, upon seeing their first stage performance and mistaking it as real, leapt upon the stage to help the supposed victims. Naive audiences in 1898 Paris and New York purportedly mistook the situation in the same way when they were frightened by films of on-rushing trains. Yet these stories did not conclude that middle-class Parisians lacked intelligence. The various audiences reacted according to their definition of the situation. Likewise, tellers of the tales defined the audiences based on assumptions about the peoples' intelligence. If anything is peculiar, it is the sophisticate's watching fourth-wall stage drama and film that involved simultaneously belief in its actuality and disbelief in it. Immersion in the story calls for the audience to simultaneously think as does the naive African and to refrain from acting as does the scoffing sophisticate.[48]

After World War II, British colonial policy shifted away from blatant racism to a policy emphasizing the positive impact of colonialism and its preparation of Africans for independence and self-government. Nevertheless, colonials in the British Federation of Central Africa (Northern and Southern Rhodesia and Nyasaland) continued to assert the inferiority of African natives. At the same time, Central African audiences became more overtly resistant to the propaganda of films shown by the mobile cinema units. Since the mobile units had an insufficient supply of custom-made films, they showed the same ones repeatedly. Understandably, Africans became increasingly bored and uninterested in attending. They also became angered by representations of white superiority and power, and increasingly critical of and hostile to the messages of films supporting unpopular colonial policies.[49]

Similar colonial policies involving film arose in French West Africa. French colonial offices did not mount as early, large, or systematic a film program as the British. Nevertheless, they were attuned to what they considered the implications of film for colonial rule. One French colonial report claimed that most moviegoers were young and thus 'more susceptible,' and proposed censoring police 'shoot-ups' and other action films that were quite popular among young Africans. As native West Africans began to attend cinemas, it led to the 1934 Laval decree establishing censorship and licensing of films shown in the colony, and even censoring film depictions of native Africans exhibited in France. Like the British after World War II, French colonial rule turned away from blatant racial stereotyping and toward a policy of cultural uplift, at least in claims about colonial policy, representing in films about native Africans the alleged beneficial effect of colonialism upon Africans having been enractured into bourgeois French values and manners.[50]

Post-Colonial Nation-Building

Through this era, colonial independence movements grew stronger. By the end of the era many former colonies were faced with the task of forging a unified nation out of polyglot peoples, in order to govern. More than for European nations, film became a strategic tool for building nations and national identities from former colonies. Even more than European elites, many colonial independence movement leaders and most post-colonial governments feared that Western culture and especially Western movies would not only infect the minds of their people, but also would poison their culture. They were as firm believers in the powerful effects and cultural hegemonic potential of film as were Europeans. However, Western Europeans, when resisting

American culture, were less vulnerable to American economic power. For nations of the colonized world, on the other hand, the situation was doubly problematic, both material and cultural. Almost all post-colonial nations remained on the periphery of the world industrial economy. The West represented a threat to their traditional culture, but at the same time seemed a necessary evil for economic development in order to feed their growing populations and overcome their marginal position in the world. Consequently, in contrast to the wariness of European nations about Americanization, some post-colonial nations actively pursued economic development through Western aid and modernization. As discussed in the Introduction, this sometimes also included acceptance and even promotion of Western values, following the advice of American economic development theorists. This made the intrusion of Western films more complicated for these nations than for Europe.[51]

A second problem for post-colonial nations was the effects of colonialism on culture and thought that continued after independence. Western points of view and ways of thinking, over long colonization, had become woven into their own culture and everyday lives. Such hybrid culture inherited from colonialism was most pronounced in entrepot cities, where migrants from the West and from the local hinterland associated. This cosmopolitan culture was an amalgam of a double contrast, city versus country and West versus East. Post-colonial nations often installed policies to constrain these Western cultural influences.[52]

Among these policies were efforts to establish a national cinema. Moroccan film-maker Moumen Smihi said a national cinema "is necessary even if only to escape servile imitation [of Western bourgeois society], to interrogate the forms and cultural traditions of this different atmosphere." Upon independence, many former colonies nationalized or heavily regulated film production and distribution within their borders, in order to contain Hollywood and harness a national cinema to the task of overcoming colonialism's effect on mind and culture and building a national identity. In the words of Indian scholar, Ashish Rajadhyaksha, "The spectatorial space produced by cinema was perceived in practically every instance of mid twentieth century nationalist decolonization as a national necessity." Thus, national cinema was an attempt to create a common *national* identity in the interest of nation building, and intended to *prescribe* the meanings to be taken from it. Post-colonial national cinema typically was used by central governments to produce a non-democratic representational public sphere in which images of the nation and national identity were defined and presented to its people.[53]

Indigenous Film: India, China, and Egypt

To obtain a deeper understanding of colonial and post-colonial film culture, we will examine more closely film cultures in three societies. In India, the largest imperial colony, a distinctive native film industry, developed early and was successful domestically. China, by contrast was slower to develop an indigenous industry, which remained small and confined to a few major cities until the 1980s reform movement. Post-colonial Egypt became a center of film production for export to other Muslim nations. Each of these represent different circumstances and outcomes, in response to similar colonial and post-colonial conditions.

India: From Mythologicals to Masala

As with nations around the world, most films shown in India were imported from Europe or the US until the 1930s. Nevertheless, unlike most colonies, there developed early a significant indigenous film industry that delivered two distinctively Indian film genres, mythologicals in the silent era and masala with the coming of sound, both of which became quite popular, even while they constituted a minority of films shown in Indian theaters at the time.[54]

Circumstances favored the development of an indigenous commercial feature film industry in India more than in other colonial and semi-colonial societies. It had a relatively strong and stable colonial central government, and, while riven with cultural and religious differences and even violence, there were no warlords nor rebel or invading armies waging military campaigns across the landscape.

In India, feature films had an enormous potential domestic market, a population of three hundred million in the 1920s, about three times the size of the US population. Even if only a small percentage of the huge population could afford movie tickets, it could produce profits. If a film could find initial finance, it could prosper while charging low admission prices and spread the modest production costs across a much larger market than in most nations, the same formula for success as Hollywood. Wealthy urban businessmen seeking investment opportunities provided the finance.

But any Indian film industry also faced two limitations in reaching that market: poverty and language barriers. Poverty was greater in rural areas where most of the population resided, and this introduced two related secondary issues, population density and transportation networks. Population density in cities meant cinemas were less dependent on transportation for their markets; walking or rickshaws were sufficient. Cinemas in the 1920s purportedly required a city of 50,000 or more, unless it was more prosperous, a university, industrial, or resort town.[55]

Growth into rural areas required adequate transport. In the last decades of colonial rule India had a very well developed rail network, far better than most colonies, for longer distance travel. But this did not help cinemas, and paved roads for passenger transport over shorter distances for moviegoers or mobile cinemas were scarce in rural areas. Traveling cinemas that carried their own tents and equipment had to use bullock carts, which were quite slow. Despite this, in the late 1920s there were roughly a hundred traveling cinemas at any one time. These were small, marginally successful businesses who showed old and worn films for a very low admissions of one or two annas, half the cost of cheap seats in cities. Even without rural markets however, numerous large cities, including several important coastal port cities, provided sufficient markets to sustain native movie industries, while the rail system and coastal shipping eased some movement of goods, such as films and film stock, necessary for the industry.[56]

Second, the subcontinent was divided by several major languages, including Hindi, Gujarati, Bengali, Tamil, Telegu, as well as dozens of minor ones, and by diverse cultures. Hindi was used by the largest population, but other major languages, such as Bengali, were spoken by tens of millions. Consequently, film production centers arose in three colonial cities to serve different language and cultural communities: Bombay (now Mumbai) for Hindi, Calcutta (Kolkata) for Bengali, and Madras (Chennai) for Tamil and Telegu. In the silent era, films often had subtitles in three languages, such as Hindi, Gujarati, and Urdu in Bombay, or Tamil, Telugu, and English in the South, and live narrators reading the local language of the movies' inter-titles for the illiterate. With the arrival of sound films in the 1930s, Indian filmmakers used new strategies; dubbing another language over the original, shooting film originals in multiple languages with the same cast, or remaking films entirely in other languages, the same story in three languages, often with three different casts, using the same sets and costumes and filming the same scene sequentially on the same day. The different language film centers shared stories and stars, thus stitching them into a single industry with similar film styles. The same stars in films of different languages welded together a multilingual fan base. In this way, film companies benefited from multiple markets.[57]

According to some, in the silent era the Indian film industry helped to knit together the nation through depictions of mythologies and histories that were already familiar to peoples of diverse languages and religions, including Muslim and Hindu. They provided vivid representations of the cultural legacy of the subcontinent's millennia of civilizations. The growing dominance of films in Hindi helped to establish Hindi as a common language. Mythologicals were frequently reissued through the 1920s, drawing large return audiences to see the movies again and again.[58]

Notwithstanding the popularity of mythologicals, most films were still imported. When World War I disrupted the supply of imported European films, American films gained a permanent foothold in India. By 1926/7 only 15 percent of films shown in India were Indian made, the rest mostly American. In the early 1920s in Madras, three genres dominated: imported serial dramas and feature films, and Indian-produced Hindu mythologicals. American serials were by far the most popular imports. However, by the late 1920s the Indian Cinematographic Committee (ICC) reported that "Public taste has changed away from serials [and] Wild West" movies. The ICC estimated that each year 250 new Indian films were made by 60 studios in the mid 1920s; by 1928 the Indian film industry was producing more films than the UK. The ICC even recommended that the industry should export its best films to Indian diaspora.[59]

In the 1930s, the arrival of sound generated a new genre, masala, which emphasized song and dance over drama. These were light-hearted entertainment, less political or religious than mythologicals, yet still grounded in Indian cultural and theatrical traditions. The indigenous industry prospered with this new genre, continuing to produce 200 or so films a year through the 1930s. Moreover, by the end of the 1930s a system of studios, stars, and distribution were in place. By the 1940s Indian film-making was the fifth largest industry within India; and by 1950 it was second only to Hollywood in film-production, making it an economic as well as a cultural force in India. India was unique among colonial societies in building such a large and successful film industry.[60]

Indian movie theaters were sites of class and status distinctions. One difference among Indians that mythological films could not overcome was educated, English-speaking Indians' distaste for illiterate, lower-class Indians. Westernized Indians generally preferred imported films and avoided Indian films as lower class. This class prejudice was reproduced in the location, architecture, management, and public perceptions of movie theaters. The ICC counted over three hundred cinemas, about a quarter to a third estimated to be Western theaters showing only imported films and catering to an "educated and better class of people." Such posh theaters, located in higher-class sections of major cities, were designed in British and American architecture styles. These theaters, often financed by Western companies and showing Hollywood films exclusively, had strikingly English names, such as Roxy Talkies, Globe, Lighthouse. Where posher Western theaters could not completely exclude 'undesirables,' they confined them to the gallery through ticket pricing, to avoid their rubbing shoulders with the preferred customers. Lower-price theaters in vernacular-speaking Indian districts showed a mix of imported 'blood and thunder' melodrama and slapstick comedy, as well as Indian films.[61]

As mentioned in Chapter 2, the ICC divided film audiences into two classes distinguished by education, tastes, and manners. Posh theater owners rejected Indian mythological films to avoid the attracting the masses to them, for fear such would alienate their higher-class patrons. One owner of several Bombay theaters testified to the ICC that screening even one Indian-produced film a week:

> will ruin that particular theater altogether, because the Indian habits and the educated man's habits are so wide apart that with the betel leaves and other things which make them equally dirty and stinking, it will take another three weeks by the time you have cleaned it well and put it in order for the better class Indians.[62]

Elite Bengali discourses from the 1920s through the 1950s similarly contrasted the masses to the 'discerning viewers' from the educated, English-speaking middle class. They considered the masses unable to distinguish "the difference between good and bad [films]" and only in pursuit of light entertainment and escape. Cultural elites, including some film-makers, blamed this illiterate mass for what elites perceived as the low quality of Indian films.[63] Yet, the sheer numbers of the mass audience made them necessary to profits for the Indian movie industry.

On the other hand, in the 1910s and 1920s, young male students, slumming in theater galleries amid the 'rabble,' shed proper behavior and joined the raucous activities there, to the dismay of middle-class clientele in the balcony and boxes below. Some of those students later wrote nostalgic accounts of their movie-going, describing the behavior of their less fortunate manual labor companions in the gallery. These 'masses' indecorously stampeded to get the better seats on the wood benches of the gallery. The few who could read the inter-titles of silent films would read out loud for their family and friends. They talked to the characters, giving warnings and advice, booed the villains and cheered the heroes. The descriptions could have easily been lifted from accounts by cultural elites slumming in American nickelodeons of the 1900s, or observing young 'gallery gods' in theaters of the late nineteenth century.[64]

The British Raj government feared the gathering of crowds of low-income Indians waiting outside cinemas for admission, and worried about their emotional incitement by the movies inside, even mythologicals that glorified pre-colonial India. The government saw these films as propaganda for independence. The ICC report noted as objectionable any film scenes that depicted challenges to authority, including "irreverence to sacred subjects," "references to controversial politics," "relations of Capital and Labor," disparaging public characters and institutions, and disrespect for, or ridicule of British officers and Britain. By the late 1920s the British government extended their concern to "cheap American films [depicting] sensational and daring murders, crimes, and divorces [that] held up Europeans to ridicule and lowered the native estimation of the white woman."[65]

China: Middle-Class Audiences

China was in political turmoil through much of the Hollywood era. In 1911 the imperial government fell and was replaced by the Republic, but it too had a relatively weak hold on its territory, with foreign concessions still controlling major ports, and local warlords and their personal armies acting independently of the central government. In 1927 dissent dissolved into civil war between the Nationalist and Communist armies, then the Japanese invaded in 1932 and remained until 1945, and civil war continued until 1949. Amid the turmoil, rural life was disrupted. Natural disasters and famines multiplied the problems further.[66]

As mentioned in Chapter 2, the spread of cinema much beyond major cities was also precluded by severe rural poverty, a lack of railroads and paved roads, and the absence of electricity to power projectors or charge batteries. A 1927 US Department of Commerce report on the motion picture market in China stated that "... vast sections of China, including many cities over 100,000 population, were entirely without facilities for showing motion pictures ... [film] has largely been confined to the treaty ports and such cities of the interior that can easily be reached and where foreign colonies, however small, exist." In the late 1920s, when there already were thousands of purpose-built movie theaters in the US and Britain, the report counted only 106 movie theaters in all of China, seating about 68,000, an average of 640 seats per theater. Even in Shanghai there were only 26 theaters for a population over one million.[67]

A small native film industry and a film subculture began to emerge within a tiny community of cinemas and literate urban movie-goers centered in Shanghai. Foreign influence was more present there than anywhere else. The foreign trade concessions in the city, including the British, French, Italians, and Americans, each had their own laws, architecture, and infrastructure. The city's commercial vibrancy attracted rural migrants who served foreign and Chinese elites, and adopted Western styles even while practicing Chinese traditions. Lesser classes in daily contact with these elites developed a metropolitan savvy, but with continuing strong ties to ancestral villages. This created Shanghai's famously cosmopolitan hybrid culture, but also its inequalities.[68]

Unequal statuses between Western and Chinese, elite and mass, urban and rural were evident among different movie houses in the 1920s and 1930s, Much as in India, although apparently encompassing a much smaller portion of the population, movie houses served specific clienteles. Western residents and Westernized, affluent Chinese attended Shanghai's posh, foreign-concession movie palaces that showed the most recent Hollywood films. Each major Hollywood studio had their own lavish house, equal to downtown movie palaces in the US. Of the one hundred or so theaters counted by the 1927 report, about twenty were first-run theaters, the remainder were cheap '10–20–30 types.'[69]

Less affluent Chinese, apparently including artists, writers, and others with cultural capital but less income, attended these lesser houses in Chinese sections and the Japanese concession that showed Chinese films as well as second or third runs of imports, and charged a tenth of the one to two yuan admission price of the palaces. These cheap houses had replaced the amusement and tea houses of the 1900s and 1910s mentioned in Chapter 2.[70]

By the 1930s Chinese companies were making quality films and buying older first-run houses in which to show them. Chinese film of the period was associated with print and thus attracted a select, literate clientele. Through the 1920s a film culture grew in conjunction with middle-brow print media of the time, read by middle-class 'petty urbanites.' The movies were advertised in Chinese and foreign papers and mailed notices, and on buses, trams, and neon signs. Chinese films of the 1920s were also influenced by 'butterfly' novels and magazine stories. Two successful Chinese film companies, Lianhua and Mingxing, even relied on literary authors for advice.[71]

The small number of movie theaters and the absence of nickelodeon-type venues, combined with minimal industrialization, suggest that the working class were unlikely to have been a significant portion of moviegoers or cinema culture, even in cities, through the Republican era (1911–1949). In 1934, a Chinese film director wrote that few workers and peasants "have the opportunity to go to the movies, and the vast majority of the audience consist of urban residents of the cities." Most manual and menial laborers in major port cities were rural migrants; a census of Hong Kong in 1931 found that two thirds were not born there. Most thought of the city as a temporary residence; home was their ancestral village. These unskilled, illiterate rural emigrants "lived a life of bare subsistence" that excluded them from "most of the facilities and conveniences a modern city offers." Those who worked in the streets, such as rickshaw pullers, were brought in proximity to city leisure by their passengers, who were almost universally of higher status. They became familiar with city life and culture and some sampled "theatrical performances, drinking establishments, brothels and teahouses" within their own price-range, especially those who were young, often teens, single and living alone in dormitories or in the streets. But histories of rickshaw pullers in Shanghai, Beijing, Canton, and Hong Kong do not mention movie-going among these amusements.[72]

So several forms of evidence point to the conclusion that movie-going in the 1920s and 1930s was still limited to more privileged commercial classes. According to the 1927 report, these middle-class Chinese audiences for Hollywood films preferred comedies and films featuring children, idyllic love stories or histories, with "happily ever after" or "triumph of right over wrong" endings. They did not favor films on social problems and clashes between parents and children. These preferences were consistent with the traditional Confucian value of harmony.[73] So while on the one hand they appeared Westernized, on the other they still expressed views typical of Chinese culture.

Even within this narrow range of movie-goers, there were still concerns about depictions of sexuality, violent crime, and anti-Chinese content in foreign films. Chinese films and fan magazines posed female actors less sexually than Hollywood did. Peking police regulations required women to be seated separately, unless escorted in stalls. There was both official and aesthetic concerns about the popularity of martial arts in film. A leading May Fourth writer in 1933 disliked the rowdiness of martial arts film audiences, "you are from the beginning to the end surrounded by the fanatic crowd ... cheering and applauding ... the mad shouting of the spectators is almost warlike."[74]

From the 1920s into the 1940s another form of drama did reach peasant villages, drama troupes from cities that traveled through the countryside to recruit peasants into the political struggles of the nation. The new form grew out of the May Fourth anti-imperialist cultural movement of the 1920s that rejected Confucian values and traditions in art and literature for social realism and political participation. During the Japanese invasion and occupation in the 1930s they urged resistance to Japanese occupation; the Guomingdang and the Communist Party both used troupes to draw peasants to their side.[75]

The troupes at first performed traditional urban plays on an outdoor stage, but these were incomprehensible to villagers unfamiliar both with stages and professional performers and with the subjects, viewpoints, and even dialects of urban plays and actors. They asked "What are you people doing up there on the stage? How come those young fellows act so recklessly? Why aren't there any gongs and drums?" Villagers did not understand or disregarded the stage's 'fourth wall,' and became bored and disinterested. This is yet another example in which the definition of the situation implicit in modern stage drama and film was not familiar to and not shared by novice audiences.[76]

Itinerant troupes soon built upon the peasants' definition of the situation and learned to write plays relevant to village life about current events and figures and to perform amid street crowds and in teahouses without stage or scenery. Most of all, they learned to use peasants' tendency to talk, emote, and interact by moving among them, actively soliciting their involvement, and even using villagers as actors in the plays. These new plays were received enthusiastically by villagers. For example, peasant audiences seeing one such play, *White Hair Girl*, wanted to attack the actor playing the evil landlord. The experience of these troupes illustrate typical behavior of peasants as audiences: vocal, participative, and unabashed about speaking out about what was represented to them.[77]

Nevertheless, the small number of troupes traveling thousands of miles still reached only a small portion of China's huge peasant population, far less than theater and vaudeville companies of the late nineteenth century US, and the ten thousand or more cinemas in the US in the 1930s and 1940s. Neither stage nor screen would become a mass medium until television in the 1980s.[78] The Chinese path differed significantly from that of the US and Britain, where film became known as a working-class amusement and only later became respectable middle-class. Instead, Chinese cinema arose first as part of cosmopolitan culture of port city elites and middle class. Once again we see that place and situation, geography and culture, make for differing histories, even while there are remarkably consistent similarities across cultures.

Egypt: History and Film

While not denying the variety of cultures across Arab nations, they have shared a long history and common cultural elements. From the late nineteenth to the mid twentieth centuries Arab Islamic nations from Morocco to the Middle East were colonies or dependencies of France or Britain. For several reasons, including its large population, its historic position as a cultural center, looser policies of its British rulers after 1922, and prohibitions or severe constraints on film in other nations, Egypt developed the first indigenous Arab film industry, which then exported films to, and later became a model for, film-making in other Arabic countries. Egypt's leading role continued into television drama production, and still today Egypt is an important screen media center for the Arabic world.[79]

Over centuries, Egypt was repeatedly ruled by other powers, from Rome to the Ottoman Turks, France, and Britain. Britain was the effective ruler of Egypt from 1882 to 1952, displacing Turkish Ottoman domination with a semi-colonial status under British suzerainty. By the turn of the century, Britain had restricted Egyptian industrialization and tied the Egyptian economy to itself, with Britain accounting for half of all of Egypt's exports and suppling 30 percent of its imports. As in China, the nation remained agricultural: in 1917 agricultural labor was 70 percent of the workforce and nearly 90 percent of the population lived in rural villages or towns under 20,000 people.[80]

Through the nineteenth century, agricultural reform had led to considerable concentration of land in the hands of urban elites, which impoverished the peasantry and increased the inequality between city and country. By 1907, 90 percent of peasants were either landless or owned too little land for subsistence, reducing them to dependence on renting land or employment by larger landowners. Resident foreigners, concentrated in the cities, owned 15 percent of the land and most of the small industrial base. Through the first half of the twentieth century, large landowners continued to dominate, as 12,000 families owned 40 percent of cultivated land; and more peasants became dependent on them. Until the 1952 land reform, population increased faster than crop production; those unable to survive on the land migrated to Cairo and Alexandria, which together grew from 1.2 million in 1917 to 3.0 million in 1937. In the cities, manufacturing jobs paid somewhat better than those left behind, but were unsafe and wages were not sufficient to sustain an adequate standard of nutrition.[81]

Economic conditions presented little prospect for indigenous film industry growth. Egypt's impoverished rural peasantry could not have afforded and probably never saw a film. The displaced peasant migrants in the cities, a nascent working class, also could not constitute much consumer demand for such pleasures as movies. Similar to China, any screen culture was confined to city elites and the small urban middle class, generating little impact on the overall culture.[82]

Film remained mostly a European expatriate pastime until the revolution of 1919.[83] The resident foreign population had fostered a hybrid urban culture in Cairo and Alexandria, as happened in Shanghai. They and native urban elites, who appropriated much of the agricultural surplus, spent it on European-style consumption. Within months of the first film exhibitions in Paris, films were shown in Alexandria and Cairo. By 1908 a handful of movie theaters had opened, owned by foreigners, and films were shown as part of a bill of stage performances. But this was a minute number of exhibition spaces confined to the two largest cities.[84]

But Egyptian film did promise potential for political mobilization. A new Egyptian middle class of bureaucrats had been gradually replacing Ottoman functionaries in government. That educated, urban middle class was growing, but many were unable to find employment, adding to their discontent. Anti-colonial sentiments in support of a nationalist movement grew among this class, in peculiar alliance with large land-holding Egyptians.[85] It stimulated a nationalist interest in supporting cultural forms by and for Egyptians, as an aide to promote independence and national identity among its citizens. It was in this context of interwar political ferment that an indigenous Egyptian film industry began, catering in particular to this native Egyptian professional and official middle class. Thus arose an Egyptian national cinema tied to nationalism and the independence movement.

However, while appealing to national identity, films tended to be indirect in their nationalist sentiments. The first, Studio Misr, was founded by a nationalist banker, who also promoted training of Egyptians for the industry. Others were owned by Syrian-Lebanese, French-educated Christians. They made commercial films to satisfy an urban Egyptian middle-class audience, with little attention to working-class or rural peoples until the Nasser era. The predominant genres were melodrama and comedy, often involving a love story and including song and dance sequences, drawing on their traditional popularity and on the fame of singers made popular in Egypt by radio broadcasts.[86] Thus the interwar film history mirrors that of China, confined to a metropolitan middle class with a hybrid culture, and little or no urban working-class or rural peasant participation. The films were divided between light-hearted and nationalist themes, as with China's apolitical butterfly and political May Fourth films, but both appealing to this small, literate metropolitan middle class, and reflecting an ambivalence toward Western influence and divided loyalty to national culture. What would distinguish Egypt's film industry was Nasser's post-war pan-Arabism that provided subsides as well as developed an export market to other Arab nations.

Patterns and Trends

During the interwar era, the American film industry consolidated rapidly into the Hollywood studio system and their control of American exhibition. European film companies lost their positions in world competition and Hollywood studios established hegemony in the nations of Europe, their Asian and African colonies and Latin America, often accounting for the overwhelming majority of all films shown in these places.

We have seen that the major Hollywood studios had clear advantages in marketing. But some audiences also seemed genuinely attracted to their films. Rhodesian miners and South African youth enjoyed westerns, even dressing the part. Richard Maltby and Ruth Vasey attribute Hollywood film success to "the deliberate adoption of strategies of semantic indeterminacy and ambiguity … [as] consumer products in search of the largest, least differentiated audience."[87] The indeterminacy enabled people to read into the film what they believed and valued, allowing very different groups to enjoy the same movie.

But movies were not a pervasive part of the general culture, so that their preferred readings were not as naturalized as in the US discussed in Chapter 3. Movies were not readily available to everyone, differing between urban and rural locales and between classes. The urban/rural difference was more muted in the US and Western Europe, where rural income, population density, and roads were more conducive to consuming by this time. In most other nations during the interwar era, however, availability of permanent theaters and Hollywood films continued to be confined mostly to major cities. Rural peasants were too poor, had less access to cash and were less able to travel to a theater. The small, industrial working classes were similarly limited in money to support theaters in neighborhoods and towns. Even in cities, most working-class people could not afford to support the kind of proliferation of venues that occurred in the US before World War I. For those who did go to movies, venues catered to particular classes or ethnicities for reasons of profit or because of location. In many cases, segregation was self-imposed; audiences chose theaters suited to their pocketbook and compatible with their cultural practices.

As for audiences in theaters, the reasons why they were there, how they behaved, and the meanings they attributed to these films and their film-going experiences tended to derive from the culture of those in the audience rather than from the films and their producers. While film production and texts in global and national markets tended to be hegemonic, what people did with film texts and movie-going experiences remained in their control to a considerable degree.

First, besides choosing a theater more welcoming to their practices, audiences defined the places through their actions when they attended. There were remarkable similarities of purpose among working-class and peasant audiences throughout the world. Urban or rural, people of less income and 'unsophisticated taste' went for pleasure rather than edification. At first, the uninitiated imported their experience with live performers and some allegedly mistook the film for reality. But as movie-going became familiar, they often defined movie-going as an opportunity and place for sociability, no matter whether the showing was in a four-anna Bombay movie house, a Johannesburg colored district or a New York nickelodeon. At the same time, posher theaters in these same places had audiences muted in their reactions, more focused during the film, having more an individual psychological experience than a sociable one.

Readings of the film text consequently differed too. First of all, working-class and peasant audiences spontaneously shared their interpretations of the film while watching, while posher audiences reserved this for ante- and post-film conversation. Readings may have differed in ways necessary to the sense-making incorporation of the movie into one's own culture – the 'gaze' not of the imagined spectator built into the film, nor of the moral entrepreneurs or nationalist boosters instructing them on good and bad films, but the gaze of the diverse audiences themselves and their own ways of seeing and meaning-making. If this was a common pattern among a group and distinct from that of another group, we can say that it is their screen culture. Reading does not become culturally significant until a large number of people share the same reading, and thus reflects their common cultural values and beliefs. It should not surprise us that reading movies, taking away a particular meaning from the text, is a differentiated activity, differing by cultural group, whether by gender, race, class, age, occupation, and so on.

Almost universally, there were 'moral panics' about Hollywood films, by different parties and for various reasons. Elites believed that film had great power to sway the minds of people, for good or bad. They were especially concerned about the effects on those allegedly more susceptible. Invariably, these were presumed to be people with less power: lower classes, subordinated races, women, and children. In Europe, an added concern was the cultural corruption and the threat to national identity. European imperial governments also were concerned for the disruptive impact on their authority over colonial natives. Leaders of independence movements had similar fears about imported films undermining nationalist sentiments and hopes that native film-making could harness this power to their nationalist goals. As we will see in succeeding chapters, post-colonial governments of newly independent nations would continue to treat screen media as valuable tools of propaganda. One or other means of censorship was introduced, most often as law and executed by government officials to suit the local concerns and goals. All in all, those holding power grumbled, while people went to the movies and enjoyed themselves.

5

Western Television in the Broadcast Era, 1945–1990

Television as a wide-spread mass medium began after World War II. There was some experimental broadcasting before, but it was halted by the war. Industrialized nations led development: the US, Britain, France and the Soviet Union, while Germany and Japan were close behind. Post-war economic prosperity provided conditions for its development in the US, while vast projects of rebuilding and adjustments to peace occasioned its development in European nations and Japan. Television spread rapidly to audiences of tens of millions.[1] In this era, television programming was dominated by national broadcast networks, who determined what these truly mass audiences would see. These networks required a constant supply of programs to fill on-air hours every day, far greater than the demand of movie theatres in Hollywood's classical era.

The spread of television in most of the rest of the world occurred a decade or more later. As late as 1972, three fourths of television audiences and four fifths of television receiver sets resided in North America and Europe (Table 5.1). Moreover, a large portion of programming seen on television in Asia and Africa involved Western-made exports, while native television production was scarce, more unevenly developed and distributed, more available to urban, higher classes, and less to rural and lower-income communities.

This chapter and the next will examine television broadcasting, texts, and audiences from the post-war beginnings through the 1980s, before digital media and the internet. We will begin with the US as the culturally hegemonic nation of this era, and move from there to the UK and Europe, then to Latin America, Asia, and Africa. This

Table 5.1. World Television Count 1972

Area	No. of TVs (millions)	Aud Size (millions)
N. America	96	
USA	89	205
W. Europe	82	246
E. Europe	45	221
Latin America	17	78
Arabic	3	12
Sub-Sahara Africa	0.2	2
Asia	30	120
Japan	23	
Total	273	884

Source: Nordenstreng and Varis, 1974[2]

chapter will include the US, Britain, and Europe; the next chapter will concentrate on Latin America, Asia, and Africa, in many cases, nations recently independent from colonial rule.

Governments generally shared an assumption, beginning with radio, that broadcasting should serve the public or national interest, even while that varied in how it was implemented.[3] In the 1920s US law and policy established that broadcasting would be an independent commercial business enterprise, with some government regulation. Most South American countries followed a similar path, although often with a closer collaborative relationship between television broadcasters and governments. In Britain and Western Europe the typical premise was that broadcasting would be a government-subsidized public service but, to varying degrees, independent of government. In Soviet-dominated Eastern Europe and in many post-colonial nations in Asia and Africa, radio and television broadcasting were overt instruments of nation-building controlled directly by the government.[4]

Across this spectrum, industries and agencies developed policies and practices in relation to issues of nationhood. Television was used to promote nationalism and a uniform national identity. Even in the US commercial system, corporate advertisers used television to promote ideas of the civic corporation and the consumer-citizen.[5] This was more notable than with many other industries because television distributed not things, but ideas. By virtue of their immense audiences and the time to repeat the same themes over and over in show after show, broadcast television texts could create a quality of 'unquestionable' truth, shaped by and in turn shaping and anchoring mainstream values and beliefs. Television texts, often implicitly and sometimes explicitly, became imbued with matters of nationhood and watching television became defined as a civic practice. The concepts of nation and national identity however, elide class, race, gender, and other statuses of inequality, by universalizing one group as the national identity.

In order to assay how much television texts repeat similar themes time after time, we will examined a wide-spread, popular genre – domestic drama serials – known colloquially as soap operas or telenovelas. Domestic drama serials provide an ideal genre on which to base comparisons of both texts and audience reception across nations, as they have been popular in almost every nation around the world. They are notable for how audiences have used these texts and how cultural elites have reacted to both texts and audiences. Whether for radio soaps in the US in the 1940s, television soaps in the US or Britain in the 1960s, telenovelas in Brazil and Argentina or India and China in the 1990s, audiences responded to these shows enthusiastically, using them to address issues of class, gender, race, and generation, and conflicts between traditional and modern values.

Drama serial audiences demonstrate that, while television has distributed texts of nationhood to many millions, delivering a message does not ensure that the same message was absorbed. For this we will look at the domestic contexts of the texts, the lived cultures of audiences. During the broadcast era, television, as with radio before it, was a domestic appliance and a stay-at-home domestic activity, in contrast to going out to a cinema. Once it became commonplace, like a cup or a comb, it could be casually picked up, set down, used for a variety of purposes or ignored, as a moment called for, a prop on the stage set of living. Sometimes it was the center of the scene, other moments it was background, but always there.

The use and meaning of television and its texts in the home grew from and shaped family interactions, relations, and culture. People singly or as couples or household groups developed television routines, using tv at scheduled times to mark particular junctures of the day or week and establishing habits of who uses the remote or chooses shows. Television can be used by people to project messages to others. Husband and wife watching together or separately expressed something about their relationship. Conversation about a show may be indirect statements to partners, children or room-mates too delicate to address directly. Viewers comment on a show's particular statements, appearances, gestures, actions, or events for purposes outside the television narrative itself, but very much in the household narrative to make a point to self or others. Television can also be another reality, created through text, into which people voluntarily and imaginatively transport themselves, but is subject to regular interruptions from its domestic context. This distinguishes television from the cinema, where a darkened theater reduced sensory and social context, so that one could be more easily transported into the film text for an extended, uninterrupted experience. It is more like nickelodeon in the living room, with people's focus moving back and forth between the screen and each other.

These parameters of the television landscape began to change dramatically in the 1980s, with the arrival of the new technologies of satellite, cable television, and vcr. Broadcast had to compete for audiences with other sources of programming, and audiences gained a greater range of choices and circumstances of viewing. At the turn of the millennium, a digital phase began, as dvrs displaced vcrs, the internet became a new means of program delivery, and television screens competed with computer screens and smartphones for viewers. These latter changes will be discussed in Chapter 7.

Living in Fifties America

Television in 1950s America was by far the cheapest entertainment of its time, and available in the comfort and convenience of home. For the price of a television set, which was affordable to most families by the mid 1950s, one could watch star performers who would be costly to see at a theater or night club. Hours of entertainment everyday were available free.

Three commercial networks, NBC, ABC, and CBS, ran the industry. They supplied polished programming with national stars about eight hours every day to over 80 percent of the nation's broadcast stations. The few stations not affiliated with one of the networks, about a seventh of all stations, could not match such programming – the same problem of small markets for recouping sunk costs as occurred with film – and frequently re-broadcast old filmed network series. The attractive shows and limited alternatives enabled the networks to attract 90 percent of the viewing audience. For this audience, affiliated stations were willing to sign restrictive contracts, giving much program control to the networks. American television was an advertising business: audiences were a commodity for sale to advertisers. The networks sold these large audiences at high prices to advertisers seeking a national market, while local stations sold the audiences in their markets to regional advertisers at similarly lucrative prices. In turn, the advertising income enabled the networks to pay for the preferred programming to continue the cycle.[6]

An important consequence was that, every night, vast audiences of tens of millions, across the whole nation, watched the same shows on the same night. More than half of the population was watching television, and overwhelmingly, one of the networks. This was an oligopoly not only of an industry market, but also of the marketplace of ideas. It is little wonder that cultural elites and social reformers began to worry about mass culture manipulating the masses.

On the positive side, the nightly ritual of watching television strengthened a national culture. To the degree that there was a common culture among all Americans, it was presented on network television. At times this rose to the level of solemn civic rituals. For example, presidential addresses were aired live on all three networks, preempting even the most popular and lucrative television series.[7] Moreover, US domestic screen culture in this era was produced almost entirely in New York and Hollywood. Foreign film and television were practically invisible in the everyday lives of Americans, with the exception of a small, niche market of 'art theaters' and a few British television programs on the anemic public broadcasting network PBS.[8] In addition, very few Americans were even aware that US film and television producers had a thriving export business.

When people watched was determined by the three networks. Network programs were available only when the network broadcast them. They were not syndicated to other stations for re-broadcast for five years. To see a particular show, people had to make themselves available on the day and time when the network chose to broadcast it. People therefore scheduled their days around the television schedule, in contrast to the time-flexible convenience of going to the movies.

What they watched also was determined by the three networks. Their contracts with affiliated stations gave the networks full control of program content, and a great deal of clout to require all affiliates to broadcast shows when the network stipulated. Adopting the weekly schedule developed for radio networks, each show appeared at the same time on the same night every week, so audiences could predict and plan. Shows ran year-round: 39 new episodes and thirteen of these re-run during the summer.

The content of these shows arose from a variety of factors pushing toward uniformity. For networks, the weekly schedule of series programs meant that during prime time, when the largest audiences garnered most profits for the networks, there were fewer than forty program decisions planned annually per network for fall debut – six half-hour slots for seven nights, mixing half-hour sitcoms with hour-long dramas. Network profits rose or fell dramatically based on those decisions. Yet the success of each show was unpredictable. Each decision then carried a large risk and networks did whatever they could to mitigate that risk. Series programming reduced some risk by providing some stability week by week. But this did not help in decisions to edit an episode or choose a new series. Consequently, network executives were wary of controversial programs or even a word or sentence of a script that would increase risk to profits. Thus 'least objectionable programming' became the norm. The vast majority of the audience would watch one of the networks; to increase its market share a network only need provide programming less objectionable than that of the other two networks in the same time slot. This pushed network decision-makers to adhere to programming similar to their competitors rather than risk offering anything substantially new and different. These pressures produced repetition of a narrow range of mainstream ideas and stereotypes year after year.[9]

The series format produced familiarity with television genres, characters and story lines through the scheduled regularity and repetition, with successful series lasting years. Television characters and popular series were a pervasive presence in almost everyone's daily life, even if they did not watch any particular show. Popular shows and characters were mentioned frequently in newspapers, magazines, and other television shows. It was nearly impossible in the 1950s for Americans not to know who Lucy, Ralph, and Sargeant Friday were. This nationwide uniformity of leisure experience meant that popular television shows and characters constituted topics for conversations with just about anyone anywhere. The same applied to the networks' national nightly news programs about dinner time. They too featured the same characters every night, 'anchormen' as they were called, cast as trustworthy authorities on the state of the nation and the world.

Network executives scheduled genres fitting time of day to gender or age. Daytime serials (soap operas) were scheduled for housewives in the afternoons, while husbands were at work and children at school, Evening prime-time programs were planned for family viewing; Saturday mornings were for children; Saturday afternoons were sports for men. Since nearly 90 percent of the audience was white, shows rarely addressed or even mentioned other races. Also, few shows specifically targeted working-class Americans, despite being a majority of the population. Class was submerged in programs, but rarely explicitly thematized.

Nevertheless, despite all the forces pushing toward uniformity and consensus, each night half the population was not watching network television, but doing something else. Moreover, the half that was watching did not react in the same way to these programs. A middle-class woman's reading of a show was likely different from that of her husband while watching together. All the more between people of different classes, races, and regions. Those identifying with a particular status regularly watched through their own lens and shared their own readings.

Yet the simultaneity of watching constituted an unprecedented textual omnipresence, further enhanced by publicity and compounded by congruent texts of other shows, so that the sheer pervasiveness of the texts' preferred reading created an appearance of consensus and 'naturalized' these ideas, as not only a cultural glue, but also a type of public pressure to accept the preferred reading and to conceal disagreement. To do otherwise would be at least unpleasant and at worst deviant. A message of such omnipresence could take on a powerful quality of fact and truth.

The experience of film was not as powerfully omnipresent. Far fewer people saw the same movie and they did not do so simultaneously on the same night; rather, their numbers accumulated only over weeks, as the movie trickled from first-run to fifth-run theaters, from center city to neighborhoods, suburbs, and small rural towns. To see a movie one had to go to a theater during its brief run there; it would be months or years before it was broadcast on television. Only a handful of the most successful movies were re-released to theaters a second time or more and accumulated larger audiences spread over years. Even these did not gain audience size on the scale of television shows. Perhaps the most notable example was MGM's *Gone With the Wind*, reputedly the all-time domestic box-office record-holder, with 200 million tickets sold domestically over decades. It demonstrated remarkable durability. It premiered in theaters in 1939 in the US, then was re-released in first-run theaters about every five to seven years thereafter to 1974. Between times, it was simply not available to the public, building pent-up demand until the next re-release. Each time it attracted packed houses and substantial profits. It did not appear on television until 1976.[10]

Compare that to perhaps the overall highest-rated television series, *I Love Lucy*, whose average audience for each episode when originally aired in 1951–57, was approximately 50 million viewers each week, roughly a third of the nation's entire population. *Lucy* gained as many viewers in four nights spread over four weeks as *Gone With the Wind* did in four decades. The latter endured and persisted, but the former was immediately pervasive as well as durably persistent over decades. American college students in the 2010s were still reliably familiar with Lucy.[11]

Suburban Television

While television quickly became a domestic appliance for the home, at first it was located in bars and other public places, as an attraction to draw in customers, a period called the 'tavern phase,' a kind of community television.[12] Its domestication in the US was made possible by greatly reduced prices for tv sets, and boosted by post-war suburbanization: massive new housing development and migration of about 12 percent of the population from older urban neighborhoods. This was a shift in the physical, social, and cultural landscape that promoted the privatization of the American family. Urban populations had lived within walking distance of schools, churches, shopping, and mass transit to work. Suburban sprawl required a vehicle for all these activities. Government policies enabled the change. During the Depression, the federal government created 'savings and loan' banks to provide home mortgages to the average working man. Low interest rates sustained by federal policy and even lower rates for World War II veterans made these mortgages affordable for middle-income families, including the skilled industrial working class. Local governments offered incentives to developers to build inexpensive housing on cheap, open land outside cities. The federal government planned an enormous expansion of roads, the interstate highway system that freed freight transport from the existing rail system tied to city centers, and eased commuting from suburban homes to city work. Lastly, the federal government initiated urban renewal that declared many older urban, working-class neighborhoods 'blighted,' and provided the funds and authority to level them, displacing and dispersing their inhabitants, some to the suburbs.[13]

These initiatives coincided with a widespread desire among people to settle down. During the Depression and World War II, young people had delayed marriage. With the war ended, many married and had children, producing a baby boom. They needed places to live and new housing in the suburbs at low prices were plentiful. Advertising and popular culture made it all seem to be the modern way to live. However, since stores and theaters were no longer within easy walking distance, the homes needed larger supplies of food and home entertainment. Refrigerators increased in size; televisions provided home entertainment. Televisions were inexpensive and provided an endless supply of entertainment every day for years. Also, time and place were fortuitous. There was full employment, a high rate of unionization, and the middle-income population was very large.[14]

The growth in the proportion of the population with middle incomes enabled the growth of suburbs, television, and the mainstream culture.

However, since television broadcasting was privately financed, more remote and smaller cities and rural areas, often poorer, were neglected in television development, sometimes having only one television station. By contrast, suburban America was well served and influential in the national culture.

Movie theaters were less compatible with suburbanization. The movie industry was heavily invested in the real estate of *urban* theaters, from metropolitan downtowns to neighborhood shopping streets. Suburbanization left these behind. Movie ticket sales plummeted from four billion in 1948 to one billion in 1960. To accommodate the suburban trend, exhibitors built inexpensive suburban drive-in theaters by the thousands for teens and families on summer nights. Drive-ins filled up, while urban, third to fifth-run neighborhood theaters began to empty.[15]

Critics complained about the uniformity and tastelessness of new suburbs. Best-selling books and even a popular song condemned the mindless sameness that their authors imagined must be suburban living. Most of this criticism was aimed at the college-educated, corporate middle class who had settled in the suburbs. John Keats' *Crack in the Picture Window* caricatured young upwardly mobile professionals who commuted to New York City. Malvina Reynold's song, *Little Boxes*, also pilloried that class, who lived in the repetitive little houses that began to march across the hillsides outside San Francisco, who went to university and now, "play golf [and] drink their martinis dry ... And the children go to school ... And they all come out the same."

Academic sociologists became public intellectuals and wrote books for public consumption on the topics of suburbia and television. C. Wright Mill's *White Collar* and William H. Whyte's *Organization Man* pointed to the workplace parallel, large corporations, that demanded conformity at home as well as at work. These confirmed some of what trade books argued, such as Sloan Wilson's *Man in the Gray Flannel Suit* and Clare Barnes *White Collar Zoo*. Bernard Rosenberg and David White's *Mass Culture* and Norman Jacobs' *Culture for the Millions* presented a range of public intellectuals highly critical of mass media and especially television. According to these critics, mass society, including massive corporations, mass-produced housing, and mass media were producing conformists and undermining democracy.

All that said, it is important to distinguish between claims about suburban life and the reality. While to some degree the claims were valid, at the same time, studies of suburban communities, particularly of working-class ones, indicated a good deal of community was constructed by the inhabitants, *despite* the limitations of sub-urban living. Herbert Gans was among the first to demonstrate this in his study of the new Levittown in Willingboro, New Jersey, built in the late 1950s. Bennett Berger, likewise found community in the alleged suburban desert. The contradictory claims of these two litera-tures contrast white-collar middle-class and working-class suburbs. Critics of conformity tended to focus on the white-collar middle class.[16]

It would seem that the conformity also would imply some sort of associated commitment to community and civic duty. Yet suburbs, cars, and television physically separated and insulated families from their neighbors. Before the 1950s, people living in urban working-class neighborhoods walked or took a trolley to work, schools, and stores. In contrast, post-war suburban design required driving to work, stores, and theaters, and riding buses to school. The home designs turned inward, eliminating the front porch and withdrawing from the street to a private rear patio. In more privileged neighborhoods, central air-conditioning sealed doors and windows from interaction with the world outside, and automatic garage-door openers made it unnecessary to exit one's car until sealed inside the attached garage – giving such neighborhoods a deserted feel, with no people in front yards or walking on sidewalks, and no sounds coming from open windows. Cultural values were changing at the same time as the shift to suburbs. People were leaving an era of intense, unified national effort, when working together for the whole was expected as civic duty, to an era that emphasized the nuclear family over neighborhood, and consumption over community service.[17]

Television complemented this turn inward, situating entertainment as a private, daily domestic activity, rather than an occasion for going out. At the same time, class cultures constructed television differently within the domestic setting. For the upper-middle class and their education and health advisors, the ideal was to separate the tv rather than embed it in household activity, so its use would be selective and limited in time and content. But most families could not afford a separate room for tv. Working-class families kept the tv in the living room and were more likely to intersperse talking and watching, giving priority to the socializing.[18]

This world of conformity began to come apart in the mid 1960s. The civil rights movement was displaced in the news by black power and black riots, a turn that alienated many whites sympathetic to civil rights advancements. The urban riots of the 1960s hastened the flight of whites to suburbs. At the same time, other groups, including Latinos, women, and the elderly, began to voice their own oppression.

In addition, revelations about the Vietnam War shattered trust in authority that was the foundation of 1950s conformity. It culminated in President Lyndon Johnson declining to seek a second term in 1968 and Richard Nixon resigning in 1974 as a result of the Watergate scandal. More people were reading against the grain of the dominant culture.

These challenges to authority may have been enabled by full employment and prosperity, a revolution of rising expectations. In the 1970s however the economy too fell apart. Stagflation, i.e. high unemployment combined with high inflation, signaled the beginning of deindustrialization in the US that would last for decades until the manufacturing economy was hollowed out, devastating unskilled and semiskilled manual workers with little education. Noticeably absent was any working-class movement; instead unions declined too as deindustrialization progressed.

Multiple forces changed the early television landscape and aided audiences reading against the grain. Among these were the spread of cable television and video cassette recorders (vcrs). By the early 1980s prosperous suburbs were wired for cable television, which provided audiences more choices and more flexibility in watching television and began to erode broadcast network dominance. Twenty or more cable networks increased the range of choices, including premium networks like HBO that offered movies well before they appeared on broadcast television.

About the same time, vcrs increased audiences' autonomy and independence and transformed people's experience of television. They no longer needed to make plans to be home for their favorite show. Now they could program the vcr to record it and watch when it suited them. Moreover, once recorded, they could skip the commercials. In addition, the vcr gave people an alternative to going to a movie theater or waiting for a movie to appear on television. By 1980, they could rent movies on pre-recorded cassettes and watch them in the comfort of their home at times convenient to them, pausing for a break whenever they chose.[19]

During the network era, critics and researchers had imagined that audiences were passive viewers consuming whole what was fed to them by television. When vcrs became widespread, it became undeniable that audiences were actively controlling what, when, where, and how they watched television. The audience defined the circumstances in which they watched, the context of television texts. As we will see in Chapter 6, the arrival of these new technologies and changes were not confined to the US, but also changed television and viewing in many nations.

Discourses about Audiences

American public discourses also shaped television screen culture. These included public worries and news reports about the effects of television, the spectator implied in the texts of shows, assumptions about audiences implied in government policies and regulations, or made by television and advertising executives and in academic research, and audiences' discourses about themselves.

The early years of television, while an era of prosperity, was also an era of anxiety about a variety of new things, such as the atomic bomb and the cold war, or teenagers and rock 'n' roll. In an era of conformity, deviance and change were cause for panics. An artificial consensus was sustained by denying the existence of deviance within one's own group, and making deviance a sin of outsiders. To sustain this belief required strict conformity within groups. Large American corporations expected loyalty and conformity from their male office employees, including such trivial matters as the color of their suits and shirts. At the same time, change and difference needed to be condemned.[20] A plethora of fears were expressed about television pouring the ills of the world into the everyone's living room, with parents unable to control it and keep the home a safe haven.

In the early 1950s, articles proliferated in homemaking magazines about the health of young children who watched in darkened rooms, instead of playing outside in sunlight and getting exercise. Critics worried that even adults were unduly influenced by television. John Frankenheimer, director of the 1962 film *Manchurian Candidate*, explained his motives in making the movie, "I think our society is brainwashed by television commercials, advertising, politicians, a censored press ..." *Saturday Review* editor Norman Cousins railed at television's tasteless menu. Public intellectuals, left and right, saw mass media, particularly television, as threats to democracy and tools of domination.[21]

Part of the foundation of any text is the implied audience, those addressed by the authors of the text. Television audiences may be implied in a variety of ways, by the time of a broadcast, type of advertising or genre and subject matter of a program. Any producer of text must begin by choosing through whose eyes they will tell the story, the subject position. The use of pronouns, 'you,' 'we' or 'they,' reveals the presumptive audience. Producers of television shows tended to be members of dominant groups (white, upper or middle-class men). Their presumptions became institutionalized, telling the story through their eyes and assumptions, as if that world view were the universal experience of every group.

For example, critics often cite award-winning television shows that "we all remember and love." A book blurb claimed: "... beloved and still-remembered family stories – *A Tree Grows in Brooklyn, I Remember Mama, Gentleman's Agreement, Death of a Salesman, Marty,* and *A Raisin in the Sun* ..." The phrasing presumes that everyone in America shared the same experience of these shows. It elides the question of whose 'beloved,' 'remembered,' and 'collective dreams': rich or poor, black or white, men or women, old or young, coastals, midwesterners or Southeners? This single blurb alone is of no consequence. However, innumerable texts that regularly imply the same audience may have had a substantial impact. The implied audience becomes an insistent demand upon others to assimilate and jettison their own point of view. It also excludes those who didn't or couldn't assimilate.

Despite uniformity of representations and subject positions, contemporary studies of actual working-class audiences indicated quite different reactions than the unanimity imagined by the book blurb. First of all, people often did not give tv their full attention. Women often watched while doing housework; husbands multitasked with newspapers; children did their homework. In addition, people selected and interpreted shows from the point of view of their own circumstance and experience.[22]

Watching tv with urban working-class men in the 1950s, sociologist Herbert Gans found that they challenged shows' definitions of who was hero and who villain. The men preferred positive portrayals of working-class men, as in *Meet McGraw*, and disliked those that were negative, such as *Dragnet,* in which they detected hostility toward working-class characters, and *The Honeymooners* and *Life of Riley* in which the husbands were characterized as buffoons. Overall, he found a skeptical attitude toward television programs and personalities, distinguishing 'them' from 'us.' He found a similar attitude in the post-war suburb, Levittown. Working-class men in a California suburb also disliked shows like *Perry Como, Ed Sullivan,* and *I Love Lucy,* which featured middle-class personalities and characters, and preferred *The Phil Silvers Show* and *Meet McGraw,* which featured working-class characters. In the early 1970s, racially prejudiced viewers of *All in the Family* tended to side with loading-dock worker Archie against his college-educated son in law. Given the correlation between class and admissions of prejudice on psychological tests, these viewers were more likely to be working class than college-educated professionals and managers. Decades later, Ellen Seiter and her colleagues observed the same reaction among working-class women watching soap operas, and Sut Jhally and Justin Lewis found both white and black working-class viewers of *The Cosby Show* were critical of this middle-class, African-American tv family.[23] These studies indicate that

American working-class viewers were guarded in their attitude towards television programs and filtered the shows through a standard that distinguished what was friendly or unfriendly to working-class people like themselves. They used television texts as raw material, re-constructing it within the framework of their everyday circumstances and lives.

Soap Opera: Daytime Serial Melodrama

To paraphrase Marx, audiences make their own screen culture, but they do so with texts presented to them by media purveyors.[24] Screen texts play a part in shaping culture, both in the explicit message presented and the subject position implied, even though they do not determine audience culture. Rarely is a single text or a specific message consequential in shaping people's views and their culture. Rather, culture is influenced only by ideas that recur in many texts and persist across time. Repetition is what persuades, simply because pervasiveness and persistence make an idea seem natural – "if everyone says it, it must be true."[25] Pervasive and persistent ideas also reach many more people and thus become generally held assumptions recycled through and reinforced by screen culture texts. And screen culture texts tend to conserve existing conventional wisdoms and the status quo.

One way this happens is by truncating reality, excluding things contrary to conventional wisdoms. For example, texts that focus on personal relationships, romances and families may sidestep issues concerning class and erase race. Television, with its small screen and close-up shots, is technically suited to genres that emphasize personal relationships. Genres focusing on such relationships can avoid thematizing class and race. Even a show depicting a working-class or black family may look less at their relation to and interaction with other classes and races. Instead, tensions are confined to gender and age strains within families that are resolved through bonds of affection.

Domestic drama serials, which focus on such relationships, are notable for their popularity and success worldwide, and provide an opportunity to compare texts and audiences across a wide array of cultures and over time. The two key traits of the genre have been the serial format, with characters and events continuing from episode to episode, and the topical focus primarily on family and romantic relationships. Continuing characters establish audience familiarity and loyalty, while the serial format draws people to the next episode to learn how the story continues. Soap opera originated as daytime serials on US network radio in the late 1920s.[26] As radio networks formed and expanded their broadcast hours they sought programs appropriate to daytime and its alleged housewife market. Other genres were developed in the 1920s and 1930s for this target audience, but the soap opera was the one that proliferated and persisted. At their peak in 1941, almost every quarter-hour segment of network daytime broadcasting from 10am to 6pm was filled with soap operas. These daytime serials neglected blue-collar workers. *None* of the forty-odd soaps of 1942 centered on blue-collar families, even though most Americans were working class at the time. Most serials featured the upper middle class.[27]

American discourses persistently ridiculed daytime soaps and the housewives who watched them. In the 1940s, social and cultural elites criticized network radio advertisers for feeding women soap operas that were, "ridiculous, sentimental bunk which has no relations to any of the realities of our lives." Humorist James Thurber caricatured soaps as "a kind of sandwich: between thick slices of advertising spread twelve minutes of dialog, add predicament, villainy, and female suffering in equal measure, throw in a dash of nobility, sprinkle with tears, season with organ music, cover with rich announcer sauce, and serve five times a week." Some claimed that listening to soap operas was psychologically unhealthy. These criticisms endured throughout the broadcast television era. Thematically, discourses about American soaps and audiences have framed the shows as women's entertainment and women listeners as mental lightweights. This perception of female audiences underlay much of television program decision-making and scheduling in the 1950s and 1960s.[28]

Contrary to criticism however, in those same decades, soap opera fans interviewed by researchers or writing fan-mail objected to this characterization and constructed an alternative positive discourse among themselves, explaining the shows' benefits to them. From the earliest studies in the 1940s, radio listeners stated that the stories provided helpful ideas about how to sort out their own relationships. Rural women in the 1930s and 1940s also described radio as a companion to ward off loneliness. The same pattern recurred with the appearance of television soaps. Much research since then has confirmed the importance of conversation among friends and fellow viewers about the shows, constructing collective representations of the shows, self-descriptions of themselves as active audiences, and asserting the benefits of their activity.[29]

British Television

In most of the world, governments took leading roles in subsidizing the cost of new television infrastructure, as well as in producing and broadcasting. There were a range of mixes of state control and commercialization across European nations, but also a general similarity in the assumption that television should serve the public interest foremost and that government should have a central role. The consequence was to favor a distinct national consciousness in television texts.[30] Even Britain, sharing a common language and much else with the US, felt compelled to defend its culture. Consequently, we will examine television in Europe by concentrating most on Britain.

The BBC, from its beginning in radio broadcasting, has been identified as the polar opposite to American's commercial broadcast model. It was publicly funded, dominated broadcast radio and television,[31] and its mission was the public good. Its founding premise and operating policies presumed a cultural hierarchy: a disdain for commercial culture and for working-class and regional cultures, and a belief in cultural uplift. John Reith, the first director of the BBC, in 1922 formulated this mission, "… our responsibility is to carry into the greatest possible number of homes everything that is the best in every department of human knowledge, endeavor, and achievement and to avoid the things which are or may be hurtful." In 1926 a government commission endorsed Reith's mission and transformed the BBC into a public monopoly supported by the state. Given this mission, the BBC established sufficient transmission and retransmission equipment for its broadcast to reach most of the population, rural or urban.[32]

Acceptance of the BBC's monopoly control was probably helped by the fact that American films accounted for 80 percent of the British box office at the time and threatened the existence of British filmmaking companies. It was hoped that BBC's monopoly power could prevent American incursion into broadcasting and could assure that a British voice and culture was broadcast to the whole population. The BBC consciously contrasted its approach to that of the US, which the BBC program director, Cecil Lewis characterized as chaotic and something to be avoided in Britain.[33]

The 1951 Beveridge Report, a post-war review of the BBC charter, reaffirmed the public service model for television, again contrasting it to the American commercial model of broadcasting. However, a new government soon introduced commercial television. Independent Television (ITV) was formed as a federation of private producers and franchised regional broadcasters. Although ITV was created as a commercial enterprise, legislation and regulation defined it as a public service "in the image of the BBC." Yet, its commercial status led it to be labeled low-brow to such a degree that its acclaimed series *Upstairs, Downstairs* was sometimes mistakenly remembered as a BBC program.[34]

Diffusion and Settling-in

The spread of television in post-war Britain and the cultural changes it engendered were similar to that in the US. Post-war television broadcasting in Britain began in 1946. There was a brief phase of community viewing before most homes had a tv, as in the US. By 1958, half of homes in England and Wales had a television; by 1961 three fourths, and by 1968, 90 percent had a tv, a diffusion rate only about four years behind the US, despite the damage of the war.[35]

Television arrived in many British homes before they had a refrigerator or a car. With limited budgets, people chose to enhance the quality of their leisure time with television, rather than increase their amount of leisure by reducing housework time. It may also have been that the housewife's work-time was considered less important than the husband's and family's leisure time. There were other reasons as well for renting or purchasing a television. Perhaps the refrigerator and automobile were less necessary for Britons in that era due to less and denser suburbanization and the continuing presence of local shops within walking distance of homes. The expense of a tv set was justified as educational or 'horizon expanding.' It also represented modernity, progress, and status. Income played a part too: In 1955 only a quarter of British working-class households had a tv set; radio remained the predominant medium. The working class afforded televisions by renting or hire-purchase schemes. Despite an improving economy, wages were low, and only three percent of the population had some post-secondary education. Nevertheless, television had settled into the domestic life of most homes and television habits were set. The daily and weekly schedules of households were fitted to the broadcast schedule.[36]

Television in the home clearly wrought adjustments in people's everyday lives. By 1955 the average viewer watched television about 1.5 hours per evening. Most affected was radio listening, as in the US. Radio listening in tv homes was one fifth of that in radio-only homes. Television viewing also displaced other activities in the home, such as cards and games, hobbies and music making. Once-a-week cinema-going reduced from 29 to 17 percent of people and never-going rose from 19 to 34 percent. Club attendance shrank by one third. Pub attendance dropped from 79 to 68 percent, but was still a robust participation. Televisions installed in pubs tended to reduce conversation in pubs, and to some degree, disrupt the settled patterns of association and behavior. But effects on conversation depended on the arrangement of the room and the makeup of the clientele. The only activity unaffected by tv ownership was sports participation and spectatorship.

Some claimed that television brought families together to watch after Sunday dinner. Yet, others claimed that television reduced conversation among family members, even when watching together. Michael Pertwee, an actor in the popular BBC soap *The Grove Family*, claimed that television "does little to create a family atmosphere and turns any parlor into a miniature cinema where conversation is frowned upon and relations and friends will sit for hours without exchanging a single word."[37]

However, tv practices and tastes varied by class, gender, and age. Teens reported that they stayed at home more and went to bed later since they had television. Women preferred serials and drama, men sports, and both liked sitcoms. Housewives reported using tv as a companion while doing housework when husbands were at work and children at school. They expressed guilt about watching, even in early evenings after chores and even while husbands used tv to relax when returning home from work.[38]

A 1958 *Sunday Times* series of articles about television changing British life reported that 59 percent of upper-middle-class respondents said that they never had tv on while eating and 66 percent considered that tv was not important in their conversations. Their furniture and family schedules were re-arranged to prevent tv from interfering with or overriding conversation, schoolwork or sleep. On the other hand, 22 percent of working-class respondents reported always having tv on during meals. A 1961 survey reported that preference for ITV over BBC was inversely related to the work-skill level of the respondent. Some respondents saw BBC announcers' 'plummy' upper-class accents as snobby. ITV in the 1950s introduced more relaxed and spontaneous modes of address that produced a more informal relation to audience. Others disliked the vulgarity they associated with ITV.[39]

Television was implicated in suburbanization as well. Britain experienced post-war suburbanization as well as the US, but on a smaller scale, spurred by the destruction of a great deal of urban housing during the war, planned and financed as public policy, and directed at the working class. Instead of rebuilding old, urban working-class neighborhoods, post-war policies favored new, publicly built and operated 'council housing estates' on the peripheries of cities.

In 1953, sociologist Michael Young observed urban working-class transplants to one of these suburbs, Debden, where "instead of going out to the cinema or the pub, the family sits night by night around the magic screen [of television] ..." Young interpreted this as a response to the destruction of the lively community culture of East London street life, pubs and clubs, and closely knit, extended-family networks, when individual families were uprooted and transplanted to a new suburb. Young wrote, "Television is something which complements and reinforces the isolation of the immediate family and the lack of opportunities for community life."[40]

The social interaction and sociability described by Young and the surveys discussed above are considered social capital, an asset of individuals and communities that enables people to work together. Reducing such assets by up-rooting a neighborhood also reduces those people's abilities to act collectively to help each other, or to advance their collective interests. It thus reduces their democratic participation. American political scientist Robert Putnam blamed television in the US for a decline in social capital, as indicated by reduced association memberships about the same time as the spread of tv in the 1950s.[41] In Young's analysis, television is an effect, not a cause of decline in social capital: in the absence of the sociability in their old urban neighborhoods, working classes in new suburban neighborhoods with little street life, bought a tv and stayed at home to watch. A related argument was that cosmopolitan 'broadened horizons,' due to the war rather than to the spread of television, loosened ties to local communities and reduced local social capital. The Lynds concluded differently, that radio in 1920s US brought cosmopolitanism that reduced social capital.[42]

Researchers have focused on the impact of social capital on collective political action. But more relevant is that social capital enhances the formation and sustenance of ground-level cultures *of* the people, rather than cultures *for* the people. That is, social interaction is the ground on which local cultures are made and sustained and where mass or global cultures are interpreted and modified to local conditions.

Serving Consumer Wants

Reactions to television were founded on two bourgeois fears: the 'enemy of culture' within, the masses, their numbers, their 'inferior' tastes and values; and the enemy without, the invasion by American commercial culture. Notable among favorite shows were imported American drama series. These two concerns were compounded by the fact that the lower classes particularly *liked* the invading American culture.[43]

Although at first a positive status symbol when it was new and expensive, television quickly became defined in published discourse as negative cultural capital. The negativity was directed less at the alleged social and psychological effects on children and more at the low-brow aesthetics of *commercial* television eroding the national culture. BBC was represented as the standard of culture and education for the nation. Perhaps more than any other organization, with the exception of public education, the BBC institutionalized a 'preferred' British culture and language for this purpose. With the advent of ITV, there arose an intense political debate about the popular and commercial. The ITV debate reiterated an old alleged contrast between high-brow BBC and low-brow American entertainment attributed to commercialism.[44]

Television had arrived as the sun set on the British empire and its world importance. Perhaps this compounded the concern about Britishness and another American cultural invasion. Labour MP Christopher Mayhew argued that the US was a danger "not only to our tv standards, but to our whole national culture and way of life ... it would be an excellent thing if we British asserted ourselves a bit against the colossal cultural impact of America." In 1956, writer John Fowles railed against ITV and its American style, "Watched commercial television for the first time ... such rubbish ... Desecration of most sacred themes – death, birth; American voices and manners."[45]

American programs were a substantial presence, especially on the fledgling ITV but also on BBC, precisely because they increased ratings. In 1956, four of the twenty top-rated series on British television were American series; in 1958 the second-highest rated show was an American western series, *Wagon Train*. In addition, British tv broadcasters bought the formats of several American game shows and adapted them to British audiences. The problem was that the British working class chose to watch the American programs.[46]

In elite British discourse, popularity and commercialism were long associated with lower classes and America. As we saw with film, there was a British upper-class aversion to both for the same reasons, to such a degree that an argument against one translated easily into an argument against the other. The nationalist rejection of American fodder and the classist rejection of working-class 'tripe' fitted together well. Much published discourse disapproved of working-class tv habits and criticized imported American shows and ITV for promoting a lack of taste and sophistication. Even anthropologist Geoffrey Gorer, who in some respects was sympathetic to the working class, excoriated working-class television taste in his *Sunday Times* column and described them as television 'addicts.' John Fowles, claiming it had a narcotizing effect, in 1956 stated "drinkers in the pub sat in silence, watching, not drinking ... Transfixed by the shimmering screen like the first cavemen to make fire."[47]

Beside American programs and working-class tastes, a third fear concerned the effects of television on children, often linked to these first two. Hilda Himmelweit, in the preface to her influential early study in the UK, *Television and the Child*, summarized the public discourse at the time before her research:

> A good deal of concern was felt about the effect of this new medium
> … that young children were intent on the screen when they should be
> out at play, that older children spent time on it that should have gone
> to their homework, and that adolescents were diverted from their youth
> clubs and their games. Some stressed the dangers arising from the
> passive character of television viewing, fearing it would make young
> people mentally lazy.[48]

Himmelweit's research concluded that these fears were overblown, but the fears remained part of public discourse nevertheless. These fears were part and parcel of policies of paternalism toward audiences and television's duty to serve citizens' and the nation's needs.

Children's programming well illustrates the public versus commercial difference in television policy between the US and Britain. In the US during the 1950s, early daytime programming for children on commercial networks was largely reruns of Hollywood's Saturday matinee films a decade or more old, especially western serials and animated cartoons. The guiding sentiment was what would attract a child audience, with little concern for its educational value. By contrast, BBC produced much of its own children's programming, and the guiding principle was socialization and education to prepare them for "an active form of citizenship and public participation."[49] This was hoped to counteract effects of both American television shows and working-class taste on British politics and culture.

These fears subsided as television became commonplace. By the 1980s during the Thatcher years, industry discourses changed, as an increasingly commercialized industry addressed audiences as consumers rather than citizens. One producer expressed the changed landscape's influence on children's programming: "they assumed in the 1950s [that] you'd put on children's television at teatime and they would sit down and that would be it, and they wouldn't watch beyond whatever. You can't schedule in that paternalistic way any longer. You've got cable and satellite and video and all the rest," new sources of television programming that spread rapidly in the 1980s and 1990s.[50]

Industry decision-makers, including advertisers, network executives, creative personnel and regulators, downplayed paternalism and serving citizen needs and emphasized serving consumers' wants. The new attitude reflected a broader neo-liberal faith in the market and consumer choice fostered by Margaret Thatcher and Tory party policies of the time.[51] Advertisers reconceived children as influencing household purchases, so that if they could be trained appropriately, they might become 'ideal consumers,' a very different goal from preparing them for "an active form of citizenship."[52] Television was re-purposed from an institution akin to government-subsidized education and cultural production to an advertising industry using programming to trawl a large audience for sale to advertisers.

British Drama Serials and Audiences

Television programming constitutes another sort of discourse about audiences, framed as the assumed audience and subject position in the text. British drama serials reveal aspects that are distinctly British in the text as well as in the discourse about their audiences.

British serial dramas were broadcast during hours that enabled the whole family to watch, in contrast to the American daytime serials that targeted housewives alone. There were two British serial sub-genres, both with roots in radio: domestic serials depicting ordinary people, several of which focused on working-class families and communities; and classic or heritage serials re-creating literary classics for television which typically featured upper-class families. The former were quite popular, sustaining high ratings for decades and in the 1980s, accounting for most of the twenty top-rated shows. The latter, not usually grouped with domestic serials, received generally critical acclaim and success as exports. The first were inexpensive dramas produced for steady income, the latter expensively produced for prestige.[53]

Two famously long-lived working-class soap operas, *Coronation Street* (ITV 1960) and *EastEnders* (BBC 1985) illustrate the first. Twice weekly *Coronation Street* was a sentimental portrait of a working-class neighborhood, probably influenced by Richard Hoggart's *Uses of Literacy* (1957). Raymond Williams described it as a "distanced and simplified evocation and prolongation of a disappearing culture: the Northern urban back-streets of the Depression and its immediate aftermath." *EastEnders* quickly became Britain's most popular tv show. Set in contemporary London's working-class East End, it was less sentimental, including storylines about thieving and some violence, yet still focused on family and community sentiments.[54]

Within this class setting, there was also a gender dimension. It is no surprise that shows built upon relationships and emotional realism were designed to attract, and indeed did attract, women more than men. As one woman viewer remarked, men "don't like [*Crossroads*] cos it's sometimes sentimental ... men are not supposed to show their emotions ... they think it's just stupid and unrealistic." The gendering also is indicated by the fact that several working-class serials were built around strong female characters, with men as secondary characters.[55]

Classic or heritage television serials began in the early 1950s, but by the 1960s more ambitious productions were made to rebroadcast and syndicate. BBC produced an adaptation of Galsworthy's *Forsyte Saga*, followed by a regular stream of lavish productions during the 1970s. ITV too produced classic serials, most famously *Upstairs, Downstairs*, which mimics a proper bourgeois Edwardian home, dress and manners.[56] These shows positioned viewers to identify with the happiness and heartbreaks of characters in financially successful families and even to enjoy vicariously the plush living and surroundings, all without class resentment.

Promotions of these serials as literary adaptations made clear their intended audience. They were the English national heritage concept applied to television, framing audiences as patriotic citizenship expressing pride of heritage, a stark contrast to the American stereotype of teary housewives watching soaps in the afternoon. Even when based on French and Russian classics, they still were presented as a product of traditional British dramatic quality, not unlike the French promotion of the auteur film.[57]

Both upper-class families of classic serials and working-class communities of soaps represented the 'emotional realism' of relationships and a common Britishness. By depicting these different classes in separate, self-contained life-worlds, the serials could present class without thematizing class conflict. Instead, they sympathetically elided class difference by emphasizing family and relationships as concerns shared by all classes. Playing up the Britishness also provided common ground to both classes.[58] In contrast, class was submerged in American shows, as we have seen, while class tension was central to Latin American telenovelas, as we will see in Chapter 6.

In one way, soap operas in Britain suffered some of the same bad reputation among elites and highbrows as in the US. The term was used to indicate any behavior or incident exhibiting melodramatic quality, in phrases such as "high politics as soap opera." *The Times* sarcastically described *Lost Empires* as a "bad case of repetition-compulsion" and *EastEnders* as "an East London Illyria of no real problems; while its residents planned a harmonious carnival, real-life Inner London was erupting in riots." At the same time, however, some soaps were treated with a certain fondness, such as the long-running *Coronation Street* and *Crossroads*. In a 1987 debate in the House of Lords on alcohol abuse, the Under Secretary for Health said that *EastEnders* set a good example in that characters were frequently shown with non-alcoholic drinks.[59] In the US, such distinctions between soaps were rare, except among their fans; they were more commonly dismissed *en masse*.

It appears too that there was less venom directed to their audiences than in the US, and to the degree that was, it seems composed of a smaller dose of misogyny and a larger dose of class, partly wrapped in the conception that the 'ignorant masses' need uplifting.[60] This seems to go hand in hand with the fact that soaps in Britain were not so ghettoized in daytime slots and identified so exclusively with women viewers, as in the US. Moreover, British soaps' domination of prime-time ratings in the 1980s made it more difficult to publicly and regularly ridicule such a large audience. Consider for example, the relative acceptance in the US of the profitable prime-time serial *Dallas*, while daytime soaps continued to be disparaged. It is not that disparagement of soaps and their audiences was absent in Britain, but rather that it was less virulent, and to a degree balanced by some public fondness as well.

In sum, two closely related cultures, sharing a language and a long shared history, yet had distinct differences in their television cultures, first in production, with differing mix of public and commercial systems, and then in consumption, differing practices in watching the same genre. Culturally sedimented discourses about television and audiences reveal yet further differences, most notably the differing treatment of class and the ridicule arising from gender-segregated soap opera.

European Television and Nationalism

Post-war television broadcasting in Europe began earlier in larger nations – France, Germany, and Italy – followed later by smaller nations – Belgium, Spain, Sweden, Switzerland, and Ireland. European television was predominantly non-commercial. Until the late 1980s, its development and operation was typically government sponsored and funded. The relationship between television ownership and operational control ranged from Britain, with the BBC alongside ITV overseeing commercial networks, to the Soviet Union, with complete government ownership and operational control. The French and German governments' control of television lay somewhere between, but closer to the British.[61] Many nations relied on American exports to fill their television broadcast hours, as they had filled the theater screens with Hollywood films.[62] This fact fed a sense of urgency in these nations to limit American programs and fund native production.

In France, the government's purpose was to use television to strengthen and unify national identity and advance nationalist agendas. The de Gaulle era in France was most notable. The Fifth Republic, new in 1958, needed to establish its legitimacy among the French people. Its first president, Charles de Gaulle used his charismatic and heroic appeal to French citizens to speak directly to the nation rather than through Parliament or political parties. His press conferences were national events broadcast by all the radio and tv stations. The de Gaulle government used television so much and so effectively that it was described as a 'teleracy.'[63]

Smaller European nations faced a greater problem of market size in supporting a national television system and supplying sufficient native programming. This was the same problem that had plagued national film industries, the cost of producing a sufficient supply for a small population, compared to larger nations where networks spread costs over much larger markets. Smaller nations were necessarily more dependent on imported programming, and less able to restrict imports, especially inexpensive American programs.[64]

For example, Sweden had a population of less than eight million and only 20 percent of households had a television as late as 1963. Sveriges, the national broadcaster that was modeled on BBC and began television broadcasting in 1956, recognized that their audiences could not generate sufficient funds to fill even a short broadcast schedule of four hours per day. Funds from exports were not a solution, since Swedish-language programs had no outside market. Therefore they planned to import a third of their programming. So, although its public service mission was explicitly to provide information and education, it actually sought American programs, which were quite cheap, about $400–800 per episode.

Sweden appeared less fearful of American cultural invasions. They upheld what they considered a higher cultural standard in rejecting some American programs and episodes as too 'sentimental and mawkish' or considered inappropriate to Swedish taste. The broadcaster carefully selected specific episodes of shows and rejected others. Sveriges was cautious about television programming, particularly violence. However, having filtered the shows, the American western genre proved popular with Swedish tv audiences. Swedes had been familiar with the genre from its predecessors in American films and dime novels even before film. A survey indicated 75 percent were 'very satisfied' with *Gunsmoke* episodes televised in 1959.[65]

One attempt to make production more affordable and to combat American imports was Eurovision, a cross-national cooperation to facilitate exchanges of programming established in 1950. At the same time, however, each nation provided its own commentaries and context of these shows to re-nationalize them for their domestic use.[66]

European Audiences

For brief periods, in pre-war Germany and Britain and post-war rural France and Italy, government policies conceived tv reception as a collective experience in theaters and public television rooms, rather than as a private domestic experience. These were experimental systems reaching only a select few people in a handful of cities. However, the small screen restricted the audience to a small number of viewers at one time, and the price of television sets dropped dramatically by the mid 1950s, making widespread private ownership of a set feasible.[67]

With a television in the home, family viewing became common in many cultures. French viewers recalled with nostalgia their nightly family rituals in front of the television in the 1950s, indicating the intimacy of that viewing experience. Italian families expressed similar experiences. It was important enough that families rearranged their everyday schedules for meals and other events in order to watch together. In this manner, television seems to have contributed to a cross-national practice in domestic life.[68]

At the same time, family and domestic settings of television often have been cited as reducing sociability and community ties, or what has been defined as a community's social capital. One concern was that it would engender fear of the outside world that increased withdrawal. However, the causal connection is unclear and the relationship bounded by social and cultural contexts.[69]

What was neglected in these claims was a continuing communal aspect found in many nations in the form not only of viewing together, but more important, of conversation *about* television programs that extended beyond the viewing context, thus constructing meanings together regardless of any preferred reading.[70] This has been most documented in the case of soap opera, when women viewers, in addition to watching with friends and neighbors, often kept each other informed and shared and compared their reactions to characters and incidents. Widely recognized but less documented by research are similar circles of men who converse about televised sports events. This latter example occurs on two levels: first, locally among family and friends as a form of bonding, and second, broadly, as a form of bridging among men used as an ice-breaker for conversation at work or in public spaces. Programs targeting men and women with different gender-identified programming have supported gender-segregated and gendered cultures that bridge racial, class and other differences among men or among women. An important implication of these observations is that television viewing as a shared culture is not reducible to a product of a preferred reading, but is based on widespread, pre and post conversations among viewers, ranging from family and friends to strangers, about television texts. At the broader level, the bridging phenomenon is linked to national identity, fostering a national culture. In these conversations, people often express feelings of national pride and identity as well, especially in relation to national news programs, televised national celebrations, and national participation in international events such as the Olympics or World Cup soccer matches.

By the 1980s, the Western television landscape was changing, with the introduction of cable television, direct broadcast satellite and the video cassette recorder (vcr) that gave viewers more program sources from which to choose and more flexibility in viewing. One impact was increased time using the television set. Another was to dis-assemble and individualize the mass audience, dispersed over dozens and more of cable or satellite networks, or dispersed across time, by watching the same show but time-shifted, and across space by watching the same movie, but at home rather at the cinema.

Still, there were cultural differences in television use. In the 1980s the French used television a bit over two hours per day. In 1991 it remained one of the least cabled countries in Europe and only 0.2 percent subscribed to satellite service. The French were also among the slowest adopters of vcr, at 20 percent of households in 1987. Of those households with a vcr, most used it to record from television; only 19 percent reported using it mostly for pre-recorded cassettes.[71]

Similar to the French, in the 1980s the average Swedish viewer watched about two hours per day. As late as 1987 only one third of Swedish homes had a vcr and only five percent had cable tv. Vcr use occurred mostly on weekends, mostly watching programs recorded off air, not pre-recorded cassettes. Women more than men viewed recorded programs; men more than women viewed cassettes. The vcr allowed adolescents greater opportunity to watch with peers separate from parents. By 1984 movie cassette rentals exceeded movie ticket sales, and tickets declined 28 percent from 1980 to 1984.[72]

Before the mid 1980s, Germans could choose from only three to four public tv channels. In 1986 the government allowed cable television and commercial broadcast. By 1987 about a third of households had a vcr. Vcr owners spent less time watching news, political discussions, current affairs, and high culture, the very programming that government-funding was supposed to encourage. But, cable and vcr did not substantially increase tv use, nor take much time away from other media or leisure.[73]

Compare these numbers to the strikingly higher consumption in the US, where in 1980 average daily use was six and half hours, and in 1987 half of all households had a vcr and half had cable service and daily use had increased to seven hours.[74]

Comparisons

American television in the network era was probably more uniform, if only because European television programs were not on American screens, while American programs were on European screens a good deal. Yet there is no evident Americanization of Europeans, other than their becoming more familiar with American accents and culture. The Beatles sang something akin to American English, but spoke Liverpudlian English. Little boys in Britain and America both watched American westerns and played with cap pistols, but British boys also played with their British soldiers. The British working class watched their fill of American television programs, but also continued to harbor a great deal of pride in their nation. Europeans watched less television than Americans, even after the arrival of cable and vcrs, but there is no clear consequence, even though it may be profound. Things changed in Europe, but their causes are speculative, not confirmed. As always with culture, it is difficult to demonstrate cause and effect. We are left with the specifics and no sweeping answers about television and cultural change.

Among Western nations, television spread fairly quickly, more so than radio, reaching a very high percentage of households by the early 1970s. Television was highly entertaining, very convenient, and very affordable, in Europe and the US. Even more than film, it was recognized as an important tool for government communication to its citizenry. This was the incentive for governments to classify broadcasting from the beginning as a public service. In Europe, governments initiated the funding and building of the physical and organizational infrastructures necessary for television broadcasts, and in some cases established schemes to subsidize household purchases of television receiver sets. Such a commitment came with expectations that this would enhance citizen identification with the nation; in effect, to convince citizens, regardless of class, race, gender, region, or other status, that their interests were congruent with each other and with those advanced by the state.

Such expectations were challenged in Europe by imported American television series that were popular among the working classes. Whatever national identity and preferred readings of native broadcasts were intended, these had to compete with other messages in an American voice. The working classes were an especial challenge. Within

Western Europe, race, gender, and regional differences had been less championed by mass movements or critical discourses and mostly overcome in the nineteenth-century by nationalist and imperialist rhetoric. On the other hand, there had arisen strong mass movements and discourses questioning and critiquing the claim that the government adequately represented working-class interests. Consequently, American appeal to European working classes was particularly threatening to governments and the class interests they represented, especially since, in the first decade or so, many government-funded television agencies needed American programs to fill their schedules.

In any case, minority viewers, whether class or otherwise, did not simply swallow preferred readings, native or imported, but constructed their own out of the television texts and the context of their own lives. For all the impressions made by America and incorporations from American imports or native productions, audience research has demonstrated thoroughly that there was no singular national reading, but rather varied readings, collective ones shared by those mobilizing the same identities, as women or children or students, in similar circumstances, for all varieties of purposes including political critique, personal venting, or simple amusement.

6

Post-Colonial Television,
1960s–1990s

[handwritten marginalia: (sec Lt.) Lower Status / Colonied + Hegemonic]

Like film, television development in nations of Asia, Africa, and Latin America were shaped by their colonial past. Most of these nations had had a subaltern status in relation to Western nations for a century or more, whether as directly ruled colonies of Western empires, such as India, or through hegemonic influence, as in China and Latin America. In the post-war era, many directly ruled colonies gained independence, and were confronting the difficulties of transition to post-colonial nationhood. Some, particularly in Latin America, continued their subaltern status under American hegemony. Many of these nations were also poor, economically 'under-developed' and dependent on foreign aid. Most did not have the resources to build nation-wide infrastructure for television broadcasting immediately. Yet, their post-colonial circumstance made television more important than in the West.

While the first broadcasts in these nations may have come shortly after those in the US and Europe, these were limited to very few major urban areas and a small portion of the population. Substantial infrastructure to reach the bulk of the population and outlying areas did not arrive until the 1980s. But when television was developed, it was frequently done so with government funding and planning and its programming often used to promote national identity and cultural changes. A confluence of economic resources and political choices brought this about.

Western colonizers had used radio and film to justify and glorify colonial rule to colonized peoples and to tie their allegiance to the ruling nation. Post-colonial governments used television broadcasting similarly as a propaganda tool, in their case, for nation-building. Nation-building involved linked projects: to develop infrastructure and increase both agricultural production and industrialization; to modernize cultural values in support of this, while preserving aspects of traditional cultures; and to unify the people in support of these goals. However, as discussed in the Introduction, colonial rulers often had drawn arbitrary borders for colonies that ignored existing tribal boundaries, so that tribal groups were separated into different nations and long-standing adversaries were re-defined as members of the same colony. Post-colonial nations inherited these boundaries and their contradictions, compounding the difficulty of forming a new nation.

Television seemed a valuable means to reach such diverse groups to forge a common national identity and to 'educate' the population into citizenship responsive to government leadership. Moreover, the very technology of television itself symbolized the modernization that governments sought. Governments faced two challenges to these plans. First, from the start, insufficient domestically produced programming was available, necessitating import of programs, even on government broadcast systems, that could contradict governments' intended messages to their peoples. A second challenge arose in the 1990s from satellite broadcasting and vcrs that could deliver programs and messages beyond control of national governments. Both of these challenges were greater for poorer and lower population nations.

Television brought modernization and its dilemmas into peoples' homes and villages, whether by governments promoting change or commercial tv depicting modern values. Those issues created tensions between men and women, young and old, religious and secularists, urban and rural dwellers, torn between their traditions and modernity. Post-colonial audiences often used television dramas to address these personal and family issues, such as arranged versus 'love' marriage. Some saw these changes as positive (youth), others as negative (elders, men), and yet others were ambivalent (women as wives versus as mothers).[2] The contradictory nature of modernization for colonial peoples and their cultures are here demonstrated by post-colonial audiences, themselves torn between modernity and tradition, secularization and religion, consumerism and subsistence.

In this chapter we will examine these issues and tensions in Brazil, India, China and Muslim nations of Africa, through the genre of telenovela and similar drama serials that were popular in these societies. We will begin with Latin America, where telenovelas originated and then were exported world-wide.[3] But first we will set the stage with a brief discussion of the two challenges to national television:

US television hegemony and satellite broadcasting and video cassette recorders.

Protecting National Sovereignty

In Chapter 2 we saw that US film export was dominant after World War I. Export of television programs began after World War II. In the early 1970s, approximately half of programming in Latin America, Africa, and the Middle East was imported. In Asia there was a wide range, with little import into Japan or China, others a third or less, but yet others, half or more. Canada imported about half, Western Europe about a third, Eastern Europe about a quarter. Britain's main customer was export to the US; France's was its former colonies in Africa.[4]

Through the post-war era into the 1970s, the US was the world leader in total export not only of film and television shows, but also many other goods. Unscathed at home by the war, American-made automobiles, household appliances, casual clothes and music were consumed around the world, due to the advantage of its huge domestic market, combined with the war's devastation of much of the industrial infrastructure of the rest of the world. In addition, the US government made export a key part of post-war planning. After the 1970s, even while the trade balance overall had reversed, for film and television, imbalance favoring the US continued. In 1993, US film export dollars were ten times the imports; for tv programs it was fifteen times the imports.[5]

US television show exports in the 1950s and 1960s were primarily to English-speaking countries, and Britain in particular. Measured by export income, four industrialized nations with well-developed television systems, Canada, Australia, Japan, and the UK, accounted for two thirds. By the early 1970s, the US was by far the largest exporter of tv programs, exporting 150,000 hours of programming per year, more than seven times that of Britain or France. A third of American exports went to Latin America, a third to East Asia, and a third to Western Europe, including Britain, with a small amount to Africa and the Middle East.[6] As with film, US hegemony in world markets of television programs engendered considerable concern among nations and elites of Asia, Africa, and Latin America.

Reactions to Western cultural hegemony came from the left against the encroachment of capitalism and weakening of socialism, and from the right against the threats of modernity to tradition. The sales success of American goods, from cars to jeans to tv shows, among peoples everywhere, seemed to suggest an acceptance of American lifestyle and values.

While recognizing the scope of the global market for television, we should also bear in mind that, by and large, imported programs or formats were still inserted into and embedded in national and local cultures, and homes and neighborhoods, and were read within the frameworks of those cultures and places. Yes, these imports brought with them foreign images and ideas; and no doubt, cumulatively, these came with other imported cultural forms (clothes, cars, capital). No doubt, they influenced national and local cultures. Yet still, it is unlikely that imports overwhelmed and drowned the local cultures that sometimes included and were sustained by the daily practices of hundreds of millions of people. International tourism, in fact, depends upon this to provide an 'exotic' experience. A typical indicator that local cultures are dissolved would be when they are preserved as museum artifacts, sideshows, and re-enactments, rather than found alive in the streets. At that point, tourism loses its destination.

Communication satellites posed a new problem for national television policy. As post-colonial national television systems began to develop and reach greater portions of their populations, communication satellites, and video cassette recorders also were spreading apace. Satellites potentially offered a solution for governments attempting to reach people in sparsely populated and remote regions. At the same time however, this would work only if such governments controlled the satellites and the programming they delivered. Yet satellite broadcasting evolved in ways that tended to challenge nation-building efforts, often embodying a vision of globalized commercialism and capitalism. Governments had to find ways to contain this.

In the mid 1970s, communication satellites began to be used as an alternative to terrestrial broadcasts for delivering television programming. In the US and, to a lesser degree, Europe, programs were uploaded to satellite and then downloaded to local cable systems that then distributed these programs via cable to subscribers' homes. Over the next decade or so, shrinking size and costs of receiver dishes made it feasible to broadcast directly from satellite to a subscriber's dish at their home, eliminating the expense of terrestrial cable distribution. By the 1990s, direct satellite broadcasting began to take root in regions where cable was not yet extensive, sometimes competing with cable as well as broadcast television, but often superseding cable television development, particularly in Asia. Satellite broadcasts also expanded

settled, sedate

the numbers and variety of tv channels, presenting a challenge to staid, paternalistic or authoritarian national public television.

Direct satellite broadcasts were not confined by borders, nor easily controlled by national regulators. Rather they disrupted national systems of broadcast and cable. Several Arab and African states planned cross-national cooperation for a news exchange program via satellite in the 1970s. But who controlled the satellites, of course, was of primary importance. The first non-military communication satellites were government funded, owned and operated in order to jump-start commercial use. By the 1990s, private ownership was within reach of large corporations: INTELSAT, owned by a consortium of several nations, began privatization and ASIASAT had the first privately owned satellites over Asia.[7] International for-profit companies, such as B-Sky satellite served Britain and Europe, and STAR-TV served East and South Asia. The interests of these businesses were not co-terminus with the several nations they served.

Nevertheless, commercial direct broadcasting fit ideologically with the neo-liberal wave that began in the 1980s to sweep across the globe, privatizing and de-regulating. Neo-liberalism changed communication policies from wide-spread twentieth-century presumptions that government should act as trustee in regulating media in the public or state interest, to a presumption that governments should withdraw regulation and allow markets to operate unimpeded. Many governments adopted neo-liberal policies, reducing government funding and approving commercial networks, including satellite. Privately funded satellite broadcast introduced an alternative for audiences and changed television programming to favor entertainment and spectacle over information, education, and cultural uplift. Combined with the withdrawal of public funding, this weakened state and non-profit television systems. Also, in this commercialized context, audiences were treated as consumers acting in proximate self-interest rather than as citizens acting in community and long-term interests, reversing nation-building priorities.[8] The consequences of this were more acute in post-colonial societies. This 'invasion from the sky' evoked centuries of colonial domination by nations far away. Elites across the political spectrum, worried about cultural imperialism and loss of control of information and framing – a national analog of parental loss of control when television invaded homes.

Commercial communication satellites seemed at first an unlimited market and an escape from national boundaries. It seemed that private companies could reach a billion or more customers with the same programming, without government controls and the huge infrastructure cost of cable. However, cultural barriers soon revealed themselves, as we will see.

Latin America: Brazil and Telenovela

In the mid twentieth century, most Latin American nations still had primarily agricultural economies and class structures dominated by a small, powerful elite. Economies were tied to the US and governments often were dependent on US aid.[9] It is no surprise, then, that Latin American nations largely adopted the American broadcasting model, emphasizing commercial television. At the same time, during rule by military juntas, governments tightly controlled media and its content, often increasing consolidation in the hands of a few families or corporations.[10] We will focus on Brazil, as it was the most populous Latin American nation, with the fourth largest television audience in the world by the late 1970s and substantial exports of tv programs to other Latin American nations.

Brazil is larger in area than the US, with vast natural resources and a population of 80 million in 1970. Its political history had been turbulent, a Portuguese colony for three centuries, and then an empire through the nineteenth century. During the years that television became a mass medium, it was ruled by a military junta (1964–84), when inequality increased and the tv industry consolidated. The junta supported the spread of television and aided its domination by one commercial network, Rede-Globo, founded in 1965. Globo continued to dominate television and influence elections after the return of democracy in the mid 1980s.

By the television era, Brazil was approaching a 'semi-industrial' economy. However, since Brazil had substantial debt to foreign lenders, raising capital for industrial expansion was difficult. The junta filled the vacuum by creating several government-owned companies, each dominating its industry, including oil, electric generation, iron mining and steel production, and motor vehicles. This increased migration to the southeast industrial center and accelerated urbanization. From 1950 to 1980, the urban share of population grew from 36 percent to 68 percent. Two contrasting major population centers arose, constituting three fourths of the population: the poor rural, agricultural Northeast and the richer urban, industrial Rio de Janeiro-São Paulo region.[11]

Television broadcasting began in Brazil in 1950, but it spread slowly. In 1960, it was still an urban elite medium, in only five percent of households. After the 1964 coup, the military government initiated construction of infrastructure for wider tv distribution, to encourage consumption and boost economic development. Households with television rose to 24 percent in 1970 and 51 percent in 1979.[12]

Cable and satellite tv were relatively minor factors in Latin American tv development. Even in the late 1990s still only five percent of Brazilian households had cable or satellite service. But vcrs arrived in the late 1980s and began to rearrange television use. Urban middle and lower classes watching telenovelas via broadcast tv saw little benefit in a buying their own vcr. They had access to vcr viewing via bars, clubs, and other spaces outside their homes. On the other hand, Latin American urban elites tended to use vcrs to view imported films, mostly American, that did not appear on broadcast television. Most rural areas still had no broadcast, cable or satellite transmissions, so vcrs provided the only source of television programming there.[13]

Although tv was a private commercial industry, the television network, Globo, had a close, cooperative relationship with the military government that enabled it to dominate Brazil's tv industry. It gained a 60 percent to 95 percent share of the prime-time viewing audience, mainly for telenovelas broadcast three per night, six nights per week. Brazil, like a few populous Latin American nations in the 1980s, rapidly increased domestic production of tv shows. Increased production enabled networks to create niche markets for different classes, segmenting the audience and resulting in separate television experiences for different classes. Upper and upper-middle classes tended to prefer US films and drama series, lower classes preferred comedies, telenovelas, and variety from Latin American producers.[14]

Telenovela has been the dominant genre on Latin American prime-time television and Brazil has been preeminent in this. Globo executive Jorge Adib wrote, "Without telenovelas, TV Globo might not exist." Globo's domination of the television industry in a large market provided it ample resources to produce a steady supply of expensive telenovelas. Since the 1980s, Brazilian telenovelas have been exported to an estimated 130 countries, including such diverse places as Russia, Bosnia, Israel, Lebanon, Ivory Coast, and the Philippines, with worldwide audiences estimated at two billion, challenging US cultural export primacy.[15]

Telenovelas, like American and UK soap operas, typically broadcast multiple days per week, focused on family and romance, and had melodramatic features. They are distinct from soap operas in the US and UK, which traditionally were day-time or early evening serials with unlimited runs continuing for years. Telenovelas have limited runs from a few months to a year, with a denouement in which the

plot lines are resolved. Broadcast in prime time, they were designed
to attract a wide viewing audience of men, women, and children.[16]

Class and social mobility were as central as gender and romance
to traditional telenovelas. Even the advertising thematized class. Product
placements showed higher-class characters using products marketed
to lower-class viewers who aspired to a higher-class style. In Brazil,
class background was determinant. Anthropologist Conrad Kottak
observed, "who you are, family, is more important than what you
do, [Brazilian] aristocratic culture has disdain for manual labor."
Telenovela themes varied, treating conflicts between tradition and
modernity, rural and urban cultures, old and young protagonists. But
regardless of these, in this era, plot-lines frequently involved mobility
through a Cinderella marriage, a move to cities, or a surprise inheri-
tance, but *not* through effort, intelligence or education, again reflecting
aristocratic values.[17]

Because production continued on new episodes while broadcasting
proceeded, Brazilian audiences often wrote to suggest future developments of the stories. In 1990 Dias Gomes, a famous and influential
scriptwriter, claimed that "The viewer has the impression that his
reaction will in some way affect the plot. The characters start to come
to life, to be real citizens involved in daily life when a telenovela is
successful. And the viewer includes them in his life." Actually there
were many influences on production, including theater, popular press,
institutional networks, marketing research organizations, the Catholic
Church, government and civic groups.[18]

At their peak of popularity in the 1980s, very successful telenovelas attracted huge audiences, 60 to 70 percent of all tv households.
Anthropologist Thais Machado-Borges noted that they are "a common
point of reference among Brazilians [that] can temporarily stop the
country." Even Rio's famous Carnival parade was delayed an hour until
a popular telenovela was finished. Women and the lower classes are the
most devoted audiences. Although men watched the shows, only 16
percent of men were avid viewers compared to 51 percent of women.
Working-class women, in particular, were proud of their knowledge
of the stories and characters, while middle-class women more often
felt guilty watching and distanced themselves from the shows, as in
the US.[19]

Urban working- and lower-class households often watched three
to four telenovelas each day. Before they could afford time-shifting
technologies like vcrs, people rushed home to watch, and meetings
and events were scheduled around these shows. Their cramped living
spaces did not allow separation of spheres, so that the whole family
necessarily watched to some degree. Even men and born-again

Christians who claimed not to watch were familiar with the storylines. Family members talked, worked, and played while watching.[20]

The stories appealed to working-class women through twin aspirations of love and wealth, combining issues of gender and class. The plots countered class envy or hate by encouraging working-class women to identify with upper-class women characters and representing upper-class life as unhappy. Women of the favelas admired even upper-class female characters who represented the idealized traditional woman (humble, patient, loyal, hard-working), and identified with their torments as wives in relationships built on mutual distrust. If a middle-class character exhibited what was perceived as a modern lifestyle – a challenge to the machismo gender order in the favelas – they were considered bad. Urban middle-class women more often accepted modern beliefs about marriage, sexuality, and a woman's place, such as seeking both family and career. Favela women, on the other hand, worked of necessity and would have preferred to be stay-at-home housewives.[21]

In sum, the stories and audiences created subject positions different than in the US where class was not thematized and viewers were positioned to identify with affluent upper-middle-class women. Instead, in Brazil, class themes emphasized adherence of characters to traditional values represented within an upper-class setting, but preferred by working-class viewers.

Audiences in the Amazon

Television did not reach rural Brazil, where a third of the population lived, until the 1980s. More remote areas offer some valuable insights due to their contrast to cities. Three generations of anthropologists documented the social history of Gurupa, a remote town in the Amazon delta, before and after the arrival of television. The town was 95 percent working-class and mostly mixed-race. In 1986 the town installed a municipal satellite dish to receive broadcasts. As late as 1999 only half the households had a tv.[22]

Before television, Gurupaenses received only sporadic information about the outside world and conversation revolved around local events and persons. This was facilitated by a nightly promenade of the townfolk, along with its music, dancing, socializing, and flirting. With the arrival of television, they were informed about the wider world, which became a new subject of conversation. When watching shows that contained some mention of Brazilians relative to other nationalities, whether news, sports, or telenovelas, Gurupaenses identified themselves with their nation.

At first television reduced participation in the nightly promenade and other events were rescheduled to not interfere with telenovela broadcasts. At that stage, tv ownership affirmed one's status. Others of higher status were invited in to watch. Those with a tv were expected to place it so that anyone could watch from the road as well. Both in the house and in the street, position in the crowd was based on status in the community. As tv became more commonplace through the 1990s, television changed from a community to a family activity. The promenade revived, although events were still postponed until after telenovela broadcasts. Families more often watched at home, without friends or neighbors, and engaged in household activities while watching.[23]

Not surprisingly, Gurupaenses preferred telenovelas that included rural life familiar to them.[24] They showed less interest in telenovelas about white, urban-middle and upper classes, often missing the producer's intended readings about social issues in these shows. While the wealthy lifestyles often depicted aroused their curiosity, they saw this as irrelevant to assessing social standing of people in their lives, where one's skills and know-how as well as one's influence over others bore far more significance for getting things or getting things done. While Gurupaenses generally did not question televisions' depictions of the outside world – youth were attracted to fashions and 'big city life' depicted in telenovelas – they resisted tv shows that contradicted local beliefs, sometimes by vocally expressing alternative viewpoints. For example, on political and social issues, Gurupaenses adhered to views of the local workers' union and the liberation theology of the local Catholic priests, and actively rejected conservative politics advocated on Globo television.[25]

Missing, ignoring, or resisting the intended meanings in shows was simply a matter of their confronting an urban elite culture distant from their own experience. Similar responses occurred in the US among working-class audiences watching shows featuring middle-class tv characters, and black Mississippi sharecroppers watching Hollywood movies.[26] As we will see, older men in patriarchal societies, such as these Brazilian rural towns or urban favelas, buttressed by religion, locale, and tribal allegiances, tend to be more resistant than young men and women to shows that represent different ways of life and contradict and challenge their status and culture.

Telenovelas, Audiences, and Modernization

The popularity of telenovelas, especially among the masses,[27] led to efforts to control the shows and their audiences. They stimulated public discussion about public issues; the Catholic Church criticized their sexual immorality; and governments exercised censorship.[28] But perhaps most notable was their use to promote modernization.

Post-colonial policy-makers in many nations saw telenovelas as a potential vehicle for social and cultural change. Latin American nations were among the pioneers of this use of telenovelas, which was also adopted in Africa and Asia as a means to spread attitudes and practices considered compatible with modernization, economic development, and nation-building. Many post-colonial nations invested in television infrastructure to reach the masses and exhort them to let go of 'backward' ideas and adopt modern values. In particular, 'education-entertainment' telenovelas focused on ameliorating women's inequality – use of birth control was often a goal – and, ironically at the same time, blaming women for defending traditional values.

These development telenovelas made assumptions about their audiences, drawn from development theory and expressed in the shows. A pioneer Mexican producer, Miguel Sabido, developed a formula for such telenovelas in the 1960s. Targeting lower-class and rural audiences who still practiced traditional values that were deemed impediments to development, they focused on everyday life of families and a central character who adopts modern values that improve her life. Other characters express traditional or extreme modern values, with story lines that illustrate the consequences of each. Sabido produced several such telenovelas in Mexico from 1967 to 1982. Sabido-style novelas were promoted for India, Kenya, Nigeria, Turkey, and Pakistan by Population Communication International, an American non-profit advocate of contraception and family planning.[29]

Some evaluation studies claimed that the telenovelas effected immediate changes in practices. However, others concluded that long-term results indicated little change of behavior. Gurupá audiences, a target population for development, for example, sometimes heeded, but at other times missed, ignored and resisted the call for a national identity and nation-building.[30]

In contrast to public disdain and policy-maker assumptions about them, however, novela audiences constructed their own images of themselves. Latin American research from the 1970s to 1990s found that audiences read the shows differently according to their demographic statuses and cultures. Urban poor women watch collectively, talk about the shows with their peers, and promote solidarity among themselves. Similar to women in earlier studies, they applied what they drew from the stories to their own gender relationships and interpersonal problems. Further, they used the shows and their talk to understand their class relationships and new roles in changing economies. The same patterns were present in 1999 when poor Afro-Brazilian women in favelas of Salvador, Brazil's third largest city, typically watched six hours a day. Talk of telenovelas was integral to their socializing and a way of 'getting by.'[31]

As we will see, these Latin audience discourses about tv were different from and similar to what anthropologists reported from other cultures. They shared issues of tradition confronting modernism. In rural India, Egypt, and West Africa and even among diaspora in urban areas of the West, women, youth, and lower classes tended to be fascinated by these exotic shows as promise of a better life with more autonomy, while others with more at stake in the status quo tended to reject the shows and their 'dangerous' messages of consumerism and modernity. Such tensions complicated post-colonial efforts to persuade people to shed some traditional values even while sustaining traditions in the face of Americanization.

Indian Telenovelas

India inherited a framework for broadcasting from the British colonial government that established strong government control of radio. The post-colonial government, through successive commissions and parliamentary acts, continued government monopoly of broadcasting and charged it with nation-building activities. Doordarshan, the post-colonial government network, stated its goals, to: "serve as an agent for national integration, agricultural development, literacy, education, health, and family welfare."[32] Entertainment was not on the list.

But television was slow to spread in India. Although Doordarshan began its first television broadcasts in 1959 in Delhi, it expanded to three other major cities only in 1972. Not until the 1990s did tv broadcasts reach 75 percent of *urban* households. In poorer rural states where traditional values remained strong, there were still fewer than twenty televisions per thousand people.[33] However by that time, a new television landscape was changing things.

In 1991, satellite television services, including Hong Kong's STAR-TV and Zee-TV in Hindi, began to beam programming into India. These were distributed on the ground through illegal and unregulated cable systems. Indian media scholar Usha Reddi wrote at the time that, with the arrival of satellite distribution, "every lane and bylane in Indian cities has a cable system, making a mockery of all attempts by government to regulate the content of television." The private, commercial satellite and cable services spurred considerable increase in the television saturation rate, and commercialized programming. These cable services attracted India's English-speaking, urban middle class that had largely ignored television before. A third of their households on weekdays and two thirds on Sundays began watching more than six hours a day, displacing other activities, including sleep. In 1993, to seek this same demographic, Doordarshan introduced an entertainment channel for a few major cities to compete with the satellite broadcasts. By then, Doordarshan depended upon advertising for 70 percent of its revenues and needed to increase its ratings.[34]

Before satellite and cable broadcast and commercialism changed Indian television, during the 1980s, a new middle class had expanded rapidly to ten percent of population, in part due to a shift in government policies from promoting heavy industry to advocating consumer goods and from reducing poverty to promoting neo-liberalism and consumerism. Most of this class were not prosperous and privileged professionals and managers and many still held traditional views. Rather they had a tenuous hold on middle-class status. Respectability as well as financial security could easily slip away. The government considered these lower middle-class households important to modernizing India and hoped to reach them via television.[35]

To do this, Doordarshan became an enthusiastic implementer of development telenovelas for nation-building and modernization, telecasting forty Indian-produced telenovelas from 1984 to 1987. Doordarshan telenovelas most often depicted this new middle class, their aspirations and struggles to acquire or maintain upward mobility and middle-class respectability. Its first telenovela, *Hum Log,*in 1984 was made specifically to persuade women to use birth control in order to ease population growth and enable development. The messages appealed to young women, but created tensions in families and communities between modernizers and traditionalists. As with Sabido's telenovelas, each episode ended with an epilogue restating the message explicitly and linking it to viewers' daily lives. The telenovelas framed the problem as people, especially women, holding on to tradition instead of adopting modern ways.[36] As commercial satellite and cable networks arrived in the 1990s, they too programmed popular telenovelas, but emphasizing consumerism rather than nation-building.

Indian Audiences

Lower middle-class audiences recently arrived in New Dehli from more rural backgrounds in 1990–1992, watched telenovelas. The families were a mix of Hindi, Muslim, and Sikh. Their apartments were tiny, as little as eight by ten feet for four adults. The women reported that television was the most easily available entertainment

for them, given their jobs and domestic responsibilities. Living in mixed neighborhoods, these immigrants from diverse parts of India were often isolated from family and found few neighbors from the same locale, language, and caste with whom to develop friendships. Telenovela serials thus were a substitute community, given the similar class location of the characters.[37]

The telenovelas promoted consumption as the measure of status for this class. Class aspirations were typically expressed through gender in the form of marriages and dowries. With television advertising promoting consumption, demands for dowries grew. Because of the insecurity of class status there was a constant pressure upon women, in particular, to sustain that status, not only through a double day of work, but also through their respectability sustained by their dress, manner, and behavior in public, especially concerning their sexuality and its containment, control and patriarchal exploitation.

The strains between tradition and modernity were evident in the 1980s among audiences for *Hum Log*, which stimulated an unprecedented flood of letters to the network, mostly from urban and suburban women. They mostly identified with two characters, a plain hard-working eldest daughter, and the selfless mother who was "treated as a doormat." The letters stressed family harmony and solidarity, and expressed concerns about social ills. They often demanded that the daughter get married or stop breaking traditions.[38]

Similar responses and ambivalences to modernity, Westernization, and consumption continued through the 1990s among the middle classes in Kolkata. While they welcomed 'modern' science, technology, and even neo-liberal economic policies and consumption of material goods, they were concerned about weakening traditional Bengali culture. While some accepted a more public role of women as consumers, at the same time, they expressed concerns about sexuality and violence on television and its influence upon youth, and supported continued traditional patriarchy in the home.[39]

Adhering to traditional values upheld *izzat* or family honor, which was paramount for Indian families, since it had such broad social and economic consequences. Behavior of each member and especially of unmarried daughters reflected on the whole family and affected the prospects of arranged marriages for all family members. Maintaining respectability and reputation then was quite important to parents and children, not unlike Victorian era Britain or the US, when young women's actions, appearance or even mere presence in the wrong place, could generate gossip and tarnish family reputation. Similarly in China, young women's public reputation was central to family respectability and marriage prospects. Even in the mid 2010s, a Chinese arranged marriage

reality tv show featured parents playing an important part in choosing who their children married.[40]

A pattern of ambivalence about television was evident in rural areas as well. Television first arrived in the mid to late 1990s in two remote villages in Maharashtra, east of Mumbai. Several changes arrived with television that may be characterized as modernity, such as taking Sundays off for leisure and being more affectionate to children. Some began accepting marriage for love and cheered tv characters who challenged arranged marriages, even while viewers planned arranged marriages for their own children. As in New Delhi, television heightened consumerism in the villages. It depicted mostly urban modern life that seemed to whet appetites for motorcycles, electric appliances, Western clothes, and non-traditional foods. To purchase these, farming villagers had to shift from non-monetary subsistence living into a money economy, becoming wage-workers to obtain cash.[41]

Tv also contributed to changes in village statuses and their relationships. As in Gurupa, Brazil when television sets first arrived, those in Maharastra who were the first tv owners could use it to reaffirm themselves as elite gatekeepers of information. Those who were invited to watch tv at those homes likewise affirmed their status. As an uninvited informant phrased it, those invited to watch, "learn a lot from tv ... they managed to become friends with the [local official] and now go to his house to watch tv every Sunday ... they meet many people at the house and make good connections." But as televisions became more common, local elites lost their positions as gatekeepers of information. Farm programs on television brought information directly to peasant farmers about fertilizers and farm loans. Television also put pressure on traditional gender roles. Maharashtra village women would leave the fields to begin cooking earlier and recruited men to help with house chores, so that they could finish their chores before their favorite tv shows began. Further, it contributed to young people leaving the villages for larger towns and cities to seek the modern life depicted on television.[42]

gatekeepers

Studies of television's first arrival in communities examine its impact on modernization. Since the tv set is absent at one time and present later, it seems to cause social change. However, such a technological focus misses an important point: It fails to consider why tv arrived at that time and place. We should ask what social conditions, processes, and changes are television a *part* of, and how did tv impede or advance those. Society and human activity are seamless processes in which many aspects advance together and one cannot separate cause and effect. Tv is an instrument of contact between two cultures, the village and the outside world. What transpires is much more complicated than a substitution of one culture for another. One indicator of this is that talk among audience members about tv shows seems to have more influence than the shows directly.[43]

Indian Diaspora

Another approach to understanding television's impact is not to compare cultures before and after tv moves in, but instead to compare the use of tv as people move from one culture to another, as do studies of diasporic migrant populations. Indians represent one of the world's largest diasporic populations. Since 1980, over one million Indians have emigrated to Britain. In the 1980s, immigrant Indian communities in Britain were early adopters of vcr to enable their watching Indian films on videotape in their homes, since theater exhibition was limited and satellite broadcasting had not begun. It was an occasion for the family to share their native culture together, and to talk about issues raised by the film. At the time, Bollywood films still tended to reinforce strong traditional values over modernity.[44]

The same generational family tensions as in India concerning marriage, parental authority, gender, and respectability were found in a Sikh neighborhood of London in the late 1980s. The tensions, tangles, and dilemmas have been a common experience in immigration from rural to urban cultures, documented, for example in Polish families in Chicago in the 1920s and by studies of many other groups since then. The Sikh parents in London felt great urgency, since their children were constantly 'tempted' by modernity, literally just outside their door. Teens tended to watch Western soaps on television, notably the Australian soap opera, *Neighbours*, with siblings and sometimes mothers, who again used them to teach moral values. When kissing or more appeared, even the young would switch channels, out of embarrassment as well as parental disapproval. Teens watching with their peers tended to choose American films, which parents also disapproved as too modern, especially about sex.[45]

The essence of soap opera is the considerable dialog about individual relationships. Scripted talk invites audiences to participate in this gossip themselves. An important pleasure for soap fans is talking about them with their friends and at work. They retell the narrative, discuss it, talk about what the character *should* have done in the situation, and what *they* would do. They recognized the value of this talk for establishing their community's shared cultural boundaries within the larger society. Even young Punjabi boys participated in such conversations with their peers. Talk often reframed the characters in terms of the group's subcultural values and expectation. For example, in the Netherlands, Dutch, Surinamese, and Turkish girls following a Dutch soap opera talked together. The girls compared soap incidents to what they might do in such situation, and explained their interpretations and claims in terms of values such as respecting your parent or child. The discussion enabled them to hear others' views and form a consensus, among themselves and across ethnicities, on acceptable and unacceptable solutions, a synthesis of their various cultures that fitted their everyday situation in Dutch society. This talk is a collective social process, not isolated housewives dealing with their psychological problems alone in their kitchens, as had been envisioned in early radio research and public discourse in the US. The collective understanding affirms shared norms, values, and beliefs.[46]

Muslim Television: Middle East, North, and West Africa

As with so many other newly independent former colonies, in the Arab nations of North Africa and the Middle East television was instrumental to post-colonial governments for promoting nationalism and pan-Arabism. In the 1960s and 1970s, its use was implemented by training personnel in this new technology and supporting local production, and eventually building satellite and terrestrial microwave links to extend broadcast to their whole territories. The substantial costs in this regard led to cross-national cooperation to achieve these ends, no doubt helped by having a common language and religion. Several Arab states formed a broadcasting union in the early 1970s to exchange programs. But such state broadcast television was challenged by alternative programming in the 1980s from video cassettes and vcrs and in the 1990s from commercial, satellite-delivered networks, stimulated in particular by popularity of the CNN news coverage of the first Gulf War in 1991.[47]

Television did not reach a mass audience in this region until the 1990s. From independence to the mid 1970s, there were few television sets in most of these nations, and terrestrial broadcast was weak or absent in outlying areas, making it commercially unviable. Even in the 1990s, access to and viewing of television was restricted mostly to higher social classes who could afford to pay for commercial satellite and cable services. The masses had to rely on government-subsidized, domestically produced television fashioned to promote national identity and tradition and Muslim religious values.[48]

For various reasons, including a large population and its leading political role in the Arab world, as well as government subsidies to promote pan-Arabism, Egypt became the principal source of Arabic film in the 1950s and 1960s. So it is no surprise that it became a production center for Arab television as well. But television's impact was limited until it reached a wider audience in the 1990s through more affordable dvds and satellite television. These provided easier and cheaper access in the home, where the privacy was more suited to family viewing in Arabic culture. With these commercial alternatives came advertising and emphasis on consumption that contrasted with the soberness and self-denial of nation-building themes. They also pushed government networks in this direction as well, in order to retain audiences.[49]

Consequently, Egypt became the principal source of *musalsalat*, the Arabic version of telenovelas. During the Mubarak regime (1981–2011), the government played an active part in producing *musalsalat* as a nation-building tool to shape the politics of the masses. These very popular serials were produced specifically to be broadcast every night of Ramadan when families gathered for the evening meal after their daily fast. Their one month duration was significantly shorter than Latin telenovelas that lasted six months or so. Once premiered during Ramadan, when the viewership was very high, the shows were then re-run at other times through the year. Like telenovelas, *musalsalat* were produced for prime-time family viewing, although women tended to be the more devoted viewers. They had a heightened significance due to their association with Ramadan, compressed length and annual peak audiences viewing as families. They were the subject of much discussion in magazines and newspapers as well as among the general population. They also were a vehicle for intensified public discussion that transcended entertainment and engaged politics. Cultural elites expressed the government view of audiences as uneducated and susceptible to government instruction through entertainment, even while screen writers sometimes saw themselves as speaking *for* the audience to government.[50]

The shows themselves have had other social import as well. They naturalized the dominant group's dialect and culture as the national identity. In many Arab states, the dominant group is higher income, formally educated, urban Sunni Arabs, in contrast to lower income, less educated Shia who tend to be villagers or migrants to cities and traditionally are manual workers such as farmers, carpenters, barbers or butchers. For example, Bahraini *musalsalat* uniformly represent the culture of the dominant Sunnis, providing a cloak of religious legitimacy to their class. Similar patterns appear in other Arab Gulf states. Younger villagers have tended to adopt that dominant culture over the village culture, while their elders remain tied to tradition.

This drift of younger villagers has created generational strains in Muslim nations.[51]

For Upper Egyptian villagers near Luxor, far from metropolitan Cairo and Alexandria, through the mid 1990s, their connection to metropolitan life was through television and *musalsalat*. The women, in particular, struggled with the tension between urban modernity and village tradition entwined in matters of nation-building and modernization. Uneducated women viewers used the shows to talk about their own circumstances and dilemmas. Together they watched a series titled, *Ummahat fi bayt al-hubb* (*Mothers in the House of Love*). This told a story of elderly women who organized to prevent the loss of their group home to the building of a hotel. It was created by a progressive Cairene woman to teach women to band together to take control of their own lives. But it represented a world and opportunities foreign to the uneducated village women. The issues were relevant, but the circumstances in the village were fundamentally different. They were not allowed a social role in the village and had few resources to mobilize. While they were attracted to some of the modern freedoms of the characters in the telenovela, these also contradicted the world within which they lived and to which they were attached, making them ambivalent. Even if they wished to act as characters did in the serial, they had no support network to help them. For the village women, the show was exotic, intriguing but not practical to implement in their lives, except for navigating interpersonal relationships.[52]

West Africa

In the mid 1990s, Africa was the least developed continent in terms of modern media. There were 1.3 billion tvs in the world, of which 37 million were in Africa, or three percent of the world's tvs for about 12 percent of world population. The principal limitations were the lack of infrastructure and an affordable cost to viewers.[53]

In French West Africa from the early 1990s, people in major cities could receive television broadcasts. Senegal formed a government television network in 1973 with French aid and programs, in the hope that it would help modernize the nation, but it reached only a few bourgeoisie in the capital, Dakar. By the mid 1990s over 40 percent of Dakar households, including many of middle and lower income, had a television and could receive terrestrial broadcasts. Satellite broadcasting arrived in 1992, but was too expensive for the vast majority. In the Ivory Coast, limited television was available in the early 1970s. By the mid 1980s tv was affordable to modest income urban households, showing mostly American shows dubbed in French.

mali

In Mali, television was confined to a few populous southern cities until the mid 1990s when Western donor organizations funded expanded transmission and low-cost Asian televisions made purchase affordable. Satellite broadcasts were available, but too expensive, so most could receive only a national television network that broadcast much imported programming.[54]

The most popular shows were Latin American telenovelas, mostly from Brazil, broadcast in prime time. The telenovelas are purported to have caused a severe decline in cinema-going, where Indian films had been popular. In the north of the Ivory Coast, American shows dubbed in French were popular among urban young people and middle-aged women, even though few understood the dialog. Brazilian and Mexican telenovelas became more popular than Nollywood videos due to their availability through broadcasts that reached about 90 percent of the urban population by the 2000s. They were broadcast in the evening as family shows and accounted for one sixth to one third of the station's entire broadcast hours. Apparently this preempted development of an indigenous video industry. A Senegal television manager claimed that the telenovelas were appealing because "they deal with social issues that are the same ones African people are facing," and in a manner acceptable to African mores.[55]

Audiences across these various African countries exhibited striking similarities in response to Latin telenovelas, as well as to urban viewers in Delhi India and to Brazilians. The underlying commonality across these diverse cultures and political conditions is people's reaction against modernist values and their defense of traditional values that are partly rooted in Islam and probably more deeply in village and tribal cultures. Urban Senegalese expressed concerned about the influence of Western programs and telenovelas on youth concerning sex, dress, respect for parents, and consumerist expectations. The men tended to think women were badly influenced, while the women worried about the children. Some criticized tv for being an expensive diversion for the affluent to adopt a 'modern' lifestyle.[56]

American soap operas and Latin American telenovelas (*filimu*) broadcast by Mali national television led to family conflicts about their deleterious influence. Malians watched intently and just as intensively debated. The shows sometimes challenged the patriarchal authority over women and youth in the Muslim family and the village. For Muslim women viewers the shows' independent women created a tension between their need for greater autonomy and patriarchal authority. Almost everyone agreed that the shows threatened the mutual obligation and solidarity that were the basis of their everyday lives.

While adults preferred telenovelas, both male and female youths were fans of American soap operas. Older men complained about the soap operas' moral indifference and about youth imitating the American culture depicted. However, the young did not uncritically accept American culture, as their elders claimed. For both youth and adults, men and women, soaps and telenovelas were a ground for examining, debating and contesting morality, manners, values, and practices. They interpreted the stories as examples of personal relationships, involving moral and other dilemmas, much like their own. They judged characters and shows based on their own values, and considered their utility or dangers in such terms. Their reactions to Western or modern values were to the behaviors of the characters, rather than a blanket anti-Western condemnation of the shows. More secular women used the shows to imagine themselves as part of a broader gender-egalitarian world, while members of a Muslim women's group used the shows as a lesson to affirm their own morals. The secularist criticized the Muslim women for their conservative views, and the Muslims accused the secularist of consumerist greed.

Such use of drama serials occurs in diverse non-Western cultures. It transcends religions and nations. The common thread across these peoples seems to be the interface between traditional, agricultural, tribal-based cultures, and an intrusive modern/post-modern, urban industrial world system, of which imported Western television shows are simply one part of a broader experience, but one that they use to observe, think about and react to the differences and implications of these alternatives.

These audiences in post-colonial settings reveal recurring self-constructions not narrowly as television audiences, but more broadly as self and identity. They use television to define themselves and their personal world, to answer what kind of wife, parent, daughter or son they are. But they also use television to locate and situate themselves in the larger world as well, rejecting or accepting, in differing degrees, that world and its globalization. This seems more important, perhaps more urgent in these settings, than it appears for Westerners, for whom this issue is moot. This may change as the flow of goods and ideas begins to reverse, creating similar crises and impositions for the West. Certainly we can see in the digital age of the new millennium that the flow has begun to shift.

China: Late Development

Chinese television developed in three centers, Hong Kong under British rule, Taiwan under the Guomintang party, and mainland China under the Communist Party. Hong Kong and Taiwan began exporting television shows in the 1970s to the Chinese diaspora. Mainland China

65-95

was late in developing television. Until the Cultural Revolution ended in 1978, a tiny few households had a television and most of the nation received no broadcast signal at all. Beijing TV had been the voice of the government for over two decades when in 1985, it was transformed into China Central Television or CCTV, the first and only equivalent of a national television network.

In the 1980s under Deng Xiaoping, the central government identified television as centrally important to the Reform Movement, which accelerated modernization and began an open-door trade policy to the outside world. Modernization meant building industrial infrastructure, developing a market economy, creating an entrepreneurial class and transforming peasants into an industrial labor force, the last involving a massive migration of more than a hundred million people from rural to urban living. The government revised the concept of socialism, stating "the socialist economy is a kind of planned commercial economy." At the same time, the government instituted a drive to 'modernize' norms and values, revaluing commerce, consumption and pursuit of private interest as beneficial to the nation. Television was the vehicle for this cultural change.[57]

China adopted policies of rapid expansion and decentralization of television, with more tv sets, more stations, more broadcast time, and telecommunication satellites. The government's goal was to reach the entire population, including isolated peasant villages. In 1987 the government introduced commercialization in the television industry, in part to pay for the expansion. Local broadcast stations, also government owned, were required to seek income through advertising, which led to pursuing larger audiences through more appealing, less overtly ideological programs, much of which local stations produced and often exchanged with other stations. At the same time, the central government, through CCTV, retained considerable control over what was produced and broadcast to assure adherence to any new party line, although censorship in the 1980s was inconsistent. Audience responses were similarly inconsistent with government hopes.[58]

Drama Serials

These changes greatly increased demand for programming. Domestic production of television drama serials increased ten-fold. These serials were short runs of a dozen or so episodes with a concluding episode providing closure, similar to those in India, Egypt and US mini series, and much shorter than Latin American telenovelas and US soap operas. They were broadcast in evening prime time when families could watch together. At first, they featured heroic and patriotic histories about Chinese social, political and economic struggles through the twentieth century to promote government policy.[59]

One early serial, *Kewang (Yearnings)* became hugely successful from its first broadcast by a Nanking station in 1990. It was consciously modeled on imported Latin and Hong Kong telenovelas. It began a new genre in China called 'indoor drama' using mostly indoor scenes and close-ups and focusing on the travails of families and personal relationships, rather than broad histories. Its popularity led other stations to broadcast it as well, quickly becoming a national phenomenon. In some areas, it drew 90 percent of the audience. People hummed the theme music in public. Audio tapes of the music quickly sold. Great crowds gathered when the actors toured around the nation. Newspapers printed numerous stories about the show and the popular response. Even a Politburo member praised the show for portraying honesty, tolerance, harmony, and mutual help, traits compatible with the new role of the masses as an industrial workforce for China's policy of economic reform, and asserted its effectiveness in influencing people as they enjoyed an entertaining story, rather than bluntly telling them what to think.[60]

Other family and romance serials followed through the 1990s and into the 2000s, fueled by their great popularity and profitability. By the mid 2000s, these domestic dramas had become standard tv fare. Yet the government also continued to emphasize the importance of television as a tool of national development, and criticized dramas "that don't describe the courageous spirit of workers–peasants–soldiers and intellectuals ... but instead pander and express unhealthy male–female love and use an uncritical, even licentious approach to extramarital love." In addition, intellectuals criticized television for its low aesthetics due to commercialization and its propagandistic tendencies due to government requirements.[61]

Through the 1990s and 2000s domestic and romance dramas evolved, as the growth of a commercial sector, massive migration to cities, sudden rise of the rich and rapid growth of a new middle class, all put great pressure on traditional values and great strains on families, albeit differently for different classes. Typical central characters were a woman who put marriage and family above herself, even as she held a job in an urban setting, and a leading man who exemplified Confucian values reinterpreted for the economic reform era. In the 2000s, 'pink dramas,' depicted the dilemmas of young, single, urban professional women also seeking marriage and family. 'Ordinary folk' dramas, modeled on *Yearnings*, focused on strains that poverty and constant work put on urban working-class and peasant families. These dramas sentimentalized a fictive, socially stable, and 'harmonious' society approved by government policy.[62]

Historical family sagas, the Chinese equivalent of British classic heritage serials, depicting the rise and fall of rich and powerful families in the Republican era (1911–1949), also had considerable success, as their stories affirmed growing national pride and the new Confucianism promoted by government policy. The first successful show, *Grand Mansion Gate* (*Da Zhaimen* 2001) redefined merchants and their pursuit of wealth as positive and even heroic.[63]

These subgenres mixed modern values with Confucian principles, with the consequent strains between individual and family, and between family and national politics, reflecting audiences' anxieties and reassuring them. In this way, the serials exemplified the same strains depicted in television shows of other non-Western nations that, too, were confronting the social and cultural dislocations of post-colonial industrialization and globalization.

China, Audience Practices

By the mid 1980s almost all urban Chinese homes possessed a television. As occurred in other nations, when television arrived, it displaced other leisure activities. People spent more time at home, where they played fewer games and listened to radio less, and they spent less leisure time in public spaces outside the home. Urban working-class families, with little money for diversions, prized television as relief from boredom and as a source of new ideas. Their living space was quite limited, often one small room that had to be rearranged for different uses through the day. When the tv was on, it was inescapable, so families used it only at specific times, in order not to disrupt other activities, such as children's homework. When television was turned on, usually after dinner, it was necessarily a family activity. When parents – most urban women had jobs – and older children were away during the day, grandparents caring for pre-school children often kept the tv on as background while engaged in other activities.

Choosing when and what to watch posed some problems. Older viewers favored traditional Chinese operas that affirmed tradition in the face of a rapidly changing urban world. Men preferred sports over drama. Younger people, especially women, favored contemporary dramas and soap operas. The strain between modernization and tradition was reflected in these generational strains over tv preferences and the modernist challenges to tradition brought into the home by television shows. Nevertheless, the still-strong Chinese traditions of harmony and primacy of family over the individual pushed family members to work together and accommodate each other. Tight living quarters in urban apartments accentuated the need for accommodation, especially in light of the intensity of densely packed urban public spaces outside the home as well.[64] This contrasts sharply to multiple televisions and individual viewing in sprawling American suburban homes. The importance of television viewing as a family bonding experience, watching together and talking about the shows, continued into the early 2000s.

Chinese public discourse has long been controlled carefully by the government shaping and censoring media content. The government used television as a representative public sphere. In this, it cast audiences as obedient subjects in harmony with the ruling party and the ancient priority of the nation and family over the individual. Government policy presumed that audiences were susceptible to 'unhealthy' influences of television and that this susceptibility could be used to teach 'healthy' attitudes and motives instead. As with the Egyptian government's use of *musalsalat* to guide the masses, the Chinese government likewise conceived television as a tool to manage cultural values.[65]

Shifting struggles about policy among high officials, and about television content among officials, intellectual elites, and television producers meant that the messages were both mixed and varying. The adherence of dramas to government positions are evident in the subject positions embedded in drama serials. The historical serials of the 1980s mostly placed audiences in the position of celebrating episodes of China's glorious past and of the Communist Party's struggles for the people, motivating them to follow the Party's lead. Later, family sagas urged audiences to support economic reform by adopting new attitudes to modernization, entrepreneurship and wealth. Ordinary folk dramas urged their patriotic participation in the industrial labor force to modernize the nation. At the same time, cultural elites criticized television for low-brow entertainment, much as critics have done in other societies, seeing it as a threat to folk traditions.

On the other hand, discourse among the general population expressed more practical hopes and fears about television, as indicated by their regulation of its use in the home. Urban parents in the 1980s expressed concerns about the effects of television on children, such as weakening children's eyes, displacing homework and teaching them violence and sexuality, similar to parental concerns in the US in the 1950s. They worried that it may also erode traditional social norms and values, as parents and elders were worried in India and Africa. At the same time, many saw television as a potential educational contribution providing information and ideas, stimulating new lines of thinking, comparing China and their lives to the rest of the world, with pride in China's advances and increased world importance. This parental image of television was heightened in the 1990s by the parent generation intensely invested in their one child.[66]

Global Patterns

Audiences across a broad range of nations responded to domestic drama serials in similar ways. There are no clear answers, supported by research, to the question: Why? Since much of their response is about family, relationships, and values, at least part of the answer must grow from the commonalities of families across cultures. Intensively interdependent and enduring relationships between spouses and between parents and children engender and bring with them common problems: the division of labor and equality between spouses, and parental responsibility for and authority over rearing and guiding children. In times of social and cultural change these issues intensify, as the solutions no longer can be taken for granted. Particularly among pre-industrial, agricultural cultures confronting Western modernity, the juxtaposition of modern and traditional norms and values in domestic drama serials brings these issues to the fore. The common use of serials to explore and understand family and intimate relationships, as well as social changes intruding on the family, then derives from practical needs; how those are resolved may differ according to cultural demands.

As to the social changes, post-colonial circumstances and the confrontation and contradictions between tradition and modernity have long been characterized as a choice between two mutually exclusive and contradictory cultures or as a progression from one to the other. However, history and anthropology indicate that peoples cannot simply choose one or the other. By the twentieth century, Western ideas in non-Western cultures had become "both indispensable and inadequate," to again use the words of historian Dipesh Chakrabarty.[67] Just as post-colonial nations could not adopt modern technologies or participate in world trade without enmeshing themselves in a whole hosts of Western institutions, Western ideas and terminology become enmeshed in post-colonial language and thinking.

Audience studies too demonstrate this. At a most elementary level, to watch a television show requires incorporating its assumptions about what is real and what an image, what is fact and what fiction. To use a television, a vcr, or a satellite dish, audiences must already be halfway into a modern world, one that is indispensable to carrying on everyday life, short of closing the door on modern technologies and media, even on the world of nations. Civilizations and cultures repeatedly have attempted closing the door and historically could not sustain it. At the same time, these modern things, ideas, and practices are inadequate to sustain, or even are destructive of, people's traditional values. One cannot segregate and insulate one from the other. Thus, choice between the two is an illusion, change is powerful, and tradition irreparably transformed.

Last, the struggle to understand and deal with the dilemmas of tradition versus modernity is not new. What is now tradition was once new. Central to the formation of Western social sciences a century ago were efforts to explain urbanization and industrialization in Europe. However, industrialization and modern culture were already upon them when Marx, Durkheim, Weber, and many others tried to explain how it happened and what was lost. A strong thread of nostalgia, which arises only after something is gone, weaves through this work. For post-colonial societies, still in the midst of their epochal upheaval, the question has been what road to take. The answer some nations have chosen is to attempt to build a road synthesizing the new and the old.

7

Digital Media in the
New Millennium

The new millennium digital age is probably the most transformative media revolution since radio. Digital mobile media and the internet have created a connectivity unlike anything seen before. Thanks to the internet and smartphone, and a few huge Silicon Valley corporations, many people carry in their pocket the world's largest library and an enormous and diverse recorded music library, plus a camera, GPS software, and a phone, all unmoored from any single place. At the same time, being able to afford it, getting connected and knowing how to find and use the information and ideas, is not straightforward and is fraught with confusion and complication. It is also a fearsome tool of surveillance of billions of people's locations, statements, choices, and actions used by corporations to profit or governments to police people.

In the 1990s, digital screen technologies were poised to transform culture in the wealthy nations of Europe, North America, Japan, and Australia.[1] Digitization was about to enable, enhance, and accelerate media convergence, mobility, and globalization. As television, satellite, and recording technologies shifted from analog to digital form, they could be integrated seamlessly with other digital technologies such as computers, internet, and mobile phones. This facilitated the movement of information not only between media, but also across the globe, as aural, visual, and linguistic representations could be transmitted by internet rather than transported by freight. This also increased the benefits of corporate mergers, creating multi-media global giants. This, in turn, aided the development of media production in numerous new centers, and the linking of old and new centers. And it fed growth of counter, bilateral, regional flows that now compete with and sometimes bypass Hollywood, challenging its long-time hegemony.

At the center of this technical revolution, digitization enabled three increasingly important features of media use today: their interactivity, mobility, and ubiquity. The internet is the heart of this new technological landscape, accessed with mobile laptops, tablets, and smartphones, and stationary desktops and televisions. These capabilities have in turn engendered habits of multi-tasking and 'always on.' As a cause and a result, boundaries between media are being replaced by convergences of technologies, industries, and end uses. Even the very notion of audiences has been destabilized by the participatory nature of these individual media and their interconnection.

This is *not* to say that technology has driven industry. Rather, the industry has driven the shape that technology has taken, most especially its data-gathering capabilities, which are effectively invisible to users. The internet began as a public non-profit utility, a free electronic mail service, just as radio broadcast initially was not commercial. By 2010 it had become an advertising business. What turned the entire technology to this purpose was the concentration of users in the hands of a few huge companies who could mine their actions and personal information to greatly refine the targeting of advertising. In this respect, the largest internet websites are simply extraordinarily efficient extensions of the television business model, grounded in selling consumer goods and services.

Lastly, computers, smartphones, and the internet have become part of *screen* culture and linked with film and television. While our primary focus is image media, and while digital communication was initially and more naturally text-based, we cannot appreciate today's screen culture without including computers, smartphones, and the internet. These technologies have become increasingly, even predominantly visual. Moreover, video has become integrated into the text, so that interactions regularly include images as messages, such as emoticons or photos. Music videos became a new form of music on television and recording in the 1980s. Skype used web cameras attached to computers for video-phoning via the internet in 2007. Smartphones have collapsed the distinction between the social interaction of the phone and the one-way reception of television, which collapses the distinction not only between word and image but also between participants and observers, users and audiences. Smartphones with digital camera and internet connection greatly accelerated image distribution. Surveillance cameras in streets, stores, and lobbies are now commonplace and taken for granted in many large cities of the US and Western Europe. Cameras are also common in homes for security and to monitor child care. Such a continual supply of easily distributed digital images invited its use across a range of digital media for a variety of purposes.

The growing use of visual imaging in the new millennium was encouraged by mobility and convergence, but the shift occurred over decades, as speed and capacity of computers grew to accommodate, first still images, then moving images. Output from mainframe computers in the 1950s through the 1970s was in the form of printed text, and the internet originally was used to transmit numerical data between mainframe computers. In the 1980s computers began to be adapted to compose word text and the internet to transmit it as messages, an alternative to type and telegraphy. Not until the late 1990s did the internet begin to become a means to transmit images. Through those same decades, computers changed from mainframe to personal and the internet changed from science and business uses to leisure use. We will explore how all this has changed the landscape within which people use these new technologies.

Digitization

Digitization here refers to the transformation of media technologies of film, audio, radio, and television from analog to digital signals.[2] An analog signal is continuous, for example, a continuous flow of sound transformed into a continuous groove of a vinyl record, or the continuous shadings of light and color that our eyes perceive are transformed by camera into continuous shadings of pigments on film. Digitization divides continuous sound, light, and color into discrete bits, each bit coded to represent a specific shade, and then those bits laid down sequentially on a screen, or stored in a dvd or computer file.

Digitization enabled integration of the technologies and industries of movies and television, phone, computers, and the internet. In the early 1960s digital computers began displacing earlier analog machines. Even through the great transformations wrought by satellite, cable, and vcr in the 1980s, television and film had remained analog. The US film and television industries began to convert to digital about the time that memory capacity and transmission speeds became fast enough for moving image download. By 2012, most television series were using digital, and 30 to 50 percent of American films were shot using digital cameras. Those shot on film stock often were converted into digital format for post-production. The infrastructure for analog film is disappearing. Camera manufacturers stopped making film cameras except on special order; Kodak, the largest manufacturer of film stock for a century, went bankrupt in 2012. American and European movie theaters are well advanced converting to digital equipment.[3]

The most visible indicator of digitization in people's lives is their internet-ready television that can display broadcast, cable, satellite, internet, and dvd. It is also evident in special effects and animation in feature films. Computer production has made animation both far cheaper and far more sophisticated than the glory days of Disney's thousands of artists hand-drawing frame by frame. Similarly, digital has made special effects far more feasible and far less costly than before, reducing the need to build models or sets and to hire hundreds of faceless actors for crowd scenes.[4]

Digitization of media also has had a substantial impact on the divide between work and leisure that industrial capitalism introduced in the nineteen century. Before the spread of personal computers and the internet to people's homes, a computer was a tool for work, while movies, radio, and television were for home and leisure. But as digitization increasingly integrates the two, maintaining a separation of work and leisure has become increasingly problematic. Companies became concerned about employees using their computers to play games, talk to friends and surf the web during work hours. At the same time, increasing portability of media and computers has led employers to expect employees to work at home as well as at work and to be available anywhere, all the time; a topic for Chapter 8.

Technical Convergence

Media and communication convergence occurred in syncrony with digitization, each feeding on and fueling the other. Media convergence is "the flow of content across multiple media platforms, the cooperation between multiple media industries, and the migratory behavior of media audiences."[5] The first, technical convergence, and second, industrial convergence are discussed here; audience convergence is discussed in Chapter 8.

Technical or infrastructural convergence is unevenly developed, geographically and economically. Its development requires the ability of a nation's government and/or the profitability of companies to build and operate the physical infrastructures of distribution, including satellites, terrestrial transmitters and transponders, and networks of communication ground cable. For individuals to participate they must be able to afford smartphones, tablets, and notebooks, and the service charges to connect to the infrastructure. Consequently this description of convergence applies to wealthier locations and classes much more than to poorer ones, in terms of the degree of participation. For example, in China even remote peasant villagers have television sets and broadcast signals, but less access to internet and smartphones. Much of the following discussion applies more fully to the US, Western Europe, and Japan, and to wealthier and middle-class inhabitants in metropolitan regions of other nations. Even there however, there are some wealthy areas quite advanced and other wealthy areas whose infrastructure lags behind for a variety of reasons.[6]

Some technical convergence preceded digitization. In the 1980s vcrs opened the door to transforming the television set into a multi-use entertainment device, enabling people to view movies in their homes as an alternative to the movie theater, to copy and time shift television programs to watch when more convenient, and to produce and view home-made videos as an alternative to 8mm film. In the 1990s video-game consoles added another use for analog television sets.

Now digitization has expanded those alternatives. Once devices as well as signals were all digitized, video content could move seamlessly between internet, tv, computer, smartphone, cameras and video-game consoles. PCs soon were used for surfing websites and playing computer games more than for numerical data manipulation and calculation. When television went digital, it linked tvs with computers. By 2011 the distinction between television and the internet had begun to blur in Europe, Japan, and the US; India, China, Latin America, and Africa, also were moving toward integrated digital systems. Digitization combined with internet access began to blur boundaries and differences between devices as their capability, content and uses converge. Conversation and entertainment are increasingly possible on the same device as well as through simultaneous use of two or more devices. These changes have had different consequences for different industries.[7]

As audiences migrate to new platforms like smartphones and laptops to view tv shows, advertising revenue threatens to shrink for broadcast and cable companies. On the other hand, production companies probably benefited by the eased distribution of digital signals compared to dvd.[8] Three features of this new media environment stand out for their dramatic impact: mobility, ubiquity, and interactivity.

Mobility and Ubiquity

Less than two decades ago, media were tethered to one place. Portable computers weighed six to seven pounds and connection to internet, cable, or most phone service required a wire, and televisions were getting bigger, designed for walls, not hands. Cordless phones had to remain within a few feet of their wired base. Since the turn of the millennium, compact and light notebook computers and smartphones have spread rapidly. Combined with wireless connection to phone networks and the internet, and including useful devices such as cameras and other sensors, they have wrought considerable changes in screen culture. Such portability and power made it possible to be 'always on,' no matter where a person was and what they were doing, thus collapsing work and play, home and away.

Mobile media require real-time location-awareness. The devices must connect wirelessly through networks of transponders and global positioning satellites that identify their physical locations. Devices that incorporate this locality capacity include not only mobile phones, computers, and tablets, but also objects embedded with tracking devices that people take with them, such as EZPass sensors in a car. These devices place users on a map and can deliver to them information about friends, places, and events (e.g. traffic) nearby. But tracking their location also allows the service provider to monetize that information.[9]

Location linked with internet connection makes these devices highly versatile for gathering data on the environments and people in the location of each phone. The aggregate location knowledge about millions of mobile devices and their users has been a valuable commodity when privately owned, which can be sold in real time to third parties, such as advertisers, nearby retail stores or governments. On the other hand, social, public goods can accrue when such aggregate data is publicly dispersed, like traffic directions that redistribute traffic and reduce street overloads. Live maps for weather, street protests, mob violence, and earthquake damage also have been constructed in this manner.[10]

Of course, as with all communication devices, their utility for social interaction depends upon sufficient numbers of people also having and using the device. Without sufficient phones operating, live maps are spotty and deliver little useful information. Their impact on society too depends on the numbers of participants engaged in the same activities at the same time. The mobility of the devices alone has not wrought dramatic change. That has come with their ubiquity and continual use.

Mobile media have disrupted traditional means to monetize audiences. Mobility changes the unit of measurement of media use from households to individuals since the device is no longer tethered to a place. It also has shrunk audiences of stationary media. In the US by 2013, 'cord-cutting,' or discontinuing land-line phones and cable and satellite television services, was significant enough to worry service providers. At the same time, people were retaining the tv set and increasing their overall time devoted to screens, by simultaneously using other media while watching television.[11]

Mobility brings ubiquity. In 1991 when computers were still mostly tools for businesses, scientists, and engineers, a researcher at Xerox's Palo Alto Research Center (PARC) imagined a world of 'ubiquitous computing,' in which computers were embedded in daily practices and everyday life.[12] That idea became a feasible reality with the wide implementation of digitization, convergence, and mobility. Computers merged with communication and media technologies, and the reality became ubiquitous media. The PARC idea of ubiquitous computing presumed stationary computers. That has been exceeded by wireless, internet-connected, mobile media. Media have become so multiplicit and omnipresent that they are the context of life, instead of life being the context of media use.[13]

Of course, mobile media would not have become ubiquitous and in continual use, if they had not offered personal benefits that appealed to the billions of people who now use them. Why buy a phone if there is no one to call? As early as 2011, the rapid adoption of mobile phones around the world was called 'mind-boggling.' As we will see in Chapters 8 and 9, among the benefits of smartphones are to remain in touch with family, friends, and work, via voice, text, photos, and videos, while on the move, and secondly, to maintain contact with information and events via mobile connection to the internet.[14]

How total the media environment is depends on the income of users and levels of governmental subsidy and regulation of infrastructure and services. But omnipresence is not confined entirely to an affluent elite. It is notable that the nations that pioneered investment in an ubiquitous media society were not the West, but Singapore and South Korea. As discussed in Chapter 9, a surprisingly large portion of the world population have access to at least some of this new media environment.[15]

Interactivity/Connectivity

Interactivity was always intrinsic to two-way communication systems, such as mail, telephones, email, and texting. One-way systems, such as film and television, are not intrinsically interactive. Interactivity was introduced first to television in the 1980s by the vcr. American consumers expressed their preferences for interactivity by overwhelmingly buying the more interactive vcr and rejecting videodisc technology that did not allow recording and time-shifting television shows. This was augmented in the 1990s by another interactive device, video game consoles connected to the tv set. In the 2010s, digitization linked televisions to the internet. Now viewers could pick their show and express their reactions via the internet, while also kibbitzing with friends via smartphone.[16]

The internet began as an open, interactive medium.[17] Yet for-profit internet websites needed to monetize their audiences/visitors, and therefore transform participation from something spontaneous and unpredictable to something manageable and measurable. An important monetizing tool for radio and television used to be demographic audience measurements, called ratings, based on samples of a few hundred to a few thousand people. Now, for smartphones and internet sites it is 'big data,' gathering every internet click by every user. The more interactive the users, the more data. As interactivity becomes increasingly visual, e.g. photos and videos, service providers are seeking algorithms to translate images into saleable data. Greatly increased size and speed of computers has made it feasible to aggregate and analyze huge amounts of detailed, real-time information on individual consumers.[18]

However, to compile this information into analyzable form, actions must be standardized, reduced to pre-defined, finite sets of categories of response that an algorithm can work with. Part of the foundation for this was laid with personal computers. An algorithm is simply a set of instructions telling a computer what to do with data fed to it. Before personal computers, the user was also the programmer who wrote the algorithms. In order to widen markets from business to home users, computers had to be simplified for people with no knowledge of programming, requiring operating system software as an interface, such as Microsoft's DOS and later Windows. Since then, innumerable 'application' programs have been laid atop this interface software. Four decades ago, computers responded to users' instructions; today, users respond to computers' instructions akin to a multiple choice format, as with TurboTax. Layers of algorithms set the agenda and frame the questions that channel user actions into these pre-defined categories.

By the 2000s, the same process was changing internet communication, which shifted from primarily participatory general-purpose tools like email, into 'platform' websites operated for profit, such as Facebook, that channeled actions into managed forms. For example, 'friending' and its levels are a means to uncover links between people and categorize their intensity. Websites contain and constrain users within a finite set of standardized rules, choices, and actions set by the website owner. This in turn produces standardized information about users that can be summed up and compared with hundreds of millions of others to sell.[19]

These websites transform the tool from serving the user to the user serving the tool, a consumer version of deskilling in industrial production that progressively removed control from workers to the machinery and its owners in the twentieth century. For the customer, like the worker, the same loss of control is evident.[20] In simple technologies, like a hammer, the tool empowers the user. It requires skill to use the tool, but the tool remains in the user's control. More complex tools that automate work reduce the need for skilled workers by having the tool control the user. A power press in a factory is a hammer in a frame to guide it stamping parts or pounding a nail or a rivet. It can do this more precisely and reliably than the best carpenters or metalworker. However, the automated press sets the pace of the work and the operator. The operator serves the machine, not the tool serving the user.

Serving the machine is familiar to media users today. Young people complain of the 'huge time suck' of tending their Facebook page. Older users of email complain of the time spent daily cleaning out the trash and unwanted emails from their virtual stalls. This problem of the device being the foreground, an end in itself, instead of being a means to the end, was recognized in the 1990s by PARC computer researchers. Today, in order to get what benefit the user wants, s/he must spend considerable time doing the particular work the website owner needs. Continual use is the labor that produces data which can be monetized. Users are the labor force – and a carefully supervised one at that.[21]

Industry Convergence

Technical convergence grew symbiotically with industry convergence, which merged several media and communication industries and created multi-media, multi-national corporations. Concentration began before digitization. By one estimate, American media industries consolidated from fifty companies accounting for most of the audience in 1983, to five companies in 2003. Since that time, mergers continued and ownership of subsidiaries has frequently changed hands. Such rapid concentration and integration in the US was a consequence of deregulation and legislation, most notably the 1996 Telecommunication Act. A turn to neo-liberal policies by many other nations, as discussed in Chapter 6, made this a world-wide phenomenon.[22]

This concentration produced horizontally and vertically integrated conglomerates that owned companies in multiple, related industries from print to film and television to phones, some of which were either suppliers or buyers for other subsidiaries in the same conglomerate. In the US, phone companies began to offer cable television and internet services as well as phone service. Cable television companies similarly began to provide all three. Television and film industries converged, as film studios, broadcast, cable, and satellite networks, and most recently internet streaming, were brought under one roof. The biggest companies became transnational. For example, Rupert Murdoch's News Corporation included Twentieth Century Fox film and television, DirectTV, B-Sky, and Star satellite tv services, as well as newspapers in Australia, the UK, and the US. During the 2010s, a few companies have come to dominate phone and internet services. Apple, Amazon, Google, Facebook, and Microsoft control the websites that account for much of internet visits and for most advertising revenue. In the US, AT&T, Verizon, Comcast, and Charter account for almost all of internet connection to homes and smartphones. Hollywood studios have become powerful global multi-media conglomerates, dominant in the US, but also with substantial stakes globally.

Such broad ownership would have been prohibited in most nations of the world four decades ago. Economists and governments have long been concerned about market concentration, and doubly concerned about media and communication industries. Market concentration in any industry concentrates economic power in the hand of a few companies, which then may rival the power of governments and breed favorable relationships with governments. But in media and communication industries this also concentrates *cultural* power over the manufacture and distribution of ideas and information. They may not dictate what people think and believe, but they determine what ideas most people are exposed to, more often and for longer periods of time. This persistence and pervasiveness, as discussed before, naturalizes ideas, giving them a taken-for-granted quality.[23]

Convergence made it feasible to shift to multi-platform delivery of movies and other entertainment through satellite, cable, broadcast, and internet to televisions, computers, and smartphones. Further, satellite and internet made it quick and economical to deliver content globally, and sensible for companies to seek international markets. Soon they promoted a 'three-screen' strategy (tv, computer, smartphone) for shows to seek and hold audiences.

These integrated companies were ideally suited to take advantage of the digital technological convergence in the new millennium. When mobile phones became smartphones, their internet capability offered an opportunity to keep in touch with audiences. Light-weight notebook computers with wireless capabilities similarly became a mobile means to access the internet. The new business strategy linked these three 'platforms' to each other, interconnecting them technically and merging their markets.

The internet provided interactive websites where fans could keep informed and express their reactions to favorite shows. Reality shows pioneered this strategy. *Big Brother*, which began in 1999 in the Netherlands, was perhaps the first show to begin streaming on the internet. In the US, the show encouraged viewers to make decisions about the show, including feeding ideas to a mole among the contestants, and voting for contestants in contests. By the end of 2011, films and tv shows were increasingly streamed through internet websites like Netflix. Nielsen and SNL Kagan industry statisticians estimated over 100,000 full-length tv shows and movies were available online by then.[24]

The three-screen strategy allowed audiences to migrate from tv set to computer screen or smartphone, enabling television shows to capture audiences anywhere and anytime, building viewer loyalty to the program brand. Audience participation via the internet became a means to involve viewers in a variety of show-related activities beyond simply watching, such as voting or texting or tweeting friends or producers while watching a show.[25] At least some of the active audience, formerly imagined as resistant to media, now cooperated with their *managed* participation.

Industry convergence, the three screen strategy, and the spread of mobile media, together feed a kind of hyper-consumption, in which people are always consuming one or more forms of media and their advertising. Internet websites, from Facebook and Google down to independent bloggers and vloggers, intensify this, as every act of participation triggers a commercial reaction by website algorithms targeting the individual user. The data gathering capability of convergent technologies and the internet enabled identifying and constantly monitoring individuals. This activity is the very core of the income business model that now sustain these industries. Marketing and advertising are now inherently founded upon a system of constant surveillance of users, to which we now turn.

Surveillance

These new digital technologies and their convergence provide valuable services with immediate, visible benefits that make life easier, more productive, and more enjoyable. Search engines quickly find information on almost any topic for work or momentary curiosity. Global positioning systems and digital maps locate places and give directions for the best route. Internet streaming delivers an enormous selection of films and television shows from around the world to users. Algorithms suggest things suited to our tastes among the millions of available choices. Online shopping, banking, and investing save numerous hours and miles of transit. Email, texting, and Facebook have made it easier and less formal to contact or stay in touch with friends, family, and work colleagues and clients. And smartphones carry all this with us to access anywhere. All these have become so pervasively used in occupations, economic activities, social relationships, and societies that they have become social necessities.

However, it is clear that these undeniable benefits do have their price, which this rich bounty entices people to pay. Of course, there is the manifest price of entry, the costs of devices and services through which people can access the benefits. But there are other, secondary prices, as well, that can be grouped under the label of surveillance. While this term has a strong negative valence in Western democracies, it accurately describes the trade-off for these services. For better or worse, billions of people are constantly being watched by corporations and governments.

Surveillance is, by definition, an invasion of privacy rooted in power. It is insidious, since it enlarges any already existing power difference between parties. Privacy is a defense against power – against what others might be able to do with what they know about you. Some have claimed that transparency is a solution, but that presumes transparency is reciprocal and power is equal. With Google, Facebook or the US National Security Administration, the transparency is aggressively one-way. However, even if transparency were mutual, that would still not resolve the power issue, since huge corporations and government agencies have enormous resources and can do much more with information about an individual than the individual can. Some awareness of the risks of revealing personal information on Facebook seems to have begun. Numerous critical news stories appeared in the US after the 2016 national elections, indicating a decided shift from positive to negative coverage of this data gathering. Recently, the percentage of New Yorkers using Facebook who hid their friend lists tripled in little more than a year.[26]

Companies gathering these data typically require some formal acquiescence to collecting their personal information before being allowed to use their website. However, when access has become a social necessity of modern life, consent becomes essentially coerced. Other factors also undermine valid consent, such as the sheer volume of work self-managing separate privacy settings for each website and the lack of information on what is being collected and what is being or will be done with it.[27]

Today, an array of panoptical technologies, including 'cookies' downloaded to computers, chips in myriad appliances and devices, and digital cameras everywhere, continually observe millions of people at millions of locations and activities, transmit that data via internet and phone networks to central computers, where it is collated and analyzed. Most of this data is gathered as part of a two-way flow of information: a visible flow from service providers to users, and a hidden flow from users to service providers. It works as Bentham's Panopticon, the unseen seer. While surveillance has a long history, the scale of it today with these new digital technologies is far greater.[28]

The value of this data lay not in the single bits of information, but rather the linking of numerous bits of information to create detailed portraits of each individual and each of their actions that can be used to determine probabilities of behaviors, and this is done continually in real time. Since the data held by corporations is proprietary and that held by government agencies is often confidential, little is known about what specific data they have, how they have integrated it, or what they do with it. We do know that corporations use it in attempts to direct our buying and political organizations to influence our opinions and voting, and from the many breaches of data, we know that this data is not secure from theft and hacking.

A most encompassing instance of surveillance is that by the US government, revealed in 2005. Under the guise of fighting terrorism after September 11, 2001, the National Security Agency began using data mining software to read emails and track phone calls of American citizens without their knowledge and with the cooperation of the largest phone companies, AT&T, Verizon, and BellSouth. One of the creators of the software noted that the program was capable of correlating data from "financial transactions, travel records, Web searches, GPS positioning," plus phone calls and emails, about every person in the US, and doing this in real time. Large corporations similarly gather and link such broad data. For example, in 2004 Walmart had 460 terabites of data on customers, larger than all of the internet content at the time.[29]

Data Gathering

Collecting and collating huge amounts of real-time data from many sources on millions of people can be done only by large organizations with regular access to millions of people.[30] It requires an army of skilled workers to program and maintain hardware and software and to utilize the data. It also requires a consumer economy in which this data is a saleable commodity. To efficiently capture and analyze such data requires supercomputers, digitization, and internet, which only coalesced in the new millennium. The costs make this data beyond the reach of and little use to the vast majority of people and organizations. So without industry concentration and technical convergence we would not have big data, for either its benefits or dangers.

Data is gathered via several communication systems.[31] Most people are aware that a range of actors, including companies, governments, and hackers, observe every click on personal computers and internet website visits.[32] However, this is only one source of data, and its information value is multiplied when combined with other data, whose nature and collection is less well known. Using a credit card for purchases enables linking the universal product bar code (UPC) of each product with the specific purchaser. UPC codes were introduced in the US in the early 1970s as a tool for on-going inventory and resupply of stores. By the new millennium when credit cards were used in most purchases, it became feasible to use UPCs to identify the specific purchaser's shopping habits. When returning an item without a receipt, stores often ask customers for identification such as a driver's license. The justification typically given is that it will reduce theft. But the license number also can link the customer to other information about him or her. Once the individual is identified, all this can be linked to credit reports and public records.

As computer chips, microphones, and cameras are proliferating in appliances and devices and creating an 'internet of things,' they have become another source of data. Customers can use the chip technology for remote control of such things using their mobile phone. Manufacturers can use the chips to schedule maintenance, diagnose problems, and improve design. But data also can be uploaded from the chips and used for other purposes, such as selling it to third parties. Automobiles now are embedded with chips that may sense speed, braking, and other data valuable to insurance companies. Chips in digital televisions have been used to track owners' use, without their knowledge. With this, not only keyboard clicks and screen touches but many other things people touch and what they say or look at in their home or car are recorded and turned into data about the individual, including children.[33]

Until recently, the data has been alpha-numeric. Cameras gather visual images. Mounted on streets and in stores, as well in homes as security system features, cameras are used for traffic control, police investigation, and home security. However, they produce so much imagery that large-scale analysis by humans is not feasible. Recent developments in facial recognition software are attempting to auto-matically search these video records and link images from cameras with the identity of a person and all the data about them. Companies such as FaceFirst are selling facial recognition software connected to retail store cameras in order to identify people as they enter the store. In addition, such software may soon be dissecting the vast quantity of photos and visual images on the internet and linking those who are in them, post them or click on them.[34]

In the US, most of these data, once captured, becomes the property of the company, with the user having few rights, not even the right to know what information the company has. In such cases, buyers may find buried in the purchase or user agreement a clause in which they acknowledge the manufacturer's right to use and sell the data to third parties. A 2017 edition of Quicken personal accounting software stated that Quicken reserves the right to store the user's personal financial data on a server anywhere in the world. In its 2016 user agreement, Facebook claimed ownership of anything posted and the right to use consumer profiles without the users' knowledge and at their own discretion. The buyer's choices are to agree or not to use the website service. Regulations in the European Union are more protective of individuals' rights concerning such data, which may result in different trajectories in its use. Nevertheless, service providers can still require agreement (opt-in) before allowing use of the service.[35]

There are two demonstrated uses that have become evident in the US. The data have significant commercial value to those who wish to sell something. Large new advertising companies, such as Axiom, use big data and algorithms to precisely target potential buyers for their clients. Most of this activity is not divulged, so we can only surmise what data and methods any particular company might use. First, data from diverse sources must be integrated, which may be done by data collectors, end-users, or intermediary companies. The more exhaustive the range of data in a dataset, the better for thick personal description of individuals: demographics, credit reports, and public records, records of purchases, websites visited, and current location. Comparing any particular individual to people with similar profiles, data analysis can project a person's probable likes and dis-likes, opinions and behavior. The goal is to identify persons most likely to buy the product or service, and to capture their attention while online or near a store so they can act immediately on the ad. To achieve this last goal, the information must be auctioned in real time to marketers who can immediately send an ad or discount offer to that person. Of course, this is only possible when done by powerful computers using personal data, including the real-time activity of millions of persons.[36]

The purpose of this marketing is to discriminate between desirable and undesirable customers. Mass marketing blanketed the entire population with the same ads. Zip-code and other demographic marketing selected particular groups, big data marketing targets specific individuals at specific moments. The preferred individuals are those who can afford to buy, the top ten percent by income that account for almost half of consumer spending in the US, or the 'emerging affluent' who are making over $100,000 before they turn 35 years old. The data is used to select individuals they seek as customers, to track their activities, entice them to interact on websites, offer incentives tailored to their profile, and cultivate the relationship with follow-up online contact. Other people, however, do not receive this privileged treatment, and some are actively discouraged.[37]

While some may experience these strategic ads and offers as a benefit, the second application appears more a strike at democratic society. It is a next stage in the progression from political 'dirty tricks' to negative campaigning to 'fake news.' It was only a matter of time before such advertising techniques would be applied to sell candidates for political office to voters. In the 2012 US presidential election and the 2014 mid-term election, consumer profiling became voter profiling. Using the same techniques as retailers, presidential campaigns began to data mine the personal lives of potential voters as a means to get them to vote for their candidate. Using the same 'big data' as advertisers use, political campaigns attempt to target individuals' vulnerable points to sway their vote. Further steps in this evolution became evident with Russian interventions in the 2016 US presidential election and in allegation that drones manufactured in China and sold in the US were sending infrastructure and other information back to the Chinese government.[38]

In these asymmetric relationships, people are managed and manipulated more than in the television era. Ads and offers pop up, based on a person's big data profile, as websites auction in real time our attention to marketers. Recommendations from Netflix and newsfeeds from Facebook reduce browsing and reinforce the algorithm's definition of oneself. Yet selecting from this 'truncated reality' is easier than searching and sorting through thousands of things from which to choose, and also tends to confirm one's views.

Individuals have little control over their personal information, and how it is used. At the same time, organizations from the US National Security and Social Security administrations to Facebook, Target, and Equifax have not established adequate security measures to keep this information private. Instead hundreds of millions of individuals' data have been hacked and could be used for property theft, identity theft, blackmail, cyberwarfare, and nationalist agendas.[39]

A Culture of Surveillance

Before digital convergence, concerns about television, video-games, and the internet focused on what these media brought *into* the home, such as sex and violence content that might influence children, distraction from homework and exercise, and contradiction of what parents taught their child. In the era of big data, the concern has reversed, focused on what private information about individuals digital devices take *from* individuals. This new turn is enveloped in issues of privacy for individuals and secrecy of organizations. The debate entangles issues of democracy, dissent, safety, and freedom.

For some time, Silicon gurus wrote of the wonders of digital technologies, and newspaper reviewers gushed about the advances in every new model. Notably in 2011, as people in Arab nations used mobile phones and Twitter to mount protests and overthrow governments, many saw this as proof of digital media's liberating potential, as discussed in Chapter 8. Gradually however, public discourse has turned to darker scenarios, as it had for other screen media in the past. Revelations a decade ago about governments reading people's emails and tracking phone calls caused a momentary pause. Now warnings have grown more common and more focused on tech companies that own and operate the digital media, notably since the 2016 US national election.[40] Several issues are addressed in the warnings: the digital divide, data privacy (data mining), data security (hacking), monopoly power, and government surveillance. It is unclear how much is a grass-roots reaction or concerns of a few privileged opinion leaders. As mentioned in the Introduction to this book, moral panics involving widespread public participation typically build on concerns about the apparent impact upon families and communities. Broader impacts on culture or democracy however, seem distant to most people and a concern more of elites and intellectuals.

An individual solution is not feasible. Not long ago, an American individual could retain their privacy and remain anonymous even in public places. Before UPC codes, credit cards, street cameras, internet activity, and chips in things, and especially before digital convergence, people could buy things and go places without being personally identified. It was relatively easy to avoid revealing personal information. Today the networks of information gathering are nigh inescapable. An early stage of change was the establishment of unique identification numbers instead of names, such as national ID cards, passports, driver licenses, as the basis of records on individuals.[41] In the US, a person's social security number, rather than their name, became the most common identifier with which other data are filed. As most of the population acquired a social security number, its use widened to other government agencies, banks and financial institutions, medical offices, and businesses to identify customers, clients, and patients.[42] To avoid divulging personal information today requires an extreme withdrawal from society, foregoing identification cards (no driver license, social security or medical insurance), using only cash and having no accounts (no gas, electricity, water, sewer, no registered property, no checkbook or credit cards, no medical records). Very few people are willing to forego all the comforts and capabilities of modern society in order to avoid surveillance.

However, these technologies are not immutable. Rather, governments and large corporations, through policies and decisions, have transformed the technologies and their capabilities from ones serving people to ones serving large, powerful organizations. By the same token, laws and policies could be changed to provide more protection to individuals. The core of the problem is how to control these monopolistic giants and their caches of data. Too much data on too many people under the trusteeship of one company is what makes these other problems threatening not only to individuals, but also to social, economic, and political stability.

There is one bright spot: data are sometimes corrupted, so the predictions of people's behavior derived from it is inaccurate. These companies do not divulge the reliability and validity of their data analysis, but some evidence suggests that it often misses its mark. Most people are aware that ads sent to them by mail, email or pop-ups, often seem ill-fitted to their needs or wants.[43] Many people also have seen the errors and identity confusion that riddle their credit agency reports. As for data from clicks on a computer, smartphone, and tv remote: Often the individual to whom the data are linked is not verified but presumed to be the owner of the device. But it may be someone else or multiple people, which would invalidate or create confused profiles. For example, when a viewer chooses and watches a movie, Netflix cannot verify that the viewer is husband, wife, child, a visitor, or all of the above. This confusion is reflected in the recommendations Netflix makes when multiple people are using one identity, such as 'Mom.' This confirms an old axiom about computerized data analysis: garbage in, garbage out. So it is not clear just how effective or ineffective this data analysis and manipulation is or will be in the future. Perhaps it is sufficient for those companies' or governments' purposes; perhaps it is enough to gain uncomfortable control over people's actions; or perhaps it's so confused as to undermine its own power.

8

Using Digital Media

In the new millennium, a bewildering number of media innovations have been rapidly shifting the media landscape at a rate measurable in months rather than years. Digitization, convergence, and mobility have made it possible for more devices to be more linked and used for much more time. By 2017, American adults spent on average about nine hours every day using a screen media device. Since 2012 almost all of the increase has been in smartphone use.[1]

The superficial consequences of the increased media use range from the mundane effect of mobile media on public places, for example, people walking and driving while staring at their screen, to the cumulative effects of social interactions of billions of people filtered through these devices, a heightened access to and everyday presence of imported cultures, and a culture of hyper-consumption. Market researchers report that in the US, younger, higher-income households use television sets mainly as dumb monitors for internet connection and video game consoles, and using the internet for a range of purposes such as paying bills, news and information, and entertainment. When watching broadcast, cablecast or streamed television, these audiences simultaneously use internet capability, via smartphone, computers, and tablets, to converse about the show. Similar trends are evident in other nations as well.[2] The sheer volume suggests that deeper cultural consequences must be significant as well.

Of course, as we have said, the main barrier to participation is the income needed in order to afford the hardware and monthly service charges. In the US, with median family income of $60,000 before taxes, many families cannot afford a full panoply of these gadgets and services that easily cost a thousand dollars or more per year. In Europe, access and subscriptions are less expensive, and in most of Asia, Africa, and South America are even less than in North America and Europe. Even in poor nations, there is significant market demand among urban middle classes. For example, a quarter of Iranians, mostly urban dwellers, had smartphones by 2017.[3] An enveloping digital environment is an experience that is widespread across many nations, even while it differs depending on class, urbanization, and education, repeating patterns we have seen in Chapters 2, 4, and 6.

Before/After

Even among the 'well connected,' before digitation and convergence and before download speeds and computer capacity gained sufficiently, the internet was not much more than email. The World Wide Web was launched in 1990, but was useful only for a limited range of professional and business purposes and included few sites of interest to the general public. Netscape, the first widely used web browser in the US, arrived in 1994. Amazon originated in 1995 with a very small presence. Netflix created its original website in 1998 to order dvds delivered by mail, and would begin streaming only in 2007. E-banking for a wide variety of services was introduced in the late 1990s and became widely accepted only in the mid 2000s. Google originated in 1998 as an internet search engine, but its usefulness depended on how much information applicable to everyday life was available on internet websites. Similarly Wikipedia, begun in 2001, took five years to reach a million articles and become a useful compendium for general use. It grew in value only as more and more people frequented the internet and began to contribute. In sum, all of these developments grew from the mid 1990s and coalesced about the mid 2000s, as they reached a critical mass of general public users and websites and a critical level of convergence. Finally, smartphones became wide-spread only in the 2010s, making mobile internet access to all these sites and features readily available.[4]

Before these tools came into widespread use among the general public, activities were geographical and corporeal, bodies and things moving from place to place, e.g. shopping in stores, going to the bank. Even at the turn of the millennium, most information that is now easily and instantly available on smartphone could be obtained only through trips to a library or archive. Films and television shows were confined to broadcast or cable delivery or a trip to a movie rental store or, even as late as the mid 2000s, via postal mail that required advance planning. On a personal level, social interaction was either face to face, by voice phone call or postal mail.

Today, both the range of entertainment and how it is delivered has changed. By mid 2017, nearly 60 percent of American homes had a device to stream video from the internet to their television set, substantially increasing the range of sources and types of recorded entertainment beyond that available from broadcast, cable, and dvr. In addition, streaming is available on mobile devices such as laptop computers, tablets, and smartphones, untethered to the home.[5] Further, streaming via the internet means anyone can watch from anywhere in the world, although still with barriers of language, censorship, and the costs for devices and services.[6] Online shopping is displacing brick and mortar stores; credit cards and electronic transfers have supplanted paper cash and checks to a significant degree; texting and Facebook messaging have supplanted talking on the phone.[7] Estonia perhaps has taken this further by establishing a government network including every citizen that gives access to all government services and information, even creating an e-resident status giving access to citizens and companies of other nations.[8]

Nowadays, digital media are commonly used both for two-way communication between people (which used to be the sole purpose of the traditional phone) and for one-way distribution of information and entertainment (which used to be the purview of traditional television). Email, texting, Facebook messaging, and voice calls are primarily two-way communication channels; Netflix, YouTube, and Google are primarily info/entertainment channels. At the same time, Facebook and other social websites have also become channels through which people receive information and entertainment as well as personal communication.[9]

Internet-connected digital mobile media have brought two things to social interaction: more interactive communication and more information. More information seems a positive development. However, the success of fake news has demonstrated that these media have brought mis-information and enhanced ability to question verifiable facts as well, to such a degree that in some democracies, opposed political camps live in different realities constructed by different media sources – illustrating the adage, "if people define a situation as real, it is real in its consequences."

The impact of interactive communication is less clear. One benefit that stands out among others is the ease of maintaining contact, both locally and over great distances, with friends and family through voice, images and messages to a degree that did not exist two decades ago. Locally, a casual glimpse around our daily lives, combined with a look at saturation and use rates, available in published reports by media ratings companies like Nielsen, suggest fairly strongly a substantial increase in contact with those in one's milieu via media devices. Even across continents and oceans such contact is now easy and cheap and can be anywhere all the time. Comparison to past communication over great distances can highlight this: In 1967 before communication satellites, an international voice call began with a request to reserve a line and then waiting for hours, even for giant international corporations. By the mid 2000s, Skype made possible inexpensive, extended trans-oceanic video and voice calls via internet, although slow transmission speeds sometimes garbled words and image. While the software technology was there, local infrastructure was sometimes insufficient.

These changes in communication capability have implications at both micro-social level of day to day social interaction, and macro-social level of social structure and social change. We will begin by examing a few implications for social interaction, and conclude by examining cases of large-scale movements to initiate social change.[10]

Mobile Mediated Interaction

First and foremost, has been the development of an '*always-on*' intensity of social interaction. Before mobile phones were widespread, when friends or family were not immediately present, but at work, school, doing errands, or in transit, the default expectation was that they were not reachable for conversation, Whereas two decades ago, computers and televisions were turned off when not in use, and phoning was moderated by a concern to not interfere with domestic and work schedules, people now often are expected to keep their mobile phones turned on always and regularly check their messages and social media pages.

Nowadays, when nearly all members of one's milieu carry a smartphone or tablet wherever they go, there has arisen a presumption that one can be reached at any place at any time, even in meetings or classrooms or with a client or patient. This presumption has morphed into an expectation that one also will respond quickly, regardless of where or when. This reciprocal expectation has accelerated use of media and induces a culture of hyper consumption of media. It also produces an existential disorientation when one's mobile device is forgotten, lost, or broken. For example in a 2016 study in Israel, people without their smartphone felt more out of date, pressured and lost, than did basic mobile users in the same population and location.

Moreover, 'always on' enforces regular, intensive servicing of phone messages and social media websites, the 'real time-suck' mentioned before, that is time consuming and often a burden.[11]

Adults as well as teens have attempted to compensate for the always-on demand by multi-tasking. As people have had to contend with continual rings for attention from several media, many people engage in multiple activities simultaneously, redefining interruption and distraction as efficient multi-tasking and making prioritizing and singular focus seem unnecessary. Multi-tasking is not new; it seems endemic to living, once we begin to notice it. Multi-tasking is matter-of-course in many everyday activities, e.g. talking while driving, singing or listening to music while working, watching television while ironing. Concerns about the inefficiency of multitasking with media also are not entirely new. In the 1920s and 1930s some expressed dismay that housewives were listening to radio while doing housework. In the 1950s parents worried about children doing their homework with the television turned on. In the 1990s, when personal computers became capable of simultaneous operation of multiple programs, multi-tasking on computer became the new normal. What is new is that multi-tasking seems to be more intensive and on-going. Throughout the day during most activities, users engage in multiple activities, moving back and forth among media devices, conversation, and other activities.

The 'always-on' phenomenon and frequent user complaints about how much time it consumes reveal it is not an individual obsession, but rather a social expectation. Only partly are expectations driven by peer pressure from those in one's immediate milieu – with everyone's face buried in some mobile medium. More important, the millions engaged in these practices indicate broader structural and cultural factors at work.

These structural forces link and shape practices among users. The structures and strictures of the websites themselves bring a common element to users in millions of personal milieux. As discussed in Chapter 7, profit-driven website companies strive to continually increase numbers of users and user time to deliver a constant flow of new data to advertisers. Websites do this by regularly adding new activities that will draw and further bind users to the site.[12] One strategy for this is the stream of 'notifications' reporting what others are doing or saying, which distract people from other activities and tempt them to respond, thus adding to the flow of data. Smartphone cameras and YouTube aid and abet the practice by providing a steady supply of new visual material that makes it easy to update their personal site.[13]

The belief in the effectiveness of multi-tasking helps to reinforce an expectation that one can be always available to respond to contact while continuing to work or do other things. Much of this however, is not actually doing two things at the same time, but rather interspersing two different activities with each other, moving back and forth between them, the consequent serial interruptions preventing concentrated and sustained focus on either activity.[14]

Despite multi-tasking, 'always on' practices necessarily take time and attention away from other activities.[15] Critics of media throughout the twentieth century have argued that each new medium, from film to radio, television, telephone, videogames, etc., displaced other more valuable activities. Once again this is the case. In particular, multi-tasking has spawned cultural tensions about expectations during face-to-face social interaction. Whether in class, dining with parents, etc., older generations, not inured to the plethora of digital media and to always-on expectations, tend to see multi-tasking as divided attention when focused attention is expected. Overall, these private website structures accelerate people's everyday lives, making them more busy, hectic, stressed, more hyped to consume, and press cultural norms to adapt.

Online Sociability

A second ramification of widely used mobile media has been the impact on the shape of sociability. Smartphones and social network sites have enabled users to incorporate much of digital media use into social interaction and social interaction into media use.[16] In the past, people frequently used screen media in ways that intertwined with social interaction. As we have seen, in the early years of film, people attended nickelodeons for sociability as much as for the films. With the arrival of sound, silence and solitude was the proper behavior for watching a movie, at least at some theaters. But the vast majority still attended in groups, as dates, friends or family. In the early days of television, people congregated to watch television and talk in public places such as pubs. Soon it became a family home activity. Only as households acquired multiple televisions, did viewing alone become common. But still, people gathered to watch sports broadcasts and daytime serial fans met to watch and kibbitz.

In the new millennium, digital mobile media and its always-on expectation has elevated the intensity and constancy of that sociability.[17] Moreover, the interactions increasingly have included not just text or voice, but also images, bountifully supplied by such tools and sources as smartphone cameras, Google Images, and YouTube.[18] For closer examination we will focus on the cultural significance of social network websites in social interaction, mobile smartphones as reshaping place, and the use of images in both.

Social network websites (SNSs), most notably Facebook, attract what used to be called audiences that number in billions per day, more than previous screen media, even for the most popular Chinese television show or for old land-line phones. Facebook and other sites provide users means to pursue information and entertainment on the one hand and communication and friendship on the other. They also enable people to easily integrate the one with the other through text and image sharing.[19] In the last decade they have rapidly expanded, in concert with the spread of internet-capable, mobile smartphones with cameras.[20] Smartphones have enabled users to visit these websites anytime, anywhere. The sheer volume and constancy of traffic and the numbers of hours spent suggest that these practices have influenced social interaction generally and perhaps reshaped cultures.

Online relationships generally do not arise *sui generis*, shaped by the structure of the website, but typically are extensions of offline relationships and cultures that individuals bring to the site.[21] The old assumption had been that 'virtual reality' was separate and independent from physical reality. But research has demonstrated the contrary, that online activity now is grounded in offline milieu. This is most clear with SNSs that enable people to remain in continual contact.

It appears that those who already have supportive offline social networks enhance their contact and strengthen the ties through SNSs. Some users claim added companionship from this online interaction itself. On the other hand, those with only weak offline networks gain less benefit. Some use SNSs predominantly to observe websites of others with whom they have little or no offline contact, a kind of para-social interaction. Such users often report loneliness and depression, rather than the sense of social support and community.[22] In other words, pre-existing offline interaction remains the primary factor for positive benefits from SNSs. This grounding in offline contact reflects a broader trend to use the internet as a convenience for localized, day-to-day activities in addition to socializing, such as shopping, banking, news and entertainment, and eliminate the need to travel to do these in person.

This also suggests that the internet sometimes strengthens bonds within groups. Smartphones and internet mediation have made it easier to sustain contact with family and friends, even after they move away, as discussed in Chapter 9. This is especially important for migratory people, as can be easily seen comparing Skype today to voice-only phone calls that were still quite expensive even into the

1990s, as well as to Skype in places where internet service is poor.[23] Friendship circles dispersed by jobs, which in the past tended to fade away for lack of regular contact, also benefit.

SNSs are frequently visited, virtual places that are wrapped into day-to-day milieux, and into situations where formulated presentations of self are expected. Facebook began as static self-portrait but steadily grew to on-going performances of self. The websites are structured around users presenting a self-conscious, regularly refreshed presentation, grounded in the person's offline life and face-to-face relationships.[24] On Facebook, features such as 'friending,' postings and photos, and 'news feeds' derive from and reflect the self that is presented. Presentations differ between various layers of 'friends,' with appropriate consideration of what is socially desirable to each sub-group, e.g. peers, family, workmates, work supervisors, the general public – hiding things that may undermine the presentation to a particular group. For example, British youth report that they take care not to be seen smoking or drinking in posted photos, as their parents may see it. Also, young users frequently present themselves in photos with peers and describe their group activities, confirming the importance of peer groups built into the 'friending' feature.[25]

Aside from the immediate milieu of family and friends and the structural constraints of websites, broader culture influences are also evident in SNS user practices. These include not only national cultures, but also urban or rural cultures and different class and gender cultures. In other words, cultures of offline places define online situations. For example, more than half of Facebook users in Western cultures are women, but only about a third of Arabic users are female, reflecting cultural differences in gender norms. There is also a greater generational difference: More than half of users in the Arab world (55%) are between thirteen and twenty-four years old, and mostly are students; in the West the same age group constitutes only a bit more than a third. In Russia, people use SNSs as an online dating space more than as a space for friends networking, whereas in the US it is the opposite. Russian women more often than US women present themselves on their website in more sexualized terms. Also, Russian men and women post substantially fewer friends than do US men and women.[26]

In more collectivist societies, such as China, Japan, and South Korea, broad cultural pressures give priority to serving the family, the group and the society over individual desires and demand individuals to present oneself in harmony with the group and avoid ideas and behavior that deviate from that. For example, in Japan, most do not use SNSs, and those who do prefer anonymity, presenting a virtual self instead. Online, as in everyday life, a mature individual should express only a 'socially expected face,' and keep true feelings to oneself. In a coerced parallel example, in Iran, people must be careful to express a politically 'expected face' online and avoid criticism of the government.[27]

Public/Private

Another facet of the recent increase in mediated social interaction is whether it occurs in appropriately public or private circumstances. This, a third ramification with perhaps a greater impact, concerns mobile media use disrupting distinctions between private and public space, and between privacy and public exposure. Public and private have multiple meanings, socially, politically, and economically.[28] We have already discussed in Chapter 7 new problems of privacy arising from growing surveillance. Here we focus on public and private *places* and situations, how the boundaries between the two have dissolved and both public and private reconfigured, with the incursion of private acts into public spaces and public into private.

What distinguishes private from public space is what is considered appropriate behavior in each situation: certain acts that, in public, make others discomfited or disrupt others' activities, should be confined to a private space, backstage. Special, private places are designated for basic bodily functions (defecation, urination, and sex acts in most societies; farting, belching, spitting in others), as well as for certain conversation (e.g. arguing, personal criticisms, and gossip) and individual expressions of strong emotions, all of which tend to be discouraged in public places.[29]

What is properly private or public space varies from culture to culture, but the boundary in most cultures is quite important, regardless where it is set. In modern Western cultures, privacy is defined more at the level of the individual, a part of individual sanctity and rights. In feudal Europe, the boundary was drawn at the level of the family. Similarly, in Muslim cultures the veiling of women is less about their individual privacy than about the reputation of the family. In contrast to both, in India the home is a space for greater sociability where individuals have little privacy from other family members and even extended family and friends can enter freely.[30]

Public and private issues have been entwined with tensions between traditional and modern values.[31] Privacy as a value in the West arose as an integral part of bourgeois individualism and more broadly, capitalist modernism, displacing traditional cultural values that gave primacy to family and community over individual rights.[32] Individual rights arose alongside the growth of markets in early modern European economies and the increasing influence of a bourgeois class.[33] Across two-plus centuries, in societies from European imperial centers to colonial peripheries, individualism and other modern values were advocated by urban, formally educated classes, while landed aristocracies and autocracies waged war against them and unschooled, rural peasants resisted in defense of traditional values in their villages. Most recently, mobile digital media have been recruited as tools by Iran's urban, educated classes in demands for democracy, against resistance in the countryside.[34]

Less clear is social media's broader impact on any shift of cultures to individualism over collectivism.[35] The balance and tension between these two have been issues in many societies discussed in previous chapters. Collectivism emphasizes bonding within groups and discourages bridging across groups.[36] Social networking sites and mobile phones, grounded in offline relationships, may foster an inward-looking attitude aligned with one's immediate milieu and little interest in the larger society and world, as some have characterized it. At the same time, however, access to internet information sites may provide knowledge of and connection to a larger world in ways and with ease previously unimagined.

How much private space can be afforded also varies with income and with traditional or modern values. In poor slums, enclosed space to allow privacy is scarce. Homes are tiny, so within the home individuals have little privacy from family. Public spaces in villages and neighborhoods also provide no anonymity. Combined with this, poverty means sharing or using public access for internet and mobile phones, which further pushes people's use into public space where others, can see what they are doing. For example, in the Philippines, 'pisonets' refer to computers outdoors on streets and alleys that offer very cheap access to internet by slotting coins into the machine at seven minutes per peso ($0.02US). The physical space enables friends to share use. The open space means passersby, including parents and neighbors, also can see what they are doing. Thus, this sharing and publicness enables enforcement of social norms, which in poor countries and neighborhoods tend to be traditional norms and values.[37]

Recently, public life – differently conceived, in contrast to the domestic sphere – has intruded into the home and private life in ways greater and different than before, due to mobile media and the internet. Work demands pursue people into their private lives. People shop online instead of at stores, and voice social and political expression individually online rather than collectively in public spaces. Complementarily, private life, and leisure pursuits intrude more into the workplace.

More visible is how private matters are displayed in and redefine public spaces. Recently in urban areas, most people on trains or buses and in waiting rooms can be seen using mobile media. Companions often appear absorbed in their smartphones more than each other. Given the widespread use of mobile media in many public places, their preponderance re-defines what is appropriate in the situation. Reactions to these recent changes in behavior indicate a clash over what is considered appropriate public behavior. Loud conversation on mobile phones are considered private matters that interfere with others' approved activities in public, such as reading, listening to a companion or public speaker, or watching a movie.[38]

These annoyances take on a different hue when we think of public spaces as the public sphere, distinct from private spheres of life in which people are expected to act in their own interest, and where they should act as citizen publics, discuss political issues and then, according to various theories, act collectively in their own or public interest.[39]

As we think about gatherings in public spaces as sociability or civic responsibility, we should reflect on observable everyday behavior. People gathered in public spaces usually do not spontaneously engage in conversations with strangers;[40] that requires an event to trigger it. Whether we call them a crowd or a public, an event draws attention and raises questions. As people attempt to understand and define the situation, they begin to talk with each other. This highlights the real issue: whether people, once they begin to talk with each other and define the situation, then go on to act collectively to resolve the problem, or does the gathering dissolve and people revert to their immediate milieu and everyday tasks. For example, the success of a public meeting can be measured by how quickly after adjournment attendees disperse rather than stay to meet and talk with each other and perhaps plan some action together.[41]

Returning again to that gathering of people, behavior in urban public space is normally non-problematic and creates no need for strangers to speak among themselves or take collective action. Rather, norms of civil inattention call for people *not* to accost strangers or intrude into their privacy and anonymity, even if they overhear a conversation.[42] This is a condition of the close quarters of urban living that makes it feasible for individuals to live among strangers. It is a situation with familiar norms in which individuals pursue their private lives, in transit or in private social interaction, while strangers are treated as objects around which individuals must maneuver through space. In small towns, local neighborhoods, and rural areas, public spaces have proportionally more acquaintances and familiar faces

Plains, GA. Billy carth in front of gas station drinking Beer.

– and less anonymity – which invites or even requires at least some minimal interaction among those present. It is in exceptional circumstances when a normal situation breaks down, such as a bus accident, which create a collective problem and a need to collectively redefine the situation, that strangers are prone to talk to each other, and in more serious circumstances, take collective action. The health of civil society is measurable in how well strangers manage this transition and resolve their problem collectively. Indeed, it is remarkable and heartening how often many people make this sudden shift and work together with strangers to aid others.

Thus, private interaction in public space is neither new with digital mobile devices nor exceptional in normal urban public space. This brings us to the question of how such devices influence interaction in exceptional circumstances that are, in terms of social and political problematic moments, the critical test whether people work collectively as a society to address collective problems. We will soon turn to such a case, the Arab Spring, where we find that the part played by digital media in the planning and then the execution and coordination is perhaps more significant than in instigating action in a spontaneous crowd.

Arab spring

In the past, a public sphere required a public space where people could assemble to engage face to face in public speech and maybe collective action. Such assemblies require legitimacy recognized by the state and other powerful forces in order to function publicly. In other circumstances, actions have been taken nevertheless, as the discontented have met in secret. In colonial America, the Sons of Liberty met secretly to plan the Boston Tea Party and other actions against the British crown government. Similarly for China's Tiananmen Square in 1989 and the Arab spring in 2011. Public or private, when such political debate was among those with a common interest, the debate was less about the problem and more about what action to take, and it often occurred in places where persons of a neighborhood or community could go in expectation of familiar faces. Such places fostered bonding over bridging and the solidarity necessary for collective action. For example, American workers in the nineteenth and twentieth centuries often held union meetings in neighborhood saloons near both their homes and their factory. Social capital in such neighborhoods was enhanced by workers sharing a common workplace, common residential locale and common places of sociability – and sometime common ethnicity and religion – where differences could be hashed out and solidarity forged. Not that these communities should be romanticized, but they potentially provided structural foundations for collective action.[43]

While they may seem to obviate the necessity of face to face gatherings, mobile media may aide action, yet they do not alone provide the structural foundation for collective action. Some consequences of this can be seen in the discussion below.

Mediating Collective Action

One of the most important features of smartphones is the camera, which has been used not only to share experiences with one's immediate milieu of friends and family, but more significantly to amplify events to the whole world and overcome government and other censorship, to plan meetings and actions, and to coordinate actions once begun.[44] Mobile smartphones enable almost anyone to record and transmit events live via the internet, and sometimes have a quite powerful influence. Entire social movements, so equipped, are even more significant. In Libya, an influential Benghazi businessman observed, "in the last 3 to 4 years we've had satellite television and the internet, but we still couldn't communicate our feelings. If we did anything to communicate with the political opposition, we'd go to jail, or be disappeared ... [now] young people watched what happened in Egypt and Tunisia on the internet, and they said, 'Why can't we do the same here?' But there was no plan for a war, or even a real plan to overthrow Qaddafi. There was no leadership."[45]

A notable distinction in the use of digital media can be seen in the contrast between China's Tiananmen Square protests in 1989 and Egypt's Tahrir Square protests in 2011. During Tiananmen Square, protesters used university computers and internet links to circumvent government censorship and transmit live coverage news, including photos, to the outside world. Little was said about computers or phones to communicate among themselves. In contrast, the lead story for the Arab Spring in Tahrir Square was the protestors' use of mobile phones to communicate among themselves in order to organize and coordinate their actions. Participants could see on their phone screens events unfolding at nearby locations and respond accordingly.[46]

However, we should not attribute these uprisings and movements to technology; digital communication simply enhanced their effectiveness.[47] Numerous riots, revolts, and revolutions have occurred over centuries without such aid.[48] Uprisings in Eastern Europe in 1956, 1968, and 1989 did not require internet and cell phones. Much resulted from word-of-mouth. Much organizational and cultural preparation preceded these events. For example, in the late 1960s in the US, an ad hoc committee of anti-war spokespersons, the Mobilization to End the War, required weeks to organize demonstrations against the Vietnam War. Digital technology accelerates the process. With the aid of the internet, organizing required only a couple of weeks for the February 15, 2003 demonstration by several million people around the world in an effort to prevent the start of the second Iraq War.[49]

The seemingly spontaneous Arab Spring uprisings also were prepared by substantial social organization. The liberation movement in Libya began in a provincial town rather than coastal cities. When young men immolated themselves in the cities, there was no rising. But when one did so in the interior town of Sidi Bousid, the whole town exploded and started the 'revolution.' While digital media were more prevalent in the cities, social ties were weak because tribes no longer had social and political importance; whereas in interior towns and villages there was still a 'country folk solidarity.'[50] In this case the organization was the village, bound by tribal ties and committed to each other, a case not unlike eighteenth-century European bread riots that grew from village traditions of moral economy.[51]

In Egypt before Tahrir Square there was a social and organization infrastructure growing for a long time. The decade before was filled with a series of protests against worsening inequality in Egypt and opposition to the US and Israel in which participants built social networks through face-to-face cooperation in confronting the government. It began in 2000 with protest in support of the second Palestinian intifada. Egyptian university and high school students led sit-ins and protests. In 2003–4 there were protests against the US invasion of Iraq. Some loosening of government restrictions on speech in 2004 led to the formation of a coalition called the Egyptian Movement for Change or Kefaya. Many key figures in the 2011 revolution had been part of its youth section. From 2006 to 2008, militant textile workers in Mahalla struck for better pay and conditions, and won concessions. In these later actions, young activists used social media and blogs to spread word to potential participants and supporters. One example was Wael Ghonim, a marketing executive for Google in Egypt, who created a Facebook group in 2010 in response to police beating to death a young man in Alexandria. It soon attracted over 200,000 members. Soon blogs appeared expressing a sense of anticipation. Finally, several groups cooperated to plan a demonstration in Tahir Square against the government on January 25, 2011. Soon it grew to millions of people in cities all over Egypt. Lastly, during the Tahrir protests, the Muslim Brotherhood, highly organized and with decades of experience, provided medical, food, and other services.[52]

Substantial organizational structure is necessary to move from initial uprisings to enduring changes. In Egypt, while the progressives who began Tahrir had only a rudimentary political organization, the Muslim Brotherhood mobilized swiftly and effectively to dominate transition negotiations, elect a new government and shunt aside the original left movement's program of progressive reform. Then, taking advantage of the disaffection of progressives and urbanites with the Morsi government, the army, the only other remaining power structure removed the Brotherhood, and re-established a military government. In Syria, the opposition to Assad's government, splintered more so by opportunistic factions with other agendas, created a multi-fronted civil war that in turn became a proxy for geo-political forces from Iran and Turkey to Russia, the EU, and the US.

History seems to show that enduring changes, in contrast to momentary protests, typically involve highly disciplined and thoroughly committed (often morally driven) organizations. The more profound the change is the goal, the more important is the organization. The organization will then find the means and implement their use, be they elections or guns, smartphones or cyberwarfare.

On the other hand, rather than requiring massive participation to bring social change, we may be in new circumstances today, so that it may be possible for a small number of people to topple governments or even global capitalism by creating digital chaos. We are in an unprecedented era in which there is an exceptional concentration of vital information in single locations and at the same time exceptional linkages to these. This makes huge, powerful systems such as global capital and its gigantic server farms dangerously vulnerable to disruption, interference and even destruction by hacking. Hackers have already demonstrated the ability to get inside almost any system.

Such an attack may be effective in destroying the status quo, but would be near useless to build a new society in its place. What takes its place and how that comes about is where well-run organizations of large numbers of strongly committed members, not simply crowds with mobile media, are needed to shape the future, for better or worse.

9

Globalized Media in the New Millennium

Globalization is, first and foremost, a matter of distribution. World-wide distribution has amplified to an entirely new level of activity and new means to achieve that, a rapid and frictionless movement over great distances of immense quantities of people, things, and ideas for the purposes of production, sale, and consumption. Technologically, this has been made possible by improved and inexpensive transportation, as well as by digitization and convergence of communication.[1]

It is easily demonstrated that trade has globalized significantly in the last half century. From the 1947 General Agreement on Tariffs and Trade (GATT) to the 1993 formation of the World Trade Organization and the 2016 Trans-Pacific Partnership, international trade agreements established political grounds by greatly reducing barriers globally. European nations, who had warred with each other for half a millennium, removed borders and barriers for moving goods and labor among themselves and created a common currency, the euro. Most recently, despite political trends in Europe and the US opposing trade agreements and immigration, one effect of the reduced trade barriers has been a lessening of Western export and an increase in regional cross-flows bypassing that hegemony and counter-flows to the West, often serving diasporas migrated there.[2]

Taking advantage of these international agreements, new transport technologies have produced a five-fold increase in actual trade of goods moved around the globe from World War II to 1990 (see Table 9.1). For example, oil has long been an international commodity, but oil tanker ship sizes increased dramatically. In 1960, a 50,000 dead-weight-ton tanker was big; by 1970 super-tankers, as they were called,

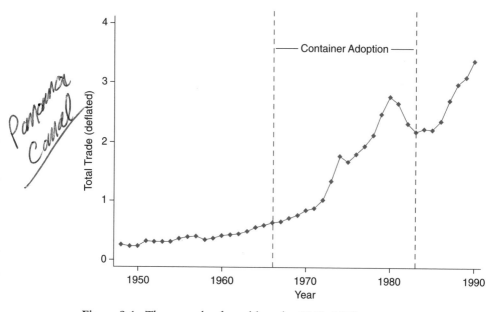

Panama Canal

Figure 9.1. The growth of world trade, 1948–1990
Source: Bernhofen, Daniel M., Zouheir El-Sahli, and Richard Kneller, "Estimating the effects of the container revolution on world trade," *Journal of International Economics*, 98 (2016): 36–50.

Super Tanker

were 250,000 and 500,000 dwt. Other commodities began to catch up when containerization increased dock efficiency in the 1980s, and when international treaties eased restrictions in the 1990s. Container ships grew accordingly. Now, they are bigger than super-tankers, carrying as many as 18,000 standard container units.[3]

Past globalization was primarily political, based on the expansion of empire and rule over other nations, with the economic benefits accruing to the colonial rulers, as discussed in the Introduction and previous chapters.[4] Today, globalization is primarily economic and cultural, the distribution of goods and ideas internationally. Much of the economic benefits still accrue to Western nations and former colonial rulers. Global communication networks, especially the internet, have made distribution of ideas and culture commonplace, principally through commercial channels. For these, the balance of exchange also still favors the West, but this is met with resistance and alternatives. As discussed in Chapter 6, global media have enabled and been enabled by the spread of neo-liberal government policies. At the same time, there has been a recent resurgence of nationalist movements that has fueled resistance to Western ideas and culture.

and as to resist foreign influence / dominance

Often discussions of globalization of cultural goods have presumed that this translated automatically into cultural hegemony. For example, economic data on imports of US culture products by nations around the world have been presented as evidence that American culture is dominant.[5] While a regular diet of American movies, television, and websites probably has effects on other cultures, the effects are filtered through the culture within which it is received and used.

In this final chapter, we will focus first on establishing the economic circumstances of media globalization, and factors favoring as well as countervailing hegemony. Then we will explore how audiences use and respond, examining the variable rates of adoption of new media in different nations and regions, and the challenges of these new media to governments as well as to global conglomerates.

Access and Affordability

In capitalist economies, population alone is not an indicator of demand. Only the portion of the population who can *afford* to purchase a product constitutes market demand. Nevertheless, overall populations are an indicator of *potential* demand, should incomes rise and prices decline. In addition, consumers must also want to buy the product.

But before people are willing to buy a product, they must have a use for it. How many people would buy an automobile if there were no roads? Who would buy a television if there was nothing to watch on it? And before they can buy it, they must have access to it. In the 1990s and 2000s there was much concern and debate about the international digital divide between rich nations with a cornucopia of media available to almost all the population, and poor nations with little infrastructure and few people who could afford these media.[6]

Access is two sided. One the one hand, governments or private investors must provide the infrastructure, electricity, and communication networks, such as land lines or transponders. This varies both between nations and between rural and urban districts within nations. On the other hand, users must have the skills to use the equipment, once purchased. At the most basic level, to use mobile phones, computers, and the internet, users must be literate, since they involve reading the screen and writing via a keyboard. Moreover, some languages, such as Chinese, are not easily adapted to keyboards.[7]

Concerning affordability, two factors seem to contradict each other. On the one hand, the devastating poverty of two and a half billion people around the globe seems to indicate that, even at the very lowest prices, such people could not afford a mobile phone and internet

2050 ? [handwritten]

access. On the other hand, surprisingly high saturation rates of these technologies and services, even in quite poor nations, suggest that a significant portion of poor people have access to these new communication media. For example, Indian censuses and national surveys of the mid 2000s indicate that half the population cannot afford a toilet and a large portion of the population is malnourished. Yet, 60 percent of India's population watched television in the previous week, and 20 percent of men had been to cinema at least once in the previous month.[8]

Media saturation data indicate that consumer media hardware have become accessible and affordable even to some quite poor populations. A United Nations survey reports that over 90 percent of world population have access to mobile phones (not necessarily owned by them nor smartphones). Nearly 40 percent have access to internet use (Figures 9.2 and 9.3). Other reports cite similar high rates of mobile phone saturation. By 2004, according to a survey by the Jamaican Office of Utilities Regulation 86 percent of Jamaicans over the age of fifteen had access to a mobile phone. The rate in the Caribbean island of Martinique in 2003 was 79 percent. These percentages may be overstated in that they count sim cards, rather than phones; and it is a custom in some places for a person to have several sim cards. That said, many field observations in poor communities report that mobile phone use is common in poor areas.[9]

one smart phone p family yes [handwritten]

every month HH that own their own smart phone [handwritten]

Sim cards in Rwanda — wonder if # of sim cards between HH's? [handwritten]

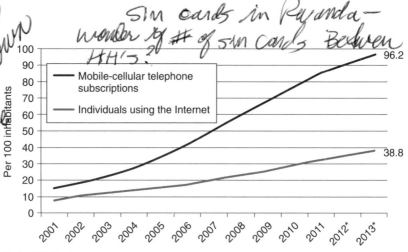

Note: * Estimate

Figure 9.2. Global saturation of mobile phone and internet use
Source: United Nations International Telecommunication Union 2013, http://www.itu.int/en/ITU-D/Statistics/Pages/stat/default.aspx

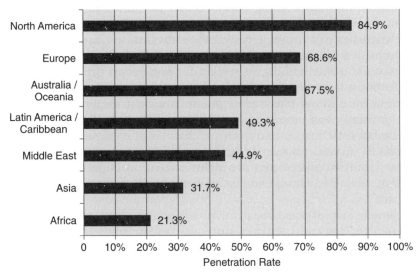

Figure 9.3. Global saturation rates for internet access by region, 2013
Source: Internet World Stats, www.internetworldststs.com/stats.htm, Miniwatts
Marketing Group

To pursue this population of low-income consumers, some private companies have provided the necessary infrastructure. For example, venture capital has financed solar-panel electrification for homes in rural equatorial Africa. This provides enough power for a few LED lights, radio, and flat screen tv, and for charging cell phones. Companies lease the equipment for $8US monthly – less than the cost of fuel for kerosene lamps. Children can study at night, farmers get weather reports, and people no longer need to walk or bike to town to charge phones. All can watch tv: village life comes to standstill for soccer and Indian telenovelas.[10]

A large part of the problem in resolving the apparent contradiction between the data on poverty and data on media saturation is that affordability is elastic.[11] Demand is not determined only by price and income, nor its utility, but also depends upon subjective priorities of potential purchasers. If a good or service or activity is highly prized or valued for symbolism or prestige or other satisfaction, people sometimes sacrifice even basic necessities to afford such things.

One way to address the matter of elasticity is to reconceive purchasing decisions in terms of *perceived* quality of life instead of costs. Subjective satisfaction differs by culture. For example, in Bangladesh, living well means being respected for benevolence, altruism, and good

character, as well as being educated and practicing religion, rather than achieving individual success and wealth. These values indicate the importance of community over the individual in this society. Consequently, a villager may strain to buy a tv so that he can invite neighbors to watch and gain respect for that generosity[12]

A robust body of research indicates that poor populations in many nations have found that mobile phones are quite useful socially and economically and emotionally satisfying. Therefore they are worth foregoing even non-discretionary purchases. For now, mobile internet access is of less concern for most people of poor nations. On the other hand, mobile phones are highly valued. In Nigeria during the 2000s, while 91 percent had text service, only 26 percent had internet service[13]

Among low-income Jamaicans, mobile phones enable them to better sustain their social networks through regular contact. When need arises, they ask for money, a bit here and a bit there. The result is a complicated system of relationships and of raising enough cash, even for small expenses. Social networks move money through the community to those whose need is most urgent, and who reciprocate on other occasions. Sustenance of such social networks through mobile phones requires a fairly high saturation rate, so that most people can be reached. Then the benefits of inclusion increase, further feeding the demand for phones. Reports of the importance of mobile phones for maintaining networks of family and friends, including those who have emigrated to cities or other nations, are familiar in many countries.[14]

While primary use of mobile phones is for social contact, researchers also have found various uses that are economically beneficial for poor people. A 2011 United Nations International Communications Union report cites Medic Mobile that helps to deliver medical care in Malawi, Ethiopia, India, and Nicaragua. Bangladesh built internet and mobile access centers to provide information for farmers. Mobile phones also reduce rural people's need to travel for information and services, such as to seek jobs or check current commodity prices. Even those who do not own mobile phones patronize pay-phone-centers for these purposes.[15]

On the other side of the market relationship, businesses are beginning to seek poorer populations as untapped markets for new media technologies. The sheer numbers of poor people in the world make them a tempting target for at least some marketers. As sales to higher income people reach saturation, to increase sales and profits, some multinationals have attempted to turn the poor into paying customers. The more viable poor customers are urban dwellers, since cities are more likely to have infra-structure for products, such as electricity or suppliers for batteries, parts, repairs, etc.[16]

The business strategy has been to pare down products to their least expensive basics and spread costs over time since, as a Nokia executive in India explained, "They don't have a cash problem – they have a cash flow problem." Nokia and Google have both developed inexpensive phones that poor people can purchase. The Nokia105 costs $20 in India, includes phone, flashlight, and radio capability, but no internet. The battery charge lasts a whole month on standby and the service is provided by prepaid SIM cards. A Philippine phone company brought down the price of phone use to 50 cents and allowed transfers of even a few cents from one account to another to accumulate a sufficient balance for a call. Many poor could manage such small outlays, enabling the phone company to reach a whole new market. In Jamaica, where 98 percent use pre-paid phone cards, the dominant mobile company, Digicel, charges by the second instead the minute. Users also have found ways to further reduce expenses. Villagers in Burkina Faso share phones, organize community phone centers, and break into phone software to annul manufacturer controls, among other strategies. In some nations, people have multiple SIM cards in order to take advantage of different rate schedules from different service providers.[17]

Costs are still a substantial, although doable, part of poor budgets. Prepaid mobile service prices from the dominant providers in sub-Sahara Africa in 2011 ranged from about $3 to $12. Prices relative to income are higher in poorer nations than in economically developed ones.[18] Nevertheless, digital technologies are spreading to lower-income populations. But the uses and benefits are not the same as for those who can afford more services and have more skills and opportunities to benefit from their use. They are not yet participating in internet screen culture that is the subject of Chapter 8. But as we will see, some participate in a film and television screen culture. Moreover, they constitute world markets numbering in the billions.

Hollywood Hegemony

In 2007–2008, half of European television programming was imported American programs. In 2011, Hollywood films accounted for 57 percent of world export box office. Several factors have helped to sustain Hollywood's hegemony over these markets of billions.[19] Digitation, a world language, a neo-liberal shift from public to private media and world-wide concentration of media ownership have had compounding effects, strengthening and being strengthened by each other.

First, satellite and internet technology, discussed in Chapter 7, has made it easier, quicker and cheaper to transmit information, including moving visual images over great distances and covering huge territories. Digitation changed the product from bulkier, heavier physical forms of films and discs delivered in days or weeks, to electronic data files delivered at the speed of light through wire and wireless transmission.[20]

Second, English is now *the* world language, through which global business is now transacted and understood by a large portion of higher-income media audiences and users world-wide. The drive toward trade globalization during the 1990s coincided with the rise of English.[21] English-language cultural products, in particular, promoted the spread of English beyond business elites. Hollywood films since the 1920s, pop music since the 1950s, the internet since the 2000s advanced the acquisition of English. Two billion English speakers, at various levels of fluency, now sustain an international market advantage for cultural products in English.

The ascent of English to an unrivalled position as the global language was rooted in the world-wide political and economic power of Britain at first and then of the United States. At the mid twentieth century, there still were other international languages established and sustained by colonial empires, since native entry into middle-class status required speaking the language of their colonial masters for politics and business. The largest and most far-flung of these empires was British. Combined with the rapid growth and spread of post-war Anglo-American popular culture, English outdistanced other languages.[22]

Third, as partly discussed in Chapter 6, a world-wide trend has reduced government ownership of media and allowed private, for-profit media. Beginning in the late 1970s, neo-liberalism began to gain ascendency, defining government as the problem and markets as the solution. New government policies catalyzed globalization and Western capitalist advantage by promoting privatization and de-regulation and eliminating trade barriers. The most notable early examples were the governments of Margaret Thatcher in the UK and Ronald Reagan in the US. But neo-liberal policy was not confined to the West. The IMF and World Bank were primary actors in imposing these shifts in South America, Africa, and Asia as a condition of loans. In Eastern Europe, they demanded austerity for government services, rapid privatization and a thorough shift to a market economy. During the Great Recession of 2008, the EU even imposed austerity and further privatization on its Mediterranean members, Spain, Italy, and Greece.[23]

At the same time, communication satellites provided the technical means for transnational corporations to deliver programming to entire nations profitably and gain a large share of those television markets. This greatly increased the world-wide markets of audience-consumers for these corporations and thus their potential for industry dominance and cultural hegemony.

Fourth, these trends contributed to concentration of media ownership. By the 1990s, a handful of multi-media corporations accounted for most sales of media content, potentially a flow of uniform information and ideas presented to billions of people every day in numerous nations around the world to a degree never existing before. Two examples of such centralization are CNN and Rupert Murdoch's companies. In the 2000s, out of one building in Atlanta, CNN distributed full program schedules for 24 networks covering North and South America, with a potential audiences of nearly a billion people. Similarly, mentioned in Chapter 7, Rupert Murdoch's satellite television empire has the potential to reach nearly half the world's population, with Star TV in East and South Asia, DirectTV in North America, B-Sky in the UK, and Sky Italia in Europe. His networks stimulated Indian tv news coverage to emphasize 'infotainment' focusing on glamour and celebrity and celebrating the benefits of a 'free market,' while shrinking coverage of rural and foreign news.[24]

At the same time, we should be cautious not to overestimate Hollywood hegemony. At least two of the four factors that had advantaged Hollywood are now beginning to benefit producers in other nations as well. Digitization has so reduced costs of reproduction and distribution that others can take advantage of them. Privatization has opened national markets to native entrepreneurs to use their distinctive cultural products to compete with Hollywood. Other languages such as Chinese and Hindi benefit from growing diasporas and regional cultural similarities to challenge English in regional markets. In addition, local speakers develop local dialects of English, contextualized in their local culture, another challenge to global English.[25]

Further, as larger portions of the populations of large nations become consumers, producers in these nations gain the advantage of domestic sales covering sunk costs, which favored Hollywood in the past. Increasing portions of China's and India's huge populations are rapidly becoming consumers, making their domestic markets triple and more the size of the US. These markets could support much greater production, a thousand new films a year rather than Hollywood's two or three hundred. With such large domestic markets, producers may even be able to ignore the US market, which no nation in international trade could do for a century.[26]

News and business discourses still tend to exaggerate the degree of integration of world markets. In 2007, Kai Hafez warned that we should temper claims about globalization, and called for empirical assessments of actual interlinks. Much of gross world production still remains national. Also, there is a considerable discrepancy between the integration of wealthier urban populations across nations and only peripherally integration of most of the world population.[27] As Hollywood attempts to move beyond exporting to Westernized audiences and reaching this far larger market, cultural factors grow in importance. In addition, global distribution faces on-the-ground realities such as widespread piracy and illegal downloads, domestic government restrictions and quotas for local films, or important domestic companies, however small globally. Diverse circumstances across nations increase costs to tailor products to each nation or group and require on-site representatives substantially familiar with local conditions.[28] We must think of globalization as a matter of gradation.

Multi-Centered Globalization

In the new millennium, multiple culture industry centers have begun to compete with US exports, first in their domestic markets, then in regional and linguistic markets, and now in European and US markets. This does not mean that American media giants are fading away–media organizations around the world are still eager to do business with Hollywood and acquire their films and tv shows – but it does mean Hollywood does not stand alone. Recognizing this, these giants are increasingly collaborating with global partners to finance and produce world screen products.

The globalization of screen industries in the twenty-first century can be seen reflected in changes in the American trade magazine, *Variety*. As recently as two decades ago, the weekly magazine reported on the film, television, and stage business by reporting on the people, events, and products in New York and Hollywood. It even included a weekly update of where important people in the industry were located, "To New York, To LA." Some events beyond US borders, such as the Cannes Film Festival, were covered because of participation from Hollywood. Global film sales were a footnote to domestic box office statistics. Today's *Variety* skews to world-wide coverage, every issue reporting on people, events, and products and box-office receipts involving other continents.

New state-of-the-art production centers provide alternatives to Hollywood. Nations around the world have long offered tax breaks and other incentives for Hollywood to shoot 'on location.' Hollywood too has sought such alternatives to sound stages, backlots, and unionized workers in Los Angeles.[29] But recently, huge new centers for film and television production and packaging have opened from Europe to China. In South India, Ramoji Film City opened in the 2000s and attracted non-Indian film productions because of its low costs and up-to-date, pre-to-post-production facilities. Bulgaria's state-owned Nu Boyana was the largest full-service film production facility in the EU when it was sold in 2005 to a Hollywood film company, Millenium, and then in 2017 to a Chinese holding company, Recon. In September 2013 the Chinese owner of the world's largest cinema chain announced plans to develop a huge film studio to produce thirty films by foreign companies and one hundred by domestic companies each year. Dubai established a film commission in 2012 and has built production facilities to attract movie-makers. The new centers offer sound stages, technical facilities, pre- and post-production, and skilled and experienced workers. These centers produce for domestic consumption and for export to culturally related nations and diaspora in Western nations, and also seek to lease their facilities to Western companies. Their ambitions are evident in that they were featured or advertised in *Variety* magazine.[30]

These centers are part of a wave of cross-flows (selling between 'peripheral' markets instead of Hollywood to periphery) and counter-flows (selling from industries in 'peripheral' nations to the US and Europe). Cross-flows have benefited from cultural proximities within regions. For two or more decades, this has characterized Latin America, sharing language, religion, and culture, as evident in the circulation of telenovelas around the continent. Within China, Japanese tv shows have been more popular than Western shows due to similar cultural values and social expectations. More striking, very recently Bollywood movies have become hits in China, encouraging Chinese companies to seek partnerships and distribution rights as well as to hire Indian directors and screen writers. The proliferation of satellite news channels from different sources in many locations around the world also has contributed to crossflows. The choices are multilayered, from global CNNI and BBC to global but regionally identified Fox, India's NDTV, and Singapore's Channel News Asia, to regional, national or even local channels.[31]

Cross-flows and counter-flows have succeeded in diasporic markets. Diasporic populations have emigrated to prospering nations in Europe, the Persian Gulf (Kuwait, Dubai) and elsewhere. Even newly prospering South Korea has begun to receive immigrant workers and wives from Southeast Asia. The world-wide Chinese diaspora is about 50 million people, half in Southeast Asia, still culturally inclined to their Chinese homeland. Satellite and internet communication has enabled them to receive entertainments from their home countries to a degree not possible before.[32]

Counter-flows from Latin America to the US have been induced by Latin immigration, constituting a diaspora of roughly 40 million potential viewers, most of whom speak Spanish. Even the younger bi-lingual population prefer Spanish networks, as they are offended by stereotypes found in English language programs. In summer 2013, Univision, partly owned by the Mexican company Televisa which supplies a third of its programming, became the highest Nielsen-rated, prime-time network in the US among adults aged 18 to 49 for all languages, surpassing ABC, CBS, NBC, and Fox. Televisa even opened offices in Santa Monica to produce programs in English for American audiences. Telemundo and Mun2 also distribute bilingual programs to the US Latino population. Indian film companies too have benefited from serving the large diaspora in Europe and the US, providing masala films, music, and dance to their emigrés. Nigerian videos also have markets among immigrants in Italy, Britain and the US.[33]

Counter-flows also have benefited from a broad increase in demand from American television networks for more new filmed product. New scripted series on US cable channels tripled to one hundred in the 2000s and to 144 in 2013. Then internet streaming drove the numbers even higher. To fulfill demand, in 2014 Netflix spent more for licenses from outside the US than domestically. Government agencies of seven Asia nations, including India, China, Japan, and Hong Kong, attended the American Film Market to seek distribution of their films in the US. Europe's demand for drama series has similarly risen, to about $6 billion in 2010, although still mostly from Hollywood.[34]

Hollywood has responded to these challenges with strategies of cooperation as much as competition. Hollywood has been participating in co-productions, including local language product intended for exhibition in specific countries as well as for global distribution. In 2014 the Swedish Svenske Filmindustri had 10 film 'partnerships' in other nations, seven of them in Hollywood. At the same time, investors from other nations are sending money to Hollywood. By the mid 2000s Hollywood films were getting financed mostly from foreign sources, one third from German banks. Reliance, an Indian entertainment company that does post-production on 80 percent of India's films, has invested $300–400 million in Dreamworks from 2006 to 2012.[35]

With international box office beginning to overshadow domestic US sales, Hollywood has striven for joint ventures for production in the export market's language rather than unaltered American films, a parallel to format sales in television discussed below. In 2012 Universal Pictures produced or made commitments to produce in local languages in Russia, Mexico, Brazil, Spain, France, and Germany. This is a minor part of their overall production, less than ten films per year, but nevertheless represents major studio interest in reaching international markets with something other than American blockbusters.[36]

US television networks too are tailoring productions for global sales. In 2011, Fox, HBO, Showtime, and Starz each sought foreign locations, international casts and storylines, and wide distribution for lavish mini series, and Universal invested in making local language films. In 2017, distinctly American television comedies such as *Grace and Frankie* included closing cast credits in several languages, suggesting an intent to export. In another defensive move, Time-Warner tendered an offer for the Dutch television producer, Endemol, whose reality show formats have been hugely successful world-wide. Twentieth Century Fox and an American private equity firm ultimately took it over in 2014.[37]

Asian and even Western European tv production companies are also eager to be in Hollywood itself. They visit and set up offices there and pursue joint ventures with Hollywood studios. To accommodate this increased production, Disney, NBC Universal, and Paramount are each expanding or upgrading their production facilities and offices in Los Angeles.[38]

Symbolic of all this internationality in film production, Hollywood's trade voice, *Variety*, published a special section of its 2014 June #4 issue that celebrated the fifteenth anniversary of the state-owned China Film Group Corporation (CFGC), the backbone of China's film industry. The section included full-page ads by Paramount, Warner Brothers, and MGM, among others, each congratulating CFGC. Since CFGC is China's sole company licensed to import films, it is the gatekeeper to the enormous Chinese market for Hollywood and everyone else. CFGC also invested in productions with Sony, Dreamworks, and Universal, the last being produced at its new production facility at Huairou, outside Beijing.[39]

International distribution is still confronted with the problem of adapting to local cultures. A variety of cosmetic changes have been tried, such as substituting local product names and images for the originals. But a more effective method of cultural adaptation for television series has been to sell the show's concept, called the format, rather than the final film product, allowing local producers to create the local product. The sale sometimes include consulting services by producers of the original show to aid in producing a new version tailored to the other country. This was done for a few US and British

Hybridity

television shows decades ago. As other nations began to build and operate national broadcasting systems, the increased demand for programs created a market for television show export. The American company Goodson-Todman Productions exported their game show formats in the 1950s. American companies too occasionally imported formats, such as Norman Lear's 1970s adaptations of two British sitcoms into very successful American sitcoms *All in the Family* and *Sanford and Son*.[40]

However, until the 1990s, format franchise sales were incidental. What distinguishes circumstances today is the regularity and success with which formats have been franchised to be remade in many other nations. Game and reality shows, in particular, have been planned from their inception as franchises to be sold internationally. *Big Brother*, one of the earliest and most successful reality shows, was created in 1999 by Endemol for Dutch television. The format was quickly adapted for numerous countries around the world. The British show *Pop Idol* also was replicated with similar success.[41]

Moreover, an entire network of organizations and conventions have arisen to foster deals, enabled by new technologies and by deregulation and privatization of television that eased importation and increased demand for programs. The result is a dense network of participants and products with deals across a complex of many nations and products flowing in many directions.

The increasing complexity of flow directions is illustrated by the Columbian telenovela *Yo soy Betty, la fea* (*Ugly Betty*). The original, produced in 2000, was a great success in Columbia, and quickly exported to other South American countries, including Venezuela, Ecuador, Bolivia, Chile, and Argentina. Next it was sold as dubbed or subtitled versions to southern and eastern European nations, Japan, and the Philippines. Then the format was re-produced in several other nations and languages. An English-language version was produced in the US and shown in the US, Canada, the UK, Hong Kong, and Australia. Another version produced in Germany was exported to several other European nations where German was spoken. Other remakes appeared in the Netherlands, Greece, Turkey, Russia, and India. Finally, Mexico remade the original and began another cycle of export and franchising.[42]

Regardless of where film products are made, who finances them and who produces them, film production is becoming a world product, woven together with parts from multiple contributors world-wide and sold globally. It is now a misnomer to describe globalized media as unidirectional, hegemonic cultural flow from center to periphery. Cultural product flows are multi-directional. They compete not only

Multi-Directional

economically, but also linguistically and culturally, as audiences consume them in a varied diet suited to their own tastes, needs, and identities.[43]

Still, geography is felt by producers and audiences, who identify themselves with a particular nation, culture, and language. They encode into or decode from media content according to these identities. Thus, while globalization and media flows are transnational and transcultural, nevertheless, crossing cultural boundaries requires not only translation but re-contextualizing from the culture of origin to the culture of consumption. The success of media export depends upon it. Recognizing the necessity to attune products to local customs is not new to today's film and television purveyors. David Jamilly, an early itinerant film exhibitor in the Far East, wrote presciently in 1909 that:

> The principal reason why the Europeans generally fail is the fact that they are utterly ignorant of [local] customs and tastes. The British showman's first move is, naturally, to exploit the larger towns where there are numbers of white residents, but in a very short time he has exhausted these, and armed with the same films and the same methods he sets out to entertain the purely native population … the films which have attained popularity for him among the Europeans will instantly doom him to dismal failure when exhibited to the native.

The same theme was echoed in a 1963 column of *Broadcasting* in which a Singapore television producer stated "what is good [programming] for the US is not necessarily good for Asia."[44] The lesson in these two comments is that film and television producers and distributors must know the cultural context of their audiences in order to successfully export their products, or in economic terms to recognize that there is no global market, only local markets to which producers must adapt their products.

The dual conclusions that films and tv shows can successfully cross cultural boundaries, but must do so by adapting to the culture of import, remind us that people find these imported media products "both indispensable and inadequate in helping us to think through various life practices."[45] They are both foreign and familiar: familiar genres with familiar personal issues, but sometimes foreign in their challenging local cultural values, as we will see below.

Local Audiences: Nollywood

To illustrate the creation of a local film product and screen industry attuned to its audience's culture, we will look more closely at the people of Nigeria and their use of media in the new millennium. By

2015, Nigeria, with 200 million people, was the most populous nation in Africa and the seventh largest in the world. It is oil rich, yet much of the population is poor. Despite the poverty, surveys claim high media saturation rates.[46]

Nigeria provides a distinctive case of films produced exclusively on videotape and dvd and exhibition via television sets rather than at cinemas, in which small-scale, local producers are personally familiar with their audiences and their circumstances.[47] Western film imports, limited by language or regional appeal, had not succeeded in the middle-class urban cinema market, and Western-controlled film distribution choked off income for indigenous vernacular films in that same market. Religious restrictions and recurring violence through the 1990s and 2000s, particularly in the more urbanized South, stunted cinema's growth too. In the absence of a corporate film industry and distribution system, video viewed in domestic circumstances displaced cinema exhibition. By the 2000s video was among the biggest indigenous industries in Nigeria. A Gallup study in 2003 concluded that two thirds of urban homes in Nigeria had a video player, while Nigerian broadcast tv offered only old imported movies.[48]

Entry into the video business was comparatively cheap and potential profits enticing. One very successful video-maker described the financial incentive, "A film that cost 3 million Naira (about $25,000) to make on Monday can earn you 10 million by Friday." In 2006, 1,600 feature-length videos were produced. Video producers were enterprising amateurs often acting as scriptwriter, producer, director, cameraman, and even actor, not unlike the artisanal period in early Western film history. Production took three to five days, shot in streets and homes and edited in back yards. Videos were sold by hawkers in local market stalls.[49]

Nollywood grew as part of an informal economy, wholly undocumented – no contracts, no insurance, no copyrights, no government regulation nor corporate control. Film-store owners, profiting from pirated copies of American and Indian films, were some of the first to bankroll production and distribute the films through their networks. This discouraged large-scale corporate investment and takeover, and sustained small video-makers. At the same time it enabled pirating of their videos too. So a film could become very popular, yet the producer received very little of the profit.[50] Piracy was accelerated by digital technology where the film master is a computer file, easily copied and distributed via the internet. Still producers could benefit from sales before news of its popularity led to piracy.

Fast local production and delivery kept Nigerian videos "closer to the public than televised production or African cinema." As with other small businesses, this video industry involved a collaborative relationship between film-makers and their audiences. Film-makers were familiar with local circumstance, people and culture, and filmed content responsive to and expressive of that local culture, quickly incorporating current local events and issues familiar to viewers. While well-educated people, with broader horizons beyond the local, initially shunned the videos as amateurish, these videos appealed to the lower-income masses in cities and villages.[51]

Video-makers tailored videos to particular groups, for north and south, in different languages, for Muslims or not, and stylistically serene or tense. Half of all Nigerian videos are in English, a third in Yoruba, and a sixth Hausa. Southern videos are fast-paced and more violent, reflecting coups and dictators, the Biafran war, oil, religious fanaticism, and general corruption endemic to that region. Hausa films from northern Nigeria, where Sharia law was established in 2000, have a slower, more contemplative pace.[52]

By the mid 1990s rural northern Hausa could choose between Hausa or Yoruba videos, Indian, Hong Kong or American films, or videos of local preachers. Indian films had been very popular, primarily for their cultural resonance to Hausa culture and their reflecting post-colonial tension that Nigerians were experiencing too: between traditional morals and arranged marriage on the one hand and rapid change, sex and romance, and Western ideas on the other. Especially older Indian films depicted rural and poorer characters, in which dress and music were not dissimilar to rural northern Nigeria. More recently, Hausa imitations of Bollywood masala films displaced the Indian originals. Watching videos in a domestic environment was also compatible with Hausa culture. While cinema had been a male public space, with television and video, film viewing moved to the female space of home and the domestic sphere, providing larger audiences and greater market demand.[53]

Nollywood's informal structure also typifies its international distribution to other African nations and to African diaspora in the US and Europe. By the 2000s Nigerian videos were delivered via satellite television to Anglophone Ghana, Kenya, Zambia, and South Africa. Nollywood videos were appealing, due to their cultural resonance and their representation of similar problems and conflicts as faced by audiences in other nations.[54]

In South Africa and Namibia many small outlets offered Nigerian videos for sale and rent. The videos offered an 'Afro-modernity' to well-to-do, young urban people, blending African culture and modern consumption. The videos evoked 'a reified African culture' set in villages, with characters that projected what young viewers consider realistic, in contrast to what they considered propagandistic American films glorifying the US. American television soap operas that were popular in the 1990s went out of favor. Instead they preferred decade-old South African soaps made to promote nation-building.[55]

Beyond Africa, Nigerian videos were sold and rented through small independent neighborhood video stores to African diaspora in the US, Britain, and Italy. African emigrants brought with them the taste for these videos and some saw an opportunity to retail videos. Efforts to establish a Nigerian film culture in cinemas for diaspora audiences in the destination nations tended to appeal to a higher class, continuing an old gulf between film auteur culture in Nigeria and the video culture serving lower classes.[56]

In Turin Italy in 2008–2009, recent low-income Nigerian immigrants found Italian beliefs and habits "strange, incomprehensible, and arbitrary" and contradictory to the Nigerians' own culture. They turned to Nollywood videos in English and set in Nigeria, often with a Pentecostal theme that sudden wealth from evil ways would bring ruin unless they were saved by religious faith. They watched in cramped rooms alone or with a small group of family or friends, rather than in community groups as in Nigeria. Like other diaspora, they used the videos "to measure themselves" against familiar Nigerian standards, to "cope with feelings of disorientation in a foreign society," and "reassess their own history and identity."[57]

Glocal: Same but Different

Anthropologists have emphasized the uniqueness of every culture and translators and semiologists have cited the 'untranslatable' qualities of languages. On the other hand, global cultural commerce seems to defy cultural barriers by succeeding at selling products across cultures. In Chapter 4 we saw that American westerns and serial films were popular in Africa and other places. As noted in Chapter 6, Latin telenovelas have demonstrated a remarkable cross-cultural portability, reaching a hundred countries in fifty languages.[58] How can we resolve this apparent contradiction between multiple peoples with differing cultures consuming the same globally distributed media? Why and how do people of diverse cultures find satisfying a cultural product from another culture beyond its mere exoticism and novelty?

Some approaches to explaining cross-cultural successes emphasize similarities of cultures, such as the 'cultural proximity' not only of the genre, but also of values expressed in media products. Another long-standing explanation concentrates on purported universal myths and archetypes rooted in human psychology or a shared human genetic component and captured in the film or tv genre. A middle path between these two proposes that international success depends on an un-specified 'denationalized or universalized' form.[59]

However, all these explanations implicitly assume a determinant product and a passive audience. I suggest instead that cross-cultural appeal depends less on production than on how audiences find a use of the show for their own practical everyday purposes.[60] To begin, we should bear in mind that the co-presence of global and local cultures is merely an enlarged case of two cultures co-existing, with people engaging in both. For example, decades of cultural studies, feminist studies and various ethnic/racial studies have documented audiences appropriating bits of dominant cultures for their own sub-cultural expression.

As to practicalities, living in groups, whether a few dozen or hundreds of millions, people inevitably must deal with and resolve problems within relationships. Both films and tv shows are largely about relationships. Even action films involve relationships between good guys and bad guys. We can understand attractions to an imported genre or particular show in terms of cross-national commonalities of situations and relationships that present problems as a regular part of everyday social interaction, and that require social skills to negotiate and to resolve. For example, women around the world express consistently that watching domestic drama serials about family and intimate relations is useful for understanding and dealing with relationships in their own lives. Men seem to gain vicarious release from watching the justified vengeance in films that they frustratingly must suppress in their real lives.

These are matters of simple practicality that are integral to social interaction in all societies and in part may explain the cross-cultural appeal of certain genres and formats. Various scholars have addressed the matter along these lines. For example, Sami Zubaida cites instrumentality as the instigating motive at the core of cultural appropriation, when one group imports an artifact or idea from another culture and adapts it to fit their own purposes.[61] Cultural appropriation and instrumentality are concepts that concentrate on the end user or audience.

This sounds a bit like the uses and gratifications approach to audiences, which tends to focus on psychological explanations for active audience behaviors of individuals.[62] But it transcends individuals, since applications from films occurs within situations and relationships that are collectively defined and encoded in cultural norms, values, and beliefs. So their practicality and use have to fit with that culture. Even pleasure, rest, and relaxation need to be fitted into the social situation. For example, the common habit of audience members discussing a reality show allows them to collectively explore consensus on distinctions between morally acceptable and unacceptable participant behaviors. Simply sharing the experience helps to bond members of a group. In many societies, people watch television in groups, either as families or more extended community groups, which spawn discussions among them, as discussed in Chapters 5 and 6.[63]

The similarities cross-culturally reveals a problem with thinking only in terms of identity and neglecting status. Focusing on identity we are led to expect that different identities based in different cultures contribute to different experiences of the same screen representation. This leaves the reasons for similarity remaining mysterious. On the other hand, focusing on status and social structure, the response transcends the individual. The reasons are situational rather than psychological. The common thread to similar responses cross-culturally is simply their practicality for cross-culturally similar situations and social interactions. Statuses holding less power and offering fewer opportunities and smaller rewards, regardless of what society or culture, will present the individual with similar practical problems and solutions for that position.

At the same time, similar situations and relationships in different societies may differ in particulars, due to their different cultures. What is the practical application of a telenovela in a Muslim village, for example, may be different from the use of the same show in a secular city. In each case women viewers may use the telenovela to 'make do,' in Michel de Certeau's sense, within the constraints of norms and values specific to that group.

Practicality may explain the cross-national popularity of various genre. People of widely different cultures have become fans of reality shows, featuring people allegedly behaving as themselves, not performing a scripted story. Fans gossip about the participants in reality shows, just as people in many cultures have long gossiped about their neighbors.[64] Sports spectating also has appeal cross culturally. Telecasts of World Cup contests in football/soccer and in Olympics competitions, draw very large and enthusiastic audiences in many nations. Sports spectators – still mostly men – tend to be emotionally identified with the game's participants, not unlike soap opera fans. Sports viewers too sometimes claim that they gain some lessons applicable to their own lives, and sports metaphors applied to other areas of life abound.[65]

It appears that cross-culturally there is an attraction to contests, whether sports or reality shows, where the outcome is not yet known and identification with one contestant is promoted. Uncertainty of outcome offers suspense and promise of success. Partisanship offers membership in an imagined community much larger than any face-to face-group and often geographically identified. Also, as with format adaptations of reality shows and drama serials, separate broadcasts, commentary, and channels of audience participation in each nation allows for adaptation of interpretation of the international contest tailored to specific national audiences.[66] Perhaps the underlying appeal is that sports and reality shows mimic contests in everyday life – between individuals, families, villages, companies – but without the risk faced in everyday life.

Thorn Birds

Notes

Introduction: A Screen Culture History

1 Graeme Turner and Jinna Tay, eds., *Television Studies After TV* (Routledge 2009).

2 Also see Lila Abu-Lughod, *Dramas of Nationhood* (University of Chicago Press 2005), p. 35; Vivian Sobchack, "The scene of the screen: Envisioning cinematic and electronic 'presence,'" in *Materialities of Communication*, eds., Hans Ulrich Gumbrecht and K. Ludwig Pfeiffer (Stanford UniversityPress), pp. 83–106. Anna Kaun and Karin Fast, "Mediatization of culture and everyday life," *Karlstad University Studies*, 13 (2014).

3 Roger Chartier *Forms and Meanings: Texts, Performances, and Audiences from Codex to Computer* (University of Pennsylvania Press 1995); W. J. T. Mitchell, *Iconology: Image, Text, Ideology* (University of Chicago Press 1986), pp. 119–121, quote p. 3. Re film see J. R. Taylor, *Cinema Eye, Cinema Ear: Some Key Film-Makers of the Sixties* (Hill and Wang 1964). Gabriel Egan, "Hearing or seeing a play: Evidence of early modern theatrical terminology," *Ben Jonson Journal*, 8 (2001): 327–347, p. 332; Jenny Sager, *The Aesthetics of Spectacle in Early Modern Drama and Modern Cinema* (Palgrave 2013), ch. 1; Herbert Blau, "The audition of dream and events," *The Drama Review*, 31(3) (1987): 59–73 on Johnson; Mitchell, *Iconology*, 121–123 on Locke.

4 Jonas Barish, *The Anti-Theatrical Prejudice* (University of California Press 1981); H. Diehl, *Staging Reform, Reforming the Stage: Protestantism and Popular Theater in Early Modern England* (Cornell University Press 1997); Fiona Price, "'Myself creating what I saw': The morality of the spectator in eighteenth-century Gothic," *Gothic Studies*, 8(2) (2006): 1–17.

5 Charles Lamb, "On the tragedies of Shakespeare, considered with reference to their fitness for stage representation," in *The Works of Charles*

and Mary Lamb (1811); Sager, *Aesthetics of Spectacle*, p. 25 n. 14 on Coleridge, n. 16 on other critics. Neil Postman, *Amusing Ourselves to Death* (Methuen 1987).

6 Norman Bryson, Michael Ann Holly, and Keith Moxey, eds., *Visual Culture: Images and Interpretations* (Wesleyan University Press 1994); Theo van Leeuwne and Carey Jewitt, eds., *Handbook of Visual Analysis* (Sage 2001).

7 Raymond Williams, *Keywords* (Oxford University Press 1976), p. 76; Stuart Hall, ed., *Representations* (Open University Press 1997), p. 3. For useful reflections on culture, symbol, and media see Michael Schudson, "How culture works," *Theory and Society*, 18 (1989): 153–180.

8 My conception of culture is based upon concepts of symbolic interaction and social constructivism. See, e.g. Herbert Blumer, *Symbolic Interaction: Perspective and Method* (Prentice Hall 1969); Erving Goffman, *Presentation of Self in Everyday Life* (Doubleday 1959); and Peter Berger and Thomas Luckmann, *The Social Construction of Reality* (Anchor 1967).

9 On culture, nations, and diaspora see John Sinclair and Cunningham, "Go with the flow: diasporas and media," *Television and New Media*, 1(1) (2000): 11–31, esp. pp. 16–18.

10 Zygmunt Bauman, *Culture in a Liquid Modern World* (Polity 2011), p. 1; Tak Wing Chan and John H. Goldthorpe, "The social stratification of cultural consumption: Some policy implications of a research project," *Cultural Trends*, 16(4) (2007): 373–384. Through the book, we will discuss class, gender, nationality, and race in terms of cultural differences.

11 Abu-Lughod, *Dramas of Nationhood*, p. 44.

12 On the links of culture with social structure, see e.g. Raymond Williams, *Marxism and Literature* (Oxford University Press 1977), and *Sociology of Culture* (Schocken 1982); Pierre Bourdieu, *Distinction*, trans. Richard Nice (Harvard University Press 1984); Arjun Appadurai, *Modernity At Large* (University of Minnesota Press 1996), p. 5.

13 Cultural geographers use the term "place"; sociologists use the term "situation." To my knowledge, the two have not been used together as I will do in this book, unless to conflate the two. The distinctions I make are not equivalent to the geographers' two terms "place" and "space." Neither space nor place are situation. Geographers use the term space to point to an objectivist abstraction, and the term place for the socially constructed features of a particular location. On place see John A. Agnew, "Space and place," in Agnew and David N. Livingstone, eds., *Handbook of Geographical Knowledge* (Sage 2011), pp. 316–330; Doreen Massey, *For Space* (Sage 2005). On situation see Blumer, *Symbolic Interaction* and Goffman, *Presentation of Self*.

14 Capitalism transformed rural agriculture in concert with creating urban industry. See David Lockwood, *The Indian Bourgeoisie: A Political History of the Indian Capitalist Class in the Early Twentieth Century* (I. B. Tauris, 2012) on India, and Raymond Williams, *The Country and the City* (Oxford University Press 1973) on England. On "rhetorical contrasts" between "traditional" country and modern city, see Williams,

Country and City, pp. 1–2, 12, 35, 46, 48, 50–51, and differently by different classes pp. 37–39, 40–43.

15 Today, cities too afford little privacy, but due to surveillance rather than peer pressure. See Ch 7.

16 On romanticization of tradition and old rural life in England, see Williams, *Country and City* (Oxford 1973). On individual differences see Joseph Henrich, Steven J. Heine, Ara Norenzayan, "The weirdest people in the world?" *Behavioral and Brain Sciences*, 33 (2010): 61–135.

17 Charles Preston, *The $64,000 Answer* (Berkley Publishing 1955); Steven Pettinga, ed., *The Best Cartoons from The Saturday Evening Post* (Harper Collins 1993); and various collections of *New Yorker* cartoons.

18 E.g. Ernesto Laclau, "Feudalism and capitalism in Latin America," *New Left Review*, 1(67) (May–June 1971); A. Haroon Akram-Lodhi and Cristóbal Kay, eds., *Peasants and Globalization: Political Economy, Agrarian Transformation and the Agrarian Question* (Routledge 2009); John Sender and Sheila Smith, *The Development of Capitalism in Africa* (Routledge 2013); Robert Brenner, "Agrarian class structure and economic development in pre-industrial Europe," *Past & Present*, 70 (February 1976): 30–75. The debates are reviewed in Kaylan Sanyal, *Rethinking Capitalist Development* (Routledge 2007) and Trevor Henry Aston and C. H. E. Philpin, *The Brenner Debate: Agrarian Class Structure and Economic Development in Pre-Industrial Europe* (Cambridge University Press 1985).

19 Harry Braverman, *Labor and Monopoly Capital* (Monthly Review Press 1974), esp. p. 276.

20 Butsch, "The commodification of leisure: The case of the model airplane hobby and industry," *Qualitative Sociology*, 7(3) (Fall 1984): 217–235; and Tim Patterson, "Notes on the historical application of Marxist cultural theory," *Science & Society* (1975): 257–291; for other examples see Eliot Wiggington, ed., *The Fox Fire Book* (Anchor Books 1972).

21 On unique properties of media products that influence global markets, see Colin Hoskins, Stuart McFadyen and Adam Smith, *Global Television and Film: An Introduction to the Economics of the Business* (Oxford University Press 1997), pp. 3–4, 31–33

22 On feminized shopping districts see William Leach, *Land of Desire: Merchants, Power, and the Rise of a New American Culture* (Vintage 1993); Erika D. Rapaport, *Shopping for Pleasure: Women in the Making of London's West End* (Princeton University Press, 2000); Michael B. Miller, *The Bon Marché: Bourgeois Culture and the Department Store, 1869–1920* (Princeton University Press 1981).

23 On the rise of cultures of consumption see Grant McCracken, *Culture and Consumption: New Approaches to the Symbolic Character of Consumer Goods and Activities* (Indiana University Press 1988); Neil McKendrick, John Brewer, and John Harold Plumb, *The Birth of a Consumer Society: The Commercialization of Eighteenth-Century England* (Indiana University Press, 1982); Colin Campbell, *The Romantic Ethic and the Spirit of Modern Consumerism* (Blackwell 1987).

24 On class representations in films see Steven Ross, *Working Class Hollywood* (Princeton University Press 1998). On product placement see Jane Gaines, "The Queen Christina tie-ups: Convergence of show window and screen," *Quarterly Review of Film and Video*, 11 (1989): 35–60; on movie palaces see Doug Gomery, *Shared Pleasures* (University of Wisconsin Press 1992).

25 Philip E. Converse and John P. Robinson, *Americans' Use of Time: 1965–1966* (Inter-University Consortium for Political and Social Research, 1980); Butsch, *The Making of American Audiences* (Cambridge University Press 2000), Appendix; *Nielsen Video 360 2017 Report* (The Nielsen Company 2017).

26 Zygmunt Bauman, *Culture in a Liquid Modern World*, trans. Laura Bauman (Polity 2011), p. 14.

27 Stanley Cohen, *Folk Devils and Moral Panics* (Routledge 2011); Howard Becker, *Outsiders: Studies in the Sociology of Deviance* (Free Press 1963).

28 For histories of media panics see Carolyn Marvin, *When Old Technologies Were New* (Oxford University Press 1988); James Gilbert, *A Cycle of Outrage* (Oxford 1986); Kristin Drotner, "Modernity and Media Panics," in Skovmand, Michael and Schroeder, Kim. *Media Cultures: Reappraising Transnational Media* (Routledge, 1992), pp. 42–62.

29 Jerry H. Bentley, *Old World Encounters: Cross Cultural Contacts and Exchanges in Pre-Modern Times* (Oxford University Press 1993) is a readable introduction. See also Anthony G. Hopkins, ed., *Globalization in World History* (W. W. Norton 2002); Barry K. Gills and William R. Thompson, eds., *Globalization and Global History* (Routledge 2006).

30 Eric Hobsbawm, *The Age of Empire* (Pantheon 1987); Immanuel Wallerstein *The Modern World System I* (Academic Press 1974). Throughout the book, I extend the term colonialism to include places such as Latin America and China, where Europeans and the US did not directly rule, but nevertheless maintained such hegemony over native governments that these societies were effectively colonized.

31 On independence movements see Chris Chase-Dunn, "Globalization from below," *Annals*, 581 (2002): 48–61; G. Teeple, *Globalization and the Decline of Social Reform* (Humanities Press 1995), p. 57. On multinationals see Samir Amin, *Capitalism in the Age of Globalization* (Zed Books 1997).

32 Anthony Sampson, *Seven Sisters: The Great Oil Companies and the World They Shaped* (Viking 1975); Francisco Parra, *Oil Politics: A Modern History of Petroleum* (I. B. Tauris, 2005).

33 Perry Anderson, *Lineages of the Absolutist State* (Routledge 1974); Eric Hobsbawm and D. Bourn, "Feudalism, capitalism and the absolutist state," *Our History*, 66 (1976); Benedict Anderson, *Imagined Communities: Reflections on the Origin and Spread of Nationalism* (Verso 1983); Eric Hobsbawm and Terrence Ranger, *Invention of Tradition* (Cambridge University Press 1992); John Breuilly, ed., *The Oxford Handbook of the History of Nationalism* (Oxford University Press 2013).

34   David Boswell and Jessica Evans, eds., *Representing the Nation: A Reader,*
      Histories Heritage and Museums (Open University 1999), quote p. 63;
      Sabina Mehelj, *Media Nation* (Palgrave 2011).
35   Michael Bommes and Patrick Wright, "'Charms of residence': The public
      and the past," in R Johnson, G. McLennan, Bill Schwarz, and David
      Sutton, eds., *Making Histories* (Hutchinson 1982), pp. 253–301; Kirk
      Savage, *Standing Soldiers, Kneeling Slaves* (Princeton University Press
      1997).
36   M. Bailey, "Rethinking public service broadcasting," in Butsch, *Media*
      and Public Spheres (Palgrave 2007), pp. 96–108; Andrew Higson, *Waving*
      the Flag (Clarendon Press 1997).
37   Inga Brandell, ed., *State Frontiers: Borders and Boundaries in the Middle*
      East (I. B. Tauris 2006); Andreas Wimmer, "Who owns the state? Under-
      standing ethnic conflict in post-colonial societies," *Nations and Nation-*
      alism 3(4) (December 1997): 631–666.
38   Partha Chatterjee, *Nationalist Thought and the Colonial World* (Zed
      Books 1986), quote, p. 38; Dipesh Chakrabarty, *Provincialising Europe*
      (Princeton University Press 2008), quote, p. 4. Also, Partha Chatterjee,
      The Nation and its Fragments: Colonial and Post-Colonial Histories
      (Princeton University Press 1993); Sheldon Pollock, "Crisis in the clas-
      sics," *Social Research*, 78(1) (Spring 2011): 21–48; Albert Memmi, *The*
      Colonizer and the Colonized, trans. Howard Greenfield (Orion Press
      1965).
39   Georg Stauth and Sami Zubaida, *Mass Culture Popular Culture and*
      Social Life in Middle East (Westview Press 1987), pp. 13–14, 171.
40   Edward Said, *Orientalism* (Vintage Books 1979). On de-Westernizing
      media studies see James Curran J. and M. J. Park, eds., *De-Westernizing*
      Media Studies (Routledge 2000); S. F. Alatas *Alternative Discourse in*
      Asian Social Science (Sage 2006); Georgette Wang, *De-Westernizing*
      Communication Research (Routledge 2011).
41   Nels Johnson, "Mass culture and Islamic populism," in Stauth and
      Zubaida, *Mass Culture*, pp. 165–187; also Stuart Corbridge and John
      Harriss, *Reinventing India: Liberalization, Hindu Nationalism and*
      Popular Democracy (Polity 2000); Richard Robison, ed., *The Neo-*
      Liberal Revolution: Forging the Market State (Palgrave 2006).
42   Said, *Orientalism*, pp. 4–7, 21.
43   E.g. Walter W. Rostow, *The Stages of Economic Growth* (Cambridge
      University Press 1960); Daniel Lerner, *The Passing of Traditional Society*
      Modernizing the Middle East (Free Press 1958). For a recent critique
      se Paul Hopper, *Understanding Development* (Polity 2012), ch. 1.
44   On the distinction between traditional and modern, see Andre Gunder
      Frank, "The development of underdevelopment," *Monthly Review*, 28(4)
      (September 1966): 17–31. On Western values and development theory
      see Andrea Cornwall and Ann Whitehead, eds., *Feminisms in Develop-*
      ment: Contradictions, Contestations and Challenges (Zed Books, 2007);
      Ralph D. Grillo and R. L. Stirrat, *Discourses of Development: Anthro-*
      pological Perspectives (Berg 1997). The divide between traditional and

modern is not clear cut, but interwoven. For example, while in many ways a peasant and even feudal society, the Indian subcontinent in the seventeenth and eighteenth centuries also had a substantial manufacturing and international trade economy based in handicraft production. In any society, dominant, residual and emergent forms co-exist. Society is a process, not a leap between one static form and another, and the sources of change are likely to be multiple and complex rather than singular and simple. On India see B. R. Tomlinson, "Introduction," *New Cambridge History of India, III* (Cambridge University Press 1993), pp. 1–29, 92.

45 William Mazzarella, "'Reality must improve': The perversity of expertise and the belatedness of Indian development television," *Global Media and Communication*, 8(3) (2012): 215–241, quote p. 219.

46 David McClelland, *The Achieving Society* (Free Press 1961); Alex Inkeles and Daniel Levinson, *National Character: A Psycho-Social Perspective* (Transaction Books 1997).

47 Steven Vertovec and Robin Cohen, "Introduction," *Conceiving Cosmopolitanism* (Oxford University Press 2002), pp. 7–14.

48 Indonesia (250 million) is so diverse in languages and dispersed across distant islands that it is effectively divided into numerous small markets. See Pankaj Mishra, "The places in between: The struggle to define Indonesia," *New Yorker*, August 4, 2014, 64–69. Also, Gerald M. Macdonald, "Third cinema and the Third World," in Stuart C. Aitken and Leo Zonn, eds., *Place, Power, Situation, and Spectacle: A Geography of Film* (Rowman and Littlefield 1994), pp. 26–45.

1   American Cinema to World War I

1 American families spent an average of $11 per year in 1917–1919 on reading materials, the earliest data available. That would be 220 admissions to a nickelodeon or about one visit per week for a family of four. Daily newspaper subscriptions in 1904 were 19 million and periodical subscriptions 17 million, each roughly one per household. See US Department of Commerce Bureau of the Census, *Historical Statistics of the United States* Part 1 (US Government Printing Office 1976).

2 Robert and Helen Merrill Lynd, *Middletown: A Study on Modern American Culture* (Harcourt Brace 1929), pp. 225–312, quote from p. 263; and *Middletown in Transition: A Study in Cultural Conflict* (Harcourt Brace 1937), pp. 242–294.

3 Daniel Cavicchi, *Listening and Longing: Music Lovers in the Age of Barnum* (Wesleyan University 2011); Sicherman, Barbara, *Well-Read Lives: How Books Inspired a Generation of American Women* (University of North Carolina Press 2010); David Paul Nord, "Working-class readers: Family, community, and reading in late nineteenth-century America," *Communication Research* 13(2) (1986), pp. 156–181.

4   Lynd, *MIddletown*, quote 263. Radio was still new; only 12% business-class and 6% working-class homes of Middletown had one in 1924.

5   E.g. Kathryn Fuller, *At the Picture Show* (Smithsonian Institution Press 1996); Gregory Waller, *Main Street Amusements* (Smithsonian 1995); Butsch, "The imagined audience in the nickelodeon era," in Cynthia Lucia, Roy Grundmann, and Art Simon, eds., *Blackwell's History of American Film*, vol. 1 (Blackwell Publishing 2012), pp. 109–129.

6   Christopher W. Wells, "The changing nature of country roads: Farmers, reformers, and the shifting uses of rural space, 1880–1905," *Agricultural History*, 80(2) (2006): 143–166; Howard Lawrence Preston, *Dirt Roads to Dixie: Accessibility and Modernization in the South, 1885–1935* (University of Tennessee Press 1991). On self-entertainment see folklore chronicles by Cecil Sharp, Alan Lomax and Charles Seeger; also Maud Karpeles, *Cecil Sharp: His Life and Work* (Faber and Faber 2012), chs. 12–13.

7   Mary Gabrielle Esteve, "Of being numerous: representations of crowds and anonymity in late nineteenth and early twentieth-century urban America" (PhD, University of Washington 1995). For example, compare Sherwood Anderson's *Winesburg Ohio* (1919) to Theodore Dreiser's *Sister Carrie* (1900). In the 1970s, psychologists were still pursuing the effects of population density. See Stanley Milgram, "The experience of living in cities," *Science*, 167 (March 13, 1970): 1461–1468; Jonathan L. Freedman, S. Heshka, and A. Levy "Population density and pathology: is there a relationship?" *Journal of Experimental Social Psychology*, 11(6) (1975): 539–552.

8   E.g. Ben Singer, *Melodrama and Modernity: Early Sensational Cinema and its Contexts* (Columbia University Press, 2001). On modernity, see Daniel Biltereyst, Richard Maltby, and Philippe Meers, *Cinema Audiences and Modernity: New Perspectives on European Cinema History* (Routledge 2011), quote p. 3; Jack Goody, *Capitalism and Modernity: The Great Debate* (Polity 2004); Ellen Meiksins Wood, "Modernity, post modernity or capitalism?" *Review of International Political Economy*, 4(3) (1997): 539–560.

9   Olivier Zunz, *The Changing Face of Inequality: Urbanization, Industrial Development, and Immigrants in Detroit 1880–1920* (University of Chicago Press 1982), quote p 1.

10 Campbell J. Gibson and Emily Lennon, "Historical census statistics on the foreign-born population of the United States: 1850–1990," Population Division Working Paper no. 29, Table 14. at http://www.census.gov/population/www/documentation/twps0029/tab02.html.

11 M. Craig Brown and Barbara D. Warner, "Immigrants, Urban Politics, and Policing in 1900," *American Sociological Review*, 57(3) (June 1992): 293–305; Paul Boyer, *Urban Masses and Moral Order in America, 1880–1920* (Harvard University Press 1978); Joseph Gusfield *Symbolic Crusade: Status Politics and the American Temperance Movement* (University of Illinois Press 1963; Moya Luckett, *Cinema and Community:*

Progressivism, Exhibition, and Film Culture in Chicago, 1907–1917
(Wayne State University Press 2013).

12 Leon Kamin, *The Science and Politics of IQ* (Lawrence Erlbaum Associates 1974); Nicole Raftner, *White Trash: The Eugenic Family Studies,
1877–1919* (Northeastern University Press 1988); Donald K. Pickens,
Eugenics and the Progressives (Vanderbilt University Press, 1968); Thomas
C. Leonard, *Illiberal Reformers: Race, Eugenics, and American Economics in the Progressive Era* (Princeton University Press 2016).

13 Charles Musser *The Emergence of Cinema: The American Screen to
1907* (University of California Press 1990), part 2; David Bordwell,
Janet Staiger, and Kristin Thompson *The Classical Hollywood Cinema:
Film Style and Mode of Production to 1960* (Routledge 1985), p. 110;
Robert C. Allen *Vaudeville and Film, 1895–1915: A Study in Media
Interaction* (Arno Press 1978).

14 On novelty see Daniel Berlyne (1950), "Novelty and curiosity as deter-
minants of exploratory behaviour," *British Journal of Psychology General
Section*, 41(1950): 68–80; Charles Spielberger and Laura Starr, "Curiosity
and exploratory behaviour," in Harold F. O'Neil and Michael Drillings,
eds., *Motivation: Theory and Research* (Lawrence Erlbaum 2009), pp.
221–244.

15 A debate soon ensued in *MPW* about suitability of drama and novels
for film. See Butsch, "Imagined audience," pp. 109–129.

16 Lewis Palmer, "The world in motion," *Survey*, June 5, 1909, quote p.
356. Such histories include, e.g. Roy Rosenzweig, *Eight Hours for what
We Will: Workers and Leisure in an Industrial City, 1870–1920* (Cambridge University Press 1983); Frank Couvares *The Remaking of Pittsburgh: Class and Culture in an Industrializing City 1877–1919* (SUNY
Press 1984); Kathy Peiss, *Cheap Amusements* (Temple University Press
1986).

17 John Corbin, "How the other half laughs," *Harper's New Monthly
Magazine*, 98 (1898): 30–48, p. 36; Carl Van Vecten, "A night with
Farfariello," *Theatre Magazine* (January 29, 1919): 32; Channing Pollock,
The Footlights Fore and Aft (Gorham Press 1911), pp. 378–93; Judith
Thissen, "Early cinema and public sphere," in Marta Braun, *Beyond
Screen* (Indiana University Press 2010), ch. 35; Butsch, *American Audi-
ences*, pp. 129–135.

18 Ray Oldenburg, *The Great Good Place* (DaCapo Press 1989); Jane
Jacobs, *The Death and Life of Great American Cities* (Vintage Press
1961); Paul Zucker, *Town and Square: From the Agora to the Village
Green* (Columbia University Press 1959).

19 Robert Putnam, *Bowling Alone: The Collapse and Revival of American
Community* (Simon and Schuster 2001); James DeFilippis, "The myth
of social capital in community development," *Housing Policy Debate*,
12(4) (2001): 781–806; Samuel Bowles and Herbert Gintis, "Social
capital and community governance," *The Economic Journal*, 112 (November 2002): F419–F436.

20 John Reps, *The Making of Urban America: A History of City Planning in the United States* (Princeton University Press 1965); Robert DeForest and Lawrence Veiller, eds., *The Tenement House Problem* (MacMillan 1903); Roy Lubove, *The Progressives and the Slums: Tenement House Reform in New York City, 1890–1917* (University of Pittsburgh Press 1963); Dominick Cavallo, *Muscles and Morals: Organized Playgrounds and Urban Reform, 1880–1920* (Philadelphia, Temple University Press 1981).

21 Quote in Corbin, "How the other half laughs." On urban immigrant working-class neighborhoods see Olivier Zunz, *The Changing Face of Inequality: Urbanization, Industrial Development, and Immigrants in Detroit, 1880–1920* (University of Chicago Press 1982), chs. 6, 7, 10.

22 Even in the later era of Hollywood classical film style, working-class movie-going seemed to be less about the films themselves than the practice of going, the event, and the place. See Chapter 3.

23 The phrase "spell-bound in darkness" implies a link to hypnosis and suggestion as made by Hugo Munsterburg, *The Photoplay: A Psychological Study* (D. Appleton 1916).

24 Butsch, *American Audiences*, pp. 130–135.

25 Joseph Medill Patterson, "The nickelodeons: The poor man's elementary course in the drama," *Saturday Evening Post* (November 23, 1907): 10–11, 38, quote from p. 10. Early film historians Benjamin Hampton, Lewis Jacobs, and Ramsay reinforced the singular focus on working-class immigrant nickelodeons as the only significant audiences. This was revived in the late 1960s and 1970s by American historians creating a new working-class history. By the late 1970s some film historians began to investigate other sites of early film exhibition, to complete the picture.

26 Nickelodeons in small cities had to appeal to almost all classes and groups in order to stay in business. They were, however, often race-segregated, excluding African Americans, or confining them to the balcony.

27 Butsch, *American Audiences*, chs. 3–9.

28 Mary Ryan, *Women in Public* (Johns Hopkins University Press 1992); John Kasson, *Rudeness and Civility* (Hill and Wang 1990).

29 Cavallo, *Muscles and Morals*; Sara Sullivan, "Child audiences in America's nickelodeons, 1900–1915," *Historical Journal of Film, Radio and Television* (hereafter *HJFRT*), 30(2) (June 2010), 155–168.

30 Butsch, *The Citizen Audience: Crowds, Publics and Individuals* (Routledge 2008), pp. 42–44; Lee Grieveson, *Policing Cinema* (University of California Press 2004); Moya Luckett, *Cinema and Community*; Biltereyst et al., *Cinema, Audiences*, pp. 26–27.

31 This section summarizes Butsch, "Imagined audience." Quote from *Moving Picture World (MPW)* "The Influence of the Pictures," December 5, 1908, 446.

32 Transition to feature-length narrative films occurred from the mid 1900s to the mid 1910s. See Musser, *Emergence*, part 4.

33 *MPW*, "Editorial: Fall outlook," September 3, 1910, 507; Sargent, Epes Winthrop, "The Triumph and the Trivial," *MPW*, September 9, 1911, 689; Stephen W. Bush, "Higher prices are possible," *MPW*, December 14, 1912: 1058. On theaters in middle-class neighborhoods see Musser, *Emergence*, part 4; Douglas Gomery "The movie palace comes to America's cities," in Butsch, *For Fun and Profit* (Temple University Press 1990), pp. 136–151.

34 Robert Grau, "A disastrous theatrical season," *MPW*, March 4, 1911, 465; *Billboard*, December 26, 1925, 7; Alfred Bernheim, *The Business of the Theatre: An Economic History of American Theatre, 1750–1932* (Benjamin Blom 1932), p. 75; n.a. "Straight picture policy," *Variety*, January 10, 1913, 11; n.a. "Pictures in summer for Shubert houses," *Variety*, December 26, 1913, 1; n.a. "Feature films turned down," *Variety*, October 17, 1913, 12; n.a. "Proctor leaving," *Variety*, March 20, 1914, 5.

35 On media message and persuasion see Carl Hovland, *Communication and Persuasion* (Yale University Press 1953); Hadley Cantril and Gordon Alport, *Psychology of Radio* (Harper and Bros. 1935).

36 Lary May, *Screening Out the Past* (University of Chicago Press 1980).

37 Staiger in Bordwell et al., *Classical Hollywood Cinema*, Part 2.

38 Steven J. Ross, *Working-Class Hollywood* (Princeton University Press 1999). Also see Steven J. Ross, "Beyond the screen: history, class and the movies," in David James and Rick Berg, eds., *Hidden Foundation: Cinema and the Question of Class* 1996, pp. 45–50.

39 Quote in Ross, *Working-Class Hollywood*, p. 50. Films about labor-capital conflicts, that sympathetically represented strikes, unions and socialism, were more threatening. These often were produced by unions and other non-profit groups, and sometimes by producers and directors who felt strongly about these issues. See Ross, "Beyond the screen," pp. 36–38, 40, 44.

40 Nan Enstad, *Ladies of Labor, Girls of Adventure: Working Women, Popular Culture, and Labor Politics at the Turn of the Twentieth Century* (Columbia University Press 1999); Shelley Stamp, *Movie-Struck Girls: Women and Motion Picture Culture After the Nickelodeon* (Princeton University Press 2000); Jane S. Smith, "Plucky little ladies and stout hearted chums," *Prospects*, 3 (October 1978): 155–174; Diana Anselmo-Sequeira. "Screen-struck: The invention of the movie girl fan," *Cinema Journal*, 55(1) (Fall 2015): 1–28.

41 These adventurous heroines had a precedent in dime novels and sensation melodramas of the post-civil war era. See Bruce McConachie, *Melodramatic Formations* (University of Iowa Press 1992), ch. 7.

42 While Enstad presumes that young working women identified with these working heroines, Shelly Stamp (p. 229 n. 106) argues that these characters were uniformly from wealthy families and that the wealthy origins likely stunted the identification.

43 Enstad, *Ladies of Labor*; Peiss, *Cheap Amusements*.

2   Global Cinema, 1900–1920

1 Gerben Bakker, "The decline and fall of the European film industry: sunk costs, market size, and market structure, 1890–1927," *Economic History Review*, 58(2) (May 2005): 310–351; Kristin Thompson, "The rise and fall of Film Europe," in Andrew Higson and Richard Maltby, eds., *"Film Europe" and "Film America"* (University of Exeter Press 1998), pp. 56–81.

2 Richard Butsch "The imagined audience in the nickelodeon era," in Cynthia Lucia, Roy Grundmann, and Art Simon, eds., *Blackwell's History of American Film*, vol. 1 (Blackwell Publishing 2012), pp. 109–129.

3 Giuliana Bruno, *Streetwalking on a Ruined Map* (Princeton University Press 1993), parts I, II, and III chapter 8; Ivo Blum, "Italy," in Richard Abel, ed., *Encyclopedia of Early Cinema* (Routledge 2005); Giorgio Bertellini, ed., *Italian Silent Cinema: A Reader* (John Libbey & Company Limited, 2013).

4 Butsch, *The Making of American Audiences* (Cambridge University Press 2000), p. 45.

5 Paul Bairoch, "International industrialization levels from 1750 to 1980," *Journal of European Economic History*, 11(1) and (2) (Fall 1982): 269–333.

6 Charles Feinstein, "What really happened to real wages? Trends in wages, prices and productivity in the United Kingdom 1880–1913," *Economic History Review*, n.s. 43(3) (August 1990): 329–355; Marghanita Laski, "Domestic Life," and W. Bridges-Adams, "Theatre," both in Simon Nowell-Smith ed., *Edwardian England 1901–1914* (Oxford University Press 1964); John Callaghan, "The Edwardian Crisis: The survival of Liberal England and the rise of a Labour identity," *Historical Studies in Industrial Relations*, 33 (2012): 1–23; Magali Gente, "Family ideology and the Charity Organization Society in Great Britain during the First World War" *Journal of Family History*, 27(3) (July 2002): 255–272.

7 On British popular culture see John M. MacKenzie, *Imperialism and Popular Culture* (Manchester University Press 1986); Luke McKernan, "Diverting time: London's cinemas and their audiences, 1906–1914," *The London Journal*, 32(2) (2007): 125–144; Asa Briggs, *Mass Entertainment: Origins of a Modern Industry* (Griffin Press 1960), p. 9; David B. Grigg, *Population Growth and Agrarian Change: An Historical Perspective* (Cambridge University Press 1980), p. 254 table 62; Michael Haines, "Industrial workers and family life cycle, 1889–1890," *Research in Economic History*, 4 (1979): 289–356; Peter Bailey, *Popular Culture and Performance in the Victorian City* (Cambridge University Press 1998); Patrick Joyce, *Visions of the People: Industrial England and the Question of Class, 1848–1914* (Cambridge University Press 1993).

8 Eugen Weber, *Peasants into Frenchmen: The Modernization of Rural France, 1870–1914* (Stanford University Press 1976), quote p. 10; Bonnie G. Smith, *Ladies of the Leisure Class: The Bourgeoisie of Northern*

France in the 19th Century (Princeton University Press 1981). On transportation, see Frank Schipper, *Driving Europe: Building Europe on Roads in the Twentieth Century* (Aksant 2008), p. 18; Philippe Reine, *Trafic automobile et réseau routier: Les autoroutes en Italie, en Allemagne et en France* (Editions A. Pedone 1944); Paul Wohl and A. Albitreccia, *Road and Rail in Forty Countries: Report Prepared for the International Chamber of Commerce* (London: Milford 1935). On artisanal production see Philip Nord, *Paris Shopkeepers and the Politics of Resentment* (Princeton University Press 1986); on welfare, Philip Nord, "The Welfare State in France 1870–1914" *French Historical Studies*, 18(3) (Spring 1994): 821–838.

9 Charles Rearick, *Pleasures of the Belle Époque: Entertainment and Festivity in Turn-of-the-Century France* (Yale University Press 1985); Leonard R. Berlanstein *The Working People of Paris, 1871–1914* (Johns Hopkins University 1984), p. 49; Michael B. Miller, *The Bon Marché: Bourgeois Culture and the Department Store, 1869–1920* (Princeton University Press 1981); Eugen Weber, *France, Fin de Siècle* (Harvard University Press, 1986), quote p. 52; Jean-Marie Mayeur and Madeleine Reberioux, *The Third Republic from its Origins to the Great War, 1871–1914*, trans J. R. Foster (Cambridge UniversityPress 1984), pp. 116–122.

10 Weber, *France, Fin de Siècle*, ch. 3; Lindsay Harris, "Photography of the 'primitive' in Italy: Perceptions of the peasantry at the turn of the twentieth century," *Journal of Modern Italian Studies*, 17(3) (2012): 310–330; Douglas Holmes, "A peasant-worker model in a northern Italian context," *American Ethnologist*, 10(4) (November1983): 734–748; Frank Snowden, *Violence and the Great Estates in the South of Italy: Apulia, 1900–1922* (Cambridge University Press 1986); Gian Piero Brunetta, *The History of Italian Cinema: A Guide to Italian Film from its Origins to the Twenty-First Century*, trans. Jeremy Parzen (Princeton University Press 2009).

11 Comparison between Belgium and Netherlands may offer further insight. See Clara Pafort-Overduin, "Distribution and exhibition in the Netherlands," in Richard Maltby, Daniel Biltereyst, and Philippe Meers, eds., *Explorations in New Cinema History* (Wiley-Blackwell 2011), pp. 125–139.

12 Gerben Bakker, *Entertainment Industrialized* (Cambridge University Press 2008), ch. 4. The survey by Carroll D. Wright, Commissioner of the US Bureau of Labor, included the US, Britain, France, Germany, Belgium, and Switzerland. See also Michael Haines, "Industrial workers," pp. 289–356; Berlanstein, *Working People of Paris*, pp. 122–37.

13 Bakker, *Entertainment Industrialized*, p. 121; also Butsch, *American Audiences*, Appendix.

14 Bakker "The European film industry in the United States," in Michael Pokorny and John Sedgwick, eds., *An Economic History of Film* (Routledge 2005), 24–47, Pathé quote p. 37.

15 Ruth Low and Roger Manvell, *History of the British Film, 1896–1906* (BFI 1948), ch. 1.

16   Bakker, *European Film Industry*; Richard Abel, *The Red Rooster Scare: Making Cinema American, 1900–1910* (1999), pp. 52–53, 57; Richard Abel, *The Ciné Goes to Town: French Cinema, 1896–1914* (University of California Press 1998); Jon Silver (2009) "Explaining Pathé's global dominance in the pre-Hollywood film industry," in Terry Flew et al., eds., *Communication, Creativity and Global Citizenship: Refereed Proceedings of the Australian and New Zealand Communication Association Conference*, 2009.

17   On Italy's film industry see: Brunetta, *History of Italian Cinema*; Angela Dalle Vacche, *The Body in the Mirror: Shapes of History in Italian Cinema* (Princeton University Press 2014); Aldo Bernardini, "An Industry in Recession: The Italian Film Industry 1908–1909," *Film History*, 3 (1989): 341–368; G. Bruno, *Streetwalking on a Ruined Map*, p. 14 on regional films.

18   As the most populous Western European nation, Germany represented an important potential film market, but developed more slowly and unevenly. Growth was limited by its affordability for urban working class and agrarian workers, even as wages rose. See Joseph Garncarz, "Origins of film exhibition in Germany," in Tim Berfelder, Erica Carter, and Deniz Gokturk, eds., *The German Cinema Book* (BFI 2002), pp. 112–20; Marc Silberman, "What is German in the German Cinema?" *Film History*, 8 (1996): 297–315; Uli Jung. "Local views: A blind spot in the historiography of early German cinema," *Historical Journal of Film Radio and Television (HJFRT)*, 22(3) (2002): 253–273; Annemone Ligensa, "Urban legend: early cinema, modernization and urbanization in Germany, 1895–1914," in Daniel Biltereyst, Richard Maltby, and Philippe Meers, eds., *Cinema, Audiences and Modernity: New Perspectives on European Cinema History* (Routledge 2012), pp. 117–129.

19   Bakker, "Decline and fall," pp. 312–313, fig. 1, 322, 337–342; Gerben Bakker, *Entertainment Industrialised. The Emergence of the International Film Industry, 1890–1940* (Cambridge University Press 2008), p. 9 fig. 1; p. 12 fig. 2; John Trumpbour, *Selling Hollywood to the World: US and European Struggles for Mastery of the Global Film Industry, 1920–1950* (Cambridge University Press, 200), p. 2, ch. 9; Jens Ulff-Moller, *Hollywood's Film Wars with France* (2001).

20   Bakker, "Decline and fall," pp. 326, 337–342; Jonathan Derek Silver, "Hollywood's dominance of the movie industry: How did it arise and how has it been maintained?" (PhD, Queensland University of Technology 2007) at http://eprints.qut.edu.au/16687/; on government protections see Trumpbour, *Selling Hollywood*; "Protest film 'invasion,'" *NYT*, July 16, 1919, 12; Editorial, "The British protest," *NYT*, August 17, 1919, 35.

21   George MacAdam, "Our new art for export" *NYT*, April 13, 1924, SM2. Non-Western film markets did not figure significantly in this shift, being less than 10% of the world market at the time (Bakker "Decline and fall," 316).

22 Bakker, "European film industry." Sunk costs includes cost of making and sales promotions of films, which do not change with the size of a market, whether a million or a billion people. Fixed cost are studio complexes and distribution networks not attached to specific films. See X. Henry Wang and Bill Z. Yang, "Fixed and sunk costs revisited," *The Journal of Economic Education*, 32(2) (Spring, 2001): 178–185. No matter the size of the market, the number of films needed per year depends on how much screen time must be filled. Alan Wood, *Mr Rank: A Study of J. Arthur Rank and British Films* (Hodder and Stoughton, 1952), p. 48.

23 On Sweden: Asa Jernudd, "Reform and entertainment: Film exhibition and leisure in a small town in Sweden at the end of the nineteenth century," *Film History*, 17 (2005): 88–105; Tor Larsson and Per Svenson, "Cultural policy in Sweden," *Journal of Arts Management, Law, & Society*, 31(1) (Spring 2001): 79–96; Jernudd, "Spaces of early film exhibition in Sweden, 1897–1911," in Biltereyst et al., *Cinema, Audiences*, pp. 19–34; Pelle Snickars and Mats Björkin, "Early Swedish (Non-fiction) cinema and cartography," *HJFRT*, 22(3) (2002): 275–290; Ulf Jonas Bjorka, "The backbone of our business": American films in Sweden, 1910–50," *HJFRT*, 15(2) (1995): 245–263.

Similarly for Spain, with a population of 18 million in 1910, film also was either imported or derivative copies of foreign films. See Joan M. Minguet Batllori, "Early Spanish cinema and the problem of modernity," *Film History*, 16(1) (2004): 92–107. Even in Germany before the war, American film serials were popular. See Marina Dahlquist, ed., *Exporting Perilous Pauline: Pearl White and the Serial Film Craze* (University of Illinois Press 2013). Large respectable cinemas screened several serial episodes together as a feature. American serials succeeded in France and Netherlands too. See Rudmer Canjels, *Distributing Silent Film Serials* (Routledge 2011).

24 On diffusion see Nigel Meadea and Towhidul Islam, "Modelling and forecasting the diffusion of innovation – A 25-year review," *International Journal of Forecasting*, 22(3) (2006): 519–545; C. Anthony Di Benedetto, "Diffusion," in V. K. Narayanan and Gina Colarelli O'Connor, eds., *Encyclopedia of Technology and Innovation Management* (Wiley-Blackwell 2010), pp. 113–117.

25 In large German cities, storefront *Ladenkinos* were quickly supplanted by *Kino-theater* and *Kinopalaste*. See Garncarz, "Origins of film exhibition"; Ligensa, "Urban legend." Budapest had a well-developed night life of cabarets, theaters, orpheums and coffee houses, where film was introduced as a novelty. But Hungary was primarily agricultural. As late as 1928 only 10% of settlements had a movie theater. Anna Manchin, "Imagining modern Hungary through film," in Biltereyst et al., *Cinema, Audiences*, pp. 64–80. Italian cinema also began as part of traveling shows, in the long tradition of *commedia della arte* and traveling carnivals. Brunetta (*History of Italian Cinema*, pp. 17–20) and Bernardini (*Industry in Recession*, p. 341) differ on claims about makeshift

nickelodeons and working class patronage. In the Netherlands exhibition began with travelling showmen, but by 1908 still only seven permanent venues appeared. By comparison, Hamburg Germany had 40 permanent cinemas, and Brussels almost 50. See Andre van der Velden and Judith Thissen, "Spectacles of conspicuous consumption," *Film History*, 22(4) (2010): 453–462.

26 American and British historians produced a large literature in the 1980s on the rise of cultures of consumption. E.g. Colin Campbell, *The Romantic Ethic and the Spirit of Modern Consumerism* (Blackwell 1987); Richard Wightman Fox and T. J. Jackson Lears, eds., *The Culture of Consumption* (Pantheon 1983); Grant McCracken, *Culture and Consumption* (Indiana University Press 1988); Richard Butsch, ed., *For Fun and Profit* (Temple University Press 1990).

27 E.g. Venessa Toulmin, "'Local films for local people': Travelling showmen and the commissioning and the commissioning of local films in Great Britain, 1900–1902." *Film History*, 13 (2001): 118–137, and Toulmin, "Cuckoo in the nest: Edwardian itinerant exhibition practices and the transition to cinema in the United Kingdom from 1901 to 1906," *Moving Image*, 10(1) (Spring 2010): 51–79; Eyles, "Exhibition and the cinemagoing experience," in Robert Murphy, *The British Cinema Book* (BFI 2009), pp. 78–84; McKernan "Diverting time"; Low and Manvell, *History of British Film*, ch. 4.

28 David Mayall, "Palaces for entertainment and instruction: A study of the early cinema in Birmingham, 1908–1918," *Midland History*, 10 (January 1985): 94–109.

29 Mayall, "Palaces for entertainment," quotes pp. 97, 98; Robert Roberts, *A Ragged Schooling* (Manchester University Press 1976), pp. 61–62.

30 Roberta Pearson, "Transitional cinema," in Geoffrey Nowell-Smith ed., *Oxford History of World Cinema* (Oxford UniversityPress 1996), pp. 23–42.

31 Nicholas Hiley, "'Nothing more than a craze': Cinema building in Britain 1909–1914," in Andrew Higson, ed., *Young and Innocent? The Cinema in Britain 1896–1930* (Exeter University Press 2002), pp. 111–127, quote p. 114; Mayal, "Palaces," p. 96

32 Hiley, "'Nothing more'." Half of all venues were non-commercial churches, schools, missions, workhouses.

33 Jon Burrows and Richard Brown, "Financing the Edwardian cinema boom, 1909–1914," *HJFRT*, 30(1) (March 2010): 1–20; Michael Hammond "Letters to America: exhibition and reception of American films in Britain," in Higson, *Young and Innocent*, pp. 128–43.

34 Jonathan Silver, "The first global entertainment company: Explaining Pathé's dominance in the pre-Hollywood film industry," *Continuum: Journal of Media & Cultural Studies*, 24(6) (2010): 877–895. Edison also probably drained capital from film companies with his patent battles.

35 Rearick, *Pleasures of the Belle Epoque*; W. Scott Haine, *The World of the Paris Café: Sociability among the French Working Class, 1789–1914* (Johns Hopkins University Press 1996).

36 Abel, *Cine*, pp. 15–17; Rearick, *Pleasures of the Belle Epoque*, pp. 189–190, 193. Méliès situated his fixed camera at the eye level of a bourgeois "gentleman in the stalls" at these boulevard theaters, thus framing his films through the eyes of that class. See Frank Kessler, "The gentleman in the stalls: Georges Méliès and spectatorship in early cinema," in Ian Christie, *Audiences: Defining and Researching Screen Entertainment* (OAPEN 2012), pp. 35–44.

37 Jean-Jacque Meusy, *Paris Palaces: Ou le temps de cinémas 1894–1918* (CRNS Editions 1995). Seeking a higher-class clientele coincided with a shift from industrial to an artisan/auteur mode of production. The term "cinephile" arose about 1910. See Annie Fee, "Gender, class and cinephilia: Parisian cinema cultures, 1918–1925" (PhD, University of Washington 2015).

38 McKernan, "Diverting time"; Hammond, "Letters to America," pp. 139, 140.

39 Peter Bailey "Conspiracies of meaning: Music-hall and the knowingness of popular culture," *Past & Present*, 144 (August 1994): 138–170; Patrick Joyce, *Visions of the People* (Cambridge University Press 1991), ch. 13; Michael Young and Peter Wilmott, *Family and Kinship in East London* (Routledge 1957); Herbert Gans, *Urban Villagers* (Free Press 1962).

40 As an example, middle-class German women had their own style of audiencing, conversing about the latest fashions displayed in the audience as well as in the film. Some men objected that their talking disrupted their follow the film story. See Andrea Haller, "Diagnosis: flimmeritis, female filmgoing in Imperial Germany, 1911–1918," in Bilтereyst et al., *Cinema, Audiences*, pp. 130–141. Similarly, mid-century American "art cinemas" tended to an upper-middle-class, quasi-intellectual clientele.

41 McKernan, "Diverting time," pp. 136–138; Hammond, "Letters to America," p. 133.

42 Hammond, "Letters to America"; McKernan, "Diverting time," p. 136.

43 Miriam Hansen, *Babel and Babylon: Spectatorship in American Silent Film* (Harvard University Press 1991); Judith Thissen, "Early cinema and the public sphere," in Marta Braun, ed., *Beyond the Screen: Institutions, Networks and Publics of Early Cinema* (John Libbey 2012), pp. 297–306.

44 Meusy, *Paris Palaces*, p. 361; Fee, "Gender, class and cinephilia," pp. 28, 31 ch. 2, pp. 68, 72, 118–120, 128, 136–138, Le Film quote pp. 13–14.

45 Fee, "Gender, class," pp. 104–105, 137.

46 Eugen Weber, *France, Fin de Siècle*.

47 Daniël Biltereyst and Roel Vande Winkel, eds., *Silencing Cinema: Film Censorship Around the World* (Springer 2013.).

48 Gareth Stedman Jones, *Outcast London: A Study in the Relationship Between Classes in Victorian Society* (Oxford University Press 1971); Peter Bailey, "Conspiracies of meaning: music-hall and the knowingness of popular culture," *Past & Present*, 144 (1994): 138–170; Dean Rapp,

"Sex in the cinema: War, moral panic, and the British film industry, 1906–1918," *Albion: A Quarterly Journal Concerned with British Studies*, 34(3) (Autumn 2002): 422–451, quote p. 425. On elite reactions to media in Britain see D. L. LeMahieu, *Culture for Democracy* (Clarendon Press 1988), part 2; Andrew Higson, *Waving the Flag: Constructing a National Cinema in Britain* (Clarendon Press 1997); Jonathan Rose, *Edwardian Temperament: 1895–1919* (Ohio University Press 1986).

49　Dean Rapp, "Sex in the cinema" (2002); James C. Robertson, *The British Board of Film Censors: Film Censorship in Britain, 1896–1950* (Croom Helm 1985); National Council of Public Morals Cinema Commission Inquiry, *The Cinema: Its Present Position and Future Possibilities* (London: Williams and Norgate, 1917), quote p. 4; Audrey Field, *Picture Palace: A Social History of the Cinema* (Gentry Books 1974), pp. 25–29, 37–40.

50　Emmanuel Plasseraud, *L'art des Foules: Théories de la réception filmique comme phénomène collectif en France 1908–1930* (Presses Universitaires du Septrentrion 2011); Abel, *Cine*, p. 42.

51　Quotes from Fee "Gender, class," pp. 2–3. This was not entirely negative: Delluc and others sometimes approved of American films and working-class cinemas in the late 1910s and early 1920s.

52　Quotes in Bernardini, "Industry in recession," pp. 350, 341; Butsch "Imagined audiences." The first film venue in Naples was a shed; the second opened in a plush shopping arcade in the city center. See Giuliana Bruno, *Streetwalking on a Ruined Map*, p. 59.

53　Quote in Bernadini, "Industry in recession," p. 355, on religions films p 356.

54　Jernudd, "Spaces of film exhibition," p. 23; Jernudd, "Reform and entertainment: film exhibition and leisure in a small town in Sweden at the end of the nineteenth century," *Film History*, 17 (2005): 88–105; Manchin, "Imagining modern Hungary," pp. 64–80.

55　Bakker, "Decline and fall," p. 316; Trumpbour, *Selling Hollywood*, p. 5.

56　Musser, *Emergence*, p. 488; Richard Abel, "In the belly of the monster," *Film History*, 5 (1993): 363–385; Richard Abel, "Booming the film business: The historical specificity of early French cinema," *BCS* (1990): 79–94; Butsch, *American Audiences* on recurring marketing strategy in the US from minstrelsy to movies.

57　E.g. Zhang Zhen, *Amorous History of the Silver Screen: Shanghai Cinema, 1896–1937* (University of Chicago Press, 2005); Manishita Dass, "The crowd outside the lettered city: Imagining the mass audience in 1920s India," *Cinema Journal*, 48(4) (Summer 2009): 77–98; V. Shafik, *Popular Egyptian Cinema: Gender, Class and Nation* (Cairo University Press 2007); Scot Barmé, "Early Thai cinema and filmmaking: 1897–1922," *Film History*, 11(3) (1999): 308–318.

58　Ana Lopez, "Early cinema in Latin American," *Cinema Journal*, 40(1) (Autumn 2000): 48–78; John King, *Magical Reels: A History of Cinema in Latin America* (Verso 1990, 2000), pp. 10–15.

59 John K. Fairbank and Merle Goldman, *China: A New History, Second Enlarged Edition* (Harvard University Press 2006). Recent sweeping plans, such as moving 250 million peasants in one decade from rural villages to industrial cities (Ian Johnson, "Chinese hit pitfalls pushing millions off farm," *NYT*, 7.14.2013, A1), are not new for China, but a reflection of this past.

60 Fairbank, *China: A New History*, ch. 9; R. Bin Wong, *China Transformed: Historical Change and the Limits of European Experience* (Cornell University Press 1997); Hanchao Lu, *Beyond the Neon Lights: Everyday Shanghai in the Early Twentieth Century* (University of California Press 1999); Wen-Hsin Yeh, *Shanghai Splendor; Economic Sentiments and the Making of Modern China, 1843–1949* (University of California Press, 2007); Kathy Le Mons Walker, *Chinese Modernity and the Peasant Path: Semi-Colonialism in the Northern Yangzi Delta* (Stanford University Press 1999). In 1920, foreigners controlled all of China's iron ore and pig iron, 90% of the railways, three fourths of the coal. In some ways, the semi-colonial status in China presaged the twentieth century multi-national corporation hegemony that supplanted colonial empires, as it paralleled the unequal trade agreements that opened the doors for Western corporations in the latter system (Walker, *Chinese Modernity*, pp. 13–14).

61 Lu, *Beyond the Neon Lights*, 1999, p. 59. On the shift from patronage to purchase in Europe see Raymond Williams, *Culture* (Fontana 1981).

62 Quote in Lu, *Beyond the Neon Lights*, p. 13.

63 Zhen, *Amorous History*, pp. 44–52, 94–100.

64 Zhen, *Amorous History*, pp. 50–60; 94–96, quote p. 65; C. J. North, "The Chinese motion picture market," Trade Information Bulletin no. 467, US Department of Commerce 1927, pp. 14, 28. Distinctions between tea house, amusement hall, and theater are unclear in the histories consulted.

65 Zhen, *Amorous History*, pp. 68, 95.

66 C. J. North, "The Chinese motion picture market" describes some of these films; Paul Pickowicz, "Melodramatic representation and the 'May Fourth' tradition of Chinese cinema," in Ellen Widmer and Dewei Wang, eds., *From May Fourth to June Fourth: Fiction and Film in Twentieth-Century China* (Harvard University Press 1993), pp. 295–325.

67 Marie-Claire Bergère, "The Chinese bourgeoisie, 1911–1937," in John King Fairbank, ed., *The Cambridge History of China*, vol. 12: *Republican China 1912–1949*, Part One (Cambridge University Press 1983), pp. 751ff. For population developments, see Liu Z. and Song J., *China's Population: Problems and Prospects* (New World Press, 1981), pp. 129–35; Walter L. Wilcox, "The Population of China in 1910," *Journal of the American Statistical Association*, 23(161) (March 1928): 18–30; http://www.stats.gov.cn/tjsj/Ndsj/2011/html/D0305e.htm. There is a broad historical and ethnographic literature on Chinese peasant poverty (see historiography in Walker, *Chinese Modernity*, Introduction).

68 C. J. North, "The Chinese motion picture market," quotes from pp. 1–2, 14. On peasant unfamiliarity with theater see Chang-tai Hung, *War and Popular Culture: Resistance in Modern China, 1937–1945* (University of California Press 1994), ch. 2.

69 This historical summary draws on David Lockwood, *The Indian Bourgeoisie: A Political History of the Indian Capitalist Class in the Early Twentieth Century* (I. B. Tauris 2012); Tirthankar Roy, "Economic History and Modern India: Redefining the Link," *Journal of Economic Perspectives* 16(3) (2002): 109–130; Barbara Metcalf, *A Concise History of Modern India*, Cambridge Concise Histories (Cambridge University Press 2006); B. R. Tomlinson, *The New Cambridge History of India, III: The Economy of Modern India, 1860–1970* (Cambridge University Press 1993).

70 On rail system see Lockwood, *Indian Bourgeoisie*, ch. 1. For a contrary conclusion on India, see Dave Donaldson, "Railroads of the Raj: Estimating the impact of transportation infrastructure," NBER Working Paper no. 16487, October 2010, pp. 7–8. A similar rail issue arose in Turkey. See Ch. 4.

71 Movements critical of the Raj also arose from the educated and elite who served British rule. See Lockwood, *The Indian Bourgeoisie*. On colonial rule's policies and impact on film in India see James Burns, *Cinema and Society in the British Empire 1895–1940* (Palgrave 2013).

72 Ashish Rajadhyaksha, "Indian cinema," in Nowell-Smith, *Oxford History of World Cinema*, p. 399; Haimanti Banarjee, "The silence of a throng: cinema in Calcutta 1896–1912," *New Quest*, 65 (September–October 1987): 261–272, 264. Watson's was located in the European section of Bombay that excluded Indians; the Novelty served prosperous Indians, in particular Persian Parsi business leaders, who would later finance Bollywood.

73 On wages see D. Bhattacharya, "Trend of wages in India, 1873–1900," *Artha Vijnana*, 7(3) (September 1965): 202–212; Tomlinson, *New Cambridge History of Modern India*, ch. 2. On poorer regions see Mike Davis, *Late Victorian Holocausts: El Nino Famines and the Making of the Third World* (Verso 1999); Dadabhai Naoroji, *Poverty and Un-British Rule in India* (Swann Sonnenschwein 1901).

74 Banerjee, "Silence of a throng," pp. 264–266; Anjali Roy, "Bhakti and Ashqi: The syncretic heritage of Hindi cinema," *Studies in South Asian Film and Media*, 2(1) (2010): 41–55; Stephen Hughes "House full: Silent film genre, exhibition and audiences in south India," *Indian Economic Social History Review*, 43 (2006): 31–62.

75 Quotes from Hughes, "House full," p. 56.

76 ... "dank" quote from Mihir Bose, *Bollywood: A History* (Tempus 2006), p. 52; Indian Committee quotes in Manishita Dass, "The crowd outside the lettered city: Imagining the mass audience in 1920s India," *Cinema Journal*, 48(4) (Summer 2009): 58–59, 78.

77 On import of US film see S. Hughes, "House full," p. 38; Miriam Sharma, "Censoring India: Cinema and the tentacles of Empire in the

early years," *South Asia Research*, 29(1) (February 2009): 41–73; Manishita Dass, *Outside the Lettered City: Cinema, Modernity, and the Public Sphere in Late Colonial India* (Oxford University Press 2015).

78 S. Hughes, "House full."
79 Quotes from Hughes, "House full," pp. 32, 45, 49.
80 Maurizio Cinquegrani, "Travel cinematography and the Indian city: The imperial spectacle of geography at the end of the long nineteenth century," *Nineteenth-Century Contexts*, 32(1) (March 2010): 65–78; Stephen Bottomore, "An amazing quarter mile of moving goals, Gems and genealogy: Filming India's 1902/03 Delhi Durbar", *HJFRT*, 15(4) (1995): 495–515; Annamaria Motrescu, "Imperial narratives displaced by Indian subaltern identities in early amateur films," *Early Popular Visual Culture*, 9(2) (May 2011): 107–121; on princely representation see Jürgen Habermas, *The Structural Transformation of the Public Sphere: An Inquiry into a Category of Bourgeois Society*, trans. Thomas Burger (MIT Press 1991), pp. 7–14; on later film and incipient nationalism see Priya Jaikumar, *Cinema at the End of Empire: A Politics of Transition in Britain and India* (Duke University Press 2006).

3   The Hollywood Studio Era, 1910s–1940s

1 W. Marston Seabury, *The Public and the Motion Picture Industry* (Macmillan 1926), quote on title page.
2 On the classic Hollywood system see David Bordwell, Janet Staiger, and Kristin Thompson, *The Classical Hollywood Cinema: Film Style and Mode of Production to 1960* (Columbia University Press 1985); Michael Storper, "The transition to flexible specialisation in the US film industry: External economies, the division of labour, and the crossing of industrial divides," *Cambridge Journal of Economics*, 13 (1989): 273–305.
3 John Ryan, *The Production of Culture in the Music Industry* (University Press of America 1985). Truffaut quote from "Sept hommes à débattre," *Cahiers du Cinéma* (December 1963–January 1964): 150–151.
4 The studies spurred no significant public discussion to regulate films. Newspapers provided brief bland reviews of the reports on their back pages.
5 Bordwell et al., *Classical Hollywood Cinema*, chs. 10, 11; on Griffith, Powell, and Sennett see Eileen Bowser, *The Transformation of Cinema, 1907–1915* (University of California Press 1990), p. 253 and Bordwell et al., *Classical Hollywood Cinema*, p. 121.
6 Richard V. Spencer, "Los Angeles as a producing center" *Moving Picture World (MPW)*, April 8, 1911, 768; Richard Koszarski, *An Evening's Entertainment* (University of California Press 1990), pp. 99–102.
7 Andrew Brodie Smith, *Shooting Cowboys and Indians* (University Press of Colorado, 2003). On Wild West shows see Joy Kasson, *Buffalo Bill's Wild West: Celebrity, Memory, and Popular History* (Hill and Wang,

2000); Richard Slotkin, *Gunfighter Nation: The Myth of the Frontier in Twentieth-Century America* (Antheneum 1992).

8 Smith, *Shooting Cowboys*, pp. 2–3. Westerns also were a leading American film export. See chs. 4, 6.

9 Mark Shiel, *Hollywood Cinema and the Real Los Angeles* (Reaktion Books 2012); Mike Davis, *City of Quartz: Excavating the Future in Los Angeles* (Pimlico 2006); quote from Ralph Hancock, *Fabulous Boulevard* (Funk and Wagnall 1949). On LA blooming in a desert see Mark Reisner, *Cadillac Desert* (Penguin Books 1993).

10 Bowser, *Transformation of Cinema*, ch. 13. Also see many articles in *Variety* and *MPW* in 1910–1911 about the patent war.

11 Bowser, *Transformation of Cinema*, pp. 224–227; Barry Langford and Douglas Gomery, "Studio genealogies: A Hollywood family tree," *Gannet Center Journal*, 3(3) (Summer 1989): 157–160; Bordwell et al., *Classical Hollywood Cinema*, pp. 401–403; Richard Koszarski, *An Evening's Entertainment*, ch. 3.

12 Gerben Bakker "The decline and fall of the European film industry: Sunk costs, market size, and market structure, 1890–1927," *Economic History Review*, 58(2) (May 2005): 336; Koszarski, *An Evening's Entertainment*, pp. 17, 21–6, 64.

13 Douglas Gomery, *Shared Pleasures* (University of Wisconsin Press 1992), quote p. 60. The FTC, TNEC, and US Department of Justice investigated the power of the major studios through much of their reign, from 1921 to the 1948 Paramount decree. See e.g. "Government sues film distributors," *NYT*, April 28, 1928, p. 4; "Will ask court order to stop block booking," *NYT*, May 15, 1928, p. 2. The Motion Picture Producer and Director Association (MPPDA) acted as a coordinator for the studios in matters from standards to export and standard contracts with independent exhibitors. In the 1990s, they reintegrated to become newly forming global multi-media companies discussed in Chapter 9.

14 Janet Staiger, "The Hollywood mode of production," in Bordwell et al., *Classical Hollywood Cinema*, Parts 2 and 5; Kristin Thompson, "Early alternatives to the Hollywood mode of production: Implications for Europe's avant-gardes," *Film History*, 5(4) (1993): 386–404; K. Mahar, "True womanhood in Hollywood," *Enterprise and Society*, 2(1) (2001): 72–110.

15 Kristin Thompson, "The formulation of the classical style," in Bordwell et al., *Classical Hollywood Cinema*, Part III. For a critique of *The Classical Hollywood Cinema* and responses see Barry King, "The classical Hollywood cinema," *Screen*, 27(6) (November–December 1986): 74–88, and, "The story continues," *Screen*, 28(3) (Summer 1987): 56–82. Responses in *Screen*, 29(1) (January 1988): Thompson, "Wisconsin project or King's projection?" pp. 48–53; Staiger, "Reading King's reading," pp. 54–70; Bordwell, "Adventures in the highlands of theory," pp. 72–97; and Barry King, "A reply to Bordwell, Staiger and Thompson," pp. 98–119. On Hollywood film style after 1960 see David Bordwell, *The Way Hollywood Tells It: Story and Style in Modern*

Movies (University of California Press 2006) and Kristin Thompson, *Storytelling in the New Hollywood: Understanding Classical Narrative Technique* (Harvard University Press 1999).

16 On style or form and content see Hayden White, *The Content of Form: Narrative Discourse and Historical Representation* (Johns Hopkins 1987). On distinction between style and form, see Seymour Chatman, *Story and Discourse: Narrative Structure in Fiction and Film* (Cornell University Press 1978), pp. 10–11. On narrative see Gérard Genette, *Narrative Discourse: An Essay in Method*, trans. Jane E. Lewin and Jonathan Culler (Cornell University Press, 1980; W. J. T. Mitchell, ed., *On Narrative* (University of Chicago Press 1981). On the point of view of the camera see Sue Thornham, *Feminist Film Theory: A Reader* (New York University Press 1999).

17 For details see Bordwell et al., *Classical Hollywood*.

18 Darkness, realism, theater policy, and sound contributed to silencing audiences; see Butsch *American Audiences* and "Movie audiences of the 1930s," *International Labor and Working Class History (ILWCH)*, 59 (Spring 2001): 106–120.

19 On immersion see Anthony Ferri, *Willing Suspension of Disbelief: Poetic Faith in Film* (Rowman and Littlefield 2007). On openness of text to varied interpretation see Bordwell, et al. and Richard Maltby, "A brief romantic interlude," in David Bordwell and Noël E. Carroll, eds., *Post Theory: Reconstructing Film Studies* (University of Wisconsin Press 1996), pp. 434–459; Stuart Hall, "Encoding, decoding," in Stuart Hall, Dorothy Hobson, Andrew Love, and Paul Willis, eds., *Culture, Media, Language* (Hutchinson 1980), pp. 128–138.

20 Quote from Bordwell et al., p. 16. For a similar analysis of the novel see Lucien Goldman *Towards a Sociology of the Novel* (Routledge, Chapman, & Hall, 1977). Richard Slotkin, *Gunfighter Nation: The Myth of the Frontier in Twentieth-century America* (MacMillan 1992).

21 On Americanizing immigrants see Butsch *The Citizen Audience*, p. 73; on exporting Americanism see Trumpbour, *Selling Hollywood*.

22 Quote from Bordwell et al., *Classical Hollywood Cinema*, p 24. For an overview and critique of subject positions and other aspects of viewer reception of film texts see Bordwell et al., pp. 37–41; Janet Staiger, *Perverse Spectators: The Practices of Film Reception* (New York University Press 2000); Christian Metz, *Film Language*, trans. Michael Taylor (Oxford University Press 1974). On stage performance see Marvin Carlson, *Performance: A Critical Introduction* (Routledge 1996).

23 Laura Mulvey, "Visual pleasure and narrative cinema," *Screen*, 16(3) (Autumn 1975): 6–18; Sue Thornham, ed., *Feminist Film Theory: A Reader* (New York University Press 1999); Stuart Hall, "Foucault: power, knowledge and discourse," in Margaret Wetherell, Stephanie Taylor, and Simeon J. Yates, eds., *Discourse Theory and Practice* (Sage 2001), pp. 72–81. On race and gender see Fatimah Tobing Rony, *The Third Eye: Race, Cinema, and Ethnographic Spectacle* (Duke University Press 1996); Aileen Moreton-Robinson, *Talkin' Up to the White Woman:*

Aboriginal Women and Feminism (University of Queensland Press 2000), ch. 5.

24 On external pressures see e.g. James Gilbert, *A Cycle of Outrage: America's Reaction to the Juvenile Delinquent in the 1950s* (Oxford University Press 1986); Richard Maltby, "The genesis of the production code," *Quarterly Review of Film and Video*, 15(4) (March 1995): 5–32; Francis Couvares, "Hollywood censorship and American culture," *American Quarterly* 44(4) (December 1992): 509–24. For a similar uniformity in post-war television see Chapter 5 and Butsch, "Why television sitcoms kept recreating white, male working-class buffoons for decades," in Gail Dines, Jean Humez, Bill and Lori Yousman, *Gender, Race and Class in Media*, 5th edn (Sage 2017), pp. 442–450.

25 Richard Maltyby "Sticks, hicks," in Melvin Stokes and Richard Maltby, eds., *Identifying Hollywood's Audiences: Cultural Identity and the Movies* (BFI 1999), quote on p. 24; on product placement see Kerry Segrave, *Product Placement in Hollywood Films: A History* (McFarland 2004). Butsch, "The imagined audience in the nickelodeon era," in Cynthia Lucia, Roy Grundmann, and Art Simon, eds., *Blackwell's History of American Film*, vol. 1 (Blackwell Publishing 2012), pp. 109–129.

26 Richard DeCordova, *Picture Personalities: The Emergence of the Star System in America* (University of Illinois Press 1990). A star system was well established before this in stage performances, thanks to P. T. Barnum and Charles Frohman, among others, who sold tickets by publicizing a specific performer. See Bruce McConachie, *Melodramatic Formations; American Theatre and Society, 1820–1870* (University of Iowa Press 1992).

27 On production codes see Richard Maltby, "The production code and the Hays Office," in Tino Balio, *Grand Design* (University of California Press 1993). The Hays office represented the interest of Hollywood at the expense of local independent exhibitors who tended to ally themselves with local reformers against Hollywood. See David Horowitz, "An alliance of convenience: independent exhibitors and purity crusades battle Hollywood, 1920–1940," *The Historian*, 59(3) (March 1997): 553–572.

28 On children at movie theaters see Richard DeCordova, "Ethnography and exhibition: The child audience, the Hays office and Saturday matinees," *Camera Obscura*, 8(2) (1990): 90–107; Guy Barefoot, "Who was that masked man?: Hollywood serial audiences in the 1930s," *HJFRT*, 31(2) (Summer 2011): 167–190; Jeffrey Klenotic, "Like nickels in a slot': Children of the American working classes at the neighborhood movie house," *Velvet Light Trap*, 48 (Fall 2001): 20–34.

29 Richard DeCordova, "Tracing the child audience: The case of Disney 1929–1933," in *Prima dei Codici 2: Alle Porte di Hays* (Venezia: Fabbri Editori 1991); Richard DeCordova, "The Mickey in Macy's window: childhood, consumerism, and Disney animation," in Eric Smoodin, ed. *Disney Discourse: Producing the Magic Kingdom* (Routledge 1994). William L. Bird *"Better Living": Advertising, Media and the New*

Vocabulary of Business Leadership, 1935–1955 (Northwestern University Press 1999) on consumer-citizens.

30 Lizabeth Cohen, *Making a New Deal: Industrial Workers in Chicago, 1919–1939* (Cambridge University Press 1990), p. 125 notes how vertical integration of distribution and exhibition stripped local and neighborhood houses of their local and class character.

31 On adhering to stereotypes see Joseph Turow, "Occupation and personality in television drama," *Communication Research*, 7(3) (1980): 295–318; Stuart Hall and Paddy Whannel, *The Popular Arts* (Pantheon Books 1965).

32 Jim Harmon and Donald Glut, *Great Movie Serials* (Doubleday 1972).

33 Donald Bogle, *Toms, Coons, Mulattoes, Mammies and Bucks: Blacks in American Films* (Continuum Books 1998); Terri Ginsberg, Chuck Kleinhans, and Dennis Broe, "Bibliography on class in film and media studies," *Jump Cut*, 47 (Winter 2005); Peter Roffman and Jim Purdy, *The Hollywood Social Problem Film* (Indiana University Press 1981); John Bodnar, *Blue Collar Hollywood* (Johns Hopkins University Press 2003); Peter Stead, *Film and the Working Class* (Routledge 1989); Tom Zaniello, *Working Stiffs, Union Maids* (ILR Press 2003). On the same observation about telenovela see Antonio La Pastina and Joseph Straubhaar, "Why do I feel I don't belong to the Brazil on TV?" *Popular Communication*, 12(2) (2014): 104–116; also see Ariel Dorfman and Armand Mattelart, *How to Read Donald Duck* (OR Books 2018).

34 Steve Ross, *Working Class Hollywood* (Princeton University Press 1999); Michael Shull, *Radicalism in American Silent Films* (McFarland 2000).

35 Lary May, *The Big Tomorrow: Hollywood and the Politics of the American Way* (University of Chicago Press 2000), quotes pp. 59, 274, 293.

36 Orson Welles summarized the sentiment of his film, *Citizen Kane*: "business plutocrats ... believed that money had automatically conferred stature to a man," in Lary May, *Big Tomorrow*, p. 56; Colin Shindler, *Hollywood in Crisis: Cinema and American Society, 1929–39* (Routledge 1996), ch. 5, quote p. 92.

37 Mark Glancy and John Sedgwick, "Cinema-going in the United States in the 1930s," in Richard Maltby, Melvin Stokes, and Robert C. Allen, eds., *Going to the Movies: Hollywood and the Social Experience of Cinema* (University of Exeter Press 2007), p. 163.

38 Koszarski, *An Evening's Entertainment*, pp. 72ff; Bowser, *Transformation of Cinema*, p. 192; Douglas Gomery, "The movie palace comes to America's cities," in Butsch, *For Fun and Profit* (Temple University Press 1990), pp. 136–151.

39 Journalists reported little on movie audiences in this era. Once palaces were commonplace and movie-going and audiences uncontroversial, newspaper coverage became focused on Hollywood and its films. The circumstances were not unlike the "imprisoned" audiences of drama theaters at the turn of the century. See Butsch, *American Audiences*, p. 80.

40   Movie palaces tended toward "tasteful" costume dramas or musicals that drew large audiences for weeks, due to Hollywood's control of most large-capacity picture palaces. See Mark Glancy and John Sedgwick, "Cinema-going in the US in the mid 1930s," in Maltby, Stokes and Allen, *Going to the Movies*, pp. 155–95; Gomery, "The picture palace: Economic sense or Hollywood nonsense," *Quarterly Review of Film Studies*, 3(1) (Winter 1978): 23–36.

41   Jeffrey Klenotic, "Four hours of hootin' and hollerin': Moviegoing and everyday life outside the movie palace," in Maltby, Stokes and Allen, *Going to the Movies*, pp. 130–154.

42   Richard Maltby, "'Perhaps everyone has forgotten just how pictures are shown to the public': Continuous performance and double billing in the 1930s," in Daniel Biltereyst, Richard Maltby, and Philippe Meers, eds., *Routledge Companion to New Cinema History* (Routledge 2018); Thomas Doherty, "This is where we came in: The audible screen and the voluble audience of early sound cinema," in Stokes and Maltby, *American Movie Audiences* (BFI 1999), pp. 143–163. Drive-in theaters became another informal option in the 1950s. See Mary Morley Cohen, "Forgotten audiences in the passion pits: drive-in theaters in post-war America," *Film History*, 6 (1994): 470–486.

43   Gregory Waller, *Mainstreet Amusement: Movies and Commercial Entertainment in a Southern City, 1896–1930* (Smithsonian 1995), p. 215; Katherine Fuller, *At the Picture Show: Small-Town Audiences and the Creation of Movie Fan Culture* (Smithsonian 1996).

44   Klenotic, "Four hours," n. 12, pp. 417–418.

45   Esther Morgan-Ellis, "Everybody sing!: Community singing in the American picture palace" (PhD, University of Georgia Press 2018). The community music movements began in the mid 1910s. See Peter W. Dykema, "The spread of the community music idea," *Annals of the American Academy of Political and Social Science*, 67(1) (September 1916): 218–223. Community sings at outdoor summer concerts in urban parks continued into the 1950s. Post-war suburbanization, television and the rise of teen culture may have helped erode these community family gatherings.

46   Morgan-Ellis, "Everybody sings"; Elizabeth Fones-Wolf, "Sound comes to the movies: The Philadelphia musicians' struggle against recorded music," *The Pennsylvania Magazine of History and Biography*, 118(1/2) (January–April 1994): 3–31.

47   "Phoney splurges," *Variety*, December 10, 1930, p. 1; "Letters," *Motion Picture Herald*, October 8, 1931; Colin Shindler, *Hollywood in Crisis*; Glancy and Sedgwick, "Cinema going in the United States," pp. 155–195. With the early decline of attendance, the big studio's heavily mortgaged theater real estate and mounting debt forced them to sell many of their theaters. The big first-run theaters in the largest cities continued their live stage performances and single feature films, but lesser theaters had to replace live shows with double features. Gomery, *Shared Pleasures*, pp. 57–66.

48 Glancy and Sedgwick, "Cinema going in the United States," p. 160; Butsch, "American movie audiences in the 1930s."
49 Klenotic, "Four hours," pp. 134–136.
50 Butsch, "American movie audiences in the 1930s," pp. 109–110; Robert Sklar *Movie-Made America: A Cultural History of American Movies* (Random House 1975), p. 153.

4 Global Hollywood, 1920s–1950s

1 Richard Maltby and Ruth Vasey, "The international language problem: European reactions to Hollywood's conversion to sound," in David W. Ellwood and Rob Kroes, *Hollywood in Europe. Experiences of a Cultural Hegemony* (University of California Press 1994), pp. 92–93.
2 Gerben Bakker, "The decline and fall of the European film industry: Sunk costs, market size, and market structure, 1890–1927," *Economic History Review*, 58(2) (May 2005): 310–351; John Trumpbour, *Selling Hollywood to the World: US and European Struggles for Mastery of the Global Film Industry, 1920–1950* (Cambridge University Press 2002), Hays quote, p. 17.
3 Thomas Guback, "Cultural identity and film in the European economic community," *Cinema Journal*, 14(1) (1974): 2–17; William Seabury, *The Public and the Motion Picture Industry* (Macmillan 1926), pp. 288–289. Even in 2011, Hollywood film majors accounted for 57% of box office receipts outside the US ("Hollywood zooms on overseas boom," *Variety*, January 9, 2012, p. 1).
4 Frank J. Lechner, *Globalization: The Making of World Society* (Wiley-Blackwell 2009), pp. 6, 25.
5 On Gainsborough, Gerben Bakker. *Entertainment Industrialised: The Emergence of the International Film Industry, 1890–1940* (Cambridge University Press 2011), p. 61; Ruth Vasey, "The world-wide spread of cinema," in Geoffrey Nowell-Smith, *Oxford History of World Cinema* (Oxford University Press 1996), p. 61 on talent drain. On three other economic factors – joint consumption of non-rivalrous goods, cultural discount, and external benefit – see Colin Hoskins, Stuart McFadyen, and Adam Smith, *Global Television and Film: An Introduction to the Economics of the Business* (Oxford University Press 1997), pp. 3–4, 31–33; Kristin Thompson, *Exporting Entertainment: America in the World Film Market, 1907–34* (BFI 1985), Preface, and ch. 2 on world familiarity with Hollywood film style. Ellen Furlough, "Selling the American way in interwar France: 'Prix Uniques' and the Salons Des Arts Menagers," *Journal of Social History*, 26(3) (Spring 1993): 491–519 on broader familiarity with American consumer products and consumer culture. On reception of American culture after World War II see Heide Fehrenbach and Uta G. Poiger, eds., *Transactions, Transgressions, Transformations: American Culture in Western Europe* (Berghahn Books 2000).

For an overview of Americanization literature see David Ellwood, *The Shock of America: Europe and the Challenge of the Century* (Oxford University Press 2012).

6 Richard Abel, *The Red Rooster Scare: Making Cinema American, 1900–1910* (1999); Andrew Higson and Richard Maltby, eds., *"Film Europe" and "Film America"* (University of Exeter Press 1998).

7 K. Thompson "National or international films?" *Film History*, 8 (1996): 281–296, quote from pp. 283–284. In 1957 when the European Economic Community was formed, it still did little for European film. See Thomas Guback, "Cultural identity and film in the European economic community," *Cinema Journal*, 14(1) (1974): 2–17.

8 Trumpbour, *Selling Hollywood*, pp. 240ff; Kristin Thompson, "Early alternatives to the Hollywood mode of production: Implications for Europe's avant-gardes," in Lee Grieveson and Peter Kramer, eds., *Silent Cinema Reader* (Routledge 2003), pp. 349–67; Frank Bösch, *Mass Media and Historical Change: Germany in International Perspective, 1400 to the Present* (Berghahn Books, 2015), pp. 118–119 re Ufa; Giuliana Bruno, *Streetwalking on a Ruined Map* (Princeton University Press 1993), pp. 18–19; Giorgio Bertellini, "Dubbing L'Arte Muta: Poetic layerings around Italian cinema's transition to sound," in Jacqueline Reich and Piero Garofalo, eds., *Re-viewing Fascism: Italian Cinema, 1922–1943* (Indiana University Press 2002), pp. 30–82, esp. nn. 11–14. On German films in interwar Central Europe, see Petr Szczepanik, "Hollywood in disguise: Practices of exhibition and reception of foreign films in Czechoslovakia in the 1930s," in Daniel Biltereyst, Richard Maltby, and Philippe Meers, eds., *Cinema Audiences and Modernity: New Perspectives on European Cinema History* (Routledge 2012), pp. 176–180.

9 "Protest film 'invasion'" *NYT*, July 16, 1919, 13; "British protests," *NYT*, August 17, 1919, editorial sec. 35; Andrew Higson, *Waving the Flag: Constructing a National Cinema in Britain* (Clarendon Press 1997), 1924 quote p. 31; Trumpbour, *Selling Hollywood*, pp. 1–2; Harm G. Schröter, *Americanization of the European Economy: A Compact Survey of American Economic Influence in Europe since the 1880s* (Springer 2005); Mark Glancy, "Temporary American citizen? British audiences, Hollywood films and the threat of Americanization in the 1920s," *HJFRT*, 26(4) (2006): 461–484; Thomas Saunders, *Hollywood in Berlin: American Cinema and Weimar Germany* (University of California Press 1994).

European responses to American imports were not uniformly hostile and defensive. For some, open markets were more important than the threat to national culture. Others argued that the solution was educating public taste rather than denying access through import quotas. Smaller nations, such as Sweden, could not supply a steady stream of films without imports. See Jonas Bjork, "'The backbone of our business': American films in Sweden, 1910–50," *HJFRT*, 15(2) (1995): 245–263.

10 E.g. Gustave Le Bon, *The Crowd* (1895). In this view, class inequality merely reflected a natural hierarchy from elites of superior character to inferior lower classes.

11 Bakker, *Entertainment Industrialized*, quote p. 61.
12 Alan Williams, ed., *Film and Nationalism* (Rutgers 2002), esp. Stephen Crofts, "Reconceptualizing national cinema," pp. 25–51, and Andrew Higson, "Concept of national cinema" pp. 52–67; Mette Hjort and Scott MacKenzie, eds., *Cinema and Nation* (Routledge 2000), esp. Higson, "The limiting imagination of national cinema," and Philip Schlesinger, "Sociological scope of 'national cinema'"; Jerry White, "National belonging: Renewing the concept of national cinema for a global culture," *New Review of Film and Television Studies* 2(2) (2004): 211–232. Higson (*Waving the Flag*, pp. 4–5) identifies four usages of the term, national cinema as: a national film production industry; exhibition and consumption preferences for domestic films; the cultural distinctiveness of a nation's films; or a representation of a nation in its films.
13 Higson, *Waving the Flag*, ch. 3; Michael Bommes and Patrick Wright, "'Charms of residence': The public and the past," in R. Johnson, G. McLennan, Bill Schwarz, and David Sutton, eds., *Making Histories* (University of Minnesota Press 1982), pp. 253–301; John Berger, *Ways of Seeing* (Penguin Books 1972) on landscape painting as heritage culture.
14 Higson, *Waving the Flag*, pp. 103, 110, 111; Patrick Joyce, *Visions of the People* (Cambridge University Press 1991), ch. 13.
15 George MacAdam, "Our new art for export," *NYT*, April 13, 1924, SM2. In some instances, people preferred their domestic films, but these were in short supply and not broadly available. See Clara Pafort-Overduin, "Distribution and exhibition in the Netherlands 1934–36," in Richard Maltby, Daniel Biltereyst, and Philippe Meers, eds., *Explorations in New Cinema History* (Blackwell 2011), pp. 125–139.
16 On English language see Trumpbour, *Selling Hollywood*, p. 10; Jeremy Tunstall, *The Media were American: US Mass Media in Decline* (Oxford University Press 2008); quote from Maltby and Vasay, in Ellwood and Kroes, *Hollywood in Europe*, pp. 92–93.
17 Ellwood and Kroes, *Hollywood in Europe*, broach the issue how much domestic films have a natural appeal in their home countries.
18 Ellen Furlough, "Selling the American way in interwar France: 'Prix uniques' and the Salons Des Arts Menagers," *Journal of Social History*, 26(3) (Spring 1993): 491–519; Robert L. Frost, "Machine liberation: Inventing housewives and home appliances in interwar France," *French Historical Studies*, 18(1) (Spring 1993): 109–130; Peter Scott, "The twilight world of interwar British hire purchase," *Past & Present*, 177 (November 2002): 195–225; also Gary Cross, *Time and Money: The Making of Consumer Culture* (Routledge 1993).
19 On women and work see Birgitte Soland, "Becoming modern: Young women and the reconstruction of womanhood in the 1920s" (Princeton University Press 2000); Laura Frader, "Engendering work and wages: The French labor movement and the family wage," in Frader and Sonya Rose, eds., *Gender and Class in Modern Europe* (Cornell University Press 1996), pp. 156–157, 163.

20 On movie admissions, Jens Ulff-Møller, *Hollywood's Film Wars with France: Film-trade Diplomacy and the Emergence of the French Film Trade Policy* (University of Rochester Press 2001), pp. 168–169; Gerben Bakker, "At the origins of increased productivity growth in services: Productivity, social savings and the consumer surplus of the film industry, 1900–1938," *Working Papers in Economic History*, 81 (Department of Economic History, London School of Economics 2004). Time of day or week and type of movie separated audiences by age and gender. Rural areas differed: People dressed to go to their local cinema as a family activity. But where there were two or more cinemas, villagers divided according to class, as in urban areas. See Judith Thissen and Clemens Zimmermann, eds., *Cinema Beyond the City: Small-Town and Rural Film Culture in Europe* (BFI 2017); Peter Miskell, *A Social History of the Cinema in Wales 1918–1951* (University of Wales Press 2006); Sue Harper "A lower middle-class taste community in the 1930s: Admission figures at the Regent Cinema, Portsmouth UK," *HJFRT*, 24(4) (2004): 565–587.

21 Philippe Meers, Daniel Biltereyst, and L. Van De Vijver, "Metropolitan vs rural cinemagoing in Flanders, 1925–1975," *Screen*, 51(3) (2010): 272–80, quotes from pp. 275, 276.

22 Andre van der Velden and Judith Thissen, "Spectacles of conspicuous consumption: Picture palaces, war profiteers and the social dynamics of movie-going in the Netherlands, 1914–1922," *Film History*, 22(4) (2010): 455–457; similarly in Britain see Nickolas Hiley, "'At the picture show': The British cinema audience, 1895–1920," in John Fullerton, ed., *Celebrating 1895: A Century of Cinema* (John Libbey 1998), pp. 96–106.

23 On movies vs soccer see Miskell, *Social History of the Cinema in Wales;* on Bolton v Brighton see John Sedgwick *Popular Film-Going in 1930s Britain* (Exeter 2000); *Mass-Observation at the Movies*, edited by Jeffrey Richards and Dorothy Sheridan (Routledge 1987), quote p. 40; on class segregation see also Sue Harper, "A lower middle taste community." Within working-class Bolton, there was a gender difference too, women drawn to romances and men to action heroes fighting for right and country.

24 Fabrice Montebello, "Hollywood films in a French working-class milieu: Longwy 1945–1960," in Ellwood and Kroes, *Hollywood in Europe*, pp. 227, 228; also Montebello, Fabrice, "Spectacle cinématographique et classe ouvrière, Longwy 1944–1960" (Doctoral thesis, Université de Lyon 2, 1997).

25 Sarah J. Smith, *Children, Cinema and Censorship* (I. B. Tauris 2005), pp. 278–280.

26 Mark Glancy "Temporary American citizen," quote pp. 469; Melvyn Stokes and Richard Maltby, eds., *Hollywood Abroad: Audiences and Cultural Exchange* (BFI 2007), pp. 3–4.

27 Van der Velden and Thissen, "Spectacles of conspicuous consumption."

28 Cassiata Ionita, "The Catholic spectator," *HJRFT*, 32(4) (December 2012): 501–520; Thunnis Van Oort, "Christ is coming to the elite cinema: Film exhibition in the Catholic south of the Netherlands, 1910s and 1920s," in Daniel Biltereyst, Richard Maltby, and Philippe Meers, eds., *Cinema, Audiences and Modernity: New Perspectives on European Cinema History* (Routledge 2012), pp. 50–63; Daniel Biltereyst, "'Healthy films from America.' The emergence of a Catholic film mass movement," in Richard Maltby, Melvin Stokes, and Robert C. Allen, eds., *Going to the Movies* (Exeter 2007), pp. 307–322. These countries had parallel institutional pillars segregated by religion, ethnicity and political ideology, that included separate political parties, newspapers, movie theaters, radio and tv stations, schools, and hospitals.

29 Robert Nye, *The Origins of Crowd Psychology* (Sage, 1975); Jaap Van Ginneken, *Crowds, Psychology, and Politics, 1871–1899* (Cambridge University Press 1992).

30 Glancy, "Temporary American citizen," p. 467

31 Glancy, "Temporary American citizen" on fan magazines; Robert James, "*Kinematograph Weekly* in the 1930s: Trade attitudes towards audience taste," *Journal of Popular British Cinema and Television*, 3(2) (2006): 229–243.

32 Quote from Kroes, "Americanization: what are we talking about?" in Rob Kroes, Robert W. Rydell, and D. F. J. Bossche, eds., *Cultural Transmissions and Receptions: American Mass Culture in Europe* (Amsterdam VU University Press 1993), p. 313; on the US see Paul Boyer, *Urban Masses and Moral Order* (Harvard University Press 1978).

33 P. Burke, *Popular Culture in Early Modern Europe*, 3rd edn (Ashgate 2009), but see the complicating Introduction.

34 R. Vasey, *The World According to Hollywood, 1918–1939* (University of Wisconsin Press 1997); Trumpbour, *Selling Hollywood*, p. 5; John Sedgwick, Michael Pokorny, and Peter Miskell, "Hollywood in the world market – evidence from Australia in the mid 1930s," *Business History*, 56(5) (2014): 689–723.

35 Nevin Coşar and Sevtap Demirci, "Incorporation into the world economy: From railways to highways, 1850–1950," *Middle Eastern Studies*, 45(1) (2009): 19–31; Dave Donaldson, "Railroads of the Raj: Estimating the impact of transportation infrastructure," *American Economic Review*, 108(4–5) (2018): 899–934; Simon Katzenellenbogen, "The miner's frontier, transport and general economic development," pp. 360–426 in Peter Duignan and L. H. Gann, eds., *Colonialism in Africa 1870–1960* (Cambridge University Press 1975), esp. pp. 392–397; López, Ana M. "Early cinema and modernity in Latin America," *Cinema Journal*, 40(1) (2000): 48–78, p. 51. About the impact of paved roads on economic development, see Daron Acemoglu and Melissa Dell, "Productivity differences between and within countries," *American Economic Journal: Macroeconomics*, 2(1) (2010): 169–188; L. Freed, "Networks of (colonial) power: roads in French Central Africa after World War I," *History*

and Technology: An International Journal, 26(3) (September 2010): 203–223.

36 James. M. Burns, *Cinema and Society in the British Empire 1895–1940* (Palgrave 2013). African patterns of cinema development were not dissimilar to that of Latin America. In Mexico in the early1920s, cinemas were concentrated in the capital where the more lucrative and larger theaters often were American owned; in the provinces, cinema was local small business. Provinces that had the most cinema seats per population were ones that were industrialized with ties to the US, such as Sonora and its mineral mining. See L. I. Serna "Exhibition in Mexico," in J. Staiger and S. Hake, eds., *Convergence Media History* (Routledge 2009), pp. 69–80.

37 Roy Armes, *Post-Colonial Images: Studies in North African Film* (Indiana University Press 2005), pp. 6–9; Noha Mellor, M. Ayish, N. Dajani, and K. Rinnawi, *Arab Media: Globalization and Emerging Media Industries* (Polity 2011), p. 104; James E. Genova, *Cinema and Development in West Africa* (Indiana University Press 2013), pp. 20–21; also Nwachukwu F. Ukadike, *Black African Cinema* (University of California Press 1994); Burns, *Cinema and Society*, pp. 8, 10; Charles Ambler, "Popular films and colonial audiences: The movies in northern Rhodesia," *American Historical Review*, 106(1) (2001): 81–105. West African Senegalese theaters were at first owned by Lebanese immigrants, who were marginal, foreign and Christian.

38 James E. Genova, *Cinema and Development*; Bill Nasson, "She preferred living in a cave with Harry, the snake-catcher': Towards an oral history of popular leisure and class expression in District Six, Cape Town, c 1920s–1950s," in Philip Bonner, Isabel Hofmeyr, Deborah James, and Tom Lodge, eds., *Holding Their Ground: Class, Locality and Culture in 19th and 20th Century South Africa* (Witwatersrand University Press 2001), pp. 285–309, quote from p. 286; Jacqueline Maingard, "Cinemagoing in District Six, Cape Town, 1920s to 1960s: History, politics, memory," *Memory Studies*, 10(1) (2017): 17–34; Charles Coulter, "The sociological problem," in J. Merle Davis, ed., *Modern Industry and the African* (London 1933), p. 72.

39 Charles Ambler, "Popular films and colonial audiences"; Charles Ambler "Cowboy modern: African audiences, Hollywood films," in Maltby Stokes and Allen, *Going to the Movies*, p. 359; Jacqueline Maingard, *South African National Cinema* (Routledge 2007), pp. 67, 68, 71, 73.

40 Ambler, "Popular films"; Bill Nasson "She preferred," quotes, p. 292

41 Nasson, "She preferred," quotes, pp. 291–292.

42 Burns, *Cinema and Society*.

43 E.g. Gustave LeBon, *The Crowd* (Viking Press 1960); Boris Sidis, *The Psychology of Suggestion* (Appleton, 1899); Edward A. Ross, *Social Psychology: An Outline and Source Book* (Macmillan 1919), ch. 2.

44 Trumpbour, *Selling Hollywood*, p. 10 on Congo ban; on Rhodesia see James M. Burns, *Flickering Shadows: Cinema and Identity in Colonial Zimbabwe* (Ohio University Press 2002).

45 A. R. Beata, "The two worlds," *Sight and Sound*, 17 (1948): 5–8.

46 Burns, *Flickering Shadows*, esp. chs. 2 and 4; Rosaleen Smyth, "The British Colonial Film Unit and sub-Saharan Africa, 1939–1945," *HJFRT*, 8(3) (1988): 285–298; on awareness see Ukadike, Nwachukwu Frank, *Black African Cinema*, p. 31.

47 Burns, *Flickering Shadows*, pp. 37–52, quote p 46; Ambler, "Popular films and colonial audiences," pp. 81–105; on the French see Genova, *Cinema and Development*. A few rejected these simplistic explanations of audience reactions and offered others grounded in the audiences' culture and colonized circumstances.

48 Manishita Dass, "The crowd outside the lettered city: Imagining the mass audience in 1920s India," *Cinema Journal*, 48(4) (2009): 77–98, 89 on Indian masses; Butsch, *American Audiences*, pp. 57–58, 114–115, 137–138, 202 on green'uns.

49 Burns, *Flickering Shadows*, pp. 126–134; also Jacqueline Maingard, *South African National Cinema*, ch. 4.

50 James E. Genova, "Cinema and development," pp. 29, 52; also Barbara Creed and Jeanette Hoorn, "Memory and history: Early film, colonialism and the French civilising mission in Indochina," *French History and Civilization*, 4 (2011). Films about Africans shown in France "legitimated the racial privileges of European workers, diverted attention from their own exploitation, and disabled impulses to solidarity with women and colonial peoples." See David H. Slavin, *Colonial Cinema and Imperial France, 1919–1939* (Johns Hopkins 2001), pp. xi, 3.

51 Turkish policy from the 1920s through the 1950s is an example. See Nezih Erdogan and Dilek Kaya, "Institutional intervention in the distribution and exhibition of Hollywood films in Turkey," *HJFRT*, 22(1) (2002): 47–59. During the Cold War, the Soviet Union presented an alternative source of help. Some post-colonial governments were able to play one against the other in order to gain some independence from both.

52 Dipesh Chakrabarty, *Provincializing Europe: Post-Colonial Thought and Historical Difference* (Princeton University Press 2007); Thiong'o, Ngugi wa, *Decolonizing the Mind: The Politics of Language in African Literature* (Heinemann 1997); Albert Memmi, *Colonizer and Colonized*, trans. Howard Greenfield (Orion Press 1974), p. 114; Rashid Khalidi, Lisa Anderson, Muhammad Muslih, and Reeva S. Simon, eds., *The Origins of Arab Nationalism* (Columbia University Press 1991), pp. 3–9; Ahmet Gurata, "Hollywood in vernacular: Translation and cross-cultural reception of American films in Turkey, 1930–1970," in Maltby, Stokes, and Allen, *Going to the Movies*.

53 Roy Armes, *Post-Colonial Images*, quote p. 87; Ashish Rajadhyaksha, *Indian Cinema in the Time of Celluloid* (Tulika Books 2009), quote p. 87. On national cinema and nationalism see Alan Williams, ed., *Film and Nationalism* (Rutgers 2002), esp. Stephen Crofts, "Reconceptualizing national cinema," pp. 25–51, and Andrew Higson, "Concept of national cinema," pp. 52–67; Mette Hjort and Scott MacKenzie, eds.,

Cinema and Nation (Routledge 2000). On representational public sphere, e.g. see Nicholas Balaisis, "Cuba, cinema, and the post-revolutionary public sphere," *Canadian Journal of Film Studies*, 19(2) (Autumn, 2010): 26–42.

54 Report of the Indian Cinematographic Committee 1927–1928, Government of India Central Publication Branch, Calcutta, 1928, vol. 1, pp. 29, 83, hereafter ICC report. Chakravarty divides the industry's history into three eras: 1897–1912 Indian topicals, 1912–1917 from first Indian feature to war, and 1918–1947 from World War I to independence and the end of the studio system. See Sumita S. Chakravarty, *National Identity in Indian Popular Cinema, 1947–1987* (University of Texas Press 2011).

55 ICC report, pp. 39–41. As late as 1941, cinema in India was seen as an urban phenomenon. See L. S. S. O'Malley, *Modern India and the West* (Oxford University Press 1941, p. 252. Yet 85% of the population was still rural. See Dennis Merrill, *Bread and the Ballot: The United States and India's Economic Development* (University of North Carolina Press 1990), p. 14.

56 ICC report, p. 25; Dave Donaldson, "Railroads of the Raj"; Shilpa Aggarwal, "Do rural roads create pathways out of poverty? Evidence from India," *Journal of Development Economics*, 133 (2018): 375–395; Donald R. Glover and Julian L. Simon, "The effect of population density on infrastructure: The case of road building," *Economic Development and Cultural Change*, 23(3) (April 1975): 453–468; James Heitzman, "Middle towns to middle cities in South Asia, 1800–2007," *Journal of Urban History*, 35(1) (November 2008): 15–38.

57 Manishita Dass, "A consuming public: Movie audiences in the Bengali imaginary," in Richard Butsch and Sonia Livingstone, eds, *Meanings of Audiences: Comparative Discourses* (Routledge 2013), pp. 97–110; Adrian Athique, *Indian Media: Global Approaches* (Polity 2012), pp. 28–30, 60, 76, 123; Ravi S. Vasudevan, "National pasts and futures: Indian Cinema," *Screen*, 41(1) (Spring 2000): 19–25.

58 ICC report, p. 34; Mihir Bose, *Bollywood: A History* (Tempus 2006), p. 139; Kaushik Bhaumik, "A brief history of cinema from Bombay to 'Bollywood'" *History Compass*, 2(1) (2004); Stephen Hughes "House full: Silent film genre, exhibition and audiences in south India," *Indian Economic Social History Review*, 43(1) (2006): 31–62.

59 Bose, *Bollywood*, pp. 61–62; ICC report, pp. 29, 88, quote from p. 23; Athique, *Indian Media*, pp. 18, 23.

60 L. O'Malley, *Modern India and the West*, p. 253; A. Rajadhyaksha and P. Willemen, *Encyclopedia of Indian Cinema* (Routledge 1999), p. 30; Chakravarty, *National Identity*, pp. 39–40.

61 ICC report, pp. 22, 39 and tables 1, 2, 5 and 6, pp. 179–182; David Vinnels and Brent Skelly, *Bollywood Showplaces: Cinema Theatres in India* (E. & E. Plumridge 2002); also Ranita Chatterjee, "Cinema in the colonial city: Early film audiences in Calcutta," in Ian Christie, ed., *Audiences: Defining and Researching Screen Entertainment Reception* (Amsterdam University Press 2012).

62 ICC report, quote p. 78.

63 Dass, "Consuming public," pp. 102, 104.

64 Dass, "Crowd outside the lettered city." Sociability remains at Bollywood movies. See Lakshmi Srinivas, "The active audience: spectatorship, social relations and the experience of cinema in India," *Media, Culture, and Society*, 24(2) (2002): 155–173; Kevin Smets, Iris Vandevelde, Philippe Meers, Roel Vande Winkel, and Sofie Van Bauwel, "Between unruliness and sociality: Discourses on diasporic audiences for Turkish and Indian films," in Butsch and Livingstone, *Meanings of Audiences* (Routledge 2013), pp. 64–79. On similar behavior in the US see Butsch, *American Audiences*.

65 ICC report quote, p. 215; Dass, "Crowd outside the lettered city," quote p. 82. The British feared that Hollywood films in the 1930s "inadvertently fanned the flames of Indian unrest" (Trumpbour, *Selling Hollywood*, p. 10). On a counter narrative see Annamaria Motrescu, "Imperial narratives *displaced* by Indian subaltern identities in early amateur films," *Early Popular Visual Culture*, 9(2) (May 2011): 107–121

66 R. Bin Wong, *China Transformed: Historical Change and the Limits of European Experience* (Cornell University Press 1997), pp. 154–163; Hanchao Lu, *Beyond the Neon Lights: Everyday Shanghai in the Early Twentieth Century* (University of California Press 1999), pp. 5–7.

67 C. J. North, "The Chinese motion picture market," *Trade Information Bulletin*, 467, US Department of Commerce 1927, quotes pp. 13–14; Changgen Zhang, M. Liu, and Y. Hu, "Shanghai: population developments since 1949," in Liu Z. and J. Song, *China's Population: Problems and Prospects* (Beijing, New World Press, 1981), pp. 129–135.

68 On cosmopolitanism, colonialism and hybridity see M. Akbar Abbas, "Cosmopolitan de-scriptions: Shanghai and Hong Kong," *Public Culture*, 12(3) (Fall 2000): 769–786; and Sheldon Pollock, Homi Babhi, Carol Breckingridge, and Dipesh Chakrabarty, "Cosmopolitanisms," *Public Culture*, 12(3) (Fall 2000): 577–589. In practice, cosmopolitanism is not egalitarian cultural relativity, but rather a kind of slumming, remaining in one's own cultural bubble while amid other cultures.

69 North, "Chinese motion picture market," pp. 9, 14. The type refers to 10, 20, or 30 cent tickets for inexpensive melodrama theaters in the US that were put out of business by the spread of movies. See Alfred Bernstein, *The Business of the Theatre* (Benjamin Blom 1932).

70 North, "Chinese motion picture market," p. 9; Leo Ou-fan Lee, *Shanghai Modern: The Flowering of a New Urban Culture in China, 1930–1945* (Harvard University Press 1999), p. 119; Zhang Zhen, *Amorous History of the Silver Screen: Shanghai Cinema, 1896–1937* (University of Chicago Press, 2005), pp. 68–69; Leo Ou-fan Lee, "The urban milieu of Shanghai cinema, 1930–1940," in Yingjin Zhang, *Cinema and Urban Culture in Shanghai 1922–1943* (Stanford University Press 1999), pp. 74–96.

71 Wen-Hsin Yeh, *Shanghai Splendor: Economic Sentiments and the Making of Modern China, 1843–1949* (University of California Press, 2007), pp. 102–103, 129ff; quote in Zhen, *Amorous History*, pp. 64–65; Lee,

"Urban milieu,"; Lee, *Shanghai Modern*, p. 83 re another US report in 1930. Some Chinese feature films in the 1920s drew on Peking opera, fairy tales, and folklore well-known "classics," similar to Indian mythology films and early European feature films. Cantonese film-making began in Hong Kong as an export industry to diaspora. See Poshek Fu and David Desser, eds., *The Cinema of Hong Kong: History, Arts, Identity* (Cambridge University Press 2000). The Japanese occupation in the 1930s stimulated patriotic films.

72   Director quote in Lee, *Shanghai Modern*, p. 111; Chi Ming Fung, *Reluctant Heroes: Rickshaw Pullers in Hong Kong and Canton, 1874–1954* (Hong Kong University 2005), pp. 9, 31–35, 59–60; Hanchao Lu, *Beyond the Neon Lights*, pp. 78, 96–97, quote p. 5; David Strand, *Rickshaw Beijing: City People and Politics in the 1920s* (University of California Press 1989), pp. 49–58. Two thirds of migrant workers were women. See Gail Hershatter, *The Workers of Tianjin, 1900–1949* (Stanford University Press 1986); Emily Honig, *Sisters and Strangers: Women in the Shanghai Cotton Mills, 1900–1949* (Stanford University Press 1986). Migrants returning to their home villages for New Year celebration with their families persists today. See *Last Train Home* (2009) documentary film directed by Lixin Fan.

73   North, "Chinese motion picture market." On Confucian social harmony see Chenyang Li, *The Confucian Philosophy of Harmony* (Routledge 2014), chs. 7, 8.

74   Lee, "Urban milieu," p. 84; North, "Chinese motion picture market," p. 28; Zhen, *Amorous History*, quote p. 237; Xiao Zhiwei, "Film censorship in China 1927–1937" (PhD, University of California at San Diego 1994), esp. ch. 2

75   Chang-tai Hung, *War and Popular Culture: Resistance in Modern China, 1937–1945* (University of California Press, 1994), ch. 2 and pp. 222–234; Ellen Widner and David Der-Wei Wang, eds., *From May Fourth to June Fourth: Fiction and Film in Twentieth-Century China* (Cambridge: Harvard University Press 1999).

76   Quoted in Hung, *War and Popular Culture*, p. 53.

77   See Richard Curt Kraus, *The Cultural Revolution: A Very Short Introduction* (Oxford University Press 2012), ch. 1.

78   Hung, *War and Popular Culture*, p. 91.

79   Viola Shafik, *Arab Cinema: History and Cultural Identity* (American University of Cairo Press, 2007), pp. 2, 9, 12–15, 26–29

80   Afaf Lutfi Al-Sayyid Marsot, *A Short History of Modern Egypt* (Cambridge University Press 1985), pp. 57–88; Roger Owen and Sevket Pamuk, *A History of Middle East Economies in the Twentieth Century* (Harvard University Press 1999), pp. 30–31.

81   Ehud Toledano, "A history of landownership in modern Egypt," in M. W. Daly, ed., *Cambridge History of Egypt; Vol 2 Modern Egypt, from 1517 to the End of the Twentieth Century* (Cambridge University Press 1996), p. 272; Kenneth Cuno, *The Pasha's Peasants: Land, Society and Economy in Lower Egypt 1740–1858* (Cambridge University Press 1992),

pp. 4, 163, 170–172; Owen and Pamuk, *History of Middle East Economies*, pp. 45–47; Nathan J. Brown, *Peasant Politics in Modern Egypt* (Yale University Press 1990); Joel Beinin, "Egypt society and economy 1923–1952," in Daly, *Cambridge History*, pp. 309–333.

82 Ella Schochat, "Egypt: Cinema and revolution," *Critical Arts*, 2(4) (1983): 22–32, p. 32 n. 5; Owen and Pamuk, *Middle Eastern Economies*.

83 The revolution gained some internal autonomy for Egypt, but did not much change class relations. Noha Mellor, *The Egyptian Dream: Egyptian National Identity and Uprisings* (Edinburgh University Press 2016); Ellis Goldberg, "Peasants in revolt, Egypt 1919," *International Journal of Middle East Studies*, 24(2) (May 1992): 261–280

84 Toledano, *History of Land Ownership*, p. 275; Jane Gaffney, "The Egyptian cinema: Industry and art in a changing society," *Arab Studies Quarterly*, 9(1) (Winter 1987): 53–75; Shafik, *Arab Cinema*, p. 10

85 Beinin, "Egypt society and economy," p. 309; Rashid Khalidi, ed., *The Origins of Arab Nationalism* (Columbia University Press 1991); Owen and Pamuk, *Middle Eastern Economies,* pp. 45–47.

86 Gaffney, "Egyptian cinema," pp. 54–57; Shafik, *Arab Cinema*, pp. 12–14. Shafik (p. 24) claims that the films blended Western with Eastern music in an amalgam that appealed to their market's desire for Western styles and goods.

87 Richard Maltby, "Introduction: The Americanization of the world," in Melvin Stokes and Richard Maltby, eds., *Hollywood Abroad: Audiences and Cultural Exchange* (BFI 2007), p 12.

5 Western Television in the Broadcast Era, 1945–1990

1 Broadcast signals (i.e. programs) are transmitted in a 360-degree direction from the source, usually located in population centers, for a distance determined by the signal's original power, enough to reach large populations spread out beyond city centers into surrounding rural areas, bringing tv to urban and rural families at one and the same time. Signals, however could be blocked by mountains, leaving some valley communities without television. In the US, a few such communities installed mountain-top antennae to receive broadcast signals and re-transmit them by cable connections to local homes and businesses.

2 Kaarle Nordenstreng and Tapio Varis, "Television traffic: A one-way street? A survey and analysis of the international flow of television programme material," Reports and Papers on Mass Communication no. 70 (UNESCO 1974), p. 13.

3 Stylianos Papathanassopoulos and Ralph Negrine, *European Media* (Polity 2011), pp. 17–19.

4 Alan Albarran, *Media Economics: Understanding Markets, Industries and Concepts* (Wiley-Blackwell 2002); Michele Hilmes, *Network Nations:*

A Transnational History of British and American Broadcasting (Routledge 2012); Papathanassopoulos and Negrine, *European Media*, pp. 17–23 on specific categories. Nevertheless, commercial broadcasts from outside broke into Britain: A 1935 survey found that 61% of British radio households listened regularly to such stations (Hilmes, *Network Nations*, p. 92). Some used pirated formats of American shows.

5 William Bird, *"Better Living": Advertising, Media and the New Vocabulary of Business Leadership, 1935–1955* (Northwestern University Press, 1999); Roland Marchand, *Advertising the American Dream: Making Way for Modernity* (University of California Press 1985).

6 On network dominance see reports by the Network Inquiry Special Staff, *An Analysis of Television Program Production, Acquisition and Distribution*, and *An Analysis of Network-Affiliate Relationship in Television* (US Federal Communication Commission 1980); Stanley Besen, Thomas Krattenmaker, A. Richard Metzger, Jr., and John Woodbury, *Misregulating Television: Network Dominance and the FCC* (University of Chicago Press 1984).

7 Richard Nixon spoke from the Oval Office 22 times in four and half years as president. By contrast Barack Obama made only two presidential addresses from the Oval Office in his first four and half years. See "Live from the Oval Office" *NYT*, July 10, 2013, A1, 14.

8 A major exception was sound, not screen, the import of British rock music in the mid to late 1960s.

9 Richard Butsch, "Why television sitcoms kept recreating male working-class buffoons for decades," in Gail Dines, Jean Humez, Bill Yousman, and Lori Bindig Yousman, eds., *Gender, Race and Class in Media*, 5th edn (Sage 2018), pp. 442–450.

10 Helen Taylor, *Scarlett's Women: Gone with the Wind and its Female Fans* (Rutgers University Press 1989).

11 Radio's audience size approached that of television. The most popular radio network shows of the 1930s and 1940s attracted about a quarter to a third of radio households during peak listening in January. See Harrison Summers, *A Thirty Year History of Radio Programs, 1926–1956* (Arno Press 1971).

12 Anna McCarthy, *Ambient Television: Visual Culture and Public Space* (Duke University Press 2001).

13 Kenneth Jackson, *Crabgrass Frontier* (Oxford University Press 1985); Barbara T. Alexander, "The US homebuilding industry: A half-century of building the American Dream," John T. Dunlop Lecture, Harvard University, October 12, 2000, p. 8. The average new house in 1950 cost $11,000 in 2016 dollars. See Mousumi Sarkar, "How American homes vary by the year they were built," Demographic Directorate Housing and Household Economic Statistics, Working Paper no. 2011–2018 (US Census Bureau 2011); Herbert Gans, *People and Plans: Essays on Urban Problems and Solutions* (Basic Books 1968).

14 Elaine Tyler May, *Homeward Bound: American Families in the Cold War Era* (Basic Books 2017); Stephen A. Marglin and Juliet B. Schor,

eds., *The Golden Age of Capitalism: Reinterpreting the Postwar Experience* (Oxford University Press 2000).

15 Douglas Gomery, *Shared Pleasures* (University of Wisconsin Press,1992), pp. 91–93.

16 Herbert Gans, *The Levittowners: Ways of Life and Politics in a New Suburban Community* (Knopf 1967); Bennett Berger, *Working Class Suburb: A Study of Auto Workers in Suburbia* (University of California Press 1968), pp. 91–105. Rosalyn Baxandall, Elizabeth Ewen, and Linda Gordon, *Picture Windows: How the Suburbs Happened* (Basic Books 2000).

17 Hidden from this view was the white, rural poverty in places such as Appalachia, and black poverty and segregation in the rural South and industrial North. Michael Harrington, *The Other America: Poverty in the United States* (Macmillan 1962); Richard Rothstein, *The Color of Law: A Forgotten History of How Our Government Segregated America* (W. W. Norton 2017).

18 Lynn Spigel, *Make Room for TV: Television and the Family Ideal in Postwar America* (University of Chicago Press 1992); Herbert Gans, *The Urban Villagers: Group and Class in the Life of Italian-Americans* (Free Press 1964).

19 Richard Butsch, "Homevideo and corporate plans," in Butsch ed., *For Fun and Profit: The Transformation of Leisure into Consumption* (Temple University Press 1990), pp. 215–235.

20 Howard Becker, *Outsiders: Studies in the Sociology of Deviance* (Free Press 1963); Stanley Cohen, *Folk Devils and Moral Panics* (Routledge 2011); Barry Glassner, *The Culture of Fear: Why Americans Are Afraid of the Wrong Things* (Basic Books 1999).

21 Vance Packard, *Hidden Persuaders* (D. McKay Co. 1957); James Gilbert, *A Cycle of Outrage: America's Reaction to the Juvenile Delinquent in the 1950s* (Oxford University Press 1986), ch. 9. Quote from Gerald Pratley, *The Cinema of John Frankenheimer* (A. S. Barnes 1969). Yet, there was no public concern about network oligopoly, even while it remained a central concern of the FCC.

22 Robert Bechtel, Clark Achepohl, and Roger Akers, "Correlates between observed behavior and questionnaire responses on television viewing," in E. A. Rubinstein, G. A. Comstock and J. P. Murray, eds., *Television and Social Behavior*, vol. IV (US Department of Health Education and Welfare, 1972).

23 Gans, *Urban Villagers* and *Levittowner*; Berger, *Working Class Suburb*; Neil Vidmar and Milton Rokeach, "Archie Bunker's bigotry: A study in selective perception and exposure," *Journal of Communication*, 24(1) (March 1974): 36–47; Ellen Seiter, Hans Borchers, Gabriele Kreutzner, and Eva-Maria Warth, "'Don't treat us like we're so stupid and naive': Towards an ethnography of soap opera viewers," in Ellen Seiter, ed., *Remote Control: Television, Audiences, and Cultural Power* (Routledge 1989); Sut Jhally and Justin Lewis, *Enlightened Racism: The Cosby Show, Audiences, and the Myth of the American Dream* (Avalon 1992).

24 John Clarke "Pessimism versus populism: The problematic politics of popular culture," in Butsch, *For Fun and Profit* (Temple University Press 1990), pp. 28–44.

25 On repetition as persuasive see, e.g. Carl Hovland, Irving Janis, and Harold Kelley, *Communication and Persuasion: Psychological Studies of Opinion Change* (Yale University Press 1953). The advertising industry's premise is to repeat the same ad or jingle over and over.

26 For definitions see, among others, Christine Garaghty, "The continuous serial – a definition," in Richard Dyer, Christine Garaghty, Marion Jordan, Terry Lovell, Richard Paterson, and John Stewart, *Coronation Street* (BFI 1981); Laura Mumford, "What is this thing called soap opera?" in Ilan Stavans, ed., *Telenovelas* (Greenwood Press, 2010), pp. 3–32. Serial fiction is at least as old as the novel. See Jennifer Hayward, *Consuming Pleasures: Active Audiences and Serial Fiction from Dickens to Soap Opera* (University Press of Kentucky 1997); Graham Law, *Serializing Fiction in the Victorian Press* (Palgrave 2000); Michael Lund, *America's Continuing Story: An Introduction to Serial Fiction, 1850–1900* (Wayne State Press 1993). Oral tradition used serial stories told over several nights, e.g. the *Iliad*.

27 Rudolph Arnheim, "The world of the daytime serial," in Paul Lazarsfeld and Frank Stanton, eds., *Radio Research, 1942–43* (Duell, Sloan, and Pearce 1944).

28 Text of speech by Yolanda Mero-Irion of the National Radio Committee, quoted in Butsch, *American Audiences*, p. 201; James Thurber, *The Beast in Me* (Hamilton 1949); Mathew Murray, "Matinee theater: Difference, compromise and the 1950s daytime audience," in Janet Tumin *Small Screen Big Ideas* (I. B. Tauris 2002), pp. 131–148.

29 Herta Herzog, "What do we really know about day-time serial listeners," in Paul Lazarsfeld and Frank Stanton, eds., *Radio Research, 1942–43* (Duell, Sloan, and Pearce 1944), pp. 3–33; Leda Summers, "Daytime serials and Iowa women" (Des Moines: WHO radio station, 1943).

30 Stylianos Papathanassopoulos and Ralph Negrine, *European Media* (Polity 2011), pp. 17–19.

31 Radio received less aesthetic criticism than tv, in part because cultural elites believed that radio encouraged listeners to exercise their imagination while visual media such as cinema and tv provided the image to a passive audience. E.g. Daniel L. LeMahieu, *A Culture for Democracy: Mass Communication and the Cultivated Mind in Britain Between the Wars* (Oxford University Press 1988), p. 192.

32 Michele Hilmes, *Network Nations*, pp. 44–45, ch. 2; LeMahieu, *Culture for Democracy*, pp. 141–154, quote p 146. See Robert Silvey, *Who's Listening* (Allen and Unwin 1974) on transmission coverage.

33 Hilmes, *Network Nations*, pp. 51–57, p. 37 on Lewis; Andrew Higson, *Waving the Flag: Constructing a National Cinema in Britain* (Oxford 1997).

34 Hilmes, *Network Nations*, pp. 172, 181–182, 208, 216; Catherine Johnson and Rob Turnock, eds., *ITV Cultures: Independent Television Over Fifty Years* (Open University Press 2005), pp. 3, 5–6, 8.

35 On war damage and austerity see Richard Titmus, *Problems of Social Policy* (HMSO 1950); David Kynaston, *Austerity Britain, 1945–1951* (Walker and Company 2008). On community tv see Tim O'Sullivan, "Television memories, and cultures of viewing, 1950–1965," in John Corner, ed., *Popular Television in Britain: Studies in Cultural History* (BFI 1991), p. 164; Kynaston, *Family Britain, 1951–1957* (Walker Publishing 2009), p. 300.

36 Sue Bowden and Avner Offer, "Household appliances and the use of time: The United States and Britain since the 1920s" *The Economic History Review*, n.s., 47(4) (November 1994): 725–748; Robert L. Fishman, "American suburbs/English suburbs, a transatlantic comparison," *Journal of Urban History*, 13(3) (May 1987): 237–251; O'Sullivan, "Television memories," pp. 158–181; David Kynaston, *Modernity Britain* (Bloomsbury 2013), p. 300; Peter Scott, "The twilight world of interwar British hire purchase," *Past & Present*, 177 (November 2002): 195–225; Peter A. Hall, "Social capital in Britain," *British Journal of Political Science*, 29(3) (July 1999): 417–461, 436 n. 52. On domestic television see Peter Collett, "The viewers viewed," *ETC: A Review of General Semantics*, 44(3) (1987): 245–51.

37 B. P. Emmett, "The television audience in the United Kingdom," *Journal of the Royal Statistical Society*, Series A (General), 119(3) (1956): 284–311; Theodore Cauter and J. S. Downham, *The Communication of Ideas: A Study of Contemporary Influences on Urban Life* (Chatto and Windus 1954), pp. 130, 154–161; also see Silvey, *Who's Listening*, pp. 149, 188. On sociability and conversation, see Peter Hall "Social capital"; Daniel Vasey, *The Pub and English Social Change* (Ams Press 1990), pp. 217–22; Pertwee quote in David Oswell, *Television, Childhood and the Home: A History of the Making of the Child Television Audience in Britain* (Oxford University Press 2002), p. 102.

38 Geoffrey Gorer, "Television in our lives," *The Sunday Times*, April 13, 20, 27, May 4 1958; O'Sullivan, "Television memories," p. 7; Kynaston, *Modernity Britain*, pp. 95–96.

39 Gorer, "Television in our lives"; on the 1961 survey see Kynaston, *Modernity Britain*, pp. 535–6; on accents see Shaun Moores, *Media and Everyday Life in Modern Society* (Edinburgh University Press 2000), pp. 19–20 and O'Sullivan.

40 Quote from Michael Young, "A study of the extended family in east London" (PhD, University of London). See also Michael Young and Peter Willmott, *Family and Class in a London Suburb* (Routledge 1960). Compare to Gans, *Levittowners*, Bennett Berger, *Working Class Suburb*, and William M. Dobriner, *Class in Suburbia* (Prentice-Hall 1963), pp. 51–55.

41 Robert Putnam, *Bowling Alone* (Simon and Schuster 2001). On studies of social capital decline in Britain and Europe, see Peter Hall, "Social capital"; Alan Warde, Gindo Tampubolon, Brian Longhurst, Kathryn Ray, Mike Savage, and Mark Tomlinson, "Trends in social capital: Membership of associations in Great Britain, 1991–1998," *British Journal of Political Science*, 33(3) (July 2003): 515–525; Dietlind Stolle and Marc Hooghe, "Inaccurate, exceptional, one-sided or irrelevant? The debate about the alleged decline of social capital and civic engagement in Western societies," *British Journal of Political Science*, 35(1) (January 2005), 149–167; Bo Rothstein, "Social capital in the social democratic welfare state," *Politics & Society*, 29(2) (June 2001): 207–241.

42 Steve Bruce and Tony Glendinning, "When was secularization? Dating the decline of British churches and locating its cause," *British Journal of Sociology*, 61(1) (March 2010): 107–126.

43 On Brits enjoying American tv shows, see O'Sullivan, "Memories," p. 163, and Richard Maltby, "Introduction: 'The Americanization of the world,'" in Melvin Stokes and Richard Maltby, eds., *Hollywood Abroad: Audiences and Cultural Exchange* (BFI 2007), pp. 3–4 on their own vivid memories. These twin concerns are found in many nations and post-colonial societies. But not all: some smaller nations, such as Sweden, seemed to feel less institutionally threatened by either, and ironically came closer to achieving what larger nations desired, a united nation with a strong native culture less vulnerable to American culture.

44 According to Silverstone, Brits generally "desire[d] to identify with the BBC, but watch[ed] ITV more." See Roger Silverstone, *Television and Everyday Life*, p. 54; Lawrence Black, "Whose finger on the button? British television and the politics of cultural control," *HJFRT*, 25(4) (October 2005): 547–575. Jeffrey Milland, "Courting Malvolio: Background to the Pilkington Committee on Broadcasting," *Contemporary British History*, 18(2) (Summer 2004): 76–102, neatly describes the ironies that Labor MPs preferred the BBC and opposed the commercial model of ITV, but were loathe to vote against ITV, which their constituents so loved. Contrariwise, Tory MPs supported the commercial model of ITV, while they personally preferred the BBC programming.

45 Janet Thumim, *Small Screens, Big Ideas: Television in the 1950s* (I. B. Tauris 2002); Black, "Whose finger?" 556; Fowles quoted in Kynaston, *Family Britain*, p. 606

46 Hilmes, *Network Nation*, p. 267; Milland, "Courting Malvolio."

47 Kynaston, *Modern Britain*, 540–1; Fowles quoted in Kynaston, *Family Britain*, p. 606; Gorer "Television in our lives," *The Sunday Times*, April 13, 1958, p. 15.

48 Hilde Himmelweit, Abraham N. Oppenheim, and Pamela Vince, *Television and the Child* (Oxford University Press 1958), p. xiii; Oswell, *Television, Childhood and the Home*.

49 Oswell, *Television, Childhood and the Home*, ch. 3, quote p. 49.

50 David Buckingham, Hannah Davies, Ken Jones, and Peter Kelley, *Children's Television in Britain: History, Discourse and Policy* (BFI 1999), p. 127, quote p. 152.

51 Buckingham et al., *Children's Television*, pp. 149, 151. This change in political discourse to neo-liberal assumptions appeared in the US and Europe in the 1980s and 1990s. The idea of consumer sovereignty is however quite different from the early nineteenth-century idea of audience sovereignty. The latter was founded on collective actions that expressed and enforced *collective* interests. The former merely presumes the arithmetic sum of *individual* interests. The two are opposite, even antagonistic ways of exercising power and political will.

52 Buckingham, *Children's Television*, p. 128; Oswell, *Television, Childhood and the Home*, p. 49.

53 David Buckingham, *Public Secrets: EastEnders and its Audience* (BFI 1987), p. 2; Robert Giddings and Keith Selby, *The Classic Serial on Television and Radio* (Palgrave 2001); Christine Geraghty. *Women and Soap Opera: A Study of Prime Time Soaps* (Polity 1991), p. 52.

54 Geraghty, *Women and Soap Opera*, ch. 5 on community in British working-class soaps; quote from R. Williams, *Television, Technology* (Fontana 1974), p. 61.

55 Quote from Dorothy Hobson, *Crossroads: The Drama of a Soap Opera* (Methuen Ltd 1982), p. 109; Richard Dyer, C. Geraghty, M. Jordan, T. Lovell, R. Paterson, and J. Stewart, *Coronation Street* (BFI 1981).

56 Giddings and Selby, *The Classic Serial*, pp. 19–20; Helen Wheatley, "Rooms within rooms," in Johnson and Turnock, *ITV Cultures*, pp. 143–158.

57 On heritage, see Michael Bommes and Patrick Wright, "'Charms of residence': The public and the past," in Richard Johnson, Gregor McLennan, Bill Schwarz, and David Sutton, eds., *Making Histories* (Hutchinson 1982), pp. 253–301; for French classics see Giddings and Selby, *The Classic Serial*, p. 56.

58 BBC historically reinforced a white, middle-class Britishness through its programs. See Glen Creeber, "Hideously white British television, glocalization, and national identity," *Television and New Media*, 5(1) (February 2004): 27–39.

59 Martin Cropper, "Soap opera in muddy waters," *The Times*, November 8, 1986; Mark Lawson, "Television: Old soap in new setting," *The Times*, October 12, 1985, np; Christine Geraghty, "Exhausted and exhausting: Television studies and British soap opera," *Critical Studies in Television*, 5(1) (2010): 82–96, p. 83. On the good influence see "*EastEnders*' good example," *The Times*, November 26, 1987. Also, Christine Gledhill, "Genre, representation and soap opera," in Stuart Hall, ed., *Representation: Cultural Representations and Signifying Practices* (Open University Press 1997), ch. 6, pp. 337–386; Charlotte Brunsdon, "Role of soap opera in feminist television scholarship," in Robert C. Allen, ed., *To be Continued: Soap Opera around the World* (Routledge 1995), pp. 49–65.

60 Mary Ellen Brown, *Soap Opera and Women's Talk: The Pleasure of Resistance* (Sage 1994).
61 Jonathan Bignell and Andreas Fickers, *A European Television History* (Blackwell 2008), p. 75; Stylianos Papathanassoloupolos and Ralph Negrine, *European Media* (Polity 2011), p. 21; Raymond Kuhn, *Media in France* (Routledge 1995), pp. 10–11; Kristin Roth-Ey, *Moscow Prime Time: How the Soviet Union Built the Media Empire That Lost the Cultural Cold War* (Cornell University Press 2014); David C. Hallin, "Neoliberalism and changes in media systems in late twentieth century," in David Hesmondhalgh and Jason Toynbee, eds., *The Media and Social Theory* (Routledge 2008), 43–58.
62 Jean K. Chalaby, "American cultural primacy in a new media order: A European perspective," *International Communication Gazette*, 68(1) (February 2006): 33–51; Daniel Biltereyst, "Resisting American hegemony: A comparative analysis of the reception of domestic and US fiction," *European Journal of Communication*, 6(4) (1991): 469–497; Els de Ben and Hedwige de Smaele, "The inflow of American television fiction on European channels revisited," *European Journal of Communication* (March 2001). US import of British shows was far less than US export to the UK. See Jeffrey Miller, *Something Completely Different: British Television and American Culture* (University of Minnesota Press 2000).
63 Kuhn, *Media in France*, pp. 114–119, 165, 185–187, 215–218, quote p. 119. In 1982, with the end of the Gaullist era, state television monopoly ended and the first commercial network, Canal Plus, a pay-television channel, began. Guallists returned to power in 1986 and moved rapidly to a neo-liberal policy of privatization with two major private operators and cable dominated by three companies.
64 For US television networks and producers these export markets were all profit, since their costs had been recovered domestically. See Valeria Camporesi, "There are no kangaroos in Kent. The American 'model' and the introduction of commercial television in Britain, 1940–1954," in David W. Ellwood and Rob Kroes, eds., *Hollywood in Europe: Experiences of a Cultural Hegemony* (VU University Press, 1994), pp. 266–282.
65 Ulf Jonas Bjork, "'Have gun, will travel': Swedish television and American westerns, 1959–1969," *HTFRT*, 21(3) (2001): 309–321.
66 Andreas Fickers, "The birth of Eurovision," in Andreas Fickers and Catherine Johnson, eds., *Transnational Television History: A Comparative Approach* (Routledge 2012), pp. 13–32.
67 Knut Hickethier "Early TV: Imaging and realizing television," in Bignell and Fickers, *A European Television History*, pp. 71–73; Monika Elsner, Thomas Müller, and Peter M. Spangenberg, "The early history of German television: The slow development of a fast medium," *HJFRT*, 10(2) (1990): 193–219; Michael Meyen and Ute Nawratil. "The viewers: television and everyday life in East Germany," *HJFRT*, 24(3) (2004): 355–364; Marie-Françoise Lévy, "Television, family and society in France, 1949–1968," *HJFRT*, 18(2) (1998): 199–212; A. G. D. West, "Development of theater television in England," *Journal of the SMPE*, 51 (1948):

127–168; H. R. Cassirer, "Audience participation, new style," *Public Opinion Quarterly*, 23(4) (1960): 529–536; J Dumazedier, *Television and Rural Adult Education* (UNESCO 1956).

68 Jerome Bourdon, "Some sense of time: Remembering television," *History and Memory*, 15(2) (Fall/Winter 2003): 5–35; John Foot, "Television and the city, Milan 1945–1960," *Contemporary European History*, 8(3) (November 1999): 379–394, and "The family and the 'economic miracle': Social transformation, work, leisure and development at Bovisa and Comasina, Milan, 1950–1970," *Contemporary European History*, 4(3) (November 1995): 315–338; Mats Bjorkin, "European television audiences," in Bignell and Fickers, *European Television History*, pp. 215–228.

69 Robert Putnam, Robert Leonardi, and Raffaella Y. Nanetti, *Making Democracy Work: Civic Traditions in Modern Italy* (Princeton University Press 1994); Robert Putnam, "Bowling alone: America's declining social capital," *Journal of Democracy*, 6(1) (1995): 65–78. But also see Bo Rothstein, "Social capital in the social democratic welfare state," *Politics & Society*, 29(2) (June 2001): 207–241 that showed no decline of social capital in Sweden since the 1950s. On fear, see George Gerbner, Larry Gross, M. Morgan, and Nancy Signorielli, "Growing up with television: The cultivation perspective," in Jennings Bryant and Dolf Zillman, eds., *Media Effects: Advances in Theory and Research* (Lawrence Erlbaum, 1994), pp. 17–41.

70 Daniel Biltereyst, "Resisting American hegemony."

71 Isabelle Pailliart, "France: Experimenting with pay tv and view data," in Lee B. Becker and Klaus Schoenbach, eds., *Audience Responses to Media Diversification: Coping with Plenty* (Routledge 1989), ch. 8.

72 Ulla Johnsson-Smaragdi, "Sweden: Opening the doors cautiously," in Becker and Schoenbach, *Audience Responses*, ch. 6.

73 Elizabeth Noelle-Neumann and Ruediger Schulz, "Federal Republic of Germany: Social experimentation with cable and commercial television," ch. 9, and Albrecht Kutteroff, Barbara Pfetsch, and Klaus Schoenbach, "Federal republic of Germany: Developing the entertainment option," ch. 10, both in Becker and Schoenbach, *Audience Responses*.

74 Butsch, *American Audiences*, p. 269, Table 18.1.

6 Post-Colonial Television, 1960s–1990s

1 Stewart Anderson and Melissa Chakars, eds., *Modernization, Nation-Building, and Television History* (Routledge 2015); Andreas Fickers and Catherine Johnson, *Transnational Television History: A Comparative Approach* (Routledge 2012), p. 1; Philip Kitley, *Television, Regulation and Civil Society in Asia* (Routledge 2003); Wanning Sun, "Dancing with chains: Significant moments on China Central Television," *International Journal of Cultural Studies*, 10(2) (2007): 187–204; Jayson

Makoto Chun, *A Nation of a Hundred Million Idiots?: A Social History of Japanese Television, 1953–1973* (Routledge 2006).

2 These issues continue to be controversial, as indicated in a 2012 documentary, *The World Before Her*, which explores recent concerns in India about Western modernization and young women (John Anderson, "The world before her," *Variety*, May 7, 2012, 43. On the shift to modernity and individualism in another large nation, see Pankaj Mishra "The places in between: The struggle to define Indonesia," *New Yorker*, August 4, 2014, 64–69.

3 On sitcom, another global genre, see Sharon Sahaf, "Welcome to the sitcom school: A globalized outlook for the study of television history," *Westminster Papers in Communication and Culture*, 4(4) (2007): 103–123.

4 Kaarle Nordenstreng and Tapio Varis, "Television traffic: A one-way street? A survey and analysis of the international flow of television programme material," *Reports and Papers on Mass Communication*, 70 (UNESCO 1974): 12–30.

5 Laurence Shoup, "Shaping the postwar world: The council on foreign relations and United States war aims during World War Two," *Critical Sociology*, 5(3) (1975): 9; "US trade in goods and services – balance of payments (BOP) basis," (US Census Economic Indicators Division, June 2, 2017), https://www.census.gov/foreign-trade/statistics/historical/gands.pdf; Colin Hoskins, Stuart McFadyen, and Adam Finn, *Global Television and Film: An Introduction to the Economics of the Business* (Oxford University Press, 1997), p. 28 table 3.2.

6 Michele Hilmes, *Network Nations* (Routledge 2012), pp. 267–268; Nordenstreng and Varis, "Television traffic," pp. 12, 30–32. The US was being challenged by the 1990s, when television was becoming a mass medium in post-colonial nations. See Chapter 9. Albert Moran, *New Flows in Global TV* (Intellect Press 2009), pp. 146–147; Dal Yong Jin, "Reinterpretation of cultural imperialism: Emerging domestic market vs continuing US dominance," *Media Culture Society*, 29(5) (September 2007): 753–771.

7 Nordenstreng and Varis, "Television traffic," p. 46; Joel Alper, "The Intelsat global satellite system," *Progress in Astronautics and Aeronautics*, 93 (1984); http://www.asiasat.com/asiasat/contentview.php?section=3&lang=0.

8 Cristine Ogan, "Media diversity and communications policy: Impact of VCRs and satellite TV," *Telecommunications Policy* 9(1) (March 1985): 63–73.

9 Jeffrey Taffet, *Foreign Aid as Foreign Policy: The Alliance for Progress in Latin America* (Routledge 2007); Gaddis Smith, *The Last Years of the Monroe Doctrine, 1945–1993* (Hill and Wang 1994), ch. 8; Victor Bulmer-Thomas. *The Economic History of Latin America Since Independence* (Cambridge University Press 2003); Nathaniel Leff, "Export stagnation and autarkic development in Brazil, 1947–1962," *Quarterly Journal of Economics*, 81(2) (1967): 286–301.

10 Elizabeth Fox and Silvio Waisbord, eds., *Latin Politics, Global Media* (University of Texas Press, 2002), ch. 1; Joseph Straubhaar, "Beyond

media imperialism: Assymetrical interdependence and cultural proximity," *Critical Studies in Mass Communication*, 8(1) (1991): 39–59; John Sinclair, *Latin American Television: A Global View* (Oxford University Press 1998).

11 George Martine and Gordon McGranahan, "Brazil's early urban transition: What can it teach urbanizing countries?" (United Nations Population Fund 2010); Ernesto Friedrich de Lima Amaral, "Brazil: Internal migration," in Immanuel Ness, *The Encyclopedia of Global Human Migration* (Blackwell 2013); Angus Maddison, *The Political Economy of Poverty, Equity, and Growth: Brazil and Mexico* (Oxford University Press 1992); Boris Fausto, *A Concise History of Brazil*, 2nd edn. trans. Arthur Brakel (Cambridge University Press 2014); Bulmer-Thomas, *Economic History of Latin America*, pp. 270–275.

12 Cacilda Rêgo and Antonio C. La Pastina, "Brazil and the globalization of telenovelas," in Daya Thussu, ed., *Media on the Move* (Routledge 2007), pp. 99–115; Conrad Kottak, "Television's impact on values and local life in Brazil," *Journal of Communication*, 41(1) (1991): 70–87; Conrad Kottak, *Prime Time Society: An Anthropological Analysis of Television and Culture* (Wadsworth 1990); Joseph Straubhaar, "Brazilian Television: The decline of American influence," *Communication Research*, 11(2) (April 1984): 221–240.

13 Joseph Straubhaar, "Brazil: The role of the state in world television," in Nancy Morris and Silvio Waisbord, eds., *Media and Globalization: Why the State Matters* (Rowman and Littlefield 2001), pp. 133–154; Joseph Straubhaar, "Context, social class and VCRs: A world comparison," in Julia Dobrow, ed., *Social and Cultural Aspects of VCR Use* (Routledge 1990), pp. 125–143. As we will see, the rural use of vcr as substitute for television broadcasts and film theaters occurred in other nations as well, most notably Nigeria.

14 Kottak, *Prime Time Society*, p. 72. On Brazilian tv ratings see Esther Hamburger, Heloisa Buarque de Almeida, Tirza Aidar, and Ananda Stucker, "Imagining audiences in Brazil: Class, race and gender," in Jérôme Bourdon and Cécile Méadel, eds., *Measuring Television Audiences Across the World: Deconstructing the Ratings Machine* (Palgrave 2014), pp. 91–105

15 Quote from Jorge Adib, Edwaldo Package, and Carlos Alberto Vizeu, *50 years of TV in Brazil* (Editora Globo); Fox and Waisbord, eds., *Latin Politics*; Rêgo and LaPastina, "Brazil and globalization of telenovelas." Globo like American producers, recovered its sunk costs domestically, enabling them to sell at low prices in export markets.

16 Laura Stempel Mumford "What is this thing called soap opera?" in Illan Stavans, ed., *Telenovela* (Greenwood Press, 2010), pp. 3–32; Mihai Zdrenghea, "Soap operas vs telenovelas" (Studia Universitatis Babes-Bolyai Romania – Philologia 1/2007); on target audiences see Rêgo and La Pastina, "Brazil and globalization," p. 104

17 Rêgo and La Pastina, "Brazil and globalization," p. 104; Thomas Tufte, "Everyday life, women and telenovelas in Brazil," in Anamaria Fadul,

Serial Fiction in TV: The Latin American Telenovelas (School of Communication and Arts University of São Paulo 1993), p. 77; Marilia Sluyter-Beltrão, "Interpreting Brazilian telenovelas: Biography and fiction in a rural-urban audience," in Fadul, *Serial Fiction*, pp. 63–76; Nico Vink, "Telenovela and emancipation: A study on television and social change in Brazil" (Royal Tropical Institute of Netherlands), p. 11; Leal Ondina and Rueben Oliven, "Class interpretations of a soap opera narrative: The case of the Brazilian novela 'Summer Sun,'" *Theory, Culture, and Society* 5(1) (February 1988): 81–99; Antonio La Pastina and Joseph Straubhaar, "Why do I feel that I don't belong to the Brazil on TV?" *Popular Communication*, 12(2) (April 2014): 104–116; quote on family in Kottak, *Prime Time Society*, pp. 58–61. Although class is a standard theme, native Americans, mestizos, and slums of the poor are never seen (Tufte, "Everyday life," p. 77).

18 Quote from Rêgo and La Pastina, "Brazil and globalization," p. 99.

19 Thais Machado-Borges, *Only for You: Brazilians and Telenovela Flow* (PhD, Stockholm Studies in Social Anthropology 2003), p. 54, quote p. 7; Vink, "Telenovela and emancipation," p. 224 on women. All classes watched to some degree: 35% of lower-middle and lower classes, 34% of middle, and 27% of upper-middle and upper classes (Machado-Borges, *Only for You*, p. 54). Both sexes watched, 60% women and 40% men (Tufte "Everyday life," p. 77). Vink, "Telenovela and emancipation," p. 221 on percentage of avid viewers. Fifty million Brazilians still watch Globo telenovelas nightly (David Segal, "Favored for the gold: Telenovelas," *NYT*, June 12, 2016, BU1, 4).

20 Vink, "Telenovela and emancipation," p. 222; Tufte, "Everyday life," p. 89; Lisa Beljuli-Brown, *Body Parts on Planet Slum: Women and Telenovelas in Brazil* (Anthem Press 2011), p. 2.

21 Vink, "Telenovela and emancipation," pp. 221–231; Tufte, "Everyday life," pp. 94–95; Leal Ondina and Rueben Oliven, "Class Interpretations of a Soap Opera Narrative," pp. 81–99. For young girls, telenovelas were their sole source of sex education (Beljuli-Brown, *Body Parts*, 2011).

22 Charles Wagley, *Amazon Town* (Macmillan 1953); Conrad Kottak, *Prime Time Society: An Anthropological Analysis of Television and Culture* (Wadsworth 1990); Richard Pace and Brian Hinote, *Amazon Town TV: An Audience Ethnography in Gurupa Brazil* (University of Texas Press 2013). A recent study in another town of the region found that patriarchal interpretations of telenovela still remain. See Antonio C. La Pastina, "Telenovela reception in rural Brazil: Gendered readings and sexual mores," *Critical Studies in Media Communication*, 21(2) (2004): 162–180. On race in Gurupa, see Fred J. Hay, "Race, culture, and history: Charles Wagley and the anthropology of the African Diaspora in the Americas," *Boletim do Museu Paraense Emílio Goeldi. Ciências Humanas*, 9(3) (2014): 695–705.

23 Pace and Hinote, *Amazon Town TV*, pp. 125–127.

24 Sluyter-Beltrao, "Interpreting Brazilian telenovelas," p. 68. Audiences
    in rural poor northeast Brazil identified with characters that conformed
    to their values, regardless of their race, class, gender, or age.
25 Pace and Hinote, *Amazon Town TV*, pp. 154–155, 170–175; Emile
    McAnany and Antonio La Pastina, "Telenovela audiences: A review
    and methodological critique of Latin America research," *Communica-
    tion Research*, 21(6) (1994): 828–849, 838.
26 Herbert Gans, *The Urban Villagers* (Free Press 1962); Hortense Pow-
    dermaker, *After Freedom: A Cultural Study in the Deep South* (University
    of Wisconsin Press 1939).
27 On poor as audience see Machado-Borges, *Only for You*, p. 10; Rêgo
    and La Pastina, "Brazil and globalization," p. 105. Ironically, Brazilian
    ratings did not count the poor, nor did India's largest ratings organiza-
    tion, TAM; Ester Hamburger et al., "Imagining audiences in Brazil,"
    pp. 91–105 and Santanu Chakrabarti, "Power games: Audience meas-
    urement as a mediation between actors in India," pp. 113–131, both
    in Bourdon and Meadel, *Measuring Television Audiences*.
28 Mauro P. Porto, "Political controversies in Brazilian TV fiction: Viewers'
    interpretations of the telenovela *Terra Nostra*," *Television and New
    Media*, 6(4) (November 2005): 342–359; Samantha Nogueira Joyce,
    Brazilian Telenovelas and the Myth of Racial Democracy (Lexington
    Books 2012); Beljuli-Brown, *Body Parts on Planet Slum*, p. 71, ch. 4;
    Nahuel Ribke, "Decoding television censorship during the last Brazilian
    military regime: The censor as negotiator and censorship as a semi-open
    interpretative process," *Media History*, 17(1) (2011): 49–61.
29 Arvind Singhal and Everett Rogers, "Educating through television,"
    Populi, 16(2) (1989): 38–47; Arvind Singhal, ed., *Entertainment-Education
    and Social Change: History, Research, and Practice* (Erlbaum 2004).
30 McAnany and LaPastina, "Telenovela audiences"; Singhal and Rogers,
    "Educating through television"; Richard Pace; "Television's interpella-
    tion: Heeding, missing, ignoring, and resisting the call for pan-national
    identity in the Brazilian Amazon," *American Anthropologist*, n.s.111(4)
    (December 2009): 407–419.
31 On the survey, McAnany and La Pastina, "Telenovela audiences"; On
    Salvador, Beljuli-Brown, *Body Parts on Planet Slum*; on getting by,
    Michel de Certeau, *The Practice of Everyday Life* (University of Cali-
    fornia Press 1984), ch. 3; on power to interpret, David Morley and
    Roger Silverstone, "Domestic communications: Technologies and mean-
    ings," *Media, Culture and Society*, 12(1) (1990): 31–55; on Mexican
    women, Karla Covarubias, "Hacia una nueva culturas televisiva: La
    telenovela Mirada de Mujer de percepcion el los publicos colimenses.
    Resultatodos de investgatione," *Estudios sobre las Culturas Contem-
    poraneas*, 2(7) (2001): 89–126.
32 Sevanti Ninan, "History of Indian broadcasting reform," *Cardozo Journal
    of International and Comparative Law*, 5 (Fall 1997): 341–364; William
    Mazzarella, "'Reality must improve': The perversity of expertise and

the belatedness of Indian television development," *Global Media and Communication*, 8(3) (2012): 215–241; Shanti Kumar, "Globalization, media privatization, and the redefinition of the 'public' in Indian television," *BioScope: South Asian Screen Studies*, 1(1) (2010): 21–5; Nikhil Sinha, "India: Television and national politics," in Marc Raboy, ed., *Public Broadcasting for the 21ˢᵗ Century* (University of Luton Press 1995), pp. 212–229.

33 Sevanti Ninan, *Through the Magic Window: Television and Change in India* (Penguin Books 1995), pp. 67–70.

34 Ninan, *Through the Magic Window*; Sinha, "India: Television"; Usha Vyasulu Reddi, "Rip Van Winkle: A story of Indian television," in David French and Michael Richards, eds., *Contemporary Television: Eastern Perspectives* (Sage 1996), pp. 231–245, quote on p. 231.

35 Purnima Mankekar, *Screening Culture, Viewing Politics: An Ethnography of Television, Womanhood and Nation* (Duke University Press 1999), pp. 75, 114.

36 Doordarshan focused on middle-class families, which drew criticism to the invisibility of the working class. See Mankekar, *Screening Culture*, pp. 77, 114. On women viewers, Chitra Krishnaswamy, "Indian women and television. A study of the women viewers of Madras, India," ERIC no. ED293523. Paper presented at the International Television Studies Conference, London, England, July 10–12, 1986. On Indian soap opera industry, Shoma Munshi, *Prime Time Soap Operas on Indian Television* (Routledge 2010). On *Hum Log* and "education-entertainment," Arvind Singhal and Everett Rogers, "Educating through television," pp. 38–47; Arvind Singhal, ed., *Entertainment-Education and Social Change: History, Research, and Practice* (Erlbaum 2004); Singhal, Rogers and William J. Brown, "Entertainment telenovelas for development: Lessons learned," in Anamaria Fadul, ed., *Serial Fiction in TV: The Latin American Telenovela* (School of Communication and Arts, University of São Paulo 1993), pp. 149–165; Veena Dass, "On soap opera: What kind of anthropological object is it?" in Daniel Miller, ed., *World's Apart: Modernity through the Prism of the Local* (Routledge 1995), pp. 169–189.

37 Mankekar, *Screening Culture*.

38 Arvind Singhal and Everett Rogers, "Television soap operas for development in India," *Gazette*, 41 (1988): 109–126, quote p. 118.

39 Timothy Scrase, "Television, the middle classes and the transformation of cultural identities in west Bengal India," *Gazette: The International Journal for Communication Studies*, 64(4) (August 2002): 323–342; Ninan, *Through the Magic Window*, pp. 187–192.

40 On *izzat* see Marie Gillespie, *Television Ethnicity and Cultural Change* (Routledge 1995), pp. 150–154. On cross cultures see Mankekar, *Screening Culture*, p. 114 n. 9; Butsch, *American Audiences*, ch. 5; John Kasson, *Rudeness and Civility: Manners in Nineteenth-Century Urban America* (Hill and Wang 1990); Francis Michael Longstreth Thompson, *The Rise of Respectable Society: A Social History of Victorian Britain,*

1830–1900 (Harvard University Press 1988); Karoline Kan, "Date show gives reins to parents in China," *NYT*, 2.20.17, A3.

41 Kirk Johnson, "Media and social change: The modernizing influences of television in rural India," *Media, Culture, and Society*, 23(2) (2001): 147–169; Y. V. Lakshmana Rao, *Communication and Development: A Study of Two Indian Villages* (University of Minnesota Press 1966); Paul Hartmann, B. R. Patil, Anita Dighe, *The Mass Media and Village Life: An Indian Study* (Sage 1989). On transitions from subsistence to consumption see Harry Braverman, *Labor and Monopoly Capital* (Monthly Review Press 1974), ch. 15.

42 K. Johnson, "Media and social change," quote p. 161.

43 Many studies have concluded this, from Paul Lazarsfeld, Bernard Berelson, and Hazel Gaudet, *The People's Choice: How the Voter Makes Up His Mind in a Presidential Campaign* (Duell Sloan 1944), to Paul Hartman et al., *Mass Media and Village Life*.

44 Ministry of Overseas Indian Affairs, "India and its diaspora" (moia. gov.in); Marie Gillespie, *Television Ethnicity*, p. 79, ch. 3. Movie-going is still about family and socializing. See Kevin Smets, Iris Vandevelde, Philippe Meers, Roel Vande Winkel, and Sofie Van Bauwel, "Between unruliness and sociality: Discourses on diasporic cinema audiences for Turkish and Indian films," in Richard Butsch and Sonia Livingstone, eds., *Meanings of Audiences* (Routledge 2013), pp. 64–79.

45 Gillespie, *Television, Ethnicity*, pp. 95–97; William I. Thomas and Florian Znaniecki, *The Polish Peasant in Europe and America* (Gorham Press 1920).

46 Gillespie, *Television, Ethnicity*, pp. 144ff; Joost De Bruin, "Dutch television soap opera, ethnicity and girls' interpretations," *Gazette*, 63(1) (2001): 41–56. On framing characters different from preferred reading, Dorothy Hobson, "Soap operas at work," pp. 150–167, and Ellen Seiter, Hans Borchers, G. Kreutzner, and E. M. Warth, "Don't treat us like we're so stupid and naive," pp. 223–247, both in Seiter et al., eds., *Remote Control: Television, Audiences, and Cultural Power* (Routledge 1989).

47 Noha Mellor, Muhammad Ayish, Nabil Dajani, Kalil Rinnawi, *Arab Media: Globalization and Emerging Media Industries* (Polity 2011), pp. 86–94; Nordenstreng and Varis, "Television Traffic," p. 46; on satellite disruption, Lila Abu-Lughod, *Dramas of Nationhood: The Politics of Television in Egypt* (University of Chicago Press 2005), p. 197. On 1990s see Kai Haifez, ed., *Mass Media Politics and Society in the Middle East* (Hampton Press 2001); on 2000s, see Haifez ed., *Arab Media: Power and Weakness* (Continuum 2008); on Arab cultures, see Samir Khalaf and Roseanne Saad Khalaf, *Arab Society and Culture: An Essential Guide* (Saqi Press 2010).

48 Haifez, *Mass Media Politics*, 2001, pp. 1–4, Table 1; Mellor et al., *Arab Media*, pp. 85–89. Marc Lynch, "Political opportunity structures: Effect of Arab media," pp. 17–32, and Hussein Amin, "Arab media audience

research: developmenst and constraints," pp. 69–90, both in Haifez, *Arab media*, each note a dearth of information in the 2000s about Arabic audiences in this region.

49   Mellor et al., *Arab Media*, pp. 104–106; Roy Armes, *Post-Colonial Images: Studies in North African Films* (Indiana University Press 2005), pp. 15, 87; Lughod, *Dramas of Nationhood*, ch. 8.

50   Aliaa Dawoud, "Egyptian audiences of *musalsalat* in the eye of the beholder," in Butsch and Livingstone, *Meanings of Audiences*, pp. 123–134. In Egypt even during the turbulence of protests and regime change in 2011, musalsalat drew large audiences. Recently, Turkish serials have become more popular among Arab nations. See Miriam Berg, "Turkish drama serials as a tool for Soft Power," *Participations*, 14(2) (November 2017), online at www.participations.org.

51   Clive Holes, "Dialect and national identity: the cultural politics of self-representation in Bahraini *musalsalāt*," pp. 52–72, in Paul Dresch and James Piscatori, eds., *Monarchies and Nations: Globalisation and Identity in the Arab States of the Gulf* (I. B. Tauris, 2005); see also Ehab Galal, ed., *Arab TV Audiences: Negotiating Religion and Identity* (PL Academic Research 2014).

52   Abu-Lughod, *Dramas of Nationhood*. Compare to the metropolitan Arabic viewers in 1980s described in Tamar Liebes and Elihu Katz, *The Export of Meaning: Cross-Cultural Readings of Dallas* (Oxford University Press 1990).

53   Estimate based on UN population statistics.

54   Jo Ellen Fair, "Francophonie and the national airwaves: A history of television in Senegal," in Lisa Parks and Shanti Kumar, eds., *Planet TV: A Global Television Reader* (New York University Press 2003), pp. 189–210; Jean-François Werner, "How women are using television to domesticate globalization: A case study on the reception and consumption of telenovelas in Senegal," *Visual Anthropology*, 19(5) (2006): 443–472; Robert Launay, "Spirit media: Electronic media and Islam among Dyula of Côte D'Ivoire," *Africa*, 67(3) (1997): 441–453; Dorothea Schulz, *Muslims and New Media in West Africa*, Indiana University Press 2012), p. 76.

55   Launay, "Spirit media"; Pierre Barrot, *Nollywood the Video Phenomenon in Nigeria* (James Currey 2008), pp. 17, 44; Werner, "How women are using television"; also Brian Larkin, *Signal and Noise: Media, Infrastructure and Urban Culture in Nigeria* (Duke University Press 2008). On Nigeria and Nollywood also see Chapter 9.

56   Werner, "How women are using television."

57   Ying Zhu, "Transnational circulation of Chinese-language television dramas," in Ying Zhu and Chris Berry, eds., *TV China* (Indiana University Press 2008), pp. 221ff; Michael Curtin, *Playing to the World's Largest Audience: The Globalization of Chinese Film and TV* (University of California Press 2007); Ying Zhu, *Two Billion Eyes: The Story of China Central Television* (The New Press 2012); quote, Yin Hong,

"Meaning, production, consumption: The history and reality of television drama in China," in Stephanie H. Donald, Michael Keane, and Yin Hong, eds., *Media in China: Consumption, Content and Crisis* (Routledge-Curzon 2002), pp. 28–40, quote p. 31.

58 Jai Yan Mi, "Visual imagined community," *Quarterly Review of Film and Video*, 22(3) (2005): 330–331; Yin Hong, "Meaning, production consumption"; Jianying Sha, *China Pop: How Soap Operas, Tabloids and Bestsellers are Transforming a Culture* (New Press 1995), 30–31; on inconsistencies, James Lull, *China Turned On: Television, Reform, and Resistance* (Routledge, 1991), pp. 132–145.

59 Ying Zhu, Michael Keane, and Ruoyun Bai, eds., *TV Drama in China* (Hong Kong University Press 2008); Hong, "Meaning, production, consumption." Demand for programming was met partly through imports from Taiwan, Hong Kong, Japan, Mexico, Brazil, and the US that were popular among urban professionals and college students (Zhu 2008, p. 72). As political winds changed, dramas sometimes were changed to fit new policy directions, criticized or even cancelled.

60 Ying Zhu, *Television in Post-Reform China: Serial Dramas, Confucian Leadership and the Global Television Market* (Routledge 2008), pp. 81–83; Hong, "Meaning, production, consumption"; Sha, *China Pop*, pp. 27–28.

61 Hong, "Meaning, production, consumption," quote p. 32; Zhu, *Television in Post-Reform China*, p. 82.

62 Shuyu Kong, "Family matters; Reconstructing the family on the Chinese television screen," in Zhu, Keane, and Bai, *TV Drama in China*, pp. 77–78.

63 Janice Hua Xu, "Family saga serial dramas and reinterpretation of cultural traditions," in Zhu, Keane, and Bai, *TV Drama in China*, pp. 34–41

64 James Lull and Se-Wen Sun, "Agent of modernization: Television and urban Chinese families," in James Lull, *World Families Watch Television* (Routledge 1988), pp. 191–236; James Lull, *China Turned On* (Routledge 1991), pp. 72–77. On the 2000s, see Tongdao Zhang, "Chinese television audience research," in Ying Zhu and Chris Berry, eds., *TV China*, pp. 168–180.

65 Yin Hong, "Meaning, production, consumption," pp. 28–40; Jingsi Wu, "From *qunzhong* to *guanzhong*: The evolving conceptualization of audience in mainland China," in Butsch and Livingstone, *Meanings of Audiences*, pp. 170–186. To compare India and China tv development see Kartik Pashupati, Hua Lin Sun, and Stephen D. McDowell, "Guardians of culture, development communicators, or state capitalists?" *Gazette: The International Journal for Communication Studies*, 65(3) (2003): 251–271.

66 Lull, *China Turned On*, pp. 165–175; Zhao Bin, "The little emperors' small screen: Parental control and children's television viewing in China," *Media, Culture, & Society*, 18(4) (1996): 639–658.

67 Dipesh Chakrabarty, *Provincializing Europe: Postcolonial Thought and Historical Difference* (Princeton University Press, 2008), p. 6.

7 Digital Media in the New Millennium

1 Only the privileged can afford and have use for the full array of mobile hardware and services. Yet, some forms and services are affordable to a surprising portion of world population. See Chapter 9.

2 Analog signals are continuous, just as a stream of water from a faucet is continuous; the volume is not broken into parts or packages. Digital signals are discrete, like the drops from a dripping faucet are separate, distinct, discrete packages of water. Analog computers are electrical models of other processes; digital computers are logical and mathematical calculators. Computers today are synonymous with digital. In 1960, one could find both digital and analog computers in the same room doing the same computations.

3 Karen Idelson, "Reel life in digital world," *Variety*, February 6, 2012, 1, 44; Andrew Horn, "Theaters at tipping point," *Variety*, June 18, 2012, 11–12. On effects of digital film see Chuck Tryon, *On-Demand Culture: Digital Delivery and the Future of Movies* (Rutgers University Press, 2013).

4 Jostein Gripsrud, ed., *Relocating Television: Television in the Digital Context* (Routledge 2010); Elsa Keslassy, "Animation maturation," *Variety*, February 28, 2011, A1. Digitization may replace many live actors in movie scenes.

5 Michael Daubs and Vincent Manzerolle, "From here to ubiquity. History of development of digitization, convergence, mobility and ubiquity," in Daubs and Manzerolle, eds., *Mobile and Ubiquitous Media: Critical and International Perspectives* (Peter Lang 2018); Henry Jenkins *Convergence Culture* (New York University Press 2006), quote p. 2.

6 On infrastructure barriers see Naman Ramachandran, "India pix face digital divide," *Variety*, April 9, 2012, 6n. On differences in access see Antonis Kalogeropoulos, Samuel Negredo, Ike Picone, and Rasmus Kleis Nielsen, "Who shares and comments on news?: A cross-national comparative analysis of online and social media participation," *Social Media & Society*, 3(4) (October–December 2017): 1–26.

7 On switch to digital television, country by country, see *International Journal of Digital Television*, 1–4, March 2000 to December 2013. On migrating audiences see Brian Lowry, "TV viewers turn on, tune out," *Variety*, September 5, 2011, 9; "No choice now but to rethink commercials," *NYT*, May 14, 2018, B4. For impact on cable and broadcast television see Robert Marich, "Should studios fret over online crack in cable window?" *Variety*, October 31, 2011, 1,10. By 2011 SNL Kagan and Nielsen reported that there already were over 100,000 tv shows and movies available online. See Marc Graser, "Cyber-bidding war,"

Variety, December 5, 2011, 1, 35. By mid 2017, nearly 60% of US homes had a TV and device to stream films and tv shows from the internet. See Neilsen Corp, Q2 2017, Total Audience Report and "Streamer things: Internet-enabled TV" *Neilsen Newswire*, November16, 2017.

8   David Carr, "More cracks undermine the citadel of TV profits," *NYT*, April 15, 2013, B1,8; Andrea Esser, "The format business: franchising television content," *International Journal of Digital Television*, 4(2) (2013): 141–158.

9   Eric Gordon and Adrianna de Souza e Silva, *Net Locality: Why Location Matters in a Networked World* (Wiley-Blackwell 2011); Graham, Mark, Matthew Zook, and Andrew Boulton, "Augmented reality in urban places: contested content and the duplicity of code," *Transactions of the Institute of British Geographers*, 38(3) (2013): 464–479; Ana Rita Morais, "Towards a new visuality of 'mobile infography,'" in Daubs and Manzerolle, *Mobile and Ubiquitous*, pp. 109–125.

10 Gordon and de Sousa e Silva, *Net Locality*; "Google Latitude: See where your friends are right now," http://www.google.com/intl/en/about/products/index.html; Adam Foster, "Don't ask why. Ask where," *NYT*, December 15, 2013, pp. 42–44, 73–75; Rich Ling, "The phases of mobile communication research," in Ana Serrano Telleria, ed., *Between the Public and Private in Mobile Communication* (Routledge 2017).

11 Robyn Weisman, "Auds time-shift future," *Variety*, March 7, 2011, 11; Nielsen, "Total audience report," Q1 2017; Farhad Manjoo, "Comcast vs the cord cutters," *NYT*, February 16, 2014, BU1,4; "Milestone marker: svod and dvr penetration are now on par with one another," *Nielsen Insights*, June 27, 2016; Hilary Atkin, "TV's social climbers," *Variety*, August 22, 2011, 3.

12 Mark Weiser, "The computer for the 21st century," *Scientific American*, 265(3) (1991): 94–104.

13 Haruhiro Kato "Japanese youth and the imagining of Keitai," in Mizuko Ito, Misa Matsuda, and kDaiske Okabe, eds., *Personal, Portable, Pedestrian: Mobile Phones in Japanese Life* (MIT Press 2005), pp. 103–122.

14 Paul Dourish and Genevieve Bell, *Divining a Digital Future: Mess and Mythology in Ubiquitous Computing* (MIT Press 2011), quote on p. 124.

15 Dourish and Bell, *Divining a Digital Future*, pp. 31–39, on Singapore and South Korea.

16 Richard Butsch, "Homevideo and corporate plans" in Butsch, ed., *For Fun and Profit* (Temple University Press 1990); "TV and social media," *Nielsen Insights*, December 18, 2017; "Media use millennials," *Nielsen Insights*, August 21, 2017.

17 Pablo Boczkowski and Eugenia Mitchelstein, "How users take advantage of different forms of interactivity on online news sites: Clicking, e-mailing, and commenting," *Human Communication Research*, 38(1) (2012): 1–22; Derek Kompare "Rerun2.0: revising repetition for multiplatform

television distribution," *Journal of Popular Film and Television*, 38(2) (2010): 79–83; Jean Burgess and Joshua Green, *YouTube: Online Video and Participatory Culture* (Polity 2009).

18 Frederick Lumley, *Measurement in Radio* (Ohio State University Press 1934), bibliography; Jerome Bourdon and Cecile Méadel, eds., *Television Audiences Across the World: Deconstructing the Ratings Machine* (Palgrave 2014); Joseph Turow, *The Daily You* (Yale University Press 2011); Anne Eisenberg, "When algorithms grow accustomed to your face," *NYT*, December 1, 2013, BU 3; Natasha Singer, "When no one is just a face in the crowd" *NYT*, February 2, 2014, BU 3.

19 Josie van Dijck, *The Culture of Connectivity* (Oxford University Press 2013).

20 Richard Edwards, *Contested Terrain* (Basic Books 1979); Harry Braverman, *Labor and Monopoly Capital* Monthly Review Press, 1974. On consumer labor see Christian Fuchs, "Dallas Smythe today – the audience commodity, the digital labour debate," *Triple C*, 10(2) (2012): 692–740; Brett Caraway, "Audience labor in the new media environment," *Media Culture & Society*, 33(5) (July 2011): 693–708; On consumer deskilling see Butsch, "The commodification of leisure," *Qualitative Sociology*, 7(3) (Fall 1984): 217–235

21 M. Weiser, R. Gold, and John Seely Brown, "Origins of ubiquitous computing research at PARC in the late 1980s," *IBM Systems Journal*, 38(4) (1999): 693–696; Weiser "Computer for the 21st century"; Eran Fisher, "How less alienation creates more exploitation. Audience labour on social network sites," pp. 180–203, and Miriyam Aouragh, "Social media, mediation and the Arab revolutions," pp. 482–515, both in Christian Fuchs and Vincent Mosco, eds., *Marx in the Age of Digital Capitalism* (Brill 2016). On continual use, see Ian Bogost, "The new iPhones are big so you won't put them down," *The Atlantic* (September 2018), www,theatlantic.com/technology/archive/2018/09/the-new-iphones-are-too-big-to-put-down.

22 Benjamin Bakdikian, *The New Media Monopoly* (Beacon Press 2004); Editorial "The national entertainment state," *The Nation*, 283(1) (July 3, 2006): 13–30; Toby Miller, Mark Crispin Miller, and Janine Jaquet Biden, "The national entertainment state," *The Nation*, 262(22) (June 3, 1996): 23–27; Littleton, Cynthia, "Ten years of tumult" *Variety*, January 3, 2010. On de-regulation see Cecelia Kang "FCC to lift rule limiting media owners," *NYT*, October 26, 2017, B6.

23 On a competitive marketplace of ideas as a solution see Barry Litman, "The television networks, competition and program diversity," *Journal of Broadcasting*, 23(4) (1979): 393–409; Philip Napoli, "Deconstructing the diversity principle," *Journal of Communication*, 49(4) (Autumn 1999): 7–34; Mara Einstein "Broadcast Network Television, 1955–2003: The pursuit of advertising and the decline of diversity," *Journal of Media Economics*, 17(2) (2004): 145–155; Jay Blumler and Caroline Spicer "Prospects for creativity in the new television marketplace," *Journal of Communication*, 40(4) (1990): 78–101.

24 Susan Young, "Riding social media wave," *Variety*, August 29, 2011, 18, 22. See discussion of *Big Brother* in Chapter 9 on adaptation of global product to local audiences; Marc Graser and Brian Lowry, "Cyberbidding war," *Variety*, December 5–11, 2011, 1, 35; Bill Carter, "Streaming and cable for *The Simpsons*," *NYT*, November 16, 2013, B1, 3; David Carr, "Amazon makes a claim for the living room and beyond," *NYT*, November 4, 2013, B1, 3.

25 Chris Morris "Nets jump into mobile stream," *Variety*, October 1, 2012, 16; Virginia Nightingale and Tim Dwyer, eds., *New Media Worlds: Challenges for Convergence* (Oxford University Press 2007). For a critique of this trend see Brian Lowry, "Tweet smell of excess," *Variety*, June 25, 2012, 7.

26 On privacy and surveillance see Barrington Moore, *Privacy: A Social and Cultural History* (M. E. Sharpe 1984); D. J. Solove, *Understanding Privacy* (Harvard University Press 2008); Joshua A. T. Fairfield and Christoph Engel, "Privacy as a public good," *Duke Law Journal*, 65(3) (December 2015): 385–457; Neil M. Richards, "The dangers of surveillance," *Harvard Law Review* 1945–1952 (2013): 126; Jose Marichal, *Facebook Democracy: The Architecture of Disclosure and the Threat to Public Life* (Routledge 2016); Daniel Trottier, *Social Media as Surveillance* (Ashgate 2012); Arne Hintz, Lina Dencik, and Karin Wahl-Jorgensen, "Digital citizenship and surveillance society," *International Journal of Communication*, 11(2017): 731–739.

27 Daniel J. Solove, "Introduction: Privacy self-management and the consent dilemma," *Harvard Law Review*, 126(7) (May 2013): 1880–1903.

28 Jeremy Bentham, *The Works of Jeremy Bentham* vol. 4, part 2: "Panopticon" (John Bowring 1843); Michel Foucault, *Discipline and Punish; The Birth of the Prison* (Vintage Books 1995).

29 Jane Mayer, "The secret sharer," *The New Yorker*, May 23, 2011, 47–57, quote p. 49; Joseph Turow, *Niche Envy* (MIT Press 2006), p. 130 on Walmart; Adam Liptak, "Wary of 'Big Brother' in a digital privacy case," *NYT*, November 30, 2017, A17.

30 Shoshana Zuboff, "Big other: Surveillance capitalism and the prospects of an information civilization," *Journal of Information Technology*, 30(1) (2015): 75–89, and *Master or Slave? The Fight for the Soul of Our Information Civilisation* (Profile Books 2018).

31 Joseph Turow, *The Daily You* (Yale University Press 2011); Eric Gordon and Adriana de Souza e Silva, *Net Locality* (Wiley-Blackwell 2011), ch. 6; Jose van Dijck, *Culture of Connectivity*.

32 Turow, *The Daily You*, ch. 2.

33 Amadou Diallo, "Is your car a privacy threat?" *Forbes Magazine*, December 16, 2013; Sapna Maheshwari, "Is your Vizio television spying on you?" *NYT*, February 8, 2017, B3; Steve Lohr, "Stepping up security for an internet-of-things world," *NYT*, October 17, 2016, B3; David E. Sanger and Nicole Perlroth, "A new era of internet attacks powered by everyday devices," *NYT*, October 23, 2016, A1, 25; Brian Chen, "Smart kitchens a tough sell," *NYT*, March 26, 2018, B1, 5; Jennifer

Valentino-Devries, "How game apps collect data on children," *NYT*, September 13, 2018, B1,7.

34   Edward Wyatt "Webcam's flaw put users' live on display," *NYT*, September 5, 2013, B1, 6; Ginger McCall, "The face scan arrives," *NYT*, August 30, 2013, A19; Natasha Singer, "When no one is just a face in the crowd," http://www.facefirst.com/advantages.

35   Quicken UPC 841798 100547. Comparing the US and EU on individual rights, see Robert Levine, "The student who stood up for privacy," *NYT*, October 11, 2015, BU1, 4.

36   Turow, *The Daily You.*

37   "On the road to riches," *Advertising Age*, May 22, 2011, online; Turow, *Niche Envy*, 180–181.

38   Charles Duhigg "Campaigns mine personal lives to get out vote," *NYT*, October 14, 2012, 1, 18; Nick Corasaniti and Ashley Parker, "G.O.P. ads chase voters at home and on the go," *NYT*, November 1, 2014, A1, 16; Sheera Frenkel, "An expert in pajamas, battling bots," *NYT*, November 13, 2018, B1, 4; Paul Mozur, "Drone maker from China clashes with US over data," *NYT*, November 30, 2017, B1, 5.

39   E.g. Scott Shane, Nicole Perlroth, and David Sanger, "Deep security breach cripples N.S.A.," *NYT*, November 13, 2017, A1, 14; "Credit firm Equifax says 143m Americans' social security numbers exposed in hack," *Guardian*, online September 7, 2017, https://www.theguardian.com/us-news/2017/sep/07/equifax-credit-breach-hack-social-security.

40   E.g. In *The New York Times* just in Fall 2017: Farhad Manjoo, "Why tech is making me uneasy," October 12, A2. Noam Cohen, "Silicon Valley is not your friend," October 15, SR1, 4–5; Nick Wingfield and Katie Thomas, "With a look by Amazon, drug firms shudder," October 28, B1, 6; Cecilia Kang, "From tech's ally to critic," October 30, B1, 9; Natasha Singer and Danielle Ivory "Tech firms entice schools with steaks and travel," November 4, A1; Cade Metz, "The rise of the machine," November 6, B1, 3; David Sax, "Our love affair with digital is over," November 19, SR10; Adam Liptak, "Wary of 'Big Brother' in a digital privacy case," November 30, A17; Ashley Boyd, "Don't give kids gifts that spy," December 9, A19.

41   James B. Rule, Douglas McAdam, Linda Stearns, and David Uglow, "Documentary identification and mass surveillance in the United States," *Social Problems*, 31(2) (December 1983): 222–234.

42   Non-cash transactions are now common in many nations. See Nathaniel Popper and Guilbert Gates, "Farewell to cash?" *NYT*, November s14, 2017, F6. On use of social security numbers since 1927, see Carolyn Puckett, "The Story of the Social Security Number," *Social Security Bulletin*, 69(2) (2009), https://www.ssa.gov/policy/docs/ssb/v69n2/v69n2p55.html. On the vulnerability of Social Security numbers for identity protection see Telis Demos and Peter Rudegeair, "After Equifax, a New Way Forward," *Wall Street Journal*, October 17, 2017, B4.

43   Suzanne Kapner, "Retailers misfire in email offers," *Wall Street Journal*, November 28, 2017, B1, 4.

8 Using Digital Media

1 http://www.nielsen.com/us/en/insights/news/2018/as-the-media-universe-grows-ad-supported-content-remains-a-preferred-source.html; Nielsen Total Audience Report Q2 2017, http://www.nielsen.com/us/en/insights/reports/2017/the-nielsen-total-audience-q2-2017.html.

2 On the US see Brian Lowry, "TV viewers turn on, tune out," *Variety*, September 5, 2011, 9; "Riding social media wave," *Variety*, August 29, 2011, 18; "TV's social climbers," *Variety*, August 22, 2011, 3; Nele Simons, Watching TV fiction in the age of digitization, *International Journal of Digital Television*, 4(2) (June 2013): 177–191. Elsewhere see Michael Daubs and Vincent Manzerolle, eds., *Mobile and Ubiquitous Media: Critical and International Perspectives* (Peter Lang 2018).

3 Koo, Gi Yeon, "Constructing an alternative public sphere: The cultural significance of social media in Iran," in Nele Lenze, Charlotte Schriwer, and Zubaidah Abdul Jalil, eds., *Media in the Middle East: Activism, Politics and Culture* (Palgrave 2018), pp. 21–43.

4 Chris Anderson, *The Long Tail* (Hyperion 2006); "Netflix to deliver movies to the PC," *NYT*, January 16, 2007; Jane Kolodinsky, Jean Hogarth, and Marianne Hilgert, "The adoption of electronic banking technologies by U.S consumers," *International Journal of Bank Marketing*, 22(4) (2004): 238–59. On the state of the internet in the mid 1990s see Barry Wellman et al., "Computer networks as social networks," *Annual Review of Sociology*, 22 (1996). Aaron Smith, "46% of American adults are smartphone owners," *Pew Internet & American Life Project* (2012).

5 n.a. "Streamer things: internet-enabled tv connected devices in US tv homes," *Neilsen Newswire* November 16, 2017. "TV streaming devices," Neilsen 2017.

6 https://www.dacast.com/blog/how-to-stream-live-video-over-the-internet-and-what-that-means/; https://www.bestsportstreaming.com/; http://www.adweek.com/tv-video/espns-millennial-ratings-for-live-sports-jump-as-much-as-33–with-streaming-and-out-of-home-viewing/; http://variety.com/2017/tv/news/espn-live-viewer-measurement-tv-advertising-upfront-2017–1202428258/; Neilsen 360 video report 8–2017; Brian Steinberg, "CBS tackles new game with super bowl 50: Digital viewers and live-streamed ads," *Variety*, January 26, 2016.

7 Roughly 90% of purchases in North America, much of Western Europe, Japan, and Korea, and half of all transactions in Russia, China, and much of South America, are now via credit or debit card and smartphone. See Nathaniel Popper and Guilbert Gates, "Farewell to cash?" *NYT*, November 14, 2017, F6.

8 Nathan Heller, "The digital republic," *New Yorker*, December 18, 2017, 84–93.

9 In late 2017 Snapchat split its user sites into two columns, left for social communication among friends etc., right for Snap-curated content from publishers, writers, celebrities and user-generated photos and videos.

Similarly, Facebook added a newsfeed. Airlines are fast moving to global inflight internet service, see www.airbornewirelessnetwork.com.

10 Claude Fischer, *America Calling: A Social History of the Telephone to 1940* (University of California Press, 1994), esp. pp. 265–68; Ellen Stock Stern and Emily Margolin Gwathmey, eds., *Once upon a Telephone: An Illustrated Social History* (Pub Overstock Unlimited Incorporated 1994); Derek R. Rutter, *Communicating by Telephone* (Pergamon Press 1987); Diane Zimmerman Umble, "The Amish and the telephone: Resistance and reconstruction," in Roger Silverstone and Eric Hirsch, eds., *Consuming Technologies: Media and Information in Domestic Spaces* (Routledge 1992), pp. 103–109; James E. Katz, *Connections: Social and Cultural Studies of the Telephone in American Life* (Transaction Publishers 1999).

11 Judy Wajcman, *Pressed for Time: The Acceleration of Life in Digital Capitalism* (University of Chicago Press 2015); Hatuka, Tali, and Eran Toch, "The emergence of portable private-personal territory: Smartphones, social conduct and public spaces," *Urban Studies*, 53(10) (2016): 2192–2208; Peter Vorderer, Dorothée Hefner, Leonard Reinecke, and Christoph Klimmt, eds., *Permanently Online, Permanently Connected* (Routledge 2017); Mirca Madianou, and Daniel Miller, "Polymedia: Towards a new theory of digital media in interpersonal communication," *International Journal of Cultural Studies*, 16(2) (2013): 169–187; Pepita Hesselberth, "Discourses on disconnectivity and the right to disconnect," *New Media & Society*, 20(5) (2018): 1994–2010.

12 Jose Marichal, *Facebook Democracy: The Architecture of Disclosure and the Threat to Public Life* (Ashgate 2012); Brett Caraway, "Audience labor in the new media environment: A Marxian revisiting of the audience commodity," *Media Culture & Society*, 33(5) (July 2011): 693–708. Technical control of labor described in Ch. 3 and Richard Edwards, *Contested Terrain: The Transformation of the Workplace in the Twentieth Century* (Basic Books 1979).

13 On continual use, see Ian Bogost, "The new iPhones are big so you won't put them down," *The Atlantic* (September 2018). About posting of pictures on Facebook see Shanyang Zhao, Sherri Grasmuck, and Jason Martin, "Identity construction on Facebook: Digital empowerment in anchored relationships," *Computers in Human Behavior*, 24(5) (September 2008): 1816–1836.

14 Both quality and efficiency of performance is reduced by multi-tasking. See Eyal Ophir, Clifford Nass, and Anthony D. Wagner, "Cognitive control in media multitaskers," *Proceedings of the National Academy of Sciences of the US*, 106(37) (September 15, 2009), 15583–15587; Nass et al., "Media use, face-to-face communication, media multitasking, and social well," *Developmental Psychology*, 48(2) (March 2012): 327–336. On past concerns see Richard Butsch, *Making of American Audiences* (Cambridge University Press 2000), chs 13 and 17. Data on current multi-tasking see "Tops of 2017: television and social media," *Nielsen Newswire*, December 18, 2017, http://www.nielsen.com/us/en/insights/news/2017/ tops-of-2017–television-and-social-media.html.

Opposite to multitasking is the use of mobile media to fill 'dead time' when there seems to be little else to do, in waiting rooms or in transit by plane, train, bus, or car.

15 Mizuko Ito, Heather Horst, Matteo Bittanti, danah boyd, Becky Herr-Stephenson, Patricia G. Lange, C. J. Pascoe, and Laura Robinson, "Living and learning with new media: Summary of findings from the digital youth project" (John D. and Catherine T. MacArthur Foundation, November 2008); http://digitalyouth.ischool.berkeley.edu/projects.

16 On interaction via smartphones: Eva Thulin, "Always on my mind: How smartphones are transforming social contact among young Swedes," *Young*, 26(5) (2017): 1–19; Shalin Misra et al., "The iPhone effect T the quality of in-person social interactions in the presence of mobile devices," *Environment and Behavior*, 48(2) (2016): 275–298: Jeffrey Hall, "When is social media use social interaction? Defining mediated social interaction," *New Media and Society*, online (July 28, 2016); Hazel Lacohée, Nina Wakeford, and Ian Pearson, "A social history of the mobile telephone with a view of its future," *BT Technology Journal*, 21(3) (2003): 203–211.

17 Much research focuses on psychological effects of smartphone and internet use on individuals, such as loneliness, depression, and addiction. Cultural approaches are less researched, but even they sometimes focus on personality traits and "national character." Two journals, *Media and Society* and *First Monday*, focus more on cultural issues. Also see note 26 below. Also Rana Abbas and Gustavo Mesch, "Cultural values and Facebook use among Palestinian youth in Israel," *Computers in Human Behavior*, 48 (2015): 644–653; Wen Gong, Rodney L. Stump, and Zhan G. Li, "Global use and access of social networking web sites: A national culture perspective," *Journal of Research in Interactive Marketing*, 8(1) (2014): 37–55.

18 As mobile media and the internet have become increasingly visual, Goffman's presentation of self has grown in relevance. E.g. Liam Bullingham and Ana C. Vasconcelos, "'The presentation of self in the online world," *Journal of Information Science*, 39(1) (2013): 101–112; Bernie Hogan, "The presentation of self in the age of social media," *Bulletin of Science, Technology, & Society*, 30(6) (2010): 377–386.

19 Facebook has become the dominant SNS worldwide. https://www.statista.com/statistics /272014/global-social-networks-ranked-by-number-of-users/.

20 "Neilsen Q2 2017 Total Audience Report" on growth of mediated interaction; Naomi Baron *Always on* (Oxford University Press 2008).

21 Before Facebook, people used the internet to reinforce offline social relationships. See Valkenburg, Peter, and Schouten, 2006.

22 Rana Abbas and Gustavo Mesch, "Do rich teens get richer? Facebook use and the link between offline and online social capital among Palestinian youth in Israel," *Information, Communication, and Society*, 21(1) (2018): 63–79; Claudia Marino, Gianluca Gini, Alessio Vieno, and Marcantonio M. Spada. "The associations between problematic Facebook use, psychological distress and well-being among adolescents and

young adults: A systematic review and meta-analysis," *Journal of Affective Disorders*, 226 (October 2017): 274–281.

23   Matthias Hofer and Viviane Aubert, "Perceived bridging and bonding social capital on Twitter: Differentiating between followers and followees," *Computers in Human Behavior*, 29 (2013): 2134–2142; Loretta Baldassar, Mihaela Nedelcu, Laura Merla, and Raelene Wilding, "ICT-based co-presence in transnational families and communities" *Global Networks*, 16(2) (April 2016): 133–144; Karina Märcher Dalgas, "Au pairs on Facebook," *Nordic Journal of Migration Research* 6(3) (2016): 175–182. Even internet use in a middle-class, tech-savvy suburb of Kuala Lumpur, Malaysia revealed bonding within and not bridging ethno-religious groups. See John Postill, *Localizing the Internet: An Anthropological Account* (Berghahn Books 2011).

24   Sherry Turkle, *Life on the Screen: Identity in the Age of the Internet* (Simon & Schuster 1995); Tetsuro Kobayashi, "Bridging social capital in online communities: Heterogeneity and social tolerance of online game players in Japan," *Human Communication Research*, 36(4) (2010): 546–69; Zhi-Jin Zhong, "The effects of collective MMORPG (Massively Multiplayer Online Role-Playing Games) play on gamers' online and offline social capital," *Computers in Human Behavior*, 27 (2011): 2352–2363. SNS ground user webpages in their offline self. Video game avatars and creative websites such as YouTube allow creation of a virtual self *not* grounded in offline self. Actual presentations range between these.

25   Ben Marder, Adam Joinson, Avi Shankar, and David Houghton, "The extended 'chilling' effect of Facebook: The cold reality of ubiquitous social networking," *Computers in Human Behavior*, 60 (2016): 582–592; Shanyang Zhao, Sherri Grassmuck, and Jason Martin, "Identity construction on Facebook," *Computers in Human Behavior*, 24 (2008): 1816–1836.

26   Khaled Saleh Al Omoush, Saad Ghaleb Yaseen, and Mohammad Atwah Alma'aitah, "The impact of Arab cultural values on online social networking," *Computers in Human Behavior* 28 (2012): 2387–2399; Skye Cooley and Lauren Reichart Smith, "Presenting me! An examination of self-presentation in US and Russian online social networks," *Russian Journal of Communication*, 5(2) (2013): 176–190. Omoush et al., p. 2388 briefly reviews research on other nations. Unfortunately, much of this research formulates national cultures in terms of predominant personality traits, such as uncertainty avoidance, more akin to "national character" of development theory than to institutionalized cultural values or norms of behavior.

27   Kenneth Farrall, "Online collectivism, individualism and anonymity in East Asia," *Surveillance & Society*, 9(4) (2012): 424–440; Jaz Hee-jeong Choi, "Approaching the mobile culture of East Asia," *M/C: A Journal of Media and Culture*, 10(1) (2007): 1–8, quote p. 4; Hiroko Tabuchi, "Facebook wins relatively few friends in Japan," *NYT*, January 9, 2011; Linda A. Jackson and Jin-Liang Wang, "Cultural differences in social networking site use: A comparative study of China and the United

States," *Computers in Human Behavior*, 29(3) (2013): 910–921; on Iran, see Koo, "Constructing an alternative public sphere"; William Davies and James Crabtree, "Invisible villages: Technolocalism and community renewal," *Renewal-London*, 12(1) (2004): 40–47.

28 Weintraub, "Theory and politics of the public/ private distinction" in Jeffrey Weintraub and Krishan Kumar, eds. *Public and Private in Thought and Practice* (University of Chicago Press 1997). On privacy and cultural values, see Barrington Moore, *Privacy: Studies in Social and Cultural History* (M. E. Sharpe 1984).

29 Moore, *Privacy*, ch. 1; John Kasson, *Rudeness and Civility: Manners in Nineteenth-Century Urban America* (Hill and Wang 1990).

30 Moore, *Privacy*. On feudal to early modern Europe see Benjamin Nelson, *The Idea of Usury: From Tribal Brotherhood to Universal Otherhood* (Princeton University Press 1949); on India see Paul Dourish and Genevieve Bell, *Divining a Digital Future: Mess and Mythology in Ubiquitous Computing* (MIT Press 2011), pp. 140–141.

31 On tradition and modernity see Introduction, nn. 15 and 16. Community, i.e. is when people define themselves with common identity (kinship/ clan, religion, nationality/race, class, gender) creating a common bond, reflecting common interests, an "us versus them" view, and a common culture. This can be a foundation for collective action (Charles Tilly, *From Mobilization to Revolution* (Addison-Wesley 1978); Charles Tilly, Douglas McAdam, and Sidney Tarrow, *Dynamics of Contention* (Cambridge University Press 2001).

32 This is reflected in some cultures today in which mobile phones are considered family property, not individual possessions. See T. T. Sreekumar, "Mobile phones and the cultural ecology of fishing in Kerala India," *The Information Society*, 27(3) (2011): 172–180.

33 Nelson, *The Idea of Usury*; Michelle Perrot, ed., *A History of Private Life: From the Fires of Revolution to the Great War* (Harvard University Press 1990); Eugen Weber, *Peasants into Frenchmen: The Modernization of Rural France, 1870–1914* (Stanford University Press 1976). On individualism see C. B. MacPherson, *The Political Theory of Possessive Individualism: Hobbes to Locke* (Oxford University Press 1962); Steven Lukes, *Individualism* (Basil Blackwell 1973).

34 Koo, "Constructing an Alternative Public Sphere."

35 Linda A. Jackson and Jin-Liang Wang, "Cultural differences in social networking site use: A comparative study of China and the United States," *Computers in Human Behavior*, 29(3) (2013): 910–921; Harry Triandis, *Individualism and Collectivism* (Westview Press 1995). According to Jackson and Wang, pp. 910–911, Eastern cultures are collectivist, China being prototypical. They give priority to family, village, and society over self. They are more likely to engage in self-effacement than self-promotion and value modesty over pride. They tend to have fewer intimate and enduring friendships than members of Western cultures. Eastern values and friendship patterns are rooted in the historical, political, and religious foundations of Confucianism, Buddhism, and Taoism (Chenyang Li,

The Confucian Philosophy of Harmony (Routledge 2014). In contrast, Western cultures are individualistic, the US being prototypic. They prioritize individual achievement over family and group. They are more likely to engage in self-promotion than self-effacement, and value pride over modesty. Members of Western cultures tend to have more friends but looser connections to them and friendships are less enduring. These values are rooted in the rugged individualism and freedom of choice that are the foundations of Western cultures. As reflected in children, see Qi Wang and Michelle D. Leichtman, "Same beginnings, different stories: A comparison of American and Chinese children's narratives," *Child Development*, 71(5) (September/October 2000): 1329–1346.

36 Abbas and Mesch, "Cultural values and Facebook," p. 646
37 Cheryll Ruth, R. Soriano, and Ruepert Jiel Cao, "Of owned, shared and public access OCT," in Ana Tellería, ed., *Between the Public and Private in Mobile Communication* (Routledge 2017), pp. 77–98.
38 Tali Hatuka and Eran Toch, "The emergence of portable private-personal territory: Smartphones, social conduct and public spaces," *Urban Studies*, 53(10) (2016): 2192–2208; Tali Hatuka and Eran Toch, "Being visible in public space: The normalisation of asymmetrical visibility," *Urban Studies*, 54(4) (2017): 984–998; Ana Tellería, ed., *Between the Public and Private*; Adriana de Souza e Silva and Jordan Frith, *Mobile Interfaces in Public Spaces: Locational Privacy, Control, and Urban Sociability* (Routledge 2012).
39 See Weintraub and Kumar, *Public and Private in Thought and Practice*; Craig Calhoun, *Habermas and the Public Sphere* (MIT Press 1992).
40 Richard Sennett, *The Fall of Public Man* (Knopf 1974) and William H. Whyte, *City: Rediscovering the Center* (Doubleday 1988) see value in urban spaces as places of strangers, whereas Ray Oldenburg, *The Great Good Place* (Paragon House 1989) values neighborhood public spaces as gathering places of friends and acquaintances. Jane Jacobs, *The Death and Life of Great American Cities* (Random House 1961) is somewhere between these.
41 On rationality in collective behavior, see Jaap van Ginneken, *Crowds, Psychology, and Politics, 1871–1899* (Cambridge University Press 1992); Charles Tilly, *Social Movements, 1768–2004* (Paradigm Publishers 2004); Butsch, "Introduction," *The Citizen Audience* (Routledge 2008).
42 Again, this differs between a downtown bar or plaza filled with strangers, and a neighborhood saloon or playground filled with familiar faces. See Lyn Lofland, *A World of Strangers: Order and Action in Urban Public Space* (Basic Books 1973).
43 On bonding in community spaces see Robert Putnam, *Bowling Alone* (Simon and Schuster); Oldenburg, *Third Places*. On foundations for collective action see Charles Tilly, McAdam, and Tarrow, *Dynamics of Contention*.
44 Recently, US Federal Communication Commission proposals and federal court decisions have considered dismantling net neutrality. See Paul

Schindler, "F.C.C. releases plan to repeal net neutrality," *NYT*, November 22, 2017, A1; Tim Wu, "The courts and net neutrality," *NYT*, November 23, 2017, A31.

45 Jon Lee Anderson, "Sons of the Revolution," *New Yorker,* May 9, 2011, 43–53, quote on p 52–53; http://www.pbs.org/mediashift/2014/02/ the-youtube-war-citizen-videos-revolutionize-human-rights-monitoring-in-syria/. The revolution soon devolved into chaos. See Frederic Wehrey, *The Burning Shores* (Farrar Straus 2018).

46 Zeynep Tufekci and Christopher Wilson, "Social media and the decision to participate in political protest: Observations from Tahrir Square," *Journal of Communication* 62 (2012), 363–379; Abdalla F. Hassan, *Media, Revolution and Politics in Egypt: The Story of an Uprising* (I. B.Tauris 2015); Asef Bayat, *Revolution without Revolutionaries: Making Sense of the Arab Spring* (Stanford University Press 2017); Miriyam Aouragh, "Social media, mediation and the Arab revolutions," in Christian Fuchs and Vincent Mosco, eds., *Marx in the Age of Digital Capitalism* (Paradigm Publishers 2016); Robert Faris, John Kelly, Helmi Noman, and Dalia Othman, "Structure and discourse: Mapping the networked public sphere in the Arab region," *Berkman Center Research Publication,* 4 (March 2016).

47 Those same digital devices also were used against protestors. See "Internet outs anonymity" *NYT*, June 11, 2014; http://www.slate.com/blogs/future_tense/2014/01/24/ ukraine_texting_euromaidan_protesters_kiev_demonstrators_receive_threats.html; Darin Barney, Gabriella Coleman, Christine Ross, Jonathan Sterne, and Tamar Tembeck, eds., *The Participatory Condition in the Digital Age* (University of Minnesota Press 2016).

48 e.g. Tilly, *Social Movements*; Jeffrey T. Schnapp and Matthew Tiews, eds., *Crowds* (Stanford University Press 2006).

49 Nancy Zaroulis and Gerald Sullivan, *Who Spoke Up? American Protest Against the War in Vietnam, 1963–1975* (Doubleday & Co., 1984); "Million march against Iraq war," BBC News World Edition, February 16, 2003, http://news.bbc.co.uk/2/hi/uk_news/2765041.stm; Chris Atton, *An Alternative Internet: Radical Media, Politics and Creativity* (Edinburgh University Press 2004); Martha McCaughey and Michael Ayers, eds., *Cyberactivism: On-Line Activism in Theory and Practice* (Routledge 2003).

50 Steven Coll, "The Casbah Coalition," *New Yorker,* April 4, 2011, 34–40, quote on pp. 37–38.

51 Edward P. Thompson, "The moral economy of the English crowd in the eighteenth century," *Past & Present*, 50 (1971): 76–136.

52 Rami El-Amine and Mostafa Henaway, "A people's history of the Egyptian revolution," *The Bullet, Socialist Project,* e-Bulletin no. 525, July 11, 2011; Wendell Steavenson, "On the Square," *New Yorker*, February 28, 2011; Peter Hassler, "Big brothers: Where is the Muslim brotherhood leading Egypt?" *New Yorker*, January 14, 2013.

9   Globalized Media in the New Millennium

1   Arjun Appadurai, *Modernity at Large: Cultural Dimensions of Globalization* (University of Minnesota Press 1996); Frank Lechner, *Globalization: The Making of World Society* (Wiley-Blackwell 2009); Joseph Straubhaar, *World Television: From Global to Local* (Sage 2007); Jean K. Chalaby, "Television for a new global order: Transnational television networks and the formation of global systems," *Gazette: International Journal for Communication Studies*, 65(6) (2003): 457–472.
2   Bernard M. Hoekman and Ernesto Zedillo, eds., *Trade in the 21st Century: Back to the Past?* (Brookings Institute Press 2018).
3   Daniel M. Bernhofen, Zouheir El-Sahli, and Richard Kneller, "Estimating the effects of the container revolution on world trade," CESifo Working Paper: Trade Policy no. 4136 (2013); Danny Hakim, "Aboard a cargo colossus," *NYT*, October 5, 2014, BU1,4; http://www.maersk.com/en/hardware/triple-e/economy-of-scale.
4   World system theory tended to focus on early modern Europe and thus single hegemons, such as Spain, Britain, or the US. See Barry Gills and Andre Gunder Frank, "World systems cycles, crises and hegemonic shifts, 1700BC to 1700AD," in Frank and Gills, eds., *The World System: Five Hundred Years or Five Thousand?* (Routledge, 1993), pp. 143–199. Pre-modern systems as early as 200 BCE tended toward trade of luxuries and goods vital to elites transported between multiple centers, e.g. from China to Europe. As ocean transportation became more reliable and regular by the sixteenth century, single hegemon nautical merchant nations came to dominate, shifting from Venice to Spain, Netherlands, and Britain. Today's globalization relies on mass-consumed goods and may be moving rapidly to multiple centers.
5   According to a UNESCO report, US exports accounted for half of the films exhibited in the EU from 1994 to 2003. See UNESCO *International Flow of Selected Cultural Goods and Services, 1994–2003* (Montreal: UNESCO 2005), pp. 47–8.
6   Neil Selwyn, "Reconsidering political and popular understandings of the digital divide," *New Media & Society*, 6(3) (June 2004): 341–362; Pippa Norris, *Digital Divide: Civic Engagement, Information Poverty, and the Internet* (Cambridge University Press 2001).
7   Elisa Oreglia, "ICT and (personal) development in rural China," *Information Technologies & International Development*, 10(3) (2014), 19–30.
8   Jean Dreze and Amartya Sen, *An Uncertain Glory: India and its Contradictions* (Princeton University Press 2013), p. 289, Table A3; Nilesh Chatterjee, Genevie Fernandes, and Mike Hernandez, "Food insecurity in urban poor households in Mumbai, India," *Food Security*, 4(4) (2012): 619–632; Habib Tiliouine and Mohamed Meziane, "Quality of life of Muslim populations: Case of Algeria," in Kenneth C. Land, Alex C. Michalos, and M. Joseph Sirgy, eds., *Handbook of Social Indicators* (Springer 2012), pp. 499–528.

9   The United Nations' International Telecommunication Union data are
     available at http://www.itu.int/ITU-D/ict/statistics/explorer/index.html.
     It obtains its data from ministries and agencies of UN nations. Gartner,
     Inc., an information technology research company, claims that in 2013
     half of mobile phone sales were smartphones (https://www.gartner.com/
     newsroom/id/2573415). See also www.internetworldststs.com/stats.html
     and World Telecommunication/ICT Indicators Database online 17th
     edn, 2013, http://www.itu.int/pub/D-IND-WTID.OL-2013. On Jamaica
     and Martinque see Heather Horst and Daniel Miller, *The Cell Phone:
     An Anthropology of Communication* (Berg, 2006), 2 and 19. On esti-
     mates of media saturation, see Bella Thomas, "What the world's poor
     watch on tv," *World Press Review*, 50 (2003).
10   Bill McKibben, "Power brokers: Africa's solar boom is changing life
     beyond the grid," *New Yorker*, June 26, 2017, 46–55; "Planning routes
     to growth in rural markets" Nielsen Insights January 30, 2018, http://
     www.nielsen.com/in/en/insights/reports/2018/planning-the-route-to-
     growth-in-rural-markets.html.
11   Himanshu and Kunal Sen, "Revisiting the great Indian poverty debate:
     Measurement, patterns, and determinants," Brooks World Poverty Insti-
     tute, University of Manchester, Working Paper 203, May 2014.
12   Laura Camfield, "Quality of life in developing countries," in Kenneth
     C. Land, Alex C. Michalos, and M. Joseph Sirgy, *Handbook of
     Social Indicators and Quality of Life Research* (Springer 2012),
     399–432.
13   Hans Peter Hahn and Ludovic Kibora, "The domestication of the mobile
     phone: Oral society and new ICT in Burkina Faso," *Journal of Modern
     African Studies*, 46(1) (March 2008): 87–109; Ebikabowei Emmanuel
     Baro and Benake-ebide Christy Endouware, "The effects of mobile phone
     on the socio-economic life of the rural dwellers in the Niger Delta region
     of Nigeria," *Information Technology for Development*, 19(3) (2013):
     249–263; Ailsa Wingfield, "Perspectives: Who exactly is Africa's con-
     suming class?" *Neilsen Newswire*, September 19, 2017, http://
     www.nielsen.com/us/en/insights/news/2017/perspectives-who-exactly-is-
     africas-consuming-class.html. In African cities, smartphones have increased
     recently.
14   Heather Horst and Daniel Miller, *The Cell Phone: An Anthropology of
     Communication* (Berg 2006), pp. 108–14. Horst and Miller and Baro
     and Endouware, "Effects of mobile phone" each cite several studies.
15   http://www.itu.int/net/itunews/issues/2011/07/11.aspx; "Local employ-
     ment in the informal economy" (Geneva: International Labour Organi-
     zation 2001); Christiana Charles-Iyoha, ed., *Mobile Telephony: Leveraging
     Strengths and Opportunities for Socio-Economic Transformation in
     Nigeria* (Lagos: Ezcell Communications 2006). Additional citations in
     Baro and Edouware, "Effects of mobile phone."
16   Stephanie Strom, "Billions of buyers," *NYT*, September 18, 2014, B1,
     6; Coimbatore K. Prahalad, *The Fortune at the Bottom of the Pyramid*
     (Dorling Kindersley 2006).

17   On mobile phone affordability see Strom, "Billions of buyers," 2014; Jamie Anderson and Costas Markides, "Strategic innovation at the base of the pyramid," *Sloan Management Review Magazine*, Fall 2007, http://sloanreview.mit.edu/article/strategic-innovation-at-the-base-of-the-pyramid/. On Jamaica see Horst and Miller, *The Cell Phone*, p. 27. On Burkino Faso see Hahn and Kibora, "Domestication of the mobile phone," pp. 104–105; on global South, Rich Ling, "The phases of mobile communication research," in Ana Serrano Telleria, ed., *Between the Public and Private in Mobile Communication* (Routledge 2017), pp. 7–24.

18   N.a., "African mobile observatory 2011: Driving economic and social development through mobile services" (London: GSM Association 2011), https://www.gsma.com/spectrum/wp-content/uploads/2011/12/Africa-Mobile-Observatory-2011.pdf. GSMA is a mobile service industry association.

19   Stylianos Papathanassopoulos and Ralph Negrine, *European Media: Sturctures: Policies and Identity* (Polity 2011), p. 95; "Hollywood zooms on overseas boom," *Variety*, January 9, 2012, 1.

20   On satellites see http://history.nasa.gov/satcomhistory.html. Alan Griffiths, *Digital Television: Business Challenges and Opportunities* (Palgrave 2003).

21   Albert Moran, *New Flows in Global TV* (Intellect Press 2009), p. 76. Global flows have reinforced cosmopolitan tendencies of entrepot cities. See Mayfair Mei-Hui Yang, "Mass media and transnational subjectivity in Shanghai," in Faye Ginsburg, Lila Abu-Lughod, and Brian Larkin, eds., *Media Worlds: Anthropology on New Terrain* (University of California Press 2002).

22   David Crystal, *English as a Global Language,* 2nd edn (Cambridge UniversityPress 2003).

23   Frank J. Lechner, *Globalization: The Making of World Society* (Wiley-Blackwell 2009), pp. 90–95; Richard Robison, ed., *The Neo-Liberal Revolution: Forging the Market State* (Palgrave 2006).

24   David McKnight, "Rupert Murdoch's news corporation: A media institution with a mission," *Historical Journal of Film, Radio and Television*, 30(3) (September 2010): 303–316; Daya Thussu, "The 'Murdochization'of news. The case of Star TV in India," *Media Culture and Society* 29(4) (2007): 593–611. The sale of 21st Century Fox to Disney will not much change his satellite reach. See Amy Chozick, "Proposed sale to Disney complicates Murdoch's succession plan," *NYT*, December 15, 2017, B1.

25   Stig Hjarvard, "Introduction," *Media in a Globalized Society* (Museum Tusculanum Press 2003). On the use of English mixed with local languages see Rani Rubdy and Lubna Alsagoff, eds., *The Global–Local Interface and Hybridity: Exploring Language and Identity,* (Multilingual Matters 2014).

26   Goldman Sachs, "BRICs and Beyond," http://www.goldmansachs.com/our-thinking/archive/archive-pdfs/brics-book/brics-full-book.pdf.

27 Appadurai, *Modernity at Large*; Kai Hafez, *Myth of Media Globalization*, trans. Alex Skinner (Polity 2007).
28 Andrew Wallenstein, "Device and conquer," *Variety*, March 5, 2014, 58; "Continental demand: Netflix faces diverse markets as it eyes European expansion," *Variety*, March 5, 2014, 61.
29 Dave McNary, "Set in California but shot where it's cheap," *Variety*, March 5, 2014, 33; Peter Caranicas, "Columbia leads Latin charge," *Variety*, November 5, 2013, 97.
30 On Ramoji see Shanti Kumar, "Mapping Tollywood," *Quarterly Review of Film and Video*, 23 (2006): 129–138; Naman Ramachandran, "Bollywood goes south," *Variety*, December 3, 2013, 66–7. On Nu Boyana see http://nuboyana.com/about-us/, and Nancy Tartaglione, "China's Recon buys 51% of millennium films for $100M," *Deadline Hollywood*, February 23, 2017, http://deadline.com/2017/02/millennium-films-acquired-by-recon-holding-chinese-firu-100–million-1201954308/. On China see Keith Bradshear, "Chinese Titan takes aim at Hollywood," *NYT*, September 23, 2013, B1,8; Hengdian was featured in Ian Johnson, "Studio city," *New Yorker,* April 22, 2013, 48–55; Daya Thussu, Hugo de Burgh, and Anbin Shi, eds., *China's Media Go Global* (Routledge 2017). On Dubai see Nick Vivarelli, "Dubai tailors its perks to foreign projects" *Variety,* December 1, 2013, 70–71. See ads in *Variety*, October 31, 2011, and March 4, 2014, pp. 10–11, 25 (Bulgaria); October 29, 2012, 71–78 (Bavaria); October 1, 2012, 5 and October 8, 2012, 8-page pullout (Dubai); March 26, 2012 (Huairu, China).
31 Indrajit Banerjee, "The locals strike back? Media globalization and localization in the new Asian television landscape," *Gazette*, 64(6) (2002): 517–535; Dal Yong Jin, "Reinterpretation of cultural imperialism: Emerging domestic market vs continuing US dominance," *Media, Culture, & Society*, 29(5) (2007): 753–771; *Jonathan Taplin*, "'Crouching tigers': Emerging challenges to US entertainment supremacy in the movie business," *Observatorio*, 1(2) (2007); Amy Qin, "A Bollywood smash hit with a twist, in China's cultural battle with India," *NYT*, October 1, 2017, 10.
32 "Where boys were king, a shift to baby girls," *NYT*, December 23, 2007; "On changing South Korea, who counts as Korean?" *NYT*, December 7, 2012, A14. On global people and media flows see Appadurai, *Modernity at Large*, 33ff.
33 On Univision see *NYT* ad, July 22, 2013, A20; on Telemundo see Anna Marie de la Fuente, "Nets put buy in bilingual," *Variety*, July 11, 2011, 1, 26; James Young, "Televisa drives US hybrids," *Variety*, August 6, 2012, 3; Elizabeth Malkin, "Leader of Televisa in Mexico steps aside," *NYT*, October 27, 2017, B3; Kevin Smets et al., in Butsch and Livingstone, *Meanings of Audiences*; Gbemisola Adeoti, "Home video films and the democratic imperative in Nigeria," *Journal of African Cinemas*, 1(1) (2009): 35–56, 37; Chukwuma Okoye, "Looking at ourselves in our mirror: Agency, counter-discourse and the Nigerian video film," *Film International*, 5(4) (2007): 20–29. T-series, India's largest music

label also advertized its Bollywood music and music videos in *Variety*, October 1, 2012, 9.

34 Emily Steel, "Emmy awards gain luster as competition stiffens," *NYT*, August 25, 2014, C1; Andrew Wallenstein, "Netflix pays to play," *Variety*, June 4, 2014, 25; Clifford Coonan, "Asian dealmakers hit the beach" *Variety*, October 29, 2012, 79.

35 A decline in Hollywood support pressed American producers to seek financing overseas. See Dave McNary, "Facts on pacts: The fallout," *Variety*, October 29, 2012, 7; on foreign financing see Clifford Coonan, "H'w'd aims to re-enter the dragon," *Variety*, February 13, 2012, 1, 8; Gregg Goldstein, "Can local lucre pay studio bills?" *Variety*, August 1, 2011, 1, 7; "Reliance," *Variety*, May 1, 2014, 47–48; "From Stockholm to the world," *Variety*, May 2, 2014, 106; Peter Bart, "Current surge of indie films defies the odds," *Variety*, January 4, 2014, 24.

36 "U Int'l revamps local strategy," *Variety*, February 6, 2012, 8; Dave McNary, "Set in California, but shot where it's cheap," *Variety*, March 1, 2014, 33. To entice production back to Hollywood, Universal Studios advertised digital backdrops at their facilities: "Any location in the world on Universal Virtual Stage 1," *Variety*, October 31, 2011, 17.

37 Stuart Levine, "Networks nation-building," *Variety*, February 28, 2011, 11,13; Diana Lodderhose, "U Int'l revamps local strategy," *Variety*, February 6, 2012, 8; Wayne Friedman, "Congloms chase big footprint," *Variety*, January 23, 2012, 1, 17, 20; "Networks nation-building," *Variety*, February 28, 2011, 1.

38 N.a., "Euro tv opens H'wood branch," *Variety*, October 3–8, 2011, 1, 16–17; Clifford Coonan "Asian dealmakers hit the beach," *Variety*, October 29, 2012, 79; Brent Lang, "A Chinese giant's drive to go Hollywood," *Variety*, November 1, 2014, 14–15; Ted Johnson, "Studios' slow build hobbles incentives," *Variety*, February 2, 2014, 38–40; Moran, *New Flows in Global TV,* 26; Stuart Cunningham, "Int'l television markets," in Theodore Newcomb, ed., *Encyclopedia of Television* (Fitzroy Dearborn 2004), pp. 1183–1184. On the other hand, Peter Bart, editor-at-large of *Variety*, argues that developing scripts, nurturing talent and backlot production are history for Hollywood. See Peter Bart, "The blockbuster model that ate Hollywood," *Variety*, 2014, 17.

39 Patrick Frater "Locomotive of local change," *Variety*, June 4, 2014, 43–44, ads on pp 42–45.

40 Albert Moran, *New Flows in Global TV;* Koos Zwaan and Joost De Bruin, eds., *Adapting Idols: Authenticity, Identity and Performance in a Global Television Format* (Ashgate 2012); Tasha Oren and Sharon Shahaf, eds., *Global Television Formats: Understanding Television Across Borders* (Routledge 2011); Timothy Havens, *Global Television Marketplace* (BFI 2006); Sharon Shahaf, "Welcome to the sitcom school: A globalized outlook for the study of television history," *Westminster Papers in Communication and Culture*, 4(4) (2007): 103–123. Moran also cites radio format sales before tv.

41 Moran, *New Flows in Global TV*; Koos Zwaan and Joost De Bruin, *Adapting Idols*.

42 Moran, *New Flows in Global TV*, pp. 84–88, 102–109.

43 Daya Thussu, "Mapping global media flow." Shanti Kumar ("Mapping Tollywood," p. 1) argues that "The location of culture is being constantly reconfigured on and off television through alternative imaginations of time, space, history, geography, identity and difference."

44 David Jamilly, "Reminiscences of the Far East with a Kine show," *The Kinematograph and Lantern Weekly*, February 25, 1909, 1153; Paul Markandan, "Far East TV production," *Broadcasting*, 64 (April 1963): 112–113.

45 Dipesh Chakrabarty, *Provincializing Europe* (Princeton University Press 2008), p. 6.

46 Ogege Sam Omadjohwoefe, "The upsurge of poverty: Obstacle to the achievement of the millennium development goals in Nigeria," *Developing Country Studies*, 3(12) (2013): 184–190; Segun Oshewolo, "Galloping poverty in Nigeria: An appraisal of government interventionist policies," *Journal of Sustainable Development in Africa*, 12.6 (2010): 264–274; Michael J. Watts, *Silent Violence: Food, Famine, and Peasantry in Northern Nigeria* (University of Georgia Press 2013). On media use see Broadcasting Board of Governors/Gallup, "Nigeria Media Use 2012," http://www.bbg.gov/wp-content/media/2012/08/gallup-nigeria-brief.pdf; P. Usman, "Cellular telephony is one of the greatest benefits of Nigeria's democracy," *Vworld*, April–June, 2005, 30; ATKearney Management Consulting, "African Mobile Observatory 2011: Driving Economic and Social Development through Mobile Services," (GSMA 2011), http://www.gsma.com/publicpolicy/wp-content/uploads/2012/04/africamobileobservatory2011-1.pdf.

47 Popular and trade press reports often cite "Nollywood" as the world's second or third largest film industry, based on numbers of films per year, but neglect to point out the inexpensive costs, ease of entry and absence of corporate structure. Economically, it is much smaller than Hollywood and Bollywood.

48 Daniel Jordan Smith, *A Culture of Corruption: Everyday Deception and Popular Discontent in Nigeria* (Princeton University Press, 2010); Pierre Barrot, *Nollywood the Video Phenomenon in Nigeria* (James Currey 2008), pp. 15–16 on Gallup; Abiodun Olayiwola, "From celluloid to video," *Journal of Film and Video*, 59(3) (Fall 2007): 58–61; Adeoti, "Home video films"; Chukwuma Okoye, "Looking at ourselves in our mirror: Agency, counter-discourse and the Nigerian video film," *Film International*, 28: 20–29; Brian Larkin, *Signal and Noise: Media, Infrastructure and Urban Culture in Nigeria* (Duke University Press 2008); Matthias Krings and Onookome Okome, eds., *Global Nollywood: The Transnational Dimensions of an African Video Film Industry* (Indiana University Press 2013), pp. 179–198. On Hausa see Catherine Coles and Beverly Mack, eds., *Hausa Women in the Twentieth Century* (University of Wisconsin Press, 1991). Emily Witt, *Nollywood: The Making*

of a Film Empire (Columbia Global Reports 2017) tries to fit Nollywood into a Hollywood model.

49 Barrot, *Nollywood*, xi, ch 6, quote on 13.

50 Barrot, *Nollywood*, 18, 58; Larkin, *Signal and Noise*; Alessandro Jedlowski, "From Nollywood to Nollyworld," in Krings and Okome, *Global Nollywood*, pp. 28–29. Compare this to film-making in the US, Chapter 3, where bank investment led to the Hollywood oligopoly.

51 Quote from Barrot, *Nollywood*, p. 58; on local issues see Okoye, "Looking at ourselves," p. 24; appeal to masses see Alessandro Jedlowski and Heike Becker, "Nollywood in urban southern Africa," in Krings and Okome, *Global Nollywood*, pp. 179–198.

52 Barrot, *Nollywood*, 19–24; Larkin, *Signal and Noise*, on northern Nigeria.

53 Larkin, *Signal and Noise*, 409–424; Barrot, *Nollywood*, ch. 4 and pp. 28–29.

54 Barrot, *Nollywood*, pp. 5, 43; Krings and Okome, *Global Nollywood*, p. 1; Okoye, "Looking at ourselves," pp. 23, 25; Jean-François Werner, "How women are using television to domesticate globalization," *Visual Anthropology*, 19(5) (2006): 443–472.

55 Jedlowski and Becker, "Nollywood in urban southern Africa."

56 Giovanna Santanera, "Consuming Nollywood in Turin Italy," in Krings and Okome, *Global Nollywood*, pp. 145–163.

57 Santanera, "Consuming Nollywood," quotes on p. 248

58 Daya Thussu, "Mapping global media flow," p. 25 on telenovelas. The seeming contradiction is also explored in Anthony Y. H. Fung, ed., *Asian Popular Culture: The Global (Dis)continuity* (Routledge, 2013).

59 On cultural proximity see Joseph Staubhaar, *World Television: From Global to Local* (Sage 2007), p. 197, and Bianca Lippert, "Betty and Lisa: alternating between sameness and uniqueness," in Janet McCabe and Kim Akass, eds., *TV's Betty Goes Global: From Telenovela to International Brand* (I. B. Tauris 2013), pp. 83–98. Explaining from myth see Betty Kaklamanidou, "The Greek *Maria I Asximi*," in McCabe and Akass, *TV's Betty Goes Global*, pp. 175–88. On translation or "trans-production," see Moran, *New Flows in Global Media*, pp. 20, 112–115. Xiaolu Ma and Albert Moran, "Towards a cultural economy of Chou Nu (Nv) Wu Di," in McCabe and Akass, *TV's Betty Goes Global*, pp. 126–142, identifies localizations as "recalibrations" of a "business" nature. Here we are more concerned with audiences' "recalibrations" of a social nature.

60 Paul S. Lee, "The absorption and indigenization of foreign media cultures," *Asian Journal of Communication*, 1(2) (1991): 52–72, and Yuri Lotman, *Universe of the Mind: A Semiotic Theory of Culture*, trans. Ann Shukman (Indiana University Press 1990) offer typologies that are abstract, but one can infer how each type may be of practical use in specific circumstances.

61 On instrumentality see Zubaida, "Components of popular culture in the Middle East," in Georg Stauth and Sami Zubaida, eds., *Mass Culture Popular Culture and Social Life in the Middle East* (Westview Press

1987), pp. 137–163. On appropriation see Hans Peter Hahn and Ludovic Kibora, "The domestication of the mobile phone: Oral society and new ICT in Burkina Faso," *Journal of Modern African Studies*, 46(1) (March 2008): 87–109; W. van Binsbergen, "Can ICT belong in Africa, or is ICT owned by the North Atlantic region?", in W. van Binsbergen and R. van Dijk, eds., *Situating Globality: African Agency in the Appropriation of Global Culture* (Brill 2004), pp. 107–155; J. Stewart, "The social consumption of ICTs: Insights from research on the appropriation and consumption of new ICTs in the domestic environment," *Cognition, Technology, and Work*, 5 (2003): 4–14.

62 E.g. Robin Nabi, Erica N. Biely, Sara J. Morgan, and Carmen R. Stitt, "Reality-based television programming and the psychology of its appeal," *Media Psychology*, 5(4) (2003): 303–330.

63 Lisa Lundy, Amanda Ruth, and Travis Park, "Simply irresistible: Reality TV consumption patterns," *Communication Quarterly*, 56(2) (2008): 208–225. Kristin Barton, "Reality television programs and diverging gratifications: The influence of content on gratification obtained," *Journal of Broadcasting and Electronic Media*, 53(3) (September 2009): 460–476.

64 E.g. Lisa Godlewski and Elizabeth Perse, "Audience activity and reality television: Identification, online activity, and satisfaction," *Communication Quarterly*, 58(2) (April–June 2010): 148–169; similarly for soap operas, see Elizabeth Perse, "Soap opera viewing patterns of college students and cultivation," *Journal of Broadcasting and Electronic Media*, 30(2) (Spring 1986): 175–193.

65 Walter Gantz, Zheng Wang, Bryant Paul, and Robert Potter, "Sports vs all comers: Comparing TV sports fans to fans of other programming genres," *Journal of Broadcasting and Electronic Media*, 50(1) (2006): 95–118.

66 Richard Giulianotti and Roland Robertson, "Globalization of football: A study in the glocalization of the 'serious life,'" *British Journal of Sociology*, 55(4) (2004): 545–568.

Index

advertising (er), 3, 11, 14, 45, 49, 78, 108, 117, 119, 123, 127, 130, 136, 152, 157–158, 162, 166, 173, 176–177, 181–182, 186–187, 194, 215
ABC television, 119, 216
achievement motivation, 18
admission price, 27, 49, 61, 78, 90, 104, 108
affordability, 12, 123, 207–208.
  mobile phone, 208, 209–211
  movie, 40, 42, 61, 81
  nickelodeon, 27
  tv, 119, 143, 162–164
African-American, 72, 128,
Afro-modernity, 221
Alexandria, 111–112, 163, 203,
algorithm, 179, 182–183, 186–187
alpha-numeric, 185
always on, 38, 173, 177, 193–195
Amazon River, 153
Amazon, Inc., 181, 191,
Americanization, 72, 83, 86, 88, 92, 102, 143, 156
analog, 172, 174, 176
animation, 175

anonymity, 7, 24, 197, 199–201
Antwerp, 89
apartheid, 96–97
appliances, home, 31, 88, 147, 159, 184–185
Arab culture, 61, 111, 162, 197
Arab nations, 110–111, 117, 149, 161–162, 188
  Shia v Sunni, 162
Arab Spring, 201–203
artisan, 26, 4, 44, 49, 52, 69, 86, 220
ASIASAT, 149
attention, 30
auteur, 4, 65, 138, 222
automobile, 22–23, 31, 49, 56, 132, 147, 185
availability, 12, 21, 29, 42, 113, 164

baby boom, 123
Barry, Iris, 92
BBC, 131–140, 215
Beijing, 109, 166, 217
Belgium, 89–90, 92, 94, 99, 139
Bengal, 104, 106, 158

Beveridge Report, 131
Big Brother, 182, 218
big data, 179, 185–187
Birmingham UK, 47–48
blog, 182, 203,
blue collar, 130
Bollywood, 57, 61, 160, 215, 221
Bombay (Mumbai), 38, 61, 63, 104, 106, 114, 159
bonding, 141, 169, 199, 201
boulevard theaters; *see* theater
bourgeoisie, 41, 51–52, 59, 87, 95, 163, 198, 199
boy(s), 53, 97, 143, 160
brand, 36, 74, 182
Brazil, 20, 84, 118, 150–154, 156, 164,
bridging, 141–142, 199, 201
Britain, 43, 160, 212, 216
    audiences, 50–51, 139,
    Empire, 40, 107, 110–111
    films, 84–85
    soap operas, 137–139
    social class, 52–53, 90–2,
    television, 130–139; *see also* BBC
B-SKY, 149, 181, 213
Buenos Aires, 38
Bulgaria, 215

cable television, 126, 161, 177, 181
    Europe, 142
    India, 156–157
    Latin America, 151
café concert, 41, 46, 49
café-chantants, 47, 54
Cairo, 38, 111–112, 163
Calcutta (Kolkata), 55, 61, 63
camera
    film, 26, 34, 70–72,
    digital, 174, 184–186, 194, 202
Canton (Quangzhou), 40, 109
Cape Town, 96-7

capitalism, 10–11, 175, 198, 204, 207, 212
    and class, 52
    and colonialism, 13–15
    and post–colonial societies
    and globalization, 12, 148
    and modernity, 24, 198
    market concentration, 24
    vs socialism, 76, 147
Capra, Frank, 77
caste, 13, 60–1, 158
Catholic Church, 53–54, 152–155
    Comite Catholique du Cinematograph, 92
CBS television, 119, 216
censorship
    film, 32, 44, 53–54, 62, 74, 83, 99, 101
    internet, 192, 202
    television, 155, 166
Chicago, 30–31, 67, 78, 160
children, 13, 15, 158–160, 209,
    movie audience, 15, 23
        affordable to, 31, 61
        and public space, 27–29
        immigrant, 28, 31, 50
        moral panic about, 31, 44, 52–55, 74–75, 91–92, 99
        unattended, 23, 79, 90–91
        working class, 28, 31, 47, 50, 90–91,
    television audience, 121, 128, 168
        as consumers, 136
        moral panic about, 127, 134–136, 160, 169
China, 20, 57–60, 107–110, 165–170, 176, 202, 215–217
China Central TV (CCTV), 166
China Film Group Corporation (CFGC), 217
cinema-chantants, 54
Cinematographic Act of, 1909 48

citizenship, 140, 146, 149, 184, 192,
        200
    and nationalism, 16–17, 87, 112,
        138, 143
    consumer, 75, 87, 117, 136–137,
        149
    corporate, 75, 117
    for immigrants, 28, 31–32
civil inattention, 200
civil rights, 125; *see* rights
class, working; *see* working class
class conflict, 138
CNN, 161, 213, 215
collectivism, 197, 199
collective action, 6, 28, 77, 134,
        200–201,
colonialism, 7, 13–18, 40, 55–56,
        95,111, 206
    and colonial native audiences, 83,
        96–98
    and film policy, 83, 95–101,
        107
commercialization, 31, 58
    television, 131, 166–167
commodification, 11
common man, 77
community, 31, 33 59, 66, 107
    and class, 124–125, 133–134,
    and sociability, 28, 141, 201
    participation, 12, 23, 27–28, 51,
        80, 96, 154
    sense of, 7, 96, 137, 160, 196
    sing, 80
    vs individual interest, 149, 198,
        210
    vs television, 141, 154, 158
    vs urbanization, 7
concentration, market, 43, 45, 69,
        111, 173, 180–181, 185, 211,
        213
Confucianism, 57, 109, 167–168
consumerism, 23, 41, 74, 125, 146,
        156–159, 164–165, 185

consumer citizen, 117, 136–137,
        149; *see also* citizenship.
consumption, 7, 10, 47, 142, 151,
        158, 166, 182, 190, 205
    , culture of, 9, 11–13, 37, 75, 162
containerization, shipping, *206*
co-production, 216
Coronation Street, 137–138
corporations, trans/multi-national,
        14–15, 20, 84, 180, 193, 213
cosmopolitanism, 6, 12, 19, 102,
        108, 134
counter-flow, media, 205, 215–216
country, 7, 10, 26, 36, 52, 58, 109,
        111, 199, 203;
    see also rural
Cousins, Norman, 127
credit card, 185, 188–189, 192,
crime and movies, 32, 53, 85, 87,
        107 109
cross flow, 205, 215
crowds, 60, 90, 97, 107, 110, 167,
        204
crowd psychology, 32, 52–53, 63, 74,
        99; *see also* suggestion
cultural appropriation, 223
cultural discount, 85
cultural proximity, 222

data-mining, 184, 188
darkness, 9, 29, 52–53, 80–81
decolonization, 102
de Gaulle, Charles, 139–140
de-industrialization, 126
demand, economic, 11, 207–210
    for movies, 26–27, 36, 39–40, 43,
        46, 59, 69, 111, 122
    for television, 116, 166, 216, 218,
        221
    for mobile phone, 191, 210
democracy, 124, 127, 150, 188, 199
de-regulation, neo-liberal, 149, 180,
        212

deskilling, 180
development, economic, 10, 17, 25,
    64, 95, 102, 151
  theory, 10, 18–19,
  telenovelas, 154–157,
diaspora, 105, 156, 205, 215
  African, 221–222
  Chinese, 165, 213, 215
  Indian, 105, 160–161, 213, 216
  Latin American, 216
digitization, 172, 174–178, 180, 185,
    213
digital video recorder (dvr), 119, 192,
director-unit, 34, 67
displacement, 9, 132, 168 195, 220;
  see leisure
domestic sphere, 8, 12, 118, 123,
    132, 141, 199, 221
dominant culture, 94, 126, 162, 223
  or mainstream, 34, 76, 123
Doordarshan, 156–157
drive-in theater, 124

EastEnders, 137–138
Eastman Kodak, 43, 174
Edison, Thomas, 27, 63, 65
effects, 1, 13
  of movies, 46, 64, 66, 81, 85, 91,
    100–101, 114
  of television, 132, 134–136, 169
  of digital media, 190, 207
Egypt, 110–13, 162–3, 169,
    202–204
electricity, 30–31, 60, 107, 159, 199,
    207, 211
Elmo the Mighty, 63
empire, 14, 38, 57, 84, 93, 145,
  British, 40, 43, 60, 96, 135
English language, 29, 31, 143, 216,
    221–222
  and global trade, 88, 147, 212–
    213, 218
  in India, 60–62, 105–106, 157

not speaking, 29, 31, 60–62,
    105–106
entrepot, 55, 59–61, 94, 102
eugenics, 25
Eurovision, 140
export, 14, 147, 205, 211
  film, 40, 42–44, 59, 84, 94, 111,
    215,
  television, 116, 137, 147, 151,
    165, 217–219

Facebook, 179–183, 186–187, 192,
    196–197, 203
facial recognition, 186
fake news, 186, 192
Famous Players, 44–45, 59, 69
fans, 36, 130, 160, 182, 224
fashion, 36, 58, 154
favela, 153–154, 156
feudalism, 15–16, 60, 198
Fields, Gracie, 87
Fifth Republic of France, 139
filimu, 164
film serials, 35–36, 51, 54, 63,
    75–76, 105; *see also* television
    serials
foreign concessions in China, 58, 107
format; *see* television series
football (soccer), 90, 224
fourth wall, 30, 100, 110
Fox, Twentieth Century, 69, 181,
    215–217
France
  cinema, 40–43, 51–54, 90, 92,
    101
  television, 139–140, 142, 147
franchise, 131, 218
friending, 179, 197

Gainsborough pictures, 84, 87, 92
games
  and television, 132, 136, 168
  video, 175–176

General Agreement on Tariffs and
    Trade (GATT), 205
Germany, 40, 85–86, 88, 91, 116,
    139, 141–142, 217
German language, 218
Ghana, 221
girls and young women, 22,
    and movies, 32, 35, 44, 74, 97
    and television, 157–158, 161
    and digital
    working class, 35–36, 51, 53, 97
glocal, 222
Gomes, Dias, 152
Gone with the Wind, 122
grandparents, 168,
Gujarati, 104
Gurupa Brazil, 153–155, 159

Hampton, Benjamin, 39
Hangkow (Wuhan), 60,
harmony, 109, 158, 167–169, 197
Hausa, 221
Hays, Will, 75, 84
heritage, 16, 87, 137–138, 168
Hindi, 61–62, 104–105, 156, 213
hire-purchase, 132
Hong Kong, 109, 156, 165, 167
Hum Log, 157–158
Hungary, 54
hybrid culture, 102, 108, 112

illiteracy, 60, 63, 104–106, 109; *see*
    literacy
I Love Lucy, 122, 128
images, 2–4, 8–9, 11, 29–30, 54,
    102, 148, 170, 173–174, 179,
    185–186, 195–196, 212
imagined community, 225
immigrant, 25, 93, 158, 215, 222;
    see also diaspora.
    to Britain, 160–161, 216
    to US, 25, 29–32, 72, 76
    African, 216

children, 28, 31
    Indian, 160–1
    Latin American, 216
immigration, 24–25, 31, 44, 52, 160,
    205
independence, 15–17, 56, 96,
    101–102, 107, 112, 145
Independent Television (ITV),
    131–137
India, 20, 60–64, 198
    English-speaking; *see* English
        language, India.
    film industry, 61, 103–105, 164,
        215–216, 221
    poverty, 60–62, 100, 103–104,
        208, 211
    telenovelas; *see* telenovelas, Indian
    television industry, 156–157, 213
    women; *see* women, India
Indian Cinematographic Committee,
    105–107
individualism, 17–18, 71–72, 77,
    198–199
Indonesia, 20 n 48
indoor drama, 167; *see also*
    telenovela.
industrialization, 7, 10, 18, 24,
    40–42, 46–47, 52, 69–70,
    108,111, 146, 171
inequality, 60–61, 66, 111, 118, 150,
    155, 203
inferiority, 17, 74, 87, 95, 99–101,
    134
informality, 28, 79, 90, 133, 220
INTELSAT, 149
inter-titles, 50, 63, 81, 104, 106
internet of things, 185
Italy, 40–42, 44, 54, 222
Ivory Coast, 163–164
izzat, 158

Jacob, Lewis, 39
Jamaica, 208, 210, 211

Japan, 40, 107–110, 116–117, 147, 197, 215

Kodak; *see* Eastman Kodak

labor, manual, 25, 47, 57, 59, 94, 106, 109, 111, 166
  wages, 27, 61
  images, 99, 169
  , distain for, 152
language, 15, 43, 105, 131, 216–217
  and colonial imposition, 15, 46, 95, 212, 215
  communities, 29, 140, 161, 213,
  barriers, 60, 104, 192
  dominant, 105, 212
  vs image; *see* image
Latin America, 56, 84, 150–6, *209*, 215–216
Laval decree, 101
leisure, 12, 23, 109, 121, 174
  as consumption, 11
  , control of, 32, 93
  skills, 9
  time, 23, 96, 132, 159, 168
  vs work, 10, *175*, 199
Lewis, Cecil, 131
Lianhua films, 108
licenses, 47, 54, 67, 91, 216, 217
literacy, 3, 58–60, 62–63, 88, 107–108, 112, 156, 207
literature, 4, 63, 109, 125
London, 11, 48, 50, 53, 133, 137–138, 160
Los Angeles (LA), 67–68, 215, 217
low-brow tastes, 53, 59, 131, 134–135, 169
Lynd, Robert, Helen, 22–23, 134

machismo, 153
Madras (Chennai), 63, 104, 105
Maghreb, 96
Mali, 164

Marx, Karl, 129, 171
masala, 105, 216, 221
masses, 16, 40, 52,
  China, 167, 169
  Britain, 83, 92, 134, 139
  , development and, 154–155
  Egypt, 161–162
  India, 61–63, 100, 106
  Italy, 54
  Nigeria, 221
  urban, 31, 61
  US, 31, 120
mass medium, 4, 20, 94, 110, 124
  television as, 20, 124, 127, 150
matinee, 35, 47, 54, 74–75, 79, 90, 136
melodrama, 30, 35, 73, 106, 112,
  soap opera, 129, 138
  telenovela, 151
mercantilism, 98
MGM, 69, 122, 217
Middletown, 22–3
milieu, 12, 77, 193–194, 196–197, 199–200, 202
Mingxing film, 108
mobile phone, 193, 200, 202, *208*, 210–11; *see also* smartphone.
mobility, social, 152
modernity, 24, 56, 132, 221
  vs tradition, 146–147, 152, 158, 160, 163, 171
modernization, 17–19, 41, 58, 102, 146, 155, 157, 166; *see also* nation–building
monetization, 177, 179–180
moral panic, 13, 25, 31, 127, 188
  about movies, 46, 91, 114
Motion Picture Patent Company (MPPC), 67–68
Motion Picture Producers and Distributors of America (MPPDA), 84, 94
Motion Picture Production Code

movie palace, 33, 69, 77–78, 80, 81,
     108
Mubarak, Hosni, 162
multi-tasking, 173, 194–195
Mumbai; *see* Bombay
Murdoch, Rubert, 181, 213
musalsalat, 162–163, 169; *see also*
     telenovela.
Music hall, 40, 46–48, 52, 87
Muslim women, 198
  and television, 164–5,
Muslim Brotherhood, 203–4
mythologicals, 61–62, 103, 105–107

narrative, 26–27, 30, 49, 56, 68, 70,
     76, 118, 160
Nasser, Gamal Abdel, 112
nationalism, 13–17, 83
  in Europe, 53, 86–87, 135,
     139–140, 144
  post-colonial, 56, 64, 102, 112,
     114, 161
nation-building, 16, 18,
  post-colonial, 101–102, 117,
     146, 148–149, 155–157,
     162–163
national cinema, 85–87, 102, 112
national culture, 14, 16, 94, 120,
     124, 142
  In Europe, 54–55, 86, 134–135,
  post–colonial, 16–17
national identity, 16–17, 41, 57, 83,
     102, 112, 117–118, 139,
     145–146, 161–162
National Trust for Places of Historic
     Interest and Natural Beauty,
     87
NBC Television, 119, 216–217
neo-liberalism, 149, 157, 212
Netflix, 187, 189, 191, 216
Netherlands, 90–92, 161, 182
New York, 11, 28, 35–36, 69, 120,
     214

News Corporation, 181
nickelodeon, 21, 27–37, 38–39,
     46–49, 54, 59, 69, 97
Nigeria, 210, 219–221
Nollywood, 219–222

oligopoly, 65–66, 69, 94, 120

Paramount Pictures, 44, 69, 78–79,
     217; *see also* Famous Players
parents, 23, 50, 78–79, 142, 168–
     169, 194, 197
  authority, 127, 160, 164, 188
  , working class, 31, 50; *see also*
     children, unattended
Paris, 11, 41, 49, 51, 100
Pathé films, 26, 43–45, 49, 55–56,
     63
PBS television, 120,
peasants, 41, 94, 113–114, 199
  China, 57–60, 108–110, 166–167,
     176
  Egypt, 111–112
  India, 60, 159
  Italy, 52
Perils of Pauline, 35, 51, 63
place, 6–9, 13, 46; *see also* situation
Pollock, Channing, 28
Pop Idol, 218
population density, 20, 57, 103,
     113
poverty, 157, 207–211
  rural, 41, 52, 59, 103, 107
practicality, 223–4
prime time, 120–121, 151, 162
privacy, 7, 162, 183, 188, 198–200
producer system, central, 70
product placement, 73, 152
profit, 10, 18, 210
  movie, 47, 55
     and class, 32, 37, 47, 55
     and women, 73
  Britain, 85

India, 103
And market size, 43–45
Nollywood, 220
television, 120–121, 149
for-profit, 149, 212
domestic dramas, 167
internet, 173, 179, 194,
progressives, 25, 27–28
propaganda,
film, 96, 98–101, 107
television, 146
public, 32–33, 52–53, 68, 88, 97,
191
discourse, 39, 66, 124, 127, 136,
155, 162, 169, 188
reaction, 30, 105
respectable, 32–33
services, 41, 117, 131, 140, 143
space, 28–29, 31, 47, 62, 123, 141,
158, 168, 190, 198–201
public sphere, 51, 102, 158, 169,
201, 221
public interest, 117, 131, 149
publicity, 54, 74, 93–94, 122

race, 82, 121, 129
and other statuses, 74, 77, 80, 91,
114, 118, 143
, subordinated, 13, 55, 74, 95, 99
exclusion, 129
, mixed, 97, 153
radio, 4, 20, 23–24, 76, 95, 129–130,
132
railroad, 60, 95, 107
Raj, British, 60
Ramadan, 162
reading, 4, 35, 48, 81,104,
, collective, 71, 114
, preferred, 1, 113, 122, 154
, alternative, 71, 114, 121–122,
126, 141–144
Reagan, Ronald, 212
reception, 6, 13 61, 118

reformers, 22, 32, 35, 75, 120
Italy, 55
Egypt, 111
Progressive, 27–29, 32, 39
Reform Movement, China's, 166
Reith, John, 131
regulation, government, 32, 117, 186;
see also de–regulation
movie, 59
China, 59, 109
Britain, 131
repetition, 33, 65, 121, 129
resistance, political, 95, 110, 206
resistance, cultural, 2, 5, 30, 199
respectability, 32, 49, 160,
And marketing, 32, 54–55, 74
And women, 31, 62, 158
Middle class, 31–32, 96, 157
Vs disreputable, 28, 32, 97
Rhodesia, 96–97, 99, 101
rickshaw, 109
rights, individual, 125, 186,
198–199
property, 215, 220
Risorgimento, 44
riots, urban, 125, 138, 203
road(s), 23, 60, 104, 107, 113,
123
Russia, 40, 187, 197, 217–218

Sabido, Miguel, 155
satellite, communication, 119, 146,
177, 181, 215–216, 221
China166
direct broadcast satellite, 142,
148–149
Egypt, 161–162
India, 156–157,
Latin America, 151, 153
West Africa, 163
saturation rates, 156, 193, *208–209*,
210, 220
Seabury, W. Marston, 65

segregation, 80
  by class, 50, 62, 89–91, 97, 113
  by race, 82
  by sex, 139, 141
Senegal, 163–164
Sikh, 157, 160
sing, community, 80
Singapore, 219
situation, 6–9, 46; *see also* place.
shadow-play, 58
Shanghai, 47, 58–59, 107–109, 112
Sharia law, 221
Silicon Valley, 172, 188
smartphone, 2, 12, 173, 181,
     190–191, 193, 195–196; *see*
     also mobile phone
soap opera, 118, 151; *see also* serials,
     domestic drama, telenovela
  British, 137–139, 160
  US radio, 129–30
  US television, 164–165
  and women, 130, 139, 141,
     160–161
soccer; *see* football
sociability, 134, 198, 200–201
  in movie theaters, 30, 36, 114
     US, 27–29,
  and television, 141
  internet, 195
social capital, 134, 141, 201
social media, 193–194, 199, 203
social network site, 195
sound, 2, 56, 81,
  and masala films, 103–105
South Africa, 96–97, 221–222
South Korea, 215
Soviet Union, 18, 116, 117, 139
spectacle, 3–4, 11–12, 58, 85, 149
spectator; *see* subject position
spellbound, 71, 81
stage entertainment, 3–4, 30–33, 35,
     38, 54, 80
  and 'green uns', 60, 100, 110

and subject position, 72
  drama, 3–4, 21–22, 25–26, 28, 35
  music hall, 52
  variety, 26, 58
  vaudeville, 38, 54
star, movie, 63, 68, 71, 74, 81, 104,
     119
STAR-TV, 149, 156, 213
streaming, internet, 182–183,
     191–192, 216
Studio Misr, 112
style, film, 58, 61, 70–71, 104, 135,
     155
subaltern states, 98, 145
subject position, 66, 72, 114, 127
subsistence production, 10, 47, 60,
     111, 159
suburbs, 123–125, 132–133
  working-class, 128, 133–134
  vs urban, 133, 169
sunk costs, 45–46, 119, 213
surveillance, 182–189

Tahrir Square, 202–204
Taiwan, 165
Tamil, 104
teen(s), 23, 32, 79, 80, 90, 124,
     194
  Britain, 133, 160
  China, 109
  Netherlands, 90
Telegu, 104
Telemundo, 216
telenovela, 118; *see also* indoor
     drama, filimu, musalsalat, soap
     opera
  Chinese, 166–168
  development, 154–156,
  Egyptian, 162–163.
  Indian, 157–158
  Latin American, 151–152,
     155–156
  export, 151, 164

popularity, 152, 164, 167
West Africa, 164–165
Televisa, 216
television serials, 118, 129–130; *see also* film serials, filimu, indoor drama, musalsalat, soap opera and telenovela
television series, 119
formats, 217–218
television audiences, 116, 118, 127
Brazil, 152–154
Britain, 132–134, 160–161
China, 168–169
Egypt, 163
Europe, 141, 142
India, 157–159, 160–161
US, 120, 122, 125–126, 142–143
discourses about, 127–31
West Africa, 164–165, 221–222
working class, 128–129, 133–135, 152–154
tent shows, 26, 38, 61, 104
Tiananmen Square, 201–202
time use, 9, 12; *see also* displacement.
Times, London, 133, 135, 138
Thatcher, Margaret, 136, 212
theater, 8,
boulevard, 49, 51, 58
drama, 25, 30, 32, 78
movie, 23, 32, 48, 55, 59, 69, 78–79, 94, 107, 112, 124; *see also* Movie palace, Drive–in
Third Republic of France, 31, 53
Thurber, James, 130
town (vs cities), 22–24, 36, 73, 78–81
Brazil, 153–154
Britain, 111
France, 42,
Hungary, 54
India, 61, 159
Libya, 203
Northern Rhodesia, 97

tradition, 26, 61, 156–157, 203; *see also* modernity; modernization
and generational strains, 168–169, 221
and nationalism, 16–17,161
and modernization, 18–19, 58, 64, 102
China, 108–110, 167
India, 157–158
and patriarchy, 61, 153, 158–159, 221
vs modernity, 7, 18, 118, 147, 155, 170–171, 198
India, 158
Muslim, 162–164,
transparency, 183
transportation; *see* railroad and roads
Truffaut, François, 65
trustee mode; *see* regulation.
Tunisia, 202
Turin, 222

ubiquity, 178
Ugly Betty, 218
uplift, cultural, 32, 87, 90–93, 131, 139
colonial, 18, 101
post–colonial, 149,
urbanization, 7,
, effects of, 7, 24, 31, 171
comparative, 42
Brazil, 150
Urdu, 104
unification, 17
China, 57
Germany, 40
Italy, 16, 41
Universal Pictures, 63, 69, 217
universal product code (UPC), 185
Univision, 216

Van Vechten, Carl, 28
variety, 21, 26–27, 46, 49, 58; *see
    also* music hall, vaudeville
vaudeville, 21, 26, 30–33, 38, 46, 54,
    78
vertical integration, 65
video cassette recorder (vcr), 126,
    142, 146, 151, 160–161, 176
village life, 11,
    Bangladesh, 210
    Burkino–Faso, 211
    China, 57–58, 60, 108–110, 176
    Cuba, 56
    Egypt, 111,
    India, 60, 159
    Libya, 203
    Muslim, 162–164
    Nigeria, 221
    Philippines, 199

wages, 27, 36–37, 40, 61–62, 89,
    111, 132
Warner Brothers, 69, 75, 217
West Africa, 96, 101, 156, 163–164,
    220–221
White Hair Girl, 110
women, 13, 28, 52, 63, 73, 99, 128,
    141, 197, 223
    Africa, West, 164–165
    Brazil, 155–157
    British, 133
    China, 109, 168
    Egypt, 162–163
    French, 142
    Indian, 60, 62, 157–159
    middle class, 11–12, 31, 152–153,
    working class, 51, 93, 128, 137,
        144, 152–153, 155–157
        young, 35–36
    young, 44, 158, 168

word (vs image), 3–4, 54, 173;
    see also image, language.
working class, 11, 41–42, 50, 90,
    114
    so Africa, 96–97
    Brazil, 152–154,
    Britain, 40, 47–8, 50, 90–91,
        132–134
    characters, 34–35, 68, 76–77,
        87, 99, 121, 130, 137, 152,
        167
    China, 112–113, 168
    control of, 91–92
    discourses about, 52–54, 92–93,
        131, 135
    France, 41, 51, 90
    India
    Italy
    neighborhoods, 50, 79, 89,
    US, 23, 27–32, 36–37, 123–125,
        128–129
World Bank, 15, 212
World Trade Organization (WTO),
    205
World War I, 51, 84, 89–91,
    105
World War II, 89, 123

Xiaoping, Deng, 166

yangjingbang, 58
yearnings, 167
Yiddish, 28,
Yoruba, 221
youth(s), 32; *see also* teens

Zambia, 221; *see also* Northern
    Rhodesia.
Zee-TV, 156

207